REAL ESTATE PRI

A STUDY MANUAL FOR OKLAHOMA REAL ESTATE

PROVISIONAL SALES ASSOCIATE
AND BROKER
LICENSE APPLICANTS

2016

DALE BAZE

Published By

B & B Publishing

405-361-4602

www.bbpublish.com

FIFTH EDITION

Copyright © 2016 by Dale Baze. All rights reserved. No part of this book may be reproduced in any manner without written permission except in the case of Laws, Rules and Forms.

SPECIAL NOTE TO STUDENTS

The requirements to sit for the state license exam and, ultimately, be issued a real estate license include several points. You must:

* **Be eighteen years of age;**
* **Complete the required pre-license course;**
* **Successfully pass the pre-license course and the qualifying examination;**
* **Be of good moral character.**
* **Submit your fingerprints along with Part A of the application for the purpose of a criminal background check.**

Since January 1, 2008, the Oklahoma Real Estate Commission requires applicants for a real estate license to obtain a fingerprint card, take it to a police department, and have your fingerprints taken. The Commission requires that you then send Part A of the application, your finger prints and a $60 fee to the Oklahoma Real Estate Commission. Students are encouraged to submit Part A as soon as possible since it may require several weeks for the criminal background check to be completed through the Oklahoma State Bureau of Investigation and the Federal Bureau of Investigation. You may get Part A from your school or the Oklahoma Real Estate Commission.

Part B of the application will be made available to you only when you have successfully completed the required course. You will obtain Part B from the school where you took the pre-license course .It must have the school director's and teacher's signatures on it in the appropriate place affirming that you have successfully completed the required course.

Part B will ask if you have been convicted of a felony, have charges pending, or are on probation. It will also ask if you are in arrears on any child support payments or in arrears on any student loans. It will also ask if you have declared bankruptcy and in which court. While some of these will not keep you from getting a real estate license, some will. If you have any of these situations in your past, please contact the Oklahoma Real Estate Commission at 405-521-3387 and discuss the matter with an investigator. He or she will likely be able to give you information which will help you with the situation. Please do not wait until you have finished the course to attend to this matter.

In addition to the above, the Oklahoma Real Estate Commission will require proof of your legal presence in the United States at the time you sit for the exam. Your school will
Give you a form from the Commission which will give you information regarding the suitable documents for such proof.

If you have questions about any of these, please discuss them with your instructor.

Wifi: Training Room
PW: CC associates

CONTENTS

INTRODUCTION TO REAL ESTATE	7
NATURE OF REAL ESTATE	19
RIGHTS AND INTERESTS IN REAL ESTATE	27
LEGAL DESCRIPTIONS	41
TITLE SEARCH, ENCUMBRANCES AND LAND USE CONTROL	51
TRANSFER OF RIGHTS	67
COMMON LAW OF AGENCY (TC)	81
BROKER RELATIONSHIPS ACT, PRINCIPLES	95
SERVICE CONTRACTS	101
VALUE AND APPRAISAL	113
MARKETING AND SELLING REAL PROPERTY	129
FAIR HOUSING	139
CONTRACT LAW OVERVIEW	145
CONTRACT LAW AND PERFORAMNCE	163
FINANCING REAL ESTATE	175
CLOSING A TRANSACTION	195
REGULATIONS AFFECTING REAL ESTATE	201
DISCLOSURES AND ENVIRONMENTAL ISSUES	283
PROPERTY MANAGEMENT AND LEASING	295
RISK MANAGEMENT	321
BASIC REAL ESTATE MATH	333

SPECIAL NOTE TO STUDENTS: Students will notice several subject headings accompanied by the notation **(TC)**. The letters **TC** stand for "test category." This does not mean that subject matter will definitely be on the test but, it does mean the possibility of it being on the test is of a greater probability than some other subjects. Students are encourage to study all material contained in this text, but are encouraged to give special attention to those areas marked **(TC)**.

FOREWORD

This manual is prepared for the use and benefit of all who may be seriously considering entering the real estate profession or upgrading their licenses to the broker level.

The license applicant must be familiar with the basic technical knowledge contained herein, as well as the wide range of ethical obligations imposed on the real estate professional. A thorough understanding of the ***Oklahoma Real Estate License Code*** and the ***Oklahoma Real Estate License Rules*** is essential for success in the real estate business.

This book is not offered as a substitute in any way for competent legal advice or services where such is needed. With the rapid changes taking place in all phases of real estate activity and changes in law, it is obvious that this book will be at least partially obsolete soon after publication.

This text is prepared according to the outlines of the courses developed by the Oklahoma Real Estate Commission and its Education Committee.

Appreciation is hereby expressed to all those who generously contributed time, knowledge, and interest in the development of this text.

Special thanks and appreciation to my wife, Nola, without whose tireless efforts, patience and endurance, this book would never have existed.

INTRODUCTION TO REAL ESTATE

REAL ESTATE ECONOMICS AND MARKETING

Real estate may well be the most important physical and economic element in the world. No everyday activity goes unaffected by it. Real estate lies at the foundation of our civilization. Upon it we eat, sleep, walk, and perform all other activities.

In Old French, the word for "thing" was "real." An individual's interest or rights to a property is referred to as "estate." Real estate is, in modern terms, the interest individuals have in the land and all that is attached thereto.

Economics is the social science concerned with the study of the allocation of scarce resources so as to maximize the satisfaction of material needs and wants. In our economic system, real estate resources are allocated by the market or price system. That is, real property goes to those who are ready, willing and able to bid the highest price to obtain it.

SUPPLY AND DEMAND

In any given market situation prices will be determined by the interaction of supply and demand. Demand is a schedule of the amounts of a good or service consumers will be willing and able to purchase at various prices. In a similar vein, supply is a schedule of the quantities of goods or services that producers or current owners will be able to make available at various prices. Thus, demand and supply represent particular relationships between prices and quantities of commodities. The LAW OF DEMAND (and common sense) tells us that as prices increase, the quantity demanded diminishes while the LAW OF SUPPLY points out that the quantity supplied tends to rise when prices increase.

Just as the economy as a whole is subject to peaks and valleys of activity that have recurred over the years with fairly reasonable regularity, the real estate industry as part of this economy has also been subjected to recurring periods of recession and prosperity.

Real estate is often the first industry to feel the adverse effects of depressed conditions in the national and local economies. It also takes the real estate industry a longer period of time to climb out of a recession than the economy as a whole because of inability to react quickly to changes in supply and demand.

A special characteristic of the real estate cycle is that the real estate industry usually attains a much higher level of activity in prosperous times than does the economy in general. Mortgage insurance programs, active secondary mortgage markets, and other contra-cyclical forces dampen the tendency toward extreme fluctuations from peaks to troughs of activity in construction and real estate investment.

Real estate, as it is known in this country, is not a necessity of life but a luxury. The amount of real estate actually needed for the bare necessity of shelter is very small. This is especially true measured in terms of dollar value rather than in dwelling units. The demand for dollars' worth of real estate, therefore, behaves very much like the dollar demand for any other luxury good.

Demand for real estate increases sharply with increased personal incomes. In this connection, it must be remembered that the increase in demand is an increase in the dollars offered for real estate. This is not necessarily an increase in the number of houses demanded; in fact, it is more likely to be an increase in the dollars that a prospective buyer will put in a single house. An increase in total demand may be accompanied by a decrease in demand for certain properties.

If the subject of real estate economics in the aggregate had to be reduced to a single theorem, it would probably be: **the most important factors in determining the price of real estate are the level of personal incomes and the competition of other luxury goods for those incomes.** For the individual, factors such as types of mortgages available, interest rates, and closing dates weigh heavily in determining the offering price.

THE REAL ESTATE MARKET

The immobility of real estate and the fact that each parcel is unique causes the real estate market to be local and therefore a highly specialized one.

The real estate market is influenced by many factors, but supply and demand are responsible for its existence. This market is somewhat different from the markets of other goods. Since real estate is immovable, its market must be a local one. If houses are selling well on the coast, the demand may exceed the supply. At the same time, a small Midwestern town may have an oversupply of housing. Housing, however, cannot be moved across the country to an area where a greater demand exists.

It must also be noted that building new structures to meet demand takes time and that supply cannot respond quickly to increased demand for real estate. Furthermore, large sums of money are needed. Funds invested in real estate are called capital. The availability or lack of such capital limits the market for real estate by controlling the effective demand.

DEMOGRAPHICS

The number of end users or consumers of real estate is of primary significance in the real estate marketplace. As a general rule, the more end users there are in a region, the higher demand (competition for supply) will be. Therefore, the higher prices will be. The location of consumers of real estate is the apparent reason the location of the real estate is so significant. In the United States, about 70% of the entire population lives within one hundred miles of a coast line. The remaining 30% inhabit the broad midlands. With this geographic distribution of our national population, it is easy to see why the price of real estate in coastal states is considerably higher than in mid-America.

CAREER OPPORTUNITIES

The sophistication of the modern real estate market causes a number of specialists to become involved in the marketplace. Perhaps one of the most difficult choices for the newcomer to real estate is to
decide which area of the business is the most interesting. The following list is not all inclusive but
should give a general idea of the proliferation of opportunities available to those interested in real estate careers.

BROKERAGE

A broker is typically defined as one who finds one who wishes to sell an item and also finds someone who wants to buy that item and brings the parties together for the purpose of a sale. The broker is paid, typically, a commission based on the amount or value of the sale. He can be paid by either the buyer or the seller. There are all kinds of brokers in the marketplace. Some deal in diamonds, cars, meat, commodities, stocks and, of course, real estate.

Because of the high cost of purchasing real estate and the complexity involved in transferring ownership from one party to another, the most commonly found expert in real estate is the broker or the associate who markets residential, commercial or some other kind real estate.

RESIDENTIAL BROKERAGE

The largest number of people in the real estate industry is involved in home sales. It is common for the general public to think only of residential sales as all there is to real estate.

COMMERCIAL BROKERAGE

Persons in commercial sales specialize in selling income-producing property. These properties usually include retail stores, warehouses, office buildings, apartment complexes, and so forth.

INDUSTRIAL BROKERAGE

Persons who specialize in industrial real estate work to find suitable land and buildings for industrial/manufacturing firms. This could include leasing the property or development of raw land.

FARM AND RANCH BROKERAGE

With the slow disappearance of the family farm and the emergence of commercial farming operations, the farm and ranch specialist should have considerable knowledge of agribusiness. In Oklahoma and this region of the country, farm and ranch sales are a significant part of the real estate industry.

PROPERTY MANAGEMENT

A property manager specializes in taking care of income producing property for investors. Property managers must be skilled in tenant relations, maintenance of property and negotiations.

In some larger cities, rental listing services help to match landlords and tenants. Most of these services make lists of available rental property and sell the lists to prospective tenants.

REAL ESTATE APPRAISING

Real estate appraisers are employed by lending institutions and others to assist in determining the estimated value of real property. In Oklahoma, appraisers are licensed or certified by the Appraisal Board, administered under the Oklahoma Department of Insurance. ODI

GOVERNMENT SERVICES

Since government is such a large land owner in the U. S., many federal, state and local government employees are in the real estate business. Some agencies such as the Park Service, Forest Service, Bureau of Land Management, Department of Agriculture, Army Corps of Engineers, and the General Services Administration are major land owners. Additionally, such agencies as Federal Housing Administration, Veterans Administration, and the Rural Development Division of the U. S. Department of Agriculture are involved in the real estate industry.

LAND DEVELOPMENT

Persons who develop raw land to complete subdivisions are called land developers. They may be "builders" who build only a few houses a year or major local, national or international companies who develop major tracts of land into housing additions.

MORTGAGE FINANCING

Persons in mortgage lending may be employees of an institution which lends money to buyers of real estate or independent mortgage brokers. Their function in either case is to connect qualified buyers with lenders by providing funds to enable the transaction.

URBAN PLANNING

Urban planners usually have an appropriate degree and are employed by local governments. They are involved in plans for the future development of a city. They plan the area of development both for commercial/industrial development and residential. They are concerned with streets, sewers, schools, parks, and the like.

CONSULTING

Real estate consultants are experts in virtually every area of real estate. They are trained to advise individuals, industry, business and government agencies on real estate matters.

EDUCATION

Opportunities in real estate education exist because of state laws requiring real estate persons to take courses and the practitioners' continual need for improving skills, increasing knowledge, and developing professionalism, for a long-term career. These courses are offered by colleges and universities, area technology centers, and privately- owned real estate schools.

INVESTORS

Real estate investors are generally non-licensed persons who buy, sell and/or manage real estate on their own accounts for a profit.

ACTIVITIES WHICH REQUIRE A REAL ESTATE LICENSE

The Oklahoma Real Estate Licensing Code requires that anyone who acts as a real estate licensee must have a license. The Commission has a Code which states that any person who performs licensed activities without a license may be fined by the Oklahoma Real Estate Commission up to $5,000.00 or the amount of the commission, whichever is greater.

The License Code defines a broker as ". . .any person, partnership, association or corporation, foreign or domestic, who for a fee, commission or other valuable consideration, or who with the intention or expectation of receiving or collecting a fee, commission or other valuable consideration, lists, sells or offers to sell, buys or offers to buy, exchanges, rents or leases any real estate, or who negotiates or attempts to negotiate any such activity, or solicits listings of places for rent or lease, or solicits for prospective tenants, purchasers or sellers, or who advertises or holds himself out as engaged in such activities."
This means that when a person attempts to sell property belonging to another, or manage property belonging to another, the person must hold an active real estate license.

A broker associate and a sales associate are licensed persons who conduct real estate activities under the supervision of the person who holds an active broker license.

ACTIVITIES WHICH DO NOT REQUIRE A REAL ESTATE LICENSE

The *Oklahoma Real Estate License Code* describes several real estate activities which do not require a license. The first of these is the owner of the property. Citizens are allowed to purchase and sell any real estate they own without having a license. Next is an attorney-in-fact who is authorized to finalize a contract. This is more commonly known as a "power of attorney" which is given by a court for a specific reason and/or function.

The next one not requiring a license is an attorney-at-law. An attorney may not list and sell real estate like a real estate broker in Oklahoma. Several states allow attorneys to broker properties, but Oklahoma is not one of them. An Oklahoma attorney may deal with any property which is within the scope of his or her agency as an attorney. For example, if the attorney is handling a divorce, bankruptcy or other activity requiring a law license, he/she may take care of that property. He/she may not, however, list and sell property unless he/she also has a real estate license.

Any person appointed by a court to tend to real estate such as a trustee, guardian, etc.

A resident manager of an apartment complex need not have a real estate license.

Those persons who purchase rights-of-ways, easements, leases, permits and licenses for such organizations as the State Department of Transportation, a utility company, a cable company, etc. need not have a real estate license.

Those persons who act for a governmental body for the purpose of purchasing property through the government's right of eminent domain do not have to have a real estate license.

INDEPENDENT CONTRACTOR VS EMPLOYEE

Broker and associate relationships.

The only person legally allowed to represent another as a real estate licensee in the transfer of real property is the broker who takes the listing. In the performance of this function, the broker may enlist the aid of other brokers to assist in the sale or may engage associates and affiliates in carrying out contracts.

As sponsors of associates, brokers are legally responsible for all actions of their associates in the brokerage relationship because the responsibility of brokerage is not delegable. Complaints filed against associates necessarily involve the broker.

Employee.

As an employer, the broker may control both what associates as employees do as well as how they are to do it. Federal law requires that the broker withhold both social security and income tax from wages paid to the employee. Further, the employing broker is liable for matching the amount on social security payments as well as the possible requirement to pay unemployment compensation taxes.

Independent contractor.

The concept of an independent contractor is substantially different from that of an employee. The basic distinction is that the broker has broad control over what the independent contractor does but cannot determine how it will be done. As an independent contractor, the associate is responsible for federal income tax payments and social security contributions as an individual.

Broker-associate agreement.

Whether an associate works for a broker as an employee or as an independent contractor, a written agreement should define the relationship between the parties. Such things as the provisions of office space for the associate, the provision of listings and assistance in servicing the listings, the relationship between the broker, the associate, and other associates with respect to commissions and their distribution, the liability for each party as to expenses, termination clauses as to the rights of the parties, and arbitration of disagreements or disputes between associates or associates and the broker are typical of relations defined in an agreement. Many brokerage firms have operating manuals which elaborate further upon the broker-associate agreement.

COMPENSATION

Each individual real estate company has a compensation plan for its associates. When associates are selecting a company with which to "hang" their licenses, they are encouraged to give special consideration to the firm's compensation plan. Typically, a company gives a portion of the commission earned to the associate. For example, in a transaction wherein there is not another company involved, the company will get a specific portion of the commission and the associate will get the rest. This "commission split" may vary from 50-50 to, ultimately, the associate getting 100% of the commission after meeting certain production goals.

In the event there is a "cross sale," meaning that one company listed the property and another sold it, thereby sharing in the commission (usually 50-50), the associate's firm may receive one half for the total commission and the other company gets the other half. In this case, most companies continue the commission split arrangement they have established with the associate. If, for example, the associate and broker have agreed that the associate is to receive 60% of the earned commission on in-house sales, the commission split will usually be the same on cross sales.

OKLAHOMA REAL ESTATE COMMISSION (TC)

Regulation of the real estate industry.

It is important to recognize that, although real estate is at the core of any private enterprise system, it is also subjected to extensive governmental regulation. Generally, the need for regulation is based upon the need to stabilize construction and real estate sales, to protect property rights, to encourage property ownership, to control institutional flows of funds into real estate-related investments, to control inflation affecting real estate markets, and to control real estate sales practices to protect the public and promote fair competition.

The regulation of the licensing and license law enforcement for the real estate industry, like most other occupational and professional businesses in the U. S., is conducted under the aegis of state government, heavily influenced by federal agency policies. Historically, legislative bodies have passed laws and relied on the executive branch to see that they were administered. The courts have served as referees when individuals questioned the constitutionality of a law, how it was being interpreted, or the way in which it was being enforced.

This model takes into account the fact that legislators lack the time, the expertise, and often the inclination to deal with complex situations. As problems of an industrialized society have grown more complicated, the existing machinery of government has proved inadequate to meet the problems that have surfaced. Administrative agencies, such as the Oklahoma Real Estate Commission, have, therefore, evolved and have been characterized as a "fourth branch of government."

After the Oklahoma Legislature formulates general policies and standards in real estate, it turns the administrative responsibility for working out details to the Commission. The Commission is in effect an extension of the Legislature with power to fill in details of the laws by making rules that have the force of law. A specialized type of law, known as Administrative Law, sets forth the ground rules by which the Commission must function to ensure orderly procedures and equal treatment for all. The real estate license law, creating the Oklahoma Real Estate Commission as a regulatory body, was passed by the Oklahoma Legislature and became effective on January 1, 1950. The primary purpose of the Oklahoma Real Estate Commission is for the protection of the public against certain illegal or unethical practices. The second major function of the Real Estate Commission is to serve the real estate industry by the regulation of standards for those persons licensed to practice real estate, enhancing the professionalism of the industry. The authority of the Commission to attain these two major purposes is contained either in the state statutes (*Oklahoma Real Estate License Code*) or is done by the adoption of regulations as determined by the Commission and known as the *Oklahoma Real Estate Commission Rules*.

The Commission is made up of seven members who are appointed by the Governor with the advice and consent of the State Senate. They serve terms of four years and may be reappointed by the Governor.

Members of the Commission may be removed from office by the Governor for inefficiency, neglect of duty or malfeasance in office in the manner provided by law for the removal of officers not subject to impeachment.

The members of the Commission elect a Chairman and a Vice-Chairman each year. The Commissioners are responsible for hiring the Secretary-Treasurer who is a full-time employee who serves at the pleasure of the Commission. The Secretary-Treasurer, usually colloquially called the Executive Director, hires the clerks and other employees necessary for the function of the Commission.

The Real Estate Commission is authorized by the Legislature to have a revolving fund which consists of all monies received by the Commission other than the Oklahoma Real Estate Education and Recovery Fund. This revolving fund is a continuing fund not subject to fiscal year limitations and is under the control and management of the Oklahoma Real Estate Commission.

ADMINISTRATIVE PROCEDURES ACT (TC)

In the exercise and performance of its duties and functions, the Commission must be in compliance with the *Administrative Procedures Act*. This act regulates the hearing process when the Commission is dealing with complaints against licensees.

The Commission has the authority under the Act to designate and employ a hearing examiner or examiners who shall have the power and authority to conduct such hearings in the name of the Commission at any time and place subject to the provisions of the law and any applicable rules of orders of the Commission. No person shall serve as a hearing examiner in any proceeding in which any party to the proceeding is a conflict of interest or potential conflict of interest. No person who acts as a hearing examiner shall act as attorney for the Commission in any court proceeding arising out of any hearing in which he/she is acting as hearing examiner.

In any hearing before the Commission, the burden of proof shall be upon the moving party. [complaining party]

POWERS AND DUTIES OF THE COMMISSION (TC)

The Legislature has enumerated by Statute the Powers and Duties of the Commission as follows:

(Title 59, Section 858-208 Powers and Duties of the Commission)
1. To promulgate rules, prescribe administrative fees by rule, and make orders as it may deem necessary or expedient in the performance of its duties;
2. To administer examinations to persons who apply for the issuance of licenses;
3. To sell to other entities of governmental bodies, not limited to the State of Oklahoma, computer testing and license applications to recover expended research and development costs;
4. To issue licenses in the form the Commission may prescribe to persons who have passed examinations or who otherwise are entitled to such licenses;
5. To issue licenses to and regulate the activities of real estate brokers, provisional sales associates, sales associates, branch offices, non-residents, associations, corporations, and partnerships;
6. Upon showing good cause as provided for in the *Oklahoma Real Estate License Code*, to discipline licensees, instructors and real estate school entities by:
    a. reprimand,

      b. probation for a specified period of time,
      c. required education in addition to the educational requirements provided by Section 858-307 of this title,
      d. suspending real estate licenses and approvals for specified periods of time,
      e. revoking real estate licenses and approvals,
      f. imposing administrative fines pursuant to Section 858-402 of this title,
      g. any combination of discipline as provided by subparagraphs a through f of this paragraph;

7. Upon showing good cause, to modify any sanction imposed pursuant to the provisions of this section and to reinstate licenses;
8. To conduct, for cause disciplinary proceedings;
9. To prescribe penalties as it may deem proper to be assessed against licensees for the failure to pay the license renewal fees as provided for in this Code;
10. To initiate the prosecution of any person who violates any of the provisions of this Code;
11. To approve instructors and organizations offering courses of study in real estate and to further require them to meet standards to remain qualified as is necessary for the administration of this Code;
12. To contract with attorneys and other professionals to carry out the functions and purposes of this Code;
13. To apply for injunctions and restraining orders for violations of the Code or the rules of the Commission;
14. To create the Oklahoma Real Estate Contract Form Committee by rules which will be required to draft and revise residential real estate purchase contracts and any related addenda capable of standardization for use by real estate licensees;
15. To enter into contracts and agreements for the payment of food and other reasonable expenses as authorized in the *State Travel Reimbursement Act* necessary to hold, conduct, or participate in meetings or training sessions as is reasonable for the administration of this Code; or
16. To conduct an annual performance review of the Executive Director and submit the report to the Legislature.

PROFESSIONAL ASSOCIATIONS/AFFILIATIONS

National Association of REALTORS®.

Not all real estate licensees are REALTORS®, and the word REALTOR® is a registered trademark. Its use is prohibited in advertising or sales efforts by any broker who is not a member of the National Association of REALTORS®.

"REALTOR®" signifies that the user thereof is a real estate licensee who is an active member of a local board also having membership in the Oklahoma Association of REALTORS® and the National Association of REALTORS®. Local boards are located throughout the state and function independently in their own communities, but each has responsibility to the national association.

The Oklahoma Association of REALTORS® (OAR), an organization formed to assist individual boards in local, state and national matters, concerns itself with matters of legislation, license law, education, etc. Each member of a local board in the state pays annual dues to become a member of the state association and the national association.

An important part of NAR is its special institutes, societies, and councils, which promote professionalism in real estate activities through educational programs and the publication of information regarding their areas of specialization. The local boards have committees on professional standards to enforce the *Code of Ethics* while various other committees within the local boards function continually to make the word REALTOR® the symbol of an honored profession.

National Association of Real Estate Brokers – NAREB-Realtist.

The National Association of Real Estate Brokers was established in 1947 (NAREB). Its members are REALTISTS and are primarily African Americans and other minority real estate licensees. Their membership is open to all qualified real estate licensees. There are local chapters in many areas. The Oklahoma City Real Estate Board is a NAREB chapter.

Association of Real Estate License Law Officials (ARELLO).

The Association of Real Estate License Law Officials (ARELLO) is an association of state licensing officials, usually the administrative staff and members of each state Commission. The main emphasis of ARELLO is the exchange of information and ideas regarding licensing and the regulation and adoption of similar policies and standards for all states.

DESIGNATIONS

Several professional associations in the real estate industry offer their members an opportunity to acquire special training and expertise in selected areas of real estate. Listed below are some of the commonly known associations:

Graduate, REALTORS® Institute – GRI: This is a designation members of the NAR may earn. The course is 90-clock hours on subjects such as marketing, servicing listings, real estate law, etc.

Institute of Real Estate Management: This is an association for people who specialize in property management. Interested persons may earn the Certified Property Management designation or the Accredited Resident Manager designation.

Building Owners and Managers Association: This is an association for persons interested in managing commercial buildings such as office buildings. They have the Building Owners and Managers Institute as their educational program.

Real Estate Educators Association: This association is for real estate teachers. Interested members can earn the Distinguished Real Estate Instructor (DREI) designation.

The Oklahoma Real Estate Educators Association: This is a separate association specifically for real estate teachers in Oklahoma. They meet on a regular basis and share information about current law changes and issues regarding teaching real estate in Oklahoma.

South Central Educators Group, Inc.: This is a group of real estate teachers from Oklahoma, Texas, Arkansas, Louisiana and Mississippi who share information and techniques about teaching real estate subjects.

Real Estate Buyer's Agent Council: Members of this association can earn the Accredited Buyer Representative (ABR) designation. Interested persons learn about representation of buyers in the real estate transaction.

Seller Agency Council: Members of this association learn about representation of sellers in the real estate transaction and earn the Accredited Seller Agency (ASR) designation.

National Association of Independent Fee Appraisers: This is an association for appraisers which conducts many conferences for the purpose of helping its members stay abreast of circumstances and changes affecting appraising.

National Association of Master Appraisers: This is also an association of appraisers for the purpose of promoting professionalism, education and awareness of current changes in the appraisal industry.

American Society of Real Estate Counselors: This association assists real estate counselors in maintaining a high level of currently applicable information about real estate for the purpose of advising their clients appropriately on real estate issues.

American Society of Home Inspectors: This association is involved in making customers aware of the necessity of home inspections and maintaining and increasing a high level of professionalism among its home inspector members.

Certified Commercial Investment Member (CCIM): This is an organization which provides in-depth courses for persons interested in learning about commercial real estate.

Ch. 1

TEST YOUR UNDERSTANDING

1. In general, when the supply of a commodity increases
    1. prices tend to rise.
    2. prices tend to drop.
    3. prices tend to stabilize.
    4. demand to increase proportionally.

2. The real estate market is subject to
    1. the cyclical changes in the national economy.
    2. the law of supply and demand.
    3. both 1 and 2.
    4. neither 1 nor 2.

3. The real estate market may be described in all of the following ways EXCEPT
    1. free market.
    2. local market.
    3. movable market. — specifically not movable
    4. market that is slow to react to changes in supply and demand.

4. The typical real estate licensee must have specialized knowledge in a variety of subjects which include all of the following EXCEPT
    1. financing.
    2. contracts.
    3. excavation.
    4. valuation.

5. The regulatory body established by the legislature and empowered to carry out the provisions of the *Oklahoma Real Estate License Code* is the
    1. Association of Real Estate License Law Officials (ARELLO)
    2. Oklahoma Real Estate Commission (OREC)
    3. Oklahoma Association of REALTORS (OAR)
    4. Oklahoma chapter of License Law Officials (OCLLO)

6. Which of the following is usually exempt from real estate licensure?
    1. Associates showing new homes of a subdivision.
    2. Owners of real estate handling their own property, or delegating such right to an attorney –in-fact.
    3. A public official handling the property of a fellow official.
    4. A self-appointed guardian selling the property of a minor.. — Can't be self appointed

7. When brokers hire associates as employees, they are responsible for paying which of the following on behalf of the associates?
    1. FICA tax
    2. State unemployment tax.
    3. Federal income tax withholding
    4. All of the above.

8. Persons who are only responsible to their employer for the results of their work are
    1. licensees.
    2. employees.
    3. independent contractors.
    4. indentured servants.

15

9. Which of the following is/are an accurate statement(s) regarding a successful career in real estate?
    1. A successful career in real estate is based on ethical conduct and services to others.
    2. A successful career in real estate is based on knowledge of a great variety of subjects.
    3. Both 1 and 2.
    4. Neither 1 nor 2.

10. The NAR *Code of Ethics* reflects the relations of the licensee to the public, licensees to fellow brokers and licensees to
    1. mortgagees..
    2. clients.
    3. abstractors.
    4. attorneys.

11. The term REALTOR is a registered trademark term and can be used by
    1. licensed brokers.
    2. full-time brokers.
    3. only members of NAR.
    4. any broker or associate.

12. Professional associations of specialist in various fields of real estate activity have been organized to serve the interests of their members. Which of the following is not expected of such organizations?
    1. Keeping members informed of developments in their field.
    2. Passing laws to regulate licensees.
    3. Providing a clearinghouse of information for licensees.
    4. Improving standards and practices.

13. ARELLO is
    1. the Association of Real Estate License Law Officials.
    2. a government agency.
    3. concerned with landlord-tenant relationships.
    4. the group that reviews real estate examinations for difficulty.

ANSWERS AND EXPLANATIONS

1. 2 A basic economic concept.

2. 3 The real estate industry is subject to the general laws of economics as are all industries dealing in commodities.

3. 3 Man must go the land. The land will not come to man.

4. 3. Successful real estate practitioners must be well informed in a wide range of subjects. Excavation is not one of them.

5. 2. The Oklahoma Real Estate Commission administers and enforces the Oklahoma Real Estate License Code and Rules.

6. 2 Exceptions to licensure include:
    1. The owner of the property.
    2. An attorney-in-fact authorized to finalize a contract.
    3. An attorney-at-law performing normal legal duties, trustees, acting under terms of a trust, or anyone acting under the direction of the court.
    4. Resident managers of apartments.

7. 4 For "employees" the broker must withhold state and federal income taxes and social security contribution. Social security withheld must be matched by the employer who must also pay state unemployment taxes.

8. 3 A broker has broad control over what the independent contractor does but cannot determine how the work will be done.

9. 3 A broad understanding of real estate and high moral standards are prerequisites to success in any phase of the real estate profession.

10. 2 The general topic areas covered in the REALTORS Code of Ethics deal with
    1. relations to the public.
    2. relationship with the client, and
    3. relations to fellow real estate practitioners.

11. 3 To use the term REALTOR in connection with a real estate business, a broker must be a member of the National Association of REALTORS as well as the local board of REALTORS and the state association.

12. 2 Although professional associations recommend and lobby for legislation, laws regulating real estate licensees are passed by the state legislature.

13. 1 ARELLO serves as a clearing house of real estate information and statistical data for the members who are real estate commissioners and real estate administrators from all fifty states and several other countries.

NATURE OF REAL ESTATE

PROPERTY

Property, defined by Oklahoma Statute, Title 60, Section 1, is a "thing of which there may be ownership." The same section of the law also states: "The ownership of property is the right of one or more persons to possess and use it to the exclusion of others."

The law divides property into two classifications, real and personal. Distinction between these types of property is important when the transfer of an interest in property is involved. Deeds transfer only the rights to real property while personal property must be identified and transferred separately, usually by a bill of sale.

REAL PROPERTY (TC)

Real property consists of land, that which is affixed to land and that which is incidental or appurtenant to land. It includes the surface of the earth, the soil beneath to the center of the earth, the airspace above to infinity, and all things provided by nature or attached by man.

Bundle of Rights. (TC)

Real property ownership or title to land is not absolute and should be considered only as a collection of "bundle of rights" which includes the rights to use, possess, enjoy, and dispose of land in any legal way, and to exclude everyone else without rights from interfering. The purchaser of real estate does not, in effect, buy the land itself but instead acquires the right to use the land in certain ways formerly held by the seller. Ownership of real property is therefore a legal concept referring to the interest, benefits, and intangible rights inherent therein.

not any way you want

The most complete collection of rights includes the right to occupy the land, the right to use the land in a particular way, and the right to convey the land to anyone at any time. Symbolic "sticks" within the bundle of rights include the rights to possess, encumber, transfer and exclude. In effect, the totality of rights give the owner the right to use, sell, lease, enter or leave, give away, and keep others away.

The ideal collection of rights never actually exists. Ownership is usually subject to taxation and possible claim of others. It is modified by private and public restrictions affecting its occupancy and use. The rights and interest in real property, also known as an estate, and the limitations placed upon them will be discussed in Chapter Three.

Land. (TC)

Oklahoma Statutes define land as "…the solid material of the earth, whatever may be the ingredients of which it is composed, whether soil, rock or other substance." Land is the part of real property that extends from the center of the earth to as high as the sky and includes the earth's surface and all things provided by nature. It does not include things attached by man. In common usage, however, the term land is synonymous with the terms "real property," "realty" and "real estate."

A thing, as defined by statute, is real property when it is attached to the land by roots (trees and shrubs), imbedded in it (fences, sewers, and the like), or permanently resting upon it (attached buildings). Ownership of such things is vested in the owner of the land to which they are attached and normally pass with the title to the land. When removed from the land, they become personal property and no longer belong to the estate.

Appurtenances. (TC)

A thing is appurtenant to land when it is used with and for the benefit of the land. This includes the rights, privileges and improvements which are adapted to the use of the real property to which they are connected or belong. When intended to be a permanent addition to the land, an appurtenance passes with title to the real property. Examples of appurtenances are easements, rights-of-ways, and condominium parking stalls.

Air Space. (TC)

The *Oklahoma Air Space Act of 1973* specifies that air space will be treated the same as other real property. Land owners are considered owners of all air space from the surface of their parcel upward. They may enjoy, alienate, exchange, partition, devise, lease or mortgage their interest in air rights. Air space is subject to taxation, zoning laws and condemnation. It is capable of being divided or subdivided. The landowner's enjoyment of air space is normally limited only by government regulations regarding flights of aircraft.

Subsurface Minerals. (TC)

Title to subsurface minerals (oil, natural gas, and coal) run with the land unless otherwise reserved. Such reserved rights may be separated from the surface rights. A landowner may own all, part or none of them. When a division takes place, title to mineral rights will run separate from title to surface rights. It is possible for one owner to have surface rights only, a second to have oil mineral rights and a third to have coal or other mineral rights.

WATER RIGHTS (TC)

Water in its natural state is real property. Title of a landowner to real property includes water rights over both surface and subsurface water, including rights to use streams, rivers, creeks, ponds and lakes. Any landowner's rights in these water sources must be weighed against the same rights of others whose land includes the same water source.

Riparian Water Rights. (TC)

The owner of land which touches on a non-navigable lake or watercourse enjoys riparian rights to use the water. While having no absolute ownership of water, rights are shared in common with all landowners along the stream or lake to use the waters in a reasonable manner. Examples of such rights are the right of swimming, boating, fishing, and the right to the alluvion deposited by the water. A riparian owner may use such water, but may not prevent the natural flow of the stream or of the natural spring from which it commences its definite course, nor pollute the water in such a way as to adversely affect others. Riparian rights give the owner of land ownership to the bed of the stream to its midpoint.

Littoral Water Rights. (TC)

Littoral rights are those held by owners of land abutting or bordering navigable bodies of water such as rivers, large lakes, oceans and seas, and include the rights to the water and ownership of the land up to the mean high-water mark.

Neither riparian nor littoral rights may be reserved by the grantor in a conveyance of land to another.

Doctrine of Prior Appropriation. (TC) *Know what it isn't!*

In states where water is scarce, water use is often decided upon the Doctrine of Prior Appropriation. Under this doctrine, water belongs to the state and is allocated to users who have filed for or obtained permits. Sometimes called the "Colorado Doctrine," the Doctrine of Prior Appropriation is applicable in several Western states.

The essence of the Doctrine of Prior Appropriation is that, while no one may own the water in a stream, all persons, corporations, and municipalities have the right to use the water for beneficial purposes. The allocation of water rests upon the theory that the first person in time has the first right to use the water. The first person to use water is called a "senior appropriator." This person has the right to its future use against later users. This first or senior appropriator has "priority" to the water use. Later users are "junior appropriators."

Since water is a scarce resource, many states have adopted detailed laws regulating the use of water. These laws are extensive and vary somewhat according to the state..

PERSONAL PROPERTY (TC)

Personal property is all property other than real property. It is sometimes referred to as chattel or occasionally as personalty. Personal property is temporary in nature and movable. Title transfers with a bill of sale. The usual evidence of ownership is possession.

Personal property may be changed to real property and, conversely, real property may be converted to personal property. Standing trees, for example, are real property. When these trees are cut down, they become personal property. If the logs are made into lumber and used to construct a house, they return to their original status as real property.

The difference between real property and personal property is not always clear. In many situations, a piece of property does not align itself perfectly into either classification. Following are some types of property that need further analysis and explanation.

Emblements. (TC)

Crops fall into two general classifications, crops by nature or crops by man. Crops by nature are those such as wild fruits, grass and perennial plants, and are usually considered real property. Crops by man, requiring annual planting or cultivation, are called emblements and normally classified as personal property. Because there is no natural, clear distinction between the classes, disputes often arise as to the classification of a particular crop.

Crop classification is generally determined by whether the crop is growing (real property) or has been severed or harvested (personal property). Even that does not always hold. For example, a contract to buy watermelons still on the vine is considered a contract for personal property. If a property is sold containing crops of any kind, the crops pass to the buyer unless specifically reserved by the seller and so stated in the sales contract. To avoid controversy over trees, growing crops, and the like, the rights of the parties involved should be clearly set forth in the purchase agreement, and, in some cases, in the deed.

Crops may be classified as **fructus industrialus** which are crops planted by human industry and are generally considered personal property and **fructus naturales** occur by nature without human effort and are generally considered real property because they are not usually harvested.

Fixtures and Trade Fixtures. (TC)

Another group of items difficult to distinguish as real property or personal property are fixtures and trade fixtures. Fixtures are considered real property while trade fixtures are considered personal property.

A fixture is an article of personal property which has been affixed to real property in such a manner that the law considers it to be a part of the real property. If an article is determined to be a fixture, it passes with the property. Since some "fixtures" can provoke disagreement, the treatment of these should be carefully stated in the purchase contract. The issue of whether or not an item is a fixture can be avoided by including the item in question in the contract. The law of fixtures addresses the basic distinction between real property and personal property. Courts apply the following tests to determine whether an article is a part of the real property.

Tests of Fixtures. (TC)

If the item was attached with the intent of making it a permanent part of the building, it is a fixture.

When personal property is firmly attached to real property, such as fence posts set in concrete, the result is a fixture. Another example is a furnace that is removable, but was attached in such a way that its removal would do serious damage to the property.

When an article is essential to the purpose of which the building is intended, such as the furnace mentioned above, it is presumed to be a fixture. If a landlord installs air conditioners into wall slots specifically designed for that purpose, the air conditioners are fixtures even though they could be readily removed.

If the parties to a contract agree, by expression or implication, that an item is or is not a fixture, the agreement will control the status of the item.

The relationship of the parties (such as landlord and tenant or buyer and seller) may aid in the ultimate decision. For example, as between a buyer and a seller in a real property contract, the issue of whether specific property is a fixture is generally resolved in favor of the buyer, particularly if the previously mentioned factors leave the issue unresolved.

A **trade fixture** or chattel is an article owned and attached by a tenant for the purpose of trade or business and is normally considered personal property. If the tenant moves out leaving a trade fixture, or the lease expires prior to removal of the trade fixture, such fixture becomes the property of the landowner. Leases generally require that, at the expiration of the lease, the tenant must return the premises to the condition existing at the time of the creation of the lease except for reasonable wear and tear.

SPECIAL CHARACTERISTICS OF LAND

PHYSICAL CHARACTERISTICS OF LAND. (TC)

The basic physical characteristics of land are its fixed location, indestructibility, and heterogeneity.

Fixed Location. (TC)

The geographical location of any given parcel cannot be changed. It is fixed. It is the immobility of land that causes only the rights in real property to be bought and sold. When land is sold, the seller cannot deliver the real property to the buyer. The buyer must go to the land.

Indestructibility. (TC)

Land is durable and indestructible. It cannot be destroyed. Improvements will depreciate and may become obsolete. Sites can be created and destroyed. The economic desirability enjoyed by a site may change as consumer preferences are altered, but the land itself remains.

Heterogeneity. (TC)

No two parcels of land are exactly alike because no two parcels of land can occupy the exact location on the earth. Because of the geographic difference, each parcel has a unique position and cannot be substituted for another. Courts have long held that a buyer cannot be compelled to accept a substitute parcel of land no matter how similar. The seller must convey ownership of a specific parcel described in the contract.

ECONOMIC CHARACTERISTICS OF LAND (TC)

The basic economic characteristics of land are its scarcity, improvements, area preference, and permanence of investment.

Scarcity. (TC)

Land in a given location or of a particular quality is becoming relatively scarce. To have an economic value, a good must be scarce or of limited supply. Usable land is a scarce commodity, though modification by man has increased the relative supply. As the supply of usable land diminishes, man finds ways to bring marginal land, once considered unusable, into production. Excessively dry land is irrigated for agricultural purposes or marshy land is drained. In urban areas, man may compensate for the scarcity of suitable land by using land more intensively. For example, single family homes may be converted into apartments, or a multi-story building may be built where a single-story building once stood. Since land is durable and immobile, it is subject to a succession of uses over the passage of time.

Improvements. (TC)

A betterment is an improvement upon the property which increases the property value and is considered a capital asset as distinguished from repairs or replacement.

The improvements or modification of one parcel of land has an effect on the value and utilization of neighboring tracts and often has a direct bearing on an entire community. For example, the improvement of a certain parcel by the placement of a manufacturing plant can greatly influence a large area. Such land improvements not only affect the land use itself, but also the value and price of the land.

Another important factor involving improvements is longevity. It is not unusual to find a building which has been standing for one hundred or more years.

Area Preference. (TC)

The economic characteristics of area preference, often referred to as situs, does not refer to a geographical location as such, but rather to choices and preferences of people for a given area within a geographic location. This preference can be created by various factors including, weather, pollution, employment, shopping and schools. Area preference, such as being on an aesthetically pleasing cul de sac, is the reason some lots within a development are sold for a premium.

Permanence of Investment. (TC)

When land has been improved, capital and labor expenditures represent a fixed investment. Once these investments, such as buildings, sewers, electric service, drainage, and water systems, have been made, they cannot be shifted economically to areas of greater demand. The fixity (permanence) of investment in land requires that careful planning precede any capital expenditure. The income return on such investments is long term, relatively stable, and usually extends over what is referred to as the economic life of the improvement.

Ch. 2

TEST YOUR UNDERSTANDING

1. A parcel of real property may include
1. land and improvements.
2. mineral rights, trees, houses and septic tanks.
3. airspace, surface, and ground beneath the surface.
4. **All of the above.**

2. Which of the following are ownership rights as contemplated in the "bundle of rights"?
1. To use, sell, or lease the property.
2. To tax, take by eminent domain, or acquire the property by escheat.
3. To enter, give away, or do nothing with the property.
4. **Both A and C.**

3. Which of the following is NOT one of the "Bundle of Rights"?
1. Right of possession.
2. Right of disposition.
3. Right of enjoyment.
4. **Right of unrestricted use.**

4. Riparian rights relate to the use and ownership of water in
1. **non-navigable rivers and streams.**
2. bays and arms of the sea.
3. subterranean cavities.
4. navigable rivers.

5. The rights to the water and ownership of the land up to the high-water mark of land abutting or bordering navigable bodies of water are
1. easement in gross.
2. **littoral rights.**
3. servient rights.
4. easements by implication.

6. Personal property is most easily distinguished from real property by its
1. permanent annexation.
2. depreciated value.
3. ownership.
4. **mobility.**

7. Owners are building a new enclosed porch on a home. The lumber dealer with whom they are contracting has just unloaded a truckload of lumber in front of their house that will be used to build the porch. At this point, the lumber is considered to be
1. **personal property.**
2. real estate.
3. an appurtenance.
4. a trade fixture.

8. In discussing the terms of a sale, a licensee makes reference to emblements. Emblements has to do with — CROPS
1. fixtures and trade fixtures.
2. monetary interest and leasehold estates.
3. water and mineral rights.
4. **crops produced annually by labor and industry.**

9. Which of the following tests would be used to determine if an item of personal property has become a fixture and, thus, real property?.
    1. The adaptation of the item to the premises.
    2. An agreement between the parties involved.
    3. The intention of the parties.
    4. All of the above.

10. The fact that no two parcels of land can occupy the same location gives land the characteristic of
    1. homogeneity.
    2. heterogeneity.
    3. mobility.
    4. indestructibility.

11. As distinguished from personal property, real property
    1. can be mortgaged.
    2. is considered permanent, fixed and immovable.
    3. can be freely transferred.
    4. is always taxed at a higher rate.

12. Man-made permanent additions to land are called
    1. chattels.
    2. parcels.
    3. improvements.
    4. trade fixtures..

ANSWERS AND EXPLANATIONS

1. 4. Real property is everything permanently attached to land. It includes everything from the center of the earth to infinity in the sky.

2. 4. Taxation, eminent domain and escheat are means of involuntary alienation exercised by various levels of government.

3. 4 The first three common to the "bundle of rights" theory.

4. 1 The owner of land which touches on a non-navigable watercourse enjoys riparian rights to use the water. He/she may use it in a reasonable manner, but cannot prevent its natural flow nor pollute the water in such a way as to adversely affect others. Examples of the rights are swimming, fishing, boating, and the right to the alluvium deposited by the water. The word "riparian" literally means "river bank."

5. 2 Littoral rights are those held by landowners adjacent or a butting navigable water courses such as lakes, large rivers, and seas, and includes the rights to the water's edge at mean high-water mark.

6. 4 Mobility is the distinguishing feature between real and personal property. Permanent annexation implies real property. Both real and personal property have ownership, and both lose value due to depreciation.

7. 1 Any property not permanently attached to real estate is considered personal property.

8. 4 The law of Emblements permits a tenant to re-enter to harvest crops grown by the tenant. Emblements are regarded as personal property even after a lease has expired.

9. 4 In addition to these tests, two other fixture tests are (1) the method of attachment and (2) the relationship of the parties. In the buyer/seller relationship, the issue is usually resolved in favor of the buyer.

10. 2 Heterogeneity implies that no two parcels of land are the same. No two may share the same location.

11. 2 Personal property can be mortgaged and is more easily transferred than real property. The tax rate for real property in relation to its value is low.

12. 3 Improvements are valuable additions made to property that amount to more than repairs, costing labor and capital, and are intended to enhance the value of the property.

RIGHTS AND INTERESTS IN REAL ESTATE

PROPERTY OWNERSHIP

The Allodial and Feudal Systems.

The system of property ownership in most of the United States had its beginning in the pre-colonial days in England. Through the centuries, the forms of land ownership have evolved through common law from ownership of land vested in the sovereign (Feudal System) to the Allodial System, free and full ownership by individuals of right in land. Technically, no one owns real estate, only the rights relative to its use. The concept of private property ownership as the basis for personal liberty is diminishing as greater emphasis is placed on the needs of society as a whole.

One of the most significant governmental actions affecting property in Oklahoma was the decision of the Continental Congress to sell to private owners the rights of parts of the vast territories acquired as a result of the Revolutionary War. A committee worked out a plan, largely attributed to Thomas Jefferson, for locating and selling land. The **Land Ordinance of 1785** established the Rectangular Survey System and guaranteed ownership in fee simple. The government described all public lands by the rectangular method before disposing of those lands through allotment, sale or homestead. The ordinance also provided that Section 16 and in some instances, Section 36, of each township be designated by law to be used for schools.

The establishment of the individual rights to own real property resulted in the creation of estates in land by which ownership interest could be divided among several individuals. Real property interests can be characterized in terms of the rights, privileges, powers and duties which may accompany them. Although persons involved in the real estate industry may not encounter all of these estates in land, it is necessary to understand the various interests which are possible and the limitations associated with them.

Interests in real property under the Allodial System can be possessory or nonpossessory. Possessory interests are those by which the owner has the physical control of land that can be enjoyed by a person. Nonpossessory interests include liens, encumbrances, easements, etc., rights which are valuable but which do not include any present right to possess or occupy the real property.

Possessory estates (corporeal rights) are classified either as freehold which means the interest lasts for an indeterminable time, or as less than freehold, which is an interest that lasts for a definite and determinable period and includes leasehold estates.

FREEHOLD ESTATES (TC)

A person holding a freehold estate has title to the real property for an indeterminable duration. Included in freehold estates are the fee simple, the fee simple defeasible, and the life estate.
The fee owner may do anything with the property that does not interfere with the rights of others. Ownership of and title to real estate are expressed in terms of the degree, quantity, nature, and extent of rights embodied in a fee simple estate.

Fee Simple Absolute.(TC) *Most common*

The fee simple absolute is the largest and most complete estate known in our legal system. It denotes the maximum legal ownership of real property and includes the greatest possible combination of rights, ownership privileges and immunities a person may have in real property. It is possible to own all rights in a parcel of real estate or only a portion of them.

Fee simple estate is limited only by governmental controls. Government has given up almost all right to absolute ownership, but it has retained certain ownership powers such as power of escheat, police power, power to tax, and the right of eminent domain. Owners have all rights except those reserved by government.

A fee simple estate is an estate of inheritance and may be willed or deeded as it is freely transferable and devisable. All other estates are derived from the fee simple. When a deed does not specify the state being conveyed, it is presumed to transfer a fee simple estate.

Qualified Estates. (TC)

Since the fee simple absolute is the only unlimited ownership interest, all the other inheritable freehold estates are limited in some way. Technically these restricted interests are called defeasible estates, which means that these interests can be defeased or defeated in the future by the happening of an event or a stated condition. In many respects, the fee simple defeasible is treated the same as the fee simple. It is an estate of inheritance and will descend to the heirs of the title holder.

A fee simple determinable estate expires automatically upon the occurrence of an event stated in the deed or will and reverts back to the grantor, his heirs or assigns. When creating the estate, words such as "so long as" or "until," followed by the event, are used. For example, property owner "A" conveying property to a church with wording "so long as the property is used for church purposes" creates a fee simple determinable estate in the church. The estate conveyed to the church will end automatically if and when the property is used for non-church purposes.

Life Estate. (TC)

Life estate is any estate in real or personal property which is limited in duration to the life of its owner or the life of some other designated person. If the estate is measured by the lifetime of a person other than its owner, it is called a life estate **pur autre vie**. Life estate is classified as a freehold estate because it is a possessory estate of indefinite duration, but it is not an estate of inheritance.

Since the interest of the grantee in life estate ends at the death of the grantee or another person, the grantor might retain a reversionary interest, which is transferable (alienable, devisable, and descendible) at all times. In the alternative, a grantor may appoint a third party to receive ownership interest at the death of the life tenant. This third person is called a remainderman, one who has a future interest, also freely alienable, and devisable. A life tenant may sell, rent, or mortgage the life estate, but can give no greater right than is owned. The right of the buyer or renter ceases immediately upon the termination of the life estate.

Life tenants owe certain duties to the owners of the vested future interest, either the reversioner or remainderman. They are obligated to maintain the property and not allow it to waste, i.e., cause exploitation of mineral deposits, destruction of buildings, or other acts resulting in permanent injury or loss of value to the property.

DOWER AND CURTESY (TC)

Curtesy is an estate in real estate recognized in common law in which a man is entitled to his wife's property upon her death. This includes land or tenements of which she was owner in fee simple and, upon her death, under curtesy, her husband inherits. This is a freehold estate.

Dower is somewhat different to curtesy Dower is the right of a wife to the property of her husband upon his death. It a form of a life estate. The law provides for a widow to have her deceased husband's property for her support and the support of any children. Under dower, she becomes a "tenant in dower" which means the wife inherits one third of her husband's property upon his death.

Tenancy by the entirety and joint tenancy have largely replaced dower and curtesy.

COMMUNITY PROPERTY (TC)

There are ten states which recognize community property. Oklahoma is not one of those. They are Alaska, Arizona, California, Idaho, Louisiana, Nevada, New Mexico, Texas, Washington and Wisconsin.

In those states which recognize community property, the partners in a marriage are considered equal participants with equal shares of ownership in property. That means the spouses have a 50% ownership of all property acquired during the marriage. Therefore, when property is disposed of, both spouses must execute any documents.

Community property laws do not necessarily recognize the right of survivorship.

Property which a spouse owned before the marriage or acquires by gift or inheritance is considered **SEPARATE PROPERTY**. Such separate property may be disposed of without the spouse's signature.

Homestead Rights. (TC)

A homestead is a tract of land which is owned and occupied as the family home. The tract may include up to 160 acres if it is an agricultural homestead or up to one acre if located within a city. Oklahoma has a homestead exemption law in which a portion of the value of the homestead property is exempted from claims of most outside creditors, except where the property is security for debt. The law also exempts $1,000 from assessed value in the calculation of taxes based on value (ad valorem) against an owner-occupied residence.

Homestead is included under the section on possessory estates because of the right of family survivors to the homestead property upon the death of the husband or wife. Upon the death of the surviving spouse, the surviving children may continue to possess and occupy the whole homestead until the youngest child reaches majority. To protect spouses individually, both husband and wife must join in executing any document conveying homestead property.

LEASEHOLD ESTATES (TC)

Leasehold estates are possessory interests created by the establishment of landlord-tenant relationships. They may last for a definite time period or for as long as the parties are willing to continue their relationship. For the duration of the lease, the lessee possesses or occupies the land with the understanding that the landlord retains full ownership of the real property. The lessor retains the reversionary rights plus the right to collect compensation. Because title does not accompany such estates, leases are considered to be personal property.

In addition to the fact that most leases contain a clause against the assignment or subletting without prior consent of the lessor, Oklahoma statutes prohibit assignment or subletting without permission from the landlord. In the absence of such restraint, tenants could indiscriminately transfer leases, introducing "strangers" to the landlord.

In an assignment, the entire interest in the property of the assignor is transferred to the assigns or assignees. The transferee comes into privity of estate with the lessor, meaning that each remains liable to the other on the covenants of the original lease. In subleasing, a lease is given by a lessee for a portion of the leasehold interest with the lessee retaining sole reversionary interest. The main difference between subletting and assigning, so far as the landlords are concerned, is that they cannot directly sue the sublessee where it is possible to bring suit against the assignee.

Estate for Years. (TC)

An estate for years is a leasehold estate expressed in terms of a specific starting time and a specific ending time. The duration can be any length of time. An estate for years does not automatically renew itself.

Periodic Tenancy. (TC)

A tenancy from period to period is an estate which continues for a fixed period (year, month, week) and for successive similar periods unless terminated by either party by proper notice. The most common example of a periodic estate is the month-to-month apartment rental. It is also called tenancy from year to year.

Tenancy at Will. (TC)

A tenancy at will may be terminated at the will of either the landlord or the tenant and has no other specified length of duration. Oklahoma statute has changed the common law in that estates at will are treated much the same as tenancy from period to period. If, for example, a tenant at will is paying monthly rent, then a thirty-day notice requirement must precede termination of the lease, just as in a tenancy from month to month.

Tenancy at Sufferance. (TC)

Tenancy at sufferance exists when a tenant, without the consent of the landlord, fails to surrender possession after termination of the lease. This is the lowest estate in real estate and no notice of termination may be required for the landlord to evict the tenant. Designed to protect the tenants from being classified as trespassers on one hand, it also prevents their acquisition of title by adverse possession on the other.

FORMS OF OWNERSHIP IN REAL PROPERTY (TC)

All real property is owned by the government, by one person alone, or with others in some form of concurrent ownership. Rights, privileges, and duties are defined in terms of the type estate held and the encumbrances and controls affecting the real property.

Ownership in Severalty. (TC)

Sole ownership of real property by a legal person is known as ownership in severalty. The term implies that the person's ownership is "severed" from all others. A natural person may own in severalty any freehold estate previously discussed. Real property owned by public corporations, such as cities, counties and school districts, is generally owned in severalty.

Concurrent Ownership. (TC)

Concurrent ownership of real property exists when more than one person has legal title to the same parcel of land. Each co-owner owns an undivided interest in the real property. Whether or not each co-owner's share is equal may determine the type of co-ownership.

Several generalities apply to all forms of co-ownership. For example, each co-owner is entitled to possess the entirety of the co-owned real property, subject to the identical rights of the others. Generally, all profits derived from the co-owned land must be divided between or among the co-owners according to the interest of each in the real property. Co-tenants cannot exclude the other co-tenant(s) or claim specific portions of the property for themselves.

Tenancy in Common. (TC)

Concurrent ownership in common exists when two or more persons own undivided interests in one parcel of land. The interest held need not be equal. For a tenancy in common to exist, only the unity of possession must be present. That is, each party must have a right of possession of the whole parcel, subject to the same rights as the other tenants. Tenants in common may deed, will, or encumber their interest in the real property as they choose.

Additionally, a tenant in common may bring a partition action to force a sale of the real property, the proceeds of such sale to be divided between or among the tenants according to their share in the real property. An action of partition may also be used to force a physical division of the co-owned property between or among the tenants where an unresolved dispute exists.

In absence of inferences otherwise, co-ownership is in tenancy in common by presumption of law.

Joint Tenancy. (TC)

The major difference between the joint tenancy and the tenancy in common is that joint tenants have the right of survivorship, the grand incident of joint tenancy. Survivorship means that upon the death of a joint tenant, title is vested in the surviving joint tenant(s). In other words, the interest of the decedent in the joint tenancy is vested to the surviving tenant(s) and is not included in the decedent's estate. Joint tenancy, sometimes referred to as a "poor man's will," defeats a will in determining the distribution of the co-owned property.

A joint tenancy exists when two or more persons own equal undivided shares in real property and when such tenants have conformed with the four unities of time, title, interest and possession. The unity of time means that each joint tenant must have acquired interest in the real property at the same time as all other joint tenants. The unity of title requires the same instrument. The unity of interest means that each joint tenant must possess the same interest in real property as to scope (the share of the interest) and duration (the estate possession) means that each joint tenant must have the same right as the other joint tenant(s). A joint tenancy will be recognized only if it was the intent of the transferor to create a joint tenancy.

Creation of Joint Tenancy. (TC)

To create a joint tenancy, specific words in a deed or will are required. Such words as "To A and B as co-owners," "to A, B and C to share and share alike," or "to A, B, C and D" are insufficient to create a joint tenancy, unless it can be otherwise specially proven. The most acceptable means of creating a joint tenancy is by stating "to A and B, as joint tenants with the sole right of survivorship, and not as tenants in common." By using such language, the intent to create a joint tenancy may be clearly proven.

An interest in a joint tenancy terminates with death. A joint tenancy is also terminated (severed) if any joint tenant deeds an interest in the joint tenancy. The grantee of the joint tenant's interest will succeed to the tenant's share, but the grantee will be considered a tenant in common. If more than one joint tenant remains, such tenants will continue to hold the remaining interest in the real property as joint tenants. For example, if "A," "B" and "C" are joint tenants and "C" conveys his interest to "X," "X" now holds an undivided one-third interest as a tenant in common with "A" and "B" who continue to be joint tenants, each with an undivided one-half interest in the remaining two-thirds interest in the real property. Termination of a joint tenancy also occurs when a joint tenant's interest is sold in foreclosure sale or in a sale to satisfy judgment creditors.

Tenancy by the Entireties. (TC)

If the four unities are present in a conveyance or devise to husband and wife, and the conveyance indicates an intent to create the right of survivorship in favor of the spouses, a tenancy by the entireties is recognized. A tenancy by the entireties is treated the same as a joint tenancy. For this tenancy to exist, however, it must be between husband and wife and cannot be terminated without the consent of both parties.

Cooperative Ownership. (TC)

Cooperative ownership is created when a nonprofit corporation is formed for the purpose of buying, converting or constructing a building in order to create individual apartment units. Shares in the corporation are sold to cooperators and, in exchange for their investment, the shareholders each receives from the corporation a proprietary lease granting them exclusive right to occupy a specific living unit in the cooperative apartment building. Cooperators do not own their living units, but are tenants in a building owned by a corporation of which they are shareholders.

Condominium Ownership. (TC)

While often thought of as a type of building or housing complex, condominium ownership or a condominium regime is a specialized form of property ownership. It is a form in which owners own their units in fee simple and share an undivided, fractional ownership of common areas with the others in the complex. Owners receive unit deeds to their own apartments entitling them to a proportionate share in the common areas.

Each owner, by purchasing a unit, is committed to absorbing a prorated share of the cost of maintaining the common area. Each pays a monthly maintenance charge to the owner's association which determines the amount for the assessment. Special assessments may also be made upon the owners from time to time to cover extraordinary expenses not covered by the normal association dues. Condominiums may be used in commercial, professional and industrial complexes, as well for residential property ownership, and are governed by legislation known as the ***Horizontal Property Act***.

Time-sharing. (TC)

Time-sharing is a specialized form of condominium ownership. As the cost of building a condominium unit outright, especially in resort areas, might be prohibitive, the developer instead sells a designated share of time in the unit to buyers who each receive a proportionate interest in the property and the right to use for specified periods of time during the year. Each owner pays a pro rata share of maintenance and management costs based on time.

The concepts for time-sharing and interval ownership of units are somewhat different. The time-sharing creates a tenancy in common among the many owners of the same unit and includes the exclusive right of each of them to use the property for specific periods. Interval ownership, on the other hand, creates a separate tenancy to the unit for a specified period each year and thereby provides the exclusive right to use the property during that time.

Townhouse. (TC)

A townhouse blends some of the characteristics of a single-family home with those of a condominium. It is a form of residential housing in which the owners own their dwellings, the land beneath and the air space above but share joint ownership of common area contiguous to the units with the other owners. "Cluster or multiple use" zoning, seeking to more fully utilize available land and provide for
higher density housing, is necessary for townhouses which feature zero lot lines where one or more of the exterior walls rest directly on the property line. A townhouse usually has a small front and/or back yard and shares common (party) walls with adjacent buildings. Under the townhouse concept, the owner's association owns and administers the common areas, rather than having individual owners hold a prorated ownership interest in them.

FORMS OF BUSINESS ORGANIZATIONS (TC)

Business organizations can take several different forms, including sole proprietorship, corporation, partnership, limited partnership, limited-liability company, syndicate and real estate investment trust. All of these business organizations can receive, hold, and convey title in the various ways previously discussed. These forms, while referred to by other names, normally take the form of tenancy in common.

Sole Proprietorship.

A sole proprietorship is a business owned by one individual. The owner of a sole proprietorship is fully liable for the business debts. If business debts exceed the assets of the business, the personal assets of the owner may be attached by creditors for satisfaction of the business debts.

Corporation.

"A corporation is an artificial being, invisible, intangible, and existing only in contemplation of law." As a creature of law, it is capable of owning real property in severalty in the corporate name. Its rights to alienate, encumber and use real property are substantially the same as those of a natural person. However, since a corporation may act only through its agents, natural persons (board of directors, members or officers) must carry out all negotiations and actions involving the transfer of corporate real property or any interest therein.

Ownership in a corporation is evidenced by shares of stock which are transferable without having to dissolve the corporation. Stockholders do not have personal liability for the debts of the corporation as only the corporate assets are subject to the claims of creditors. Corporations are subject to double taxation as they are taxed on corporate earnings and stockholders are further taxed on dividends when received.

General Partnership.

A general partnership is a form of business organization in which the business is owned by two or more persons called partners. In a general partnership, the partners are personally liable for partnership debts exceeding partnership assets. Partners are jointly and severally liable. That is, any individual partner is personally liable for the partnership debts exceeding partnership assets as well as all the partners being jointly liable.

Limited Partnership.

A limited partnership exists when some of the partners are limited in their financial liability to the amount of their contribution to the partnership. Limited partners are "silent partners" and cannot take
a role in management of the partnership. The limited partnership is not taxed as such. The individual owners are taxed on their portion of the partnership earnings. Each limited partnership must have at least one general partner who conducts business for the entity and may be held liable for all losses and obligations not met by the other partners.

Limited Liability Company.

A limited liability company is a form of a corporation which is more suitable for smaller business operations. It is similar to a corporation in that it limits the liability to the company assets but has restricted numbers of owners who are called members.

Syndicate.

A syndicate is a term to describe a combination of investors who pool funds for investment. The usual form of syndicates are joint ventures, general partnerships and limited partnerships.

Joint Venture.

The joint venture and general partnership are alike in that all partners are liable for a partnership's debts and all partners normally have a voice in management of the group. The ownership of the group is not taxed (as a corporation would be) but passes through all benefits and/or losses to each partner. The difference between the joint venture and general partnership is that the partnership is normally established to carry on business for an indefinite period while a joint venture is a single or limited purpose partnership, usually for a short time period.

REIT.

Real estate investment trusts are unincorporated trusts or associations of investors. They are managed by one or more trustees responsible for making various income-producing investments in real property so that such income may be distributed to holders of the beneficial interest of the real property (trust beneficiaries). To qualify as REIT under the ***Internal Revenue Code*** which exempts REITs from taxation at corporation rates on income distributed to beneficiaries, certain requirements must be met. This necessitates intricate legal advice.

Ch. 3

TEST YOUR UNDERSTANDING

1. Full and complete ownership of land exists most nearly in a(n)
    1. absolute.
    2. fee simple absolute.
    3. leasehold.
    4. dominant tenement.

2. A fee simple estate includes an owner's right to do all of the following with the property except to
    1. sell it.
    2. condemn it.
    3. lease it.
    4. finance it.

3. Lis Pendens, a widow, devised a piece of property through her will to the Church of the Holy Fellow for so long as the property is to be used for church purposes. Several years later, the church conveyed this property to Chico El Bueno who began restaurant operations. Chico El Bueno received
    1. a fee simple interest in the property.
    2. a remainder interest in the property.
    3. a determinable fee in the property.
    4. no interest at all in the property.

4. A life estate may be granted
    1. only when it is for the grantee's life.
    2. for the duration of the life of the grantee or the life of someone other than the grantee.
    3. for a definite term.
    4. only to a grantee over the age of majority.

5. Winkin conveys a house to Blinkin for life, then to Lincoln. Blinkin's heirs have
    1. no estate interest.
    2. an interest equivalent to Blinkin.
    3. a reversion.
    4. a remainder.

6. In order to protect a family from the financial irresponsibility of the head of the household, Oklahoma provides a form of relief from creditors called
    1. credit insurance.
    2. moratorium on all debt repayments.
    3. homestead exemption.
    4. low interest rate debt consolidation loans.

7. In order to create a homestead right in Oklahoma, the claimant must
    1. be married.
    2. have been an Oklahoma resident for five years.
    3. have at least one child.
    4. own and occupy the property as the principle residence.

8. The declaration of homestead in Oklahoma, filed by the head of a family by March 15, will exempt from the assessed valuation of the property the amount of
    1. $1.00
    2. $10.00
    3. $100.00
    4. $1,000.00

9. Regarding homestead rights
   1. all real property owned is kept from being sold to satisfy creditors.
   2. **when homestead property is sold, both spouses should sign the deed.**
   3. death of the head of the household will terminate homestead exemption.
   4. either spouse may convey the rights of the other.

10. A person holding title to real property in severalty would most likely have
   1. a life estate.
   2. an estate for years.
   3. ownership in common.
   4. **sole ownership.**

11. Real property owned by public corporations, such as cities, counties, and school districts, is generally owned in
   1. **severalty.**
   2. tenancy in common for the benefit of all citizens.
   3. tenancy in partnership among elected officials.
   4. joint tenancy for the benefit of all citizens.

12. Concurrent ownership of real property by two or more persons, each of whom has an undivided interest (not necessarily equal) without right of survivorship is
   1. a tenancy in partnership.
   2. a tenancy by the entireties.
   3. **a tenancy in common.**
   4. a tenancy in sufferance.

13. Ann and her brother, Bob. Inherited under their mother's will title to a house in joint tenancy. Ann married and had title to her share put in joint tenancy with her husband. Bob is now
   1. a joint tenant with Ann and her husband.
   2. sole owner of the property.
   3. a tenant in common owning an undivided 1/3 interest.
   4. **a tenant in common owning an undivided ½ interest.**

14. Marlene and Alice own property as tenants in common. This means that if Marlene dies, she can leave her interest to
   1. Alice only.
   2. **anyone she wants to.**
   3. her husband only.
   4. her children only.

15. Tenants in common must
   1. **share possession of the property.**
   2. take title at the same time.
   3. share equal interests.
   4. take title through the same instrument.

16. Which is true if two sisters, Mary and Kate, inherit real property with no conditions except the stipulation that one-third of the property is to go to Mary and two-thirds to Kate?
   1. Mary and Kate are joint tenants of the property.
   2. Kate may not mortgage her interest in the property without Mary's consent.
   3. **Mary and Kate are tenants in common.**
   4. Mary and Kate are tenants in entirety.

17. A, B, and C are joint tenants, each enjoying a one-third share of their jointly owned property. C dies suddenly. In her will she specified that her husband, D, who is not a member of the joint tenancy, should inherit her share of the property. A and B, meanwhile, protest that the deceased tenant's share is rightfully theirs, to be split equally between them. Which of the following is true?
   1. The court will rule in A' and B's favor.
   2. A and B are now co-equal joint tenants.
   3. Husband D acquires no interest in the tenancy as the result of his wife's will.
   4. All of the above.

18. In order to create a joint tenancy, the
   1. deed or will must definitely state the intention to create a joint tenancy.
   2. four unities of time, title, interest and possession must be present.
   3. Both 1 and 2.
   4. Neither 1 nor 2.

19. The so called "grand incident" of the joint tenancy is the right of
   1. inheritance.
   2. limited freehold.
   3. survivorship.
   4. possession.

20. Mrs. Quirk is now a widow whose husband owned an office building jointly with right of survivorship with Tom Thug and Sam Sleazy. Upon her husband's death, his will devised all his property to her. Mrs. Quirk is
   1. an owner in severalty of the building.
   2. a tenant in common with Thug and Sleazy.
   3. a joint tenant with right of survivorship in the building with Thug and Sleazy.
   4. none of the above. She has no interest at all.

21. Spice and Zesty bought a building and took title as joint tenants. Spice died testate. Zesty now owns the building
   1. as a joint tenant with right f survivorship.
   2. in severalty.
   3. in absolute ownership under the law of descent.
   4. subject to the terms of Spice's will.

22. To mortgage property held in a tenancy by the entireties, it is necessary to have the mortgage signed by the husband
   1. alone, because he is the head of the household under law.
   2. and wife both. Because neither alone has the power to deal with the property.
   3. Both 1 and 2.
   4. Neither 1 nor 2.

23. The establishment of a condominium
   1. is accomplished by a series of deeds to various owners, establishing fee simple interest in their respective properties.
   2. must be done in strict accordance with state statutes because the condominium is not recognized under common law.
   3. Both 1 and 2.
   4. Neither 1 nor 2.

24. Max Meander sells his house and moves into a condominium. Shortly after moving in, he learns that, Noah Count, his next door neighbor has failed to pay his real estate taxes. If Count does not pay his taxes
   1. there is a general lien against the condominium, including Meander's unit.
   2. the only lien that can be placed against the property is against Count's unit and his interest in the common areas.
   3. there is no lien against Meander's unit, but a lien is placed against all the common areas.
   4. the only lien that an be placed against the property is against Count's unit. No lien can be placed against any interest in the common areas.

25. Which is true concerning apartment ownership?
    1. Ownership in a cooperative apartment usually requires purchase of shares of stock in the cooperative association.
    2. individual apartments in a condominium are conveyed and are financed as if they were single family dwellings on separate pieces of land.
    3. Both 1 and 2.
    4. Neither 1 nor 2.

26. Time-sharing is best explained as
    1. a condominium owner sharing an individual unit.
    2. title to property or the right to use property for a specific interval each year.
    3. an easy payment plan used in purchasing goods.
    4. None of the above.

27. Estates owned by those who lease property from others are
    1. defeasible fee estates.
    2. leasehold estates.
    3. fee simple estates.
    4. estates in remainder.

28. A tenant's lease has expired. The tenant has neither vacated nor negotiated a renewal lease and the landlord does not want the tenant to remain in the building. The tenant is a
    1. casual occupant.
    2. periodic visitor.
    3. tenant at will.
    4. tenant at sufferance.

29. Which of the following are personally liable to creditors for debt of the business?
    1. Shareholders of a corporation.
    2. Trust beneficiaries.
    3. Members of a general partnership.
    4. None of the above.

30. In order to enjoy some of the benefits of incorporation, yet retain the partnership form of ownership, it is possible to form a "limited partnership." This can be achieved only by filing a formal certificate. Limited partners
    1. may participate in management.
    2. may allow their names to be used in the business.
    3. must have at least two persons who function as general partners.
    4. are not responsible for firm debts beyond their individual investment.

ANSWERS AND EXPLANATIONS

1. 2. Fee simple is the maximum possible estate one can possess in real estate.

2. 2. Condemnation is the administrative proceeding in the exercise of the eminent domain, but the others are standard rights of fee simple ownership.

3. 4. A fee simple determinable is an estate in real property that exists "so long as," "while," or "during the period" that a certain prescribed use continues.

4. 2. Life estate may be granted for the life of a designated person. If the estate is measured y the lifetime of a person other than the life tenant, it is called a "life estate por autre vie."

5. 1. Lincoln is the remainderman. Blinkin is the life tenant whose interest ceases automatically at his demise. Life estate is not an estate of inheritance.

6. 3. One purpose of the state homestead law is to protect the family against eviction by general creditors.

7. 4. To enjoy homestead rights a claimant must own and occupy the property as a family home as of January first.

8. 4.. An exemption of $1,000 is deducted from the assessed valuation of real estate in determining ad valorem taxes for one who has been approved for homestead exemption.

9. 2. Only the home in which the owner is living is protected from judgments of creditors. To protect spouses individually, both husband and wife must join in executing any conveyance of homestead property.

10. 4. Severalty means sole ownership of real property. In this form of ownership, the title to the property is held by one person or by an artificial entity such as a corporation, university, city, state, etc. and is "severed" from anyone else.

11. 1. Most corporations, public or private, hold title to real property under tenancy in severalty.

12. 3. A good definition of tenants in common.

13. 4. Ann's transfer of interest terminated the joint tenancy. Bob still owns half of the property.

14. 2. Marlene's interest will go to her heirs or assigns. By will, she can give it to whomever she designates.

15. 1. Tenants in common can have different interest and need not acquire the property at the same time or from the same instrument. The only unity required is that of possession, an undivided interest to possess the entire parcel.

16. 3. The unequal interest indicates a tenancy in common. Either may mortgage interest in the property without the consent of the other.

17. 4. Joint tenancy defeats a will. Upon the death of C, her interest in the estate vests in the survivors of the joint tenancy.

18. 3. A joint tenancy can be created only by grant, purchase (by a deed of conveyance), or by devise (will). It cannot be created by operation of law. Four unities are required to create a joint tenancy: unity of title, unity of time, unity of interest, and unity of possession. Unless all four unities are present, a joint tenancy is not created.

19. 3. The "grand incident' of joint tenancy is the right of survivorship by which the survivors immediately inherit the interest of the one deceased.

20. 4. Thug and Sleazy are joint tenants, each holding 50% interest in the building.

21. 2. As each successive joint tenant dies, the remaining tenants acquire the interest of the deceased. The last survivor takes title in severalty, fully inheritable at death.

22. 2. In tenancy by the entirety, neither spouse can convey interest or form a partition during the lifetime of the other, without the consent of the other spouse.

23. 3. Each condominium unit is a statutory entity that may be mortgages, taxes, sold or otherwise transferred in ownership, separately and independently of all other units in the structure. Since title is in fee simple, transfer is normally by deed. Each condominium owner has exclusive ownership of the individual unit, but must nevertheless, comply with the requirement of the declaration, bylaws, and house rules set up for the protection and comfort of all the condominium owners.

24. 2. Units are separately assessed and taxed, based on the combined value of the individual living unit and the proportionate ownership of the common areas. A unit can be separately foreclosed upon in case of default n the mortgage note or other lienable payments.

25. 3. These are the primary distinctions between condominium and cooperative ownership.

26. 2. Timesharing permits multiple purchasers to buy an undivided interest in real property (usually in a resort condominium or hotel) with the right to use the facility for a fixed or variable time period.

27. 2. A lessee's interest is called the leasehold estate and consists of the right to the exclusive use and occupancy of the estate.

28. 4. Tenancy at sufferance is the lowest form of estate.

29. 3. The primary disadvantage of a partnership is that each general partner is personally liable for all the debts of the business. This is called unlimited liability.

30. 4. A "limited partnership" limits the liability to the individual investor, but the limited partner cannot be a part of the firm's management nor permit the name to be used in the business. A limited partnership need not have more than one general partner.

LEGAL DESCRIPTIONS

An all important matter in real property law is that the description of real property be stated in such a way that the property is identifiable to a knowledgeable person. The validity of a deed depends upon its containing an adequate description of the real property.

There may be a difference between a technically correct description and a legally correct description of real property. It is not uncommon for a house and lot to be described by using only a street address. This is an informal description and not generally acceptable as an adequate legal description of the house or building in question. Descriptions should be definitely ascertainable and should describe boundaries which are not subject to movement. A wrong description in an otherwise valid document could render the document legally ineffective. The importance of proper descriptions of the land to be conveyed cannot be over-emphasized.

METHODS OF DESCRIBING REAL PROPERTY (TC)

Real property can be described in any one of three generally accepted methods: (1) metes and bounds and monuments, (2) U. S. Government Survey System, (3) recorded plats.

Metes and Bounds and Monuments. (TC)

Description by metes and bounds is used as the primary means of describing real estate in twenty states including the thirteen original states, Hawaii, North Carolina, South Carolina, Tennessee, Texas, West Virginia and Kentucky, as well as parts of Ohio. A description by metes (length) and bounds (direction) is one which starts at a designated point of beginning and then proceeds to define the tract by reference to units of measurement and direction. A metes and bound description can use either a surveyor's approach or a monuments approach. The surveyor's method uses compass directions (90 degrees, 0 minutes, 0 seconds for Due East) while the monuments approach uses physical attributes such as rivers, and trees. Physical monuments are subject to destruction, removal, shifting, and do not provide lasting identification. An example of a description by metes and bounds using monuments is:

"A tract of land located in Alfalfa County, Oklahoma, described as follows: Beginning at the confluence of the Medicine and Salt Fork Rivers, thence north 660 feet along the center line of said Medicine River; thence due west 2,475 feet, more or less, to Highway 58/8; thence south 675 feet, more or less, along said center of the Salt Fork River, then east 2,460 feet, more or less, along said center line back to the point of origin."

If there is a discrepancy between the actual distance to a stated monument and the linear distance, the actual distance to the monument will prevail. A parcel can be described accurately regardless of what happens to monuments provided there is a fixed, permanently identifiable point of beginning (POB), such as a reference to sections, townships, or ranges from the Government Survey System.

Permanent reference marks (PRM) or bench marks are located throughout the country to aid surveyors in work involving elevation and altitude. A bench mark is a reference point of known elevation and location established by the U. S. Geodetic Survey, and usually identified by a marker of stone or other durable material permanently fixed in the ground. Where there is no datum (assumed point) in an area, surveyors may begin at an established bench mark for location and elevation.

U. S. Government Survey System. (TC)

The United States Government Survey System, or Rectangular Survey System, as it is usually called, is a means of describing land in thirty states, including Oklahoma. Description in terms of the Government Survey System is based upon a system adopted by Congress in 1785 which consists of lines running true north and south, called principal meridians, and lines running east and west, called base lines. The point of intersection of a principal meridian and a base line is called an initial point. Each principal meridian is identified by a name or a number and is intersected by its own base line, creating only one initial point on each principal meridian.

Land in Oklahoma is described in reference to two principal meridians. The Panhandle uses the Cimarron Meridian, while the rest of the state is described using the Indian Meridian. The Cimarron Meridian is the actual border between Oklahoma and

New Mexico and its base line is the border between the Oklahoma Panhandle and Texas. Its initial point is at the intersection of the Oklahoma, New Mexico and Texas borders. The Indian Meridian is approximately seven miles west of Davis Oklahoma, with its base line being a line which runs through Sulphur and Duncan. The Indian Meridian initial point was established by surveyors Barrett and Darling in 1871.

Standard parallels are established at 24-mile intervals north and south of the base line. The standard parallels are parallel at all points to the base line and at all point perpendicular to the meridians. Each standard parallel is referenced whether north or south of the base line (i.e., 1st Standard Parallel North). Guide meridians are established at 24-mile intervals east and west of the principal meridians running true north and perpendicular to the base line and standard parallels. Each guide meridian is referenced either east or west of the principal meridian (i.e., 1st Guide Meridian West). Guide meridians are not continuous as parallels are, but extend only from standard parallel to standard parallel. Correction lines compensate for the curvature of the earth.

Each 24-mile square unit bordered by two guide meridians and two standard parallels is referred to as a quadrangle or a surveyor's check. Each quadrangle is in turn divided into 16 squares called townships each measuring six miles on each side. The rows of townships extending east and west are numbered from the base line north or south and are referred to as townships or tiers. An example would be Township 2 North, symbolically represented by T2N. A column of townships extending north and south is called a range, and ranges are numbered from the principal meridian east or west. An example would be Range 2 East, symbolically represented R2E.

All townships are further divided into 36 squares, each called a section. Each township contains 25 full sections of approximately 640 acres each. There are 11 fractional sections (Sections 1-7, 18, 19, 30 and 31) of less than 640; acres in each township due to the correction lines which compensate for the curvature of the earth. Sections are numbered within a township starting with Number 1 at the northeast corner and proceeding to the west boundary, then down to the next row, numbering to the east boundary, then down and so on in a serpentine manner.

If less than a section is being described, smaller measures within a section may be described. When working with a description such as "the east half of the southwest quarter of the southeast quarter" of a section, it is easier to locate the parcel by reading the description backward. Thus, to locate the property, start by finding the southeast quarter of the section. Then find the southwest quarter of that, and then the east half. The size of a tract can be determined by dividing the fractions of a section into 640 acres. The tract would have 640 ÷ ¼ = 160 ÷ ¼ = 40 ÷ ½ = 20 for a total of 20 acres.

Not all sections contain exactly 640 acres. Some are smaller because of the curvature of the earth, but some may be larger or smaller than 640 acres due to historical accommodations or survey errors dating back more than a century. For a legal description of virtually every specific parcel of land to be accurate as to quantity, the words "approximately" or "more or less" should be included in the description. This helps to avoid claims that might be made later by one of the parties in an effort to rescind a contract on grounds that the quantity in a parcel was not precisely as indicated.

Government Lots. (TC)

Because of converging meridians, parcels along the north side of township Sections 1 to 6, inclusive, and along the west side of Sections 6, 7, 18, 19, 30, and 31 are fractional tracts, containing less than 40 acres each and are called government lots. They are numbered 1, 2, 3, and 4, running from east to west in Sections 1 to 6 inclusively, and from north to south along the west sides of Sections 7, 18, 19, 30, and 31. In Section 6, these "lots" are numbered 1, 2, 3, and 4, running along the north side and 4, 5, 6, and 7 along the west side. These tracts are legally and correctly described as being, for example, "Lot 4, Section 4," and "containing 39.95 acres, more or less."

Many other irregular tracts and odd amounts of acreage are also identified as government lots. These are usually found where townships border on Indian reservations, national parks, government established town sites and similar parcels of land. Government lots are also used where meandering streams course through sections so that normal-sized quarter sections cannot be established.

In the original survey, lakes, streams, or other land features were sometimes encountered that created fractional pieces of land less than a quarter-section in size. Government lots were used to delineate the area.

Because of the curvature of the earth, the square of sixteen townships (a quadrangle) is slightly narrower at the north than at the south. The shortage is taken from sections on the north and west boundary of a township so that all other sections are surveyed to exactly one mile square.

RECORDED PLATS (TC)

Land is often described in terms of its location within a certain subdivision. A plat of the subdivision will be recorded (and given a name) and such will be entered in the plat book. The plat will reveal the shape of each lot in relation to other lots, and all lots and blocks will be numbered. The main essentials are:

1. A definite starting point, clearly set out, with the corners marked accurately with permanent monuments set out on the plat. The plat corners must accurately fit the tract of land.

2. A careful and accurate survey of the tract into streets, parks (if any), lots, alleys, and the placing of permanent stones or iron stakes at the corner of all blocks and similar stakes at the corners of lots.

3. Platting of the subdivision on paper showing all blocks, lots, streets, alleys, etc. The exact size or dimension of each lot, block, alley, or street, and any other information which, in later years, may be of assistance in definitely locating any property in the subdivision.

The plat must be executed and acknowledged by the owner with streets, parks, etc., dedicated to the public. After the plat has been filed, it cannot be rescinded or vacated without all of the property owners in the addition joining in the vacation, or unless a successful suit filed in the District Court asking for a cancellation or vacation of the plat, in which case, service is required by the statutes of Oklahoma relative to the vacation of plats on all owners.

Original additions or parts thereof are sometimes later re-subdivided or amended. For instance, the size of the lots are changed or made to face a different direction. An amended plat or re-subdivision of less than the entire original addition, however, will not have the effect of waiving or changing the restrictions in the original plat. The legality of such re-plats, or re-subdivision is often questioned by attorneys, and frequently a lot will be described in more than one way or by metes and bounds description to cure such objections.

A typical lot and block description would be: "Lot 1, Block 1A, amended re-plat of the Brentwood Addition to Edmond, (Oklahoma County) Oklahoma, according to the recorded plat thereof." It is also important to be sure that the appropriate number of the addition is used. If, in the public records, there were Brentwood First and Second, the example description would not be adequate.

MEASUREMENTS

A good understanding of units of measurements is an important part of legal descriptions.

Rod	=	16 ½ feet (320 Rods = 1 mile)
Chain	=	66 feet or 100 links
Mile	=	5,280 feet (1,760 yards)
Acre	=	43,560 square feet (160 square rods)
Section	=	1 square mile (640 acres)

memorize

MEASUREMENT CALCULATIONS (TC)

A lot which is 660 feet long and 330 feet wide contains how many acres?

660 X 330 = 217,800 square feet.

Since an acre contains 43,560 square feet, divide 217,800 square feet by 43,560 square feet. The lot contains 5 acres.

How many square feet are in 2 ½ acres?

Since one acre contains 43,560 square feet, two times that amount will equal 87,120 square feet. One half of 43,560 square feet is 21,780 square feet. Add the number of square feet in two acres (87,120) to the number of square feet in one half acre (21,780) and the answer will be 108,900 square feet in 2 ½ acres.

How many acres are contained in the following legal description?

W 1/2 of SW ¼ & W ½ of E ½ of SW ¼ of Section 20 T11N, R2W

To read a legal description, begin from the left side and read as you normally would in and English sentence. However, to "work the problem" (find out how many acres are contained in the legal description), begin with the section number and work to the left, dividing as you go. For example:

Section 20 contains 640 acres.

The SW ¼ of section 20 would be ¼ of 640 or 160 acres.
The E ½ of the SW ¼ is one half of the SW ¼ or 80 acres.

The W ½ of the E ½ is one half of the E ½ or 40 acres.

NOTE: when working these kinds of problems an ampersand (&) means to add the two parts together. Therefore the second half of the problem is as follows:

The SW ¼ on the left side of the "and" sign (&) is the same SW ¼ at the beginning of this problem. It is the same 160 acres.

The other half of the problem is asking for the W ½ of the same SW ¼ of section 20. Therefore, one half of the SW ¼ is 80 acres.

Add the 40 acres on the right side of the problem to the 80 acres on the left side of the problems and the total number of acres in the legal description is 120 acres.

44

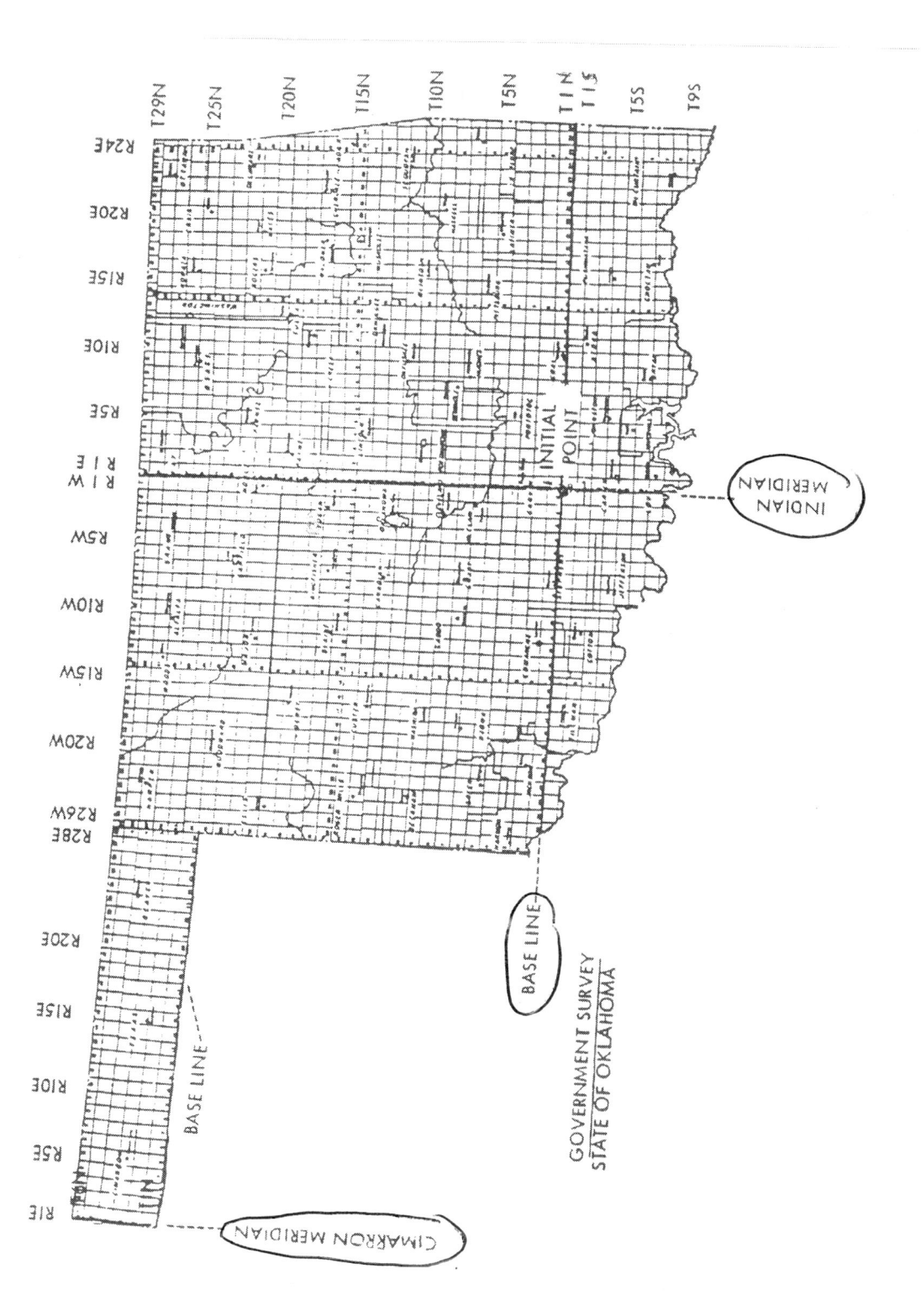

GOVERNMENT SURVEY
STATE OF OKLAHOMA

Quadrangle Division (Townships)

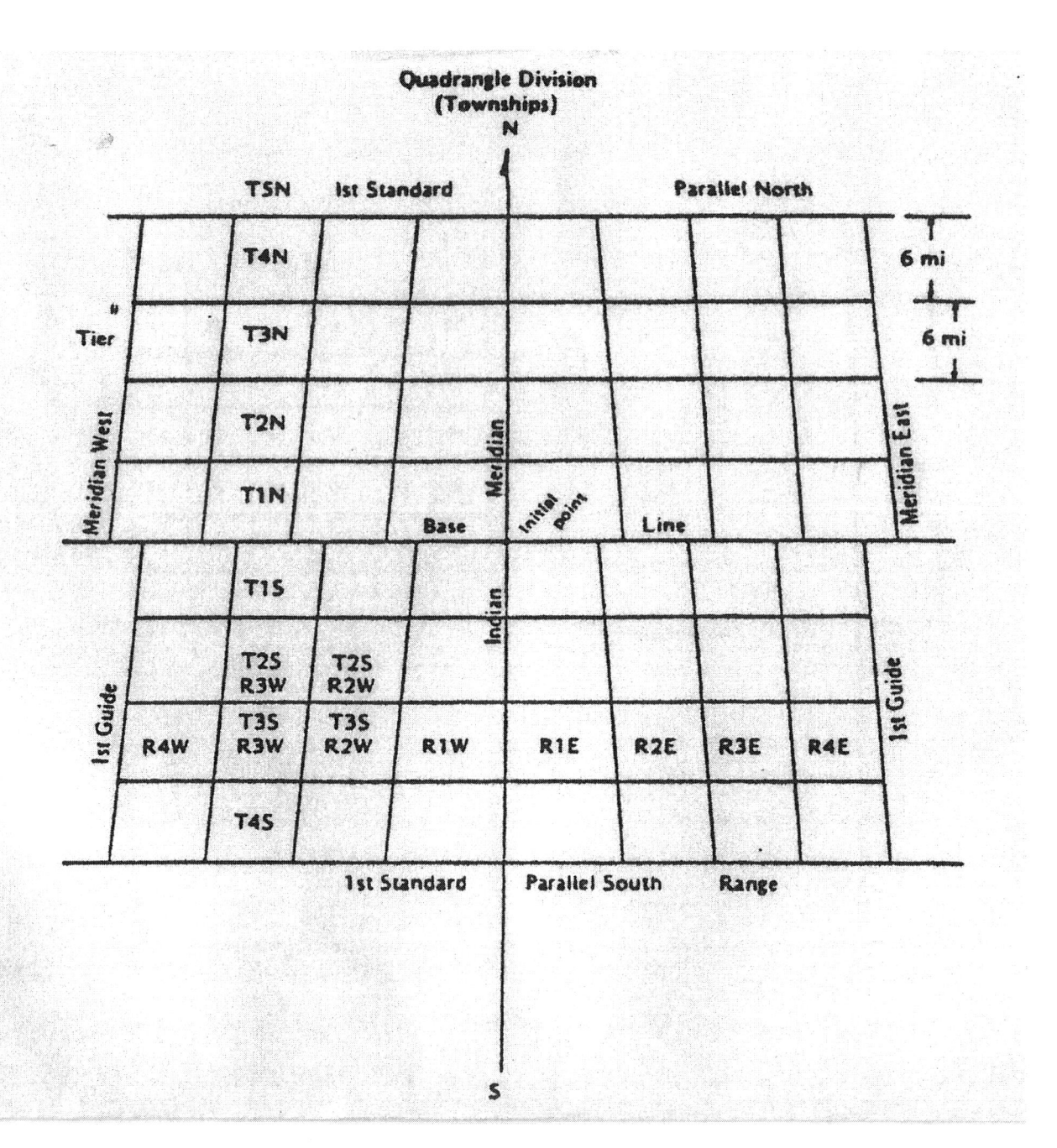

	T5N	1st Standard		Parallel North			
	T4N						
	T3N						
	T2N						
	T1N		Base	Initial point	Line		
	T1S						
	T2S R3W	T2S R2W					
R4W	T3S R3W	T3S R2W	R1W	R1E	R2E	R3E	R4E
	T4S						

Tier — Meridian West — Meridian — Indian — Meridian East

1st Guide — 1st Standard Parallel South — Range — 1st Guide

6 mi / 6 mi

N / S

Township Division
(Sections)

6	5	4	3	2	1
7	8	9	10	11	12
18	17	16	15	14	13
19	20	21	22	23	24
30	29	28	27	26	25
31	32	33	34	35	36

T2S R3W | T2S R2W

T3S R2W

Range Line | Township Line

6 mi | 1 mi

Ch. 4

TEST YOUR UNDERSTANDING

1. **Land in Oklahoma, under the governmental survey system, is described by**
    1. the Cimarron Meridian.
    2. the Indian Meridian.
    3. Both 1 and 2
    4. Neither 1 nor 2..

2. **The main base line in Oklahoma**
    1. runs north and south in the western part o the state.
    2. runs east and west in the southern part of the state.
    3. runs north and south in the eastern part of the state.
    4. runs east and west in the northern part of the state.

3. **The point of intersection of a principal meridian and a base line is the**
    1. point of no return.
    2. initial point.
    3. major intersection.
    4. crossroads.

4. **An example of a government lot is**
    1. tract along the west or north side of a township which, because of the curvature of the earth, contains less than 40 acres.
    2. any parcel of real property owned by the state or by a political subdivision of the state.
    3. a parcel of land along the shore of a lake or river, usually containing less than 40 acres.
    4. Both 1 and 3.

5. **A township is**
    1. 6 miles square.
    2. 6 square miles.
    3. 36 miles square.
    4. 24 miles square.

6. **The sections in a township are numbered in a serpentine pattern that always begins in which corner of the township?**
    1. The SW corner.
    2. The SE corner.
    3. The NE corner.
    4. The NW corner..

7. **The section of land that is locate immediately to the east of Section 1 would be Section**
    1. 2.
    2. 6.
    3. 12.
    4. 7.

8. **All of the following are true statements about metes and bounds descriptions, EXCEPT**
    1. legal description by metes and bounds is often used when the subject property is not included in a duly recorded map.
    2. the primary advantages of a metes and bounds description are brevity, simplicity and uniform interpretations.
    3. metes and bounds descriptions are valid even if the property could be described otherwise.
    4. metes and bounds descriptions are sometimes used because of peculiar shapes of the subject properties.

9. **In a metes and bounds description,**
    1. boundaries are established on the basis of actual distance between monuments.
    2. the boundary must return to the point of beginning (POB).
    3. the method may be highly complicated.
    4. All of the above.

10. A monument may be
 1. any physically identifiable object.
 2. a concrete marker on an iron pipe.
 3. Both 1 and 2.
 4. Neither 1 nor 2.

11. How many square feet are in 1 ¼ acres?
 1. 10,890.
 2. 44,649.
 3. 54,450.
 4. 152,460.

ANSWERS AND EXPLANATIONS

1. 3 Oklahoma has two principal meridians. The Indian Meridian runs north and south near the center of state. The Cimarron Meridian runs along the New Mexico/Oklahoma border.

2. 2 The main base line in Oklahoma intersects the Indian Meridian. A second base line is the Texas/Oklahoma border in the Panhandle.

3. 2 The initial point for the Indian Meridian is west of Davis, Oklahoma. The initial point for the Cimarrom Meridian is the southwest corner of the Panhandle where the Texas, Oklahoma and New Mexico borders meet.

4. 4 A government lot is an irregular-sized parcel of land, usually containing less than 40 acres.

5. 1 Six square miles include only six sections. A check is 24 miles square.

6. 3 Numbering of sections in townships begin in the NE corner and end in the SE corner.

7. 2 This would be in the adjacent township.

8. 2 Metes and bounds descriptions are frequently complex, lengthy, and difficult to understand.

9. 4 A metes and bounds description is based on distances between points and the description must "close." It is rarely a simple description.

10. 3 A monument is an identifiable landmark that serves as a corner of a property.

11. 3   43,560 X 1 ¼ = 54,450.

TITLE SEARCH, ENCUMBRANCES AND LAND USE CONTROL

EVIDENCE OF TITLE (TC)

A prudent person buying real estate will want to know the exact state of the title of the seller and will demand that the seller furnish evidence of ownership in accordance with prevailing title standards. The fact that a seller can produce a deed to the property naming the seller as the grantee is not adequate title as there may be some lesser degree of ownership. The title may be technically free and clear or it may be legally un-merchantable. The title may be heavily encumbered by liens and restrictions. In addition, the lenders will be greatly concerned with the state of the title as they will normally be accepting a mortgage on this property as security for the repayment of the loan.

Public Record. (TC)

The only "true evidence of title" is the county's records. The purpose of recording any instrument is to give notice to the world of the transaction. Recording a deed or any document that affects ownership in land is not compulsory, but is a right of the holder. If such documents are recorded, the chain of title continues on record.

The recorder will note on the instrument the filing number and the exact time at which the document was filed, including the year, month, day, hour, and minute that it was received. The contents of the document are then reproduced and filed in the appropriate book of records. The original instrument is returned to the person who left it to be recorded. The recorded instrument is a matter of public record and anyone desiring to examine information regarding a particular parcel of property may do so by visiting the county courthouse where the document is recorded.

Present interests in real property are protected if documents affecting the title are recorded. All subsequent recordation of instruments affecting the same property will be subordinate to the right of the present interest holder. Recordation of subsequent interest in real property protects the interest against claimants whose interests have not yet been recorded. This conforms to the general recording maxim, "first to record is first in right." Known as the race notice concept, "the first to record is first in right."

Recording Title. (TC)

A properly executed deed is effectual between the parties without recording, but in order to be effectual against the world, it must be recorded in the proper office. The principal office for recording is the office of the county clerk of the county in which the real property is located. The seventy-seven county clerks in Oklahoma are charged with the duty of maintaining public records relating to rights
and duties associated with real estate. However, not all documents affecting real property appear in the county clerk's records. Court decrees, for example, which may profoundly affect titles, may be found in a different office.

Notice. (TC)

Title recordation acts as a means of protecting title to real property against all persons who may later claim a right against the property.

Actual Notice. (TC)

In previous times the seller would take the new owner around and introduce him/her to the neighbors and tell them this was the new owner of the property. This is referred to as "actual" notice, the conveying of information by word of mouth regarding possession of the property.

Constructive Notice. (TC)

Recording is constructive notice to the world, a legal presumption that everyone in the world has been informed of the existence and content of the document being recorded. This provides documentation in a county office for reference by any interested party.

Inquiry Notice.

Inquiry notice has to do with information or facts concerning a property which would put a reasonable person on notice that he/she should investigate the issue or matter to a greater extent.

Chain of Title. (TC)

A chain of title is a record of a property's grantors and grantees, linking one owner to the next throughout the legal history of the parcel of land. Whenever the link is broken or unclear, a cloud is created and there is a flaw in the title. All recorded instruments affecting a parcel of real property are a part of the chain of title, indexed in the order of their actual occurrence.

ABSTRACT OF TITLE (TC)

As recorded documents are extremely difficult and time-consuming to examine, the major evidence of title has become the abstract. To the average purchaser, the abstract affords no knowledge of the state of the title to the real estate. An attorney's opinion is needed to inform the prospective purchaser of the nature of the seller's title and of any defects, liens, encumbrances, or other rights which might be disclosed by the abstract.

All counties in the state provide for the recording, in a public office, of every document by which any estate or interest in land is created, transferred, encumbered, or otherwise affected. These public records furnish a reliable history of the title or ownership of the tract of land. The abstract of title is a summary or a copy of every recorded instrument affecting the title to the tract of real estate covered
by the abstract and is compiled by a duly licensed abstractor who conducts a title search. If covered by the abstractor's certificate, "filed" instruments which are not technically recorded instruments may also be included. These are such documents as security agreements, financing statements, chattel mortgages and certain liens.

Innocent Purchaser/Unrecorded Documents.

The law provides that no document affecting the right in real estate shall be valid against any person who does not have actual knowledge of the rights of the parties unless that document is recorded. Therefore, an innocent and unknowing purchaser or encumbrancer who acts in ignorance of an unrecorded instrument is reasonably protected. However, for an innocent buyer to become a bona fide purchaser, and prevail over a prior purchaser of the same real property, three conditions must exist:

1. The innocent purchaser must be without knowledge of the prior claim at the time of purchase;

2. The purchase must be for value; and

3. The document must be the first recorded.

In effect, the purchaser for value must win the race to the recording office and be without notice of the prior claim at the time value was given.

TITLE OPINION (TC)

Marketable title to real property is generally determined by an examination of an abstract of title. The examiner will issue an opinion of title containing views as to the interest of grantors and their parties in a parcel of real estate.

The buyer's title opinion, generally called the purchaser's title opinion, is the chief instrument upon which the buyer relies. It represents an attorney's comments, opinions, and requirements concerning the state of the title to the property, as disclosed in the abstract delivered. It is written solely for the buyer from the buyer's point of view.

The buyer should not rely on a mortgagee's title opinion since it is written with an entirely different goal in mind. Many defects are of no interest to the mortgagee but may be of great concern to the purchaser who may have to pay later to have them cleared.

The mortgagee will try to obtain a title opinion relating to the mortgaged property making sure that there are no outstanding liens or encumbrances which may be superior to that of the intended mortgage. The mortgagee is simply looking for "security" for the investment. It will not be the mortgagee's problem or expense to render the title marketable.

The abstractor is not a guarantor of the title to the real estate. The law imposes upon the abstractor only the duty to exercise due care in searching the title and in the preparation of the abstract. The abstractor can be held liable for any loss caused the purchaser as a result of negligence in omission of a document from the abstract or the incorrect summarization to the content of the instrument. Likewise, an attorney can only be held liable for damages which are caused by negligence in the examination of the abstract. For example, the attorney is liable for any loss caused by failure to discover an existing recorded lien contained in the abstract.

No evidence of title can completely and conclusively reveal the exact state of the title to real property. For instance, an abstract may indicate that the seller has clear title, but the chain of title may contain a forged deed. There is no way of knowing from the abstract whether or not a deed is forged and, of course, such deed passes no title. Also, an abstract will not reveal the rights of parties in possession. The abstract may show title in one person but another may have a superior right through adverse possession. With an abstract and an opinion, together with an examination of the property itself, the buyer can be reasonably certain that a good title can be obtained.

CLOUD ON TITLE (TC)

The usual means of curing a defect or a cloud on the title to the property are by the obtaining quitclaim deeds from all other parties who might have an interest in the property or bringing an action to quiet title.

TITLE INSURANCE (TC)

Title insurance is a contract which protects the insured against loss occurring through defects in the title to real property. The risk of loss, as in other policies of insurance, is transferred from the property owner to a responsible insurer. A title company will not insure a bad title any more than a life insurance company will insure a person who is terminally ill.

Basically, a title insurance policy provides that the company will indemnify the owner against any loss sustained as a result of a defect in the title to the real estate, provided that the defect is not specifically excluded in the policy. Further, the company usually agrees to defend at its expense any lawsuit attacking the title where such attack is based on a claimed defect covered by the insurance provisions.

Examples of typical standard exclusions which the title policy does not insure against are:

1. Rights and claims of parties in possession not shown of record, including unrecorded easements.

2. Any statement of facts an accurate survey would show.

3. Mechanic's liens, or any rights thereto, where no notice of such liens or rights appear of record.

4. Taxes and assessments not yet due or payable and special assessments not yet certified to the treasurer's office.

For additional consideration, all-inclusive owner's title policies may be obtained covering standard exclusions.

Should the title insurance company pay a loss within the scope of the policy, the principle of subrogation provides that the company may attempt to collect the loss from a third party in the place of the insured.

OWNER'S AND MORTGAGEE'S POLICY (TC)

Title insurance companies will issue policies to both the owner and the mortgagee. The fee or premium of the title policy, unlike other insurance, is paid only once and the policy continues in force without further payment. The premium, as with other insurance, is based upon the amount of insurance purchased. The owner's title policy is not transferable. Therefore, when the property is resold, the new purchaser should obtain a reissue title policy.

The mortgagee's title policy does not protect the owner's interest in the property. A mortgagee's policy will protect only the mortgagee and only to the extent of the mortgagee's interest, whatever that may be. The equity of the owner is protected only by an owner's title policy. In the case of mortgagee's policy, if the insurer pays the mortgage, the insurance company could enforce the mortgage against the mortgagor.

ENCUMBRANCES AFFECTING THE PHYSICAL CONDITION OR USE OF REAL PROPERTY (TC)

Encumbrance. (TC)

An adverse interest affecting title is known as an encumbrance. It is the right or interest in property held by others who are not the legal owners of the property. An encumbrance is any claim, lien charge, or liability attached to and binding on real property which may affect its value, or burden, or obstruct, or impair the use of the property. Although it may lessen the value of the title, it does not necessarily prevent the transfer of ownership.

Public and private actions can have the effect of limiting the ability of the landowner to exercise absolute control over the condition and use of real property. Deed restrictions, easements, licenses, water rights, and encroachments are all examples of such encumbrances or controls.

Deed Restrictions/Restrictive Covenants. (TC)

Restrictions are placed in the deed to control a land owner's use of real property. The grantor may place restrictions upon the right to use the real estate conveyed. Such restrictions must be reasonable and not contrary to public policy. The use of restrictions, usually called deed restrictions or restrictive covenants, is an old practice arising from the rights of property. Owners have the right of free alienation; that is, they may dispose of their estates in any manner they may elect. Deed restrictions, once established, normally run with the land and are a limitation upon the use of all future grantees.

Restrictions are most frequently encountered in the development of subdivisions wherein the limitation is for the benefit of all the landowners. Typical restrictions deal with the minimum size of
the house, type of material that may be used, and exclusion of commercial establishments. Well formulated restrictions have a stabilizing effect upon property value. Home owners are protected against forbidden uses. They can rely on the knowledge that a business will not be established next door and that their neighbor's house must conform to certain minimum standards. Violations of restrictions can be enjoined through a court action brought by any party for whose benefit the restrictions were imposed.

Court enforcement of just deed restrictions is possible to the extent that it can be proven that a restriction has been violated. Any action may be brought to require the violator to conform to the deed restrictions. Enforcement may be sought by the parties to the original deed which contained the restriction and by those persons who are not parties to the agreement if the restriction is imposed for their benefit (e.g., lot buyers within a subdivision).

Deed restrictions may be given an express lifetime by expressing their duration in the deed. Otherwise, such restrictions will terminate by material change in the neighborhood, by unanimous agreement between or among affected parties, and by merger in which one land owner acquires the interest of all persons owning subject to the restriction. Court action will usually be required to properly effect such termination.

Easements. (TC)

An easement is a right-of-way or right to use another's real property or a portion thereof. An easement holder claims no title to the real property over which the easement exists; rather, an easement carries with it the right to enter and use the property within definable limits.

There are two general types of easements. The easement may be either appurtenant or it may be in gross. An easement appurtenant attaches to and runs with ownership of land. An easement in gross belongs to its owner personally and such right does not pass with transfer of ownership of land.

Easements may be created by a voluntary act or by operation of law. A voluntary act would be by deed or by contract. If an easement is created by contract, the contract must be in writing to be enforceable because easements are interests in real property covered by the Statute of Frauds. An easement may be created by granting such right in a deed, or it may arise through a specific deed reservation of an easement by the grantor of real property.

Easements may also come into existence by implication or by prescription. An easement by implication would be recognized in buyers who purchase land which is totally inaccessible to a public highway except across land retained by the seller. Since the buyers have access rights, right to ingress and egress to and from their land, the buyers obtain an easement by implication over the seller's land (this is also called an easement by necessity). An easement by prescription is one obtained by continuous use of another's property for the statutory period (fifteen years in Oklahoma).

Dominant and servient parcels are common terms used in connection with easements. An easement appurtenant to travel across a neighbor's property is a dominant tenement. Property over which an easement runs in favor of another parcel of real estate is the servient tenement.

An easement may be terminated by a written release given by the easement owner to the affected landowner. The writing could be by quitclaim deed which is a conveyance by the easement owner of legal right, title, and interest in the affected parcel, an easement may be terminated by merger in which the owner of either the dominant or servient parcel acquires ownership of the other parcel. Mutual agreement, abandonment, end of the necessity (regarding an easement by necessity), destruction of the servient estate, acquisition of the servient estate by a bona fide purchaser (a person having neither actual or constructive knowledge of the easement), and severance are other means of terminating easements.

License. (TC)

A license is neither a right nor an estate in land, nor is it an encumbrance against land. It is a personal privilege to make reasonable use of the real property of the licensor. Unlike an easement, a license is revocable by the granting party at any time. A license may be oral or in writing, and it may or may not be based upon a contract. Death of either party will terminate a license. Examples of a license would be the privilege to hunt on the property of a neighbor or to park an automobile in a parking lot. Also in this category are tickets to theaters or sporting events.

Encroachments. (TC)

An encroachment is the wrongful extension of a structure or other improvement into the property of another. Buildings, fences, and other structures may encroach on adjacent land. Most encroachments are revealed by an accurate land survey. The party encroached upon, may or may not have the ability to have the encroachment removed, depending upon the circumstances.

If an encroachment has been present for the statutory period (fifteen years), the owner of the encroaching structure may assert a right to the affected land on the basis of adverse possession (title by prescription). If the owner of such structure cannot claim adverse possession, the party encroached upon may bring action to have the encroachment removed on the grounds of trespass.

ENCUMBRANCES AFFECTING TITLE

Liens. (TC)

A lien is a right given to a creditor to have a debt or charge satisfied out of the real or personal property belonging to a debtor. It always arises from a debt and can be created by agreement of the parties (such as in a mortgage) or by operation of law (such as in tax liens). A lien may be a general lien, affecting all of the debtor's property, as in the case of a judgment lien. It can also be a special lien, affecting only a specific property, as when a mortgage is given on one piece of property.

Liens can be statutory or equitable, voluntary or involuntary. For example, a mechanic's lien is an involuntary, statutory, special lien, whereas a mortgage is a voluntary, equitable, special lien.

At the initiation of a law suit, the plaintiff who wishes to make known the claim against the property may do so by filing a statutory notice of lis pendens or pendency of action. This should be filed in the county in which the property is located, giving constructive notice of a claim against the real property of the debtor.

Liens do not transfer title to the property. Until foreclosure, the debtor retains title. Certain statutory liens (mechanic's liens and judgments) become unenforceable after a lapse of time from origination or recording unless a foreclosure suit is filed. The senior or prior lien is normally determined by the date of recordation. State property tax liens and assessments, however, take priority over all liens, even those previously recorded.

Mortgages. (TC)

The mortgage is the most typical encumbrance against real property. It is a voluntary lien, in that the property owner voluntary gives a lien, a mortgage, to a lender to secure the lender's risk in making the loan. A mortgage is a means, recognized by law, by which property is pledged as security for the payment of debt.

Lien and Title Theory. (TC)

There are two different systems for securing a lender's interest (loan) in real property in the United States. One is called "Lien Theory of Mortgages" and the other is called "Title Theory of Mortgages."

In Oklahoma, and most other states, Lien Theory is the practice. In Lien Theory, the borrower enters into a contract with a lender to borrow money. This contract is called a "note" and specifies the amount of the loan, the interest rate, the duration of the loan, method of repayment and many other terms. Once the borrower and lender enter into a loan (note) the lender will request the borrower to give (to the lender) a mortgage for the purpose of securing the lender's interest in the property. This is called "securitizing the debt." Essentially, the borrower gives the lender the right to foreclose (take through legal means) the property should the borrower fail to pay back the loan.

In Lien Theory, the ownership rights are conveyed to the buyer through a deed. The deed is then recorded in the County Clerk's Office in the name of the buyer.

In those few states which practice Title Theory, a deed of trust is used. A deed of trust is an instrument which conveys ownership rights to a third party, usually a trust company, as security for the debt. Essentially, a deed of trust serves as a common law mortgage, though it is not a mortgage.

The parties involved in a deed of trust are the TRUSTOR, the borrower, the BENEFICIARY, the lender, and the TRUSTEE, the neutral third party.

In the deed of trust arrangement, the borrower gives the lender a note (the instrument of indebtedness) and the deed (of trust) is conveyed to a third party, the trustee, where it is held until the note is paid off. The deed of trust is recorded in the county where the property is located for the purpose of constructive notice.

In the deed of trust situation, the owner is said to have NAKED or BARE title because the purchaser has the usual rights of ownership such as possession, use and the right to sell. When the purchaser pays off the debt, the lender will authorize request of re-conveyance and the trustee will cancel the note and issue a re-conveyance or release deed which conveys the deed to the borrower. This document is then recorded by he borrower.

Property Taxes. (TC)

Unpaid state, county, municipal, or quasi-public (e.g., school board) real estate taxes may result in a special lien against the taxed real property. The taxing entity may ultimately conduct a tax sale of the affected real property to satisfy the debt.

Certain real property is exempted in whole or in part from real estate taxation. The most typical of tax exempt property are public libraries, free museums, public cemeteries, non-profit schools and colleges, and property used exclusively for religious or charitable purposes.

Ad Valorem Taxes. (TC)

Real property taxes (ad valorem taxes) are apportioned according to the value of nonexempt property. The determination of the property value is the duty of the county assessor, or duly elected county officer. There are generally two methods of determining the assessed valuation of real estate.

The first method values property at fair market value and deducts exemptions to determine the taxable valuation (assessment). This is a market value assessment.

The second method values property at fair market value then applies a fractional percentage against the value to determine the assessment in which exemptions are deducted to determine the net assessed valuation. Such assessment is then used to determine the tax liability imposed against each parcel of real property in the county. Oklahoma is a fractional assessment state since all taxable real property in the state is assessed annually at not less than 10 % nor more than 13 ½% (by state Constitution) of its fair cash value, estimated at the price it would bring at a fair voluntary sale. The Oklahoma Supreme Court has determined that fair cash value is synonymous with fair market value.

The tax rate is described in terms of millage or mills (a mill is one thousandth of a dollar). The millage applied to the valuation of a particular parcel of land determines the tax liability of that parcel. There are generally two methods used by various states to determine their tax rate. They may set a fixed rate in the constitutional and statutory laws. They may also allow the tax rate to increase or decrease (float) based on the budgets submitted and the net assessed valuation. Oklahoma uses a fixed tax rate system for the general funds for each specific taxing jurisdiction as set out in Article 10 of the Oklahoma Constitution.

Tax Liens. (TC)

Tax liens are usually enforced through forced public sales of the affected real property. Generally, the owner of the property is given a period of redemption during which time he/she may buy back the real
property for the sale price plus a penalty assessed as a percentage of the price brought from the public sale. Tax (and special assessment) liens are prior, superior, and paramount to all other liens, claims, or encumbrances of whatever character, including those of a mortgagee, judgment creditor, or other lien holder whose rights were performed prior to the date that the tax lien was filed in the District Court judgment docket, located in the office of the count clerk.

Special Assessments. (TC)

Special assessments are taxes or levies customarily imposed against only those specific parcels of realty that will benefit from a proposed public improvement. Whereas property taxes are levied for the support of the general functions of government, special assessments cover the cost of specific local improvements such as streets, sewers, irrigation, and drainage.

The owner usually has the option of paying special assessments in installments over several years with interest or paying the balance in full at the beginning.

When property is sold, the sales contract should specify which party is responsible for payment of the assessments, if any, at the time of closing. Because of the increased property value generally resulting from the improvement, the seller usually pays for all improvements substantially completed by the closing date. Improvements not substantially completed but authorized by the closing date are usually assumed by the buyer.

Special assessments are generally apportioned according to benefits received, rather than by the value of the land and buildings being assessed. For example, in a residential subdivision, the assessment for installation of storm drains, curbs and gutters is made on a front-foot basis. The property owners are charged for each foot of that lot that abuts the street being improved. In the case of a street being paved for the first time, all nearby properties may share in the assessment in some proportion based on proximity to the improvement.

Owners of condominiums may be subject to special assessments if major improvements are made to the building such as installation of automatic elevators or corridor carpeting.

Mechanic's Liens. (TC)

A mechanic's lien is a statutory lien (created by the legislature) in favor of those who furnish labor or materials for the improvement of real property, not repairs. These liens tend to improve the chances of such persons receiving compensation for the labor and materials provided.

The lien obtained by a person furnishing materials for such an improvement is called a materialman's lien, but the law relating to both liens is the same, and both liens will be treated the same in this discussion. Such statutory liens may be obtained by all persons, including day laborers, who provide labor or materials for the improvement of real property.

A person has a maximum of four months from the last date that labor or materials were furnished to file a mechanic's lien. The lien is filed at the county clerk's office of the county in which the real property is located. This four month limitation applies to persons who are in a direct contract relationship with the owner of the real property (generally the contractor). Those who furnish labor or materials and are not involved directly in a contract with the owner of the real property (sub-contractors) have ninety days after the date labor or materials were last furnished to file their mechanic's lien. Under certain circumstances, a laborer may file a lien within eight months after labor is performed.

A mechanic's lien is superior to all liens which were filed subsequent to the commencement of such
labor or provision of materials by the lien holder. This lien is also superior over any lien of which the lien holder had no notice, and which was unrecorded at the time of the commencement of the work or the providing of materials by the lien holder. If the underlying debt is paid to the lien holder, the lien is terminated or if the lien is proven invalid in a court of law, the lien is terminated. If a valid lien exists, such lien may be discharged by the person against whose interest such lien was filed by depositing with the county clerk the amount of such claim in cash and executing a bond to the claim. In the case of a lien in question, the same process may be used until the court can make a determination.

Failure to pursue a mechanic's lien within one year will terminate the lien. If enforcement is pursued and payment on the debt is not forthcoming, the lien holder may have the affected real property sold to satisfy the debt. If the affected property is a homestead, certain conditions must have been met before the lien may attach to force sale of the property (i.e., the improvements must have been agreed to by both husband and wife).

Other Special Liens. (TC)

Other liens affecting only one parcel of land include vendee's lien, available to the buyer (vendee) of real property in the event of the seller's breach, vendor's lien, available to the seller (vendor) where buyer does not pay the seller the purchase price, and attachment of surety bond liens.

Unpaid Specific Taxes. (TC)

Nonpayment of tax liabilities based upon such taxes as state and federal income and/or estate taxes, corporate franchise taxes, etc., generally causes a lien to be placed on all property owned by the nonpaying party. If the specific tax is a state tax and the estate has not paid such a tax, a lien is placed over all of the real and personal property included in the estate. Clear title to a property cannot be given until tax liens are discharged.

Decedent's Debts. (TC)

The debts of a decedent must be paid out of the estate. It is not uncommon for the decedent to have included a provision in a will which sets aside money or assets to pay outstanding debts. If no such

provision is present, or if a decedent dies intestate, the property of the estate must be used to satisfy debts. A lien against all estate property, except homestead property, exists on the basis of all just debts
acquired by the decedent while living. Personal property will be resorted to first to satisfy such debts,
but in the event that the personal property is insufficient to pay the debts, resort may be had to real property contained in the state of the debtor.

Judgments. (TC)

A judgment is a special determination in a legal action as to the rights and liabilities of the parties. The most common legal judgment is one for the money damages. Once a money judgment is obtained, the judgment creditor (the person who has obtained the judgment) acquires a lien over all the property of the judgment debtor, except homestead property, if the property is located in the same county as the court where such judgment was rendered. By properly filing (docketing) such judgment lien in other counties in which the judgment debtor owns property, the judgment creditor may obtain a lien over most property owned by the debtor.

If the debtor fails to pay on the judgment, the creditor may bring an action to have the debtor's property sold to satisfy the judgment debt. The debtor's personal property will be sold first, but if the sale of the personal property is insufficient to cover the judgment, the real property over which the creditor has obtained a judgment lien will be sold to satisfy the debt.

PUBLIC LAND USE CONTROL (TC)

Property continues to be limited by government powers including the power of taxation, police power, the right of eminent domain and escheat. The power of taxation, which is complicated, involved and ever changing, was covered earlier in this chapter. The right of eminent domain and escheat relate to involuntary transfer of property. Police power is the right of the public to control and limit an owner's use of private property.

Police Power. (TC)

Police power is the constitutional authority and inherent power of government to adopt and enforce laws and regulations to promote and support the public health, safety, morals, and general welfare. It is in essence, policy power, controlling such functions as zoning, city planning, subdividing, building codes and environmental protection.

Zoning. (TC)

Zoning authority is the power of government officials to specify the types of uses to which properties may be put in specific areas. Zoning generally divides land use into the four broad categories of residential, commercial, industrial, and agricultural.

In addition to specifying the land use, zoning laws may impose additional restrictions, such as size of structures, minimum square feet, height limits and set back requirements.

Zoning laws are enforced by requiring a building permit from an appropriate governmental authority. Nonconforming use is permitted when that use was previously lawfully established and maintained. In case of substantial destruction by fire or other means, the zoning statutes probably will prohibit reconstruction for nonconforming use caused by a change in zoning.

New usage not conforming to established regulations will require a variance or an amendment to the ordinance.

City Planning. (TC)

City planning is an attempt to regulate in a general way the long-range physical geography of the city. These plans will incorporate such items as land use, flood control, sewage disposal, streets, recreation, and solid waste disposal into a comprehensive plan which will guide the city as it is required to make specific decisions about proposed projects, population growth, and other matters affecting the public welfare. Private actions which may contravene a city "master or comprehensive" plan will be prohibited by a planning commission unless those initiating such action can carry the burden of showing that the action is in substantial compliance with the plan.

Private development or subdividing of land may be regulated at the federal, state or local level. ***The Oklahoma Subdivided Land Sales Code*** generally requires private developers of subdivisions located outside the state and containing twenty lots or more to make certain disclosures in all subdivision sales transactions. The subdivisions must be registered as security with the Oklahoma Securities Commission.

Master Plan. (TC)

A municipality may call the master plan by other names, Frequently, the master plan is called a comprehensive plan or a general plan. No matter by which name it is called, the master plan is developed according to the direction of the municipality's planning commission. The first thing the planning commission will do to develop its master plan is to conduct a survey of the physical and economic characteristics of the area. The physical survey will map the roads, utility lines, and developed and undeveloped lands in the area. The economic survey looks at the economic base of the community and its potential for future economic development. The results these two surveys become the basic information upon which the master plan is developed.

The master plan will be developed with a view to the future development of the municipality. Social, recreational and cultural opportunities as well as jobs and housing are considered. The aim is generally, to develop a plan which will allow the future development of the municipality in a balanced and effective way.

The master plan becomes a foundational instrument for which future zoning and developmental plans may be made. Inherent in this is the intent of the planners to look to the future fifteen to twenty-five years of anticipated growth and development including the economic and social aspects of the community's development.

Government is in the infrastructure business. Municipalities' master plans are essential in the growth and development of the infrastructure on which its citizens depend. The master plan considers the addition of new housing developments, shopping and industrial areas, electric grid, sewer systems, streets and transportation facilities, schools, entertainment districts, commercial areas, etc.

Building Codes. (TC)

Building codes are designated to provide minimum standards to safeguard the health, safety, and welfare of the public by regulating and controlling the design, construction, quality, use and occupancy, location and building line, and maintenance of all buildings and structures. Although Section 324.8, Title 74, Oklahoma Statutes, sets minimum standards, rules established by local governments for building restrictions are not uniform and vary widely from community to community.

Violations of building codes may render a property unmarketable. Proposed construction must conform to local zoning and building codes, and must generally be inspected and approved before completion and occupancy. Upon satisfactory completion, an occupancy certificate may be issued. Nonconformance to building codes can result in forced demolition.

Environmental Protection. (TC)

With regard to cleanliness and pollution, local and state health departments control commercial ventures such as restaurants, heavy industry, and transportation. State and federal environmental laws and regulations have been passed to control both public and private pollution. The primary regulating body at the federal level is the Environmental Protection Agency. This agency has the power to regulate and enforce such laws as the **Clean Air Act**, the **Water Pollution Control Act**, the **Solid-Waste Disposal Act**, and others. If private development is such that environmental factors are endangered or conservation of natural resources is jeopardized, the EPA will most likely have jurisdiction to oversee and regulate such development.

At the state level, the State Health Department, Water Resources Board and the Department of Environmental Quality are the primary agencies charged with regulation of environmental matters. These agencies have the power to regulate actions, especially purely intra-state actions, which may have an impact on the environment. Municipalities may also play a role in environmental control through ordinances and zoning.

Wet Lands. (TC)

The national Resources Conversation Service has identified wetlands which are other than swamps, floodplains and marshes. However, wetlands are those which have enough water on the surface to allow the growth of a water plant community. These are generally subject to flooding and are protected by federal, state and local environmental controls.

Tidelands. (TC)

Tidelands are those areas near the ocean where the tide periodically ebbs and flows. If the land is not subject to the flow of the tide, it is considered beach. Typically these tidewater lands are federal properties.

Coastal and Shoreline Regulations. (TC)

The Coastal Zone Management Act went into effect in 1972. Its intent is to preserve and
enhance the management, use, protection and development of the Great Lakes and
saltwater coastal zones. It encourages states to plan for the use and development of land and water resources in coastal zones.

Utility and Tax Districts. (TC)

In Texas, and some other states, municipalities form Municipal Utility Districts, called a "MUD." In jurisdictions which have "MUD's" they are formed to provide water, sewage, drainage and other services in the district. They are frequently under the overall jurisdiction of the state's environmental quality regulation agency such as the Texas Commission of Environmental Quality.

In general, these Municipal Utility Districts are formed because the citizens of a community petition the state agency for its creation. A public hearing is held and, publicly elected board of directors continues the supervision of the MUD.
A Municipal Utility District is supported by taxes on real property. MUDs may also develop conservation, irrigation, electrical generation, firefighting, waste collection and disposal and recreational projects as funds collected allow.

Flight Paths. (TC)

The term "avigation easement" is of relative recent origins. The term applies to the space around airports which contributes to the organized, safe movement of aircraft into and out of airports. Avigation easements are acquired by local governments when the noise and inconvenience of low flying aircraft interfere with the use and enjoyment of property in the flight paths of airports. These avigation easements may come into existence through the exercise of eminent domain.

Stigmatized Properties. (TC)

Stigmatized properties are also called psychologically impacted properties. These are properties wherein a violent crime or even the suspicion that it is haunted. In some states, even the proximity of gang-related activity or even a nuclear power plant may cause a property to be stigmatized. Included in this classification is such diseases as AIDS and other diseases which may not be transferred by occupancy.

Some states require the disclosure of certain stigmas such as violent crimes and gang-related activities. However, such things as AIDS and other health issues are not to be disclosed. Both state and federal laws prohibit disclosure of another person's health information without that person's permission. In Oklahoma the Real Estate License Code specifically forbids a licensee to discuss the issue of psychologically impacted properties. Rather, the licensee must require the prospective purchaser to put the question in writing and it will be delivered to the seller who may or may not answer.

Megan's Law. (TC)

Megan's Law passed n 1996 and requires registration of sex offenders with local law enforcement upon their release from prison. Offenders are classified by their offense at level 1, 2 or 3. Level 1 must report annually for 15 years. The individual receives a verification letter from the state and must register within 10 days.. Level 2 must report every 6 months for 25 years. The individual receives a verification letter and must register within 10 days. Level 3 must report every 90 days for life. There is a verification letter from the state and must register within 10 days. If an individual repeats the offense or fails to register the individual is classified at the next higher level. Should the sex offender be designated a s habitual or aggravated (use of force or a child under 12, for example) authorities may notify the neighbors by posting a flyer, going door to door. The offender's driver's license is marked. Many police departments post offender's photographs in their stations.

Ch. 5

TEST YOUR UNDERSTANDING

1. The recording system was established to
    1. preserve instruments of title and give evidence of voluntary execution.
    2. give public notice of change or ownership or the existence of liens thereon.
    3. **Both 1 and 2.**
    4. Neither 1 nor 2

2. Recordation of instruments which transfer or encumber a parcel of real property will do all of the following EXCEPT
    1. give constructive notice of the contents of the instruments to persons who have not consulted the records.
    2. create presumption of delivery of instruments.
    3. **give actual notice of the instruments to third parties who may be affected by the related transactions.**
    4. assist title insurance companies in maintaining their title plants.

3. A collection of all recorded instruments, chronologically arranged, affecting title to real property is a(n)
    1. conglomeration.
    2. guaranteed title policy.
    3. **abstract of title.**
    4. certificate of title.

4. A "chain of title" is a(n)
    1. measurement of land.
    2. form of title insurance.
    3. **record of a property's grantors and grantees.**
    4. encumbrance on a title.

5. The abstract
    1. will compensate the grantee in case of failure.
    2. guarantees the seller's ability to pay under the warranties found in the deed.
    3. will contain all unrecorded documents concerning the property.
    4. **will do none of the above.**

6. Under the abstract method of assurance of title, the
    1. abstractor determines the title's quality.
    2. **attorney determines whether any liens which existed have been satisfied.**
    3. Both 1 and 2
    4. Neither 1 nor 2

7. A title search done by an attorney will
    1. **generally locate defects in title.**
    2. protect the title owner from any financial loss.
    3. Both 1 and 2
    4. Neither 1 nor 2

8. Happy Beyer is in the process of purchasing a new home. To protect its interest Ms. Beyer's mortgagee decided to take out title insurance. The title insurance policy
    1. is proof of title.
    2. **indemnifies the holder against some, but not all, of the possible defects in title.**
    3. Both 1 and 2
    4. Neither 1 nor 2

9. The cost of title insurance is
    1. paid only at the time of issuance of the policy.
    2. **a non-recurring premium.**
    3. amortized monthly.
    4. Both 1 and 2

10. When the title search indicates a clear title
    1. the seller owns the property debt free.
    2. a policy of title insurance becomes unnecessary.
    3. the seller is assured of a marketability of the property.
    4. the buyer still cannot be absolutely certain that the title is good.

11. Any interest in, or right to, land by third persons, adversely affecting the value of the property, is an
    1. encumbrance.
    2. encroachment.
    3. appurtenance.
    4. escrow.

12. In the states such as Oklahoma which practice "lien theory" in mortgages, title to the real property which is mortgaged is in the
    1. mortgagee.
    2. vendor.
    3. mortgagor.
    4. trustee.

13. A mechanic's lien claim arises when a general contractor has performed work or provided material to improve a parcel of real estate on the order of the owner, and the owner has not paid for it. Such contractor has a right to
    1. tear out the work.
    2. record a notice of mortgage.
    3. record a mechanic's lien and file a court suit within the time required by state law.
    4. have personal property of the owner sold to satisfy the lien.

14. The priority of a mechanic's lien over such liens as mortgages and other non-tax liens is determined by the date of
    1. valid notice of completion is recorded.
    2. work of improvement commences.
    3. claim of lien is recorded.
    4. action to foreclose is filed.

15. Public notice that an action at law is pending that may affect the title to specific land or other property is known as
    1. lis pendens.
    2. nolo contendere.
    3. caveat emptor.
    4. habeas corpus.

16. What is the difference between a general and a specific lien?
    1. A general lien cannot be enforced in court, while a specific lien can be enforced.
    2. A specific lien is held by one person, while a general lien is held by at least two persons.
    3. A general lien is a lien against all of the debtor's property, while a specific lien covers only a certain piece of property.
    4. A specific lien is a lien against real estate, while a general lien is a lien against personal property.

17. The illegal, wrongful extension of a structure or of any improvement, partly or wholly, on the property of another is a(n)
    1. restriction.
    2. easement.
    3. encumbrance.
    4. encroachment.

18. Should a person erect an improvement on the land of another by mistake and in good faith, the owner of the land on which the encroachment has occurred
    1. would acquire title by accession.
    2. may sell the improvement
    3. may cause the improvement to be removed and may collect for any damage to the property caused by the removal.
    4. can destroy the entire improvement even if it requires the damage of a portion of the improvement not encroaching on the land.

19. An acquired legal privilege or right of use or enjoyment, falling short of actual ownership, which a party may have in the land of another is
   1. a divestment.
   2. an assurance right.
   3. an easement.
   4. usage privilege.

20. Restrictions placed on property by sub-dividers which limit a landowner's ability to exercise absolute control over the condition and use of real property are.
   1. condominiums.
   2. deed restrictions.
   3. absentee ownership.
   4. encroachments.

21. Queenie, owner of a 40-lot tract of land, conveys each lot with a restrictive covenant requiring the owner to use the land for residential purposes. One of her grantees, Prince, later sells his lot to Duke, who wants to build a gas station. Which of the following is true?
   1. Prince's covenant is personal with Queenie and will not bind Duke.
   2. Duke will have to ask the local zoning board of appeals for a writ of non-conformance.
   3. Duke will be bound by the restrictive covenants in Prince's deed.
   4. Duke may build the station, the doctrine of estoppel will prevent Queenie from enforcing the covenant.

22. The ability of the state to enact and enforce zoning ordinances stems from its
   1. police powers.
   2. tax powers.
   3. power of eminent domain.
   4. authority to condemn.

23. Which statement about building codes is true?
   1. They have been standardized throughout the United States.
   2. They establish minimum standards in design, structural systems, and construction materials.
   3. Both 1 and 2
   4. Neither 1 nor 2

24. Should landowners develop their land without first obtaining building permits, they could be
   1. given jail sentences.
   2. forced to tear down the buildings.
   3. Both 1 and 2
   4. Neither 1 nor 2

25. Even though an area is zoned for single-family dwelling units only, some commercial use may be permitted if
   1. the commercial use was a per-existing non-conforming use.
   2. a variance is authorized by the zoning board for a new non-conforming use.
   3. Both 1 and 2.
   4. Neither 1 nor 2

ANSWERS AND EXPLANATIONS

1. 3 The seventy-seven county clerks in Oklahoma are charged with the duty of maintaining public records relating to rights and duties associated with real property. These records are for the protection and other interest in real property because once an instrument is validly recorded, such recordation serves as constructive notice to all persons of that interest.

2. 3 Actual notice must be actually and expressly or by implication given and received.

3. 3 A good definition of abstract of title.

4. 3 An abstractor searches and notes the chain of title (also called running the chain of title) in the examination of the title at the office of the county clerk, tracing he title from the original grant up to the present ownership.

5. 4 The abstract of title does not guarantee or assure the validity of the title of the property. It merely discloses those items about the property which are of public record, and thus does not reveal such things as encroachments, forgeries, and so on.

6. 2 The abstractor merely searches the title as recorded and copies the various instruments affecting the property and arranges them in the chronological order of recording. An opinion as to the status of the title is given by a person competent in examining titles, usually a title attorney.

7. 1 The purpose of a title search is to locate defects in the title and determine the quality of title. It is no guarantee of quality and offers no protection from financial loss.

8. 2 Although it is the assurance of clear title, title insurance is not proof of title. Harpy's interest is not covered by a mortgagee's policy – only the lender's interest.

9. 1 Title insurance premium is a one-time payment, usually made at closing.

10. 4 A buyer can never be absolutely certain that title is good. An opinion of title and title insurance remain the best assurances available.

11. 1 An encumbrance is any claim, lien, charge, or liability attached to and binding on real property which may lessen it value, or burden, obstruct, or impair the use of the property.

12. 3 "Title Theory" holds that legal title passes to a third party escrow agent upon the signing of a promissory note by a borrower. Oklahoma is a "Lien Theory" state in which title remains with the mortgagor

13. 3 In Oklahoma, a person who is in a direct contract relationship with the owner of the real property (generally a contractor) has a maximum of four month from the last date that labor or materials were furnished to file the mechanic's lien. Those who furnish labor or materials and are not involved directly in a contract with the owner of the real property (sub-contractors) have 90 days after the date labor or materials were last furnished to file their mechanic's lien. Failure to pursue a mechanic's lien within one year will terminate the lien.

14. 2 The effective date of a lien is usually the time of visible commencement of operations; that is, when enough work is performed to give notice that the real property is being improved or is about to be improved.

15. 1 "Nolo contendere" means "no contest." Lis pendens is a Latin term which means "action pending" and is in the nature of a quasi lien. It is a recorded legal document which gives constructive notice that n action affecting a particular piece of property has been filed in court.

16. 3 The main difference between a general and a specific lien is the scope of claim. The general lien is on all the real and personal property of the debtor, while a specific lien is restricted to a specified parches of real or personal property.

17. 4 A good definition of an encroachment.

18. 3 Only this option is possible. For remedy, if a friendly settlement cannot be obtained an owner may bring civil suit against a neighbor for removal of an encroachment or the grounds of trespass.

19. 3 A good definition of an easement.

20. 2 A deed restriction, sometimes called private zoning, is created by means of a restrictive covenant written into real property instruments. Such covenants might restrict the number and size of structures to be placed on the land, the cost of structures, fence heights, setbacks, the use of the property for the sale of intoxicating beverages, etc. Restrictive covenants which discriminate by limiting the conveyance to, or used by, individuals of a specified race, sex, color, religion, familial status, or ancestry are void.

21. 3 Deed restrictions run with the land are binding on all subsequent owners. Also, when a conflict between private restrictions and public restrictions exist, the most restrictive will prevail.

22. 1 Police power is a constitutional authority and inherent power of a state to adopt and enforce laws and regulations to promote the support the public health, safety, morals, and general welfare. It is, in essence, policy power.

23. 2 Building codes are designed to provide minimum standards to safeguard the health, safety, and the welfare of the public by regulating and controlling the design, construction, quality, use and occupancy, location, and maintenance of all buildings and structures. Rules are established by local governments and vary widely from area to area.

24. 2 Violations of building codes may render a property unmarketable. Nonconformance to building codes could result in forced demolition. Proposed construction must conform to local zoning and building codes, and must generally be inspected and approved upon completion.

25. 3 Nonconforming use is permitted when that use was previously lawfully established and maintained, although it no longer conforms to the current use regulations because of a change in zoning. In case of substantial destruction by fire of otherwise, the zoning statutes probably will prohibit reconstruction. A variance will permit nonconforming use.

TRANSFER OF RIGHTS

ACQUISITION OF RIGHTS

Sovereign nations acquire original title to land by discovery, occupancy, conquest, or cession. The grant of title by a governmental body to individual persons is known as a patent.

Subsequent transfer of legal title to real property occurs by alienation, whereby the ownership, title or interest in real estate is conveyed to an aliened who receives the same legal rights, obligations, and remedies as the grantor. Usually, the transfer occurs by voluntary alienation (execution), normally by a deed or by will. The transfer may also come from involuntary alienation (against the will of the owner), such as transfer by a tax sale or nonpayment of taxes, by adverse possession, or by eminent domain.

Contracts representing agreements between two or more parties to sell or buy real estate are, in essence, gap fillers. Legal title or ownership of rights to land is not transferred until the transaction is actually closed. The purpose of a sales contract is to provide the rules governing the rights and duties of the parties between the time the contract is signed and the transaction is completed. A contract for sale does, however, serve to transfer equitable title, an interest held by the contract buyer allowing the buyer to sue for specific performance if the seller refuses to sell after the contract is signed and the buyer tenders performance.

VOLUNTARY TRANSFER (ALIENATION) (TC)

In the acquisition of rights to real property, the most commonly encountered voluntary conveyance is a deed. Accession may also be by will, by descent should the owner die without a will, and by the direction or action of a court.

Title (TC)

The concept of title is an abstraction. In real estate, ownership or title is the possession of "rights" Frequently, the ownership rights are described as a "bundle of rights" meaning the "owner" (possessor) has the right of possession, exclusion, occupy and use, restrict use, devise by will, etc.

Original title is held by the state. Derivative title is held by individual or others than the state.

Equitable title is held by a buyer in a purchase contract, contract for deed or other installment sales contract. Equitable title is transferable by assignment and, upon performance of the contract, may become legal title.

Deeds. (TC)

A deed is a written legal instrument which, when properly executed and delivered, conveys all rights, title, and interest in realty from the grantor to the grantee. It is a form of contract and the requirements relating to contracts apply. Although there are many types of deeds, the most common classifications are (1) general warranty deeds, (2) special warranty deeds, and (3) quitclaim deeds. One type does not transfer any greater interest in title than another. The difference among the several types of deeds is the variation of guarantee of ownership and the quality of title assured.

General Warranty Deed. (TC)

The grantor in a general warranty deed warrants or guarantees the title against defects existing before the grantor acquired title or arising during the grantor's ownership. Besides receiving title to the real property, the grantee receives the grantor's personal covenant that the grantor will defend the grantee and the grantee's heirs, personal representatives, and assigns against any claim to the title, no matter how far back in the chain of title. The general warranty deed is the most extensively used form of deed and, because there are more assurances, is the safest deed that can be received.

The Oklahoma statutes provide a form for the general warranty deed. A warranty deed made in substantial compliance with the statutory form conveys the whole interest of the grantors and makes the following covenants or promises which are binding upon the grantors, their heirs, and personal representative.

Covenant of Seizen. (TC)

The grantors covenant or promise that they hold good right, full power, and absolute authority to convey title to the real property, as specified in and by the deed. (They are legally seized).

Covenant against Encumbrances. (TC)

The grantors warrant that the property being conveyed is free of all liens and encumbrances, except for those specifically stated in the deed.

Covenant of Quiet Enjoyment. (TC)

The grantors promise quiet and peaceable possession of the property by the grantees. The grantor warrants that the grantees acquired title is good, not only as against the grantor, but also as against all third parties.

Covenant of Further Assurance. (TC)

The grantors agree to perform such acts as may be necessary to perfect title in the grantees.

Covenant of Warranty Forever. (TC)

The grantors promise to defend the title against all persons who may lawfully claim the same title.

Special Warranty Deed. (TC)

A special warranty deed is one in which the grantors warrant or guarantee the title only against defects arising during the period of their tenure and ownership of the property, and not against defects existing before that time. No statutory form exists for special warranty deeds which are most often used by a person holding title for someone else, such as a trustee or guardian. In recent years, such deeds have been given by employers who have purchased the home of a transferred employee.

Quitclaim Deed. (TC)

A quitclaim deed warrants nothing. It conveys only the present interest, if any, of the grantor in the land. Although it transfers in full whatever interest the grantor may have, it is normally used to clear technical defects in the chain of title or to release lien claims against the property. The Oklahoma statutes provide a form for a quitclaim deed.

Among the other types of deeds is the trust deed (deed of trust), in which title to real property is conveyed to a trustee who holds the land for those named as beneficiaries. As in the case of a bank trust, the trustee holds title on behalf of the beneficiaries until certain conditions are met, such as a contract for deed. A trustee's deed is one given by a trustee conveying property under trust. A sheriff's deed is given by court order in connection with the sale of property to satisfy a judgment.

Usual and Essential Elements. (TC)

To convey title, a valid deed must be delivered to and accepted by the grantee during the lifetime of the grantor. The usual elements of a deed are:

*1. **Written Instrument**.
 2. Date.
*3. **Parties, Grantor and Grantee**.
 4. Recital of Consideration.
*5. **Words of Conveyance**.
*6. **Description of the Property**.
 7. Exceptions and Restrictions.
 8. Warranties and Covenants.
*9. **Signature of the Grantor**.
*10. **Delivery and Acceptance**.
 11. Acknowledgement.
 12. Recording.

For a deed to be valid, only six of the usual elements, identified by the asterisks above, are absolutely essential. These include: written instrument, identity of the parties (grantor and grantee), words of conveyance, description of the property, signature of the grantor, and delivery and acceptance. Although making a conveyance a matter of public records is not required in order to transfer title, recording is necessary to protect the interest of the grantee in the real property against the claims of third persons.

Written Instrument. (TC)

There is no deed unless it is in writing. If a deed is altered in any manner after delivery to the grantee, it may be set aside by the courts. In case of printed forms, all blanks should be properly completed according to the requirements of law and according to the intention of the parties.

Date. (TC)

Although it is the universal custom to date all deeds, a date is not absolutely essential for a valid deed. Inclusion of the date may prevent future questions or controversy concerning the time of delivery.

Parties, Grantor and Grantee. (TC)

To be valid, a deed must have a name or otherwise clearly identified grantor who is conveying an interest in the property. The name of the grantor should be identical to that appearing in the conveyance by which title was received. Otherwise, it will create a cloud on the title, and although certain minor discrepancies will not invalidate the deed, possible litigation can be avoided by exercising care. The grantor, if a natural person, should be of legal age and sound mind. Otherwise, the grantor can, at a later date, have the deed set aside and recover the property. A grantee must be named or indicated with reasonable certainty or the deed is void.

Recital of Consideration. (TC)

The matter of consideration is a technical requirement. As a contract, a consideration must be stated in a deed. However, a person may make a gift of a parcel of real estate and lack of consideration does not render the conveyance void. While most contracts must be supported by a valuable consideration, a good consideration (love and affection) is sufficient to support a gift deed.

If no consideration is given, the grantee cannot enforce covenants of warrant against the grantor. A gift deed given to defraud creditors may be set aside by the grantor's creditors.

So that the information will remain private and not be made a matter of public record, most deeds do not show the full purchase price paid. The use of a nominal sum in the recital of consideration satisfies the technical requirement of contract law that there be some consideration.

Words of Conveyance. (TC)

Without some clearly expressed intention to transfer ownership of real estate, a deed may be ineffective in accomplishing its purpose or may at best create ambiguity as to its purpose. This portion of the deed should clearly state any limitations or reservations that are intended. The standard form deeds in common use utilize terms such as "convey and warrant" in general warranty deeds, "convey and specially warrant" when a deed of limited warranty is intended, or "release and quitclaim" when no warranties of any kind are intended.

The habendum clause following the granting clause defines or limits the extent of ownership to be enjoyed by the grantee, such as fee simple, life estate or easement. The words "to have and to hold" introduce the clause. The description of the estate in the agendum clause should agree with the description in the granting clause.

Description of the Property. (TC)

To correctly identify the property being conveyed, the property must be described with a reasonable degree of accuracy. No doubt should be left as to its identification. Although several ways are acceptable for describing property, to avoid discrepancies in the records, the legal, technical description should be the same as used in previous conveyances.

All improvements to the land go with the land as appurtenances. In transferring a house and lot, it is necessary only to describe the land upon which the house is situated. It is common, however, to add, following the description, words indicating that all the appurtenances go with the land.

Exceptions and Restrictions. (TC)

The grantor is assumed to be conveying the property free and clear of all encumbrances and restrictions, except for those specifically mentioned in the deed. Therefore, the deed usually contains a provision that the grantor conveys the property free and clear of all encumbrances. Then follows a specific enumeration of the exceptions, such as: "subject to a mortgage (giving complete description)," "subject to an easement" (with a detailed description) or "subject to all encumbrances and restrictions of record."

Warranties and Covenants. (TC)

Warranties and covenants are not essential requirements of a valid deed. The grantor may convey an interest in land by a quitclaim deed wherein no warranty of any kind is given, or the grantor may convey by a general warranty deed wherein numerous warranties are made to the grantee.

Signature of the Grantor. (TC)

To transfer title effectively by a deed, it must be signed by the grantor with the intent that ownership of some interest in land be transferred to a designated grantee. In the event there are co-owners, and the agreement is to transfer the interest of each of the owners, each must sign the deed.

If the property is homestead property, the owner's spouse must join in the conveyance. The rules in practice require the signatures of both husband and wife on any deed to property owned by only one of them.

The execution of a deed to property owned by a partnership can be accomplished by the signature of any general partner on the deed. For corporations, a resolution of the board of directors will give authority to certain officers to execute deeds on behalf of the company.

Delivery and Acceptance. (TC)

A deed is not effective until it is delivered by the grantor and accepted by the grantee. For there to be an effective delivery, the grantor must intend to pass title to the grantee. A deed given to the grantee, affording an opportunity to examine, does not constitute delivery.

For delivery of a deed to be effective, it must be made during the lifetime of the grantor. If the grantor executes a deed, retains it and directs that upon death, it is to be delivered to the grantee, the deed does not pass title. Effective delivery may be made to some third person for the benefit of the grantee, but the grantor must surrender all right and control or recovery of the deed. When a deed is recorded, Oklahoma law presumes effective delivery.

Acknowledgement. (TC)

An acknowledgement is a formal declaration made by a person (in the case of a deed, by the grantor) to a notary public or another public official authorized to take acknowledgements, and to affirm that the execution of the instrument was an act of free will, voluntarily given. The notary public, or other authorized officer, fills out the certificate of acknowledgement customarily printed on the instrument. The statutory form of acknowledgement also provides that the declarer is known by the notary or other authorized officer to be the identical person who executed the instrument.

A deed is valid between the parties without being acknowledged, but in Oklahoma, the deed cannot be recorded unless it has been acknowledged. Since an unrecorded title can lead to serious difficulties, it is advisable to have the deed acknowledged so that it can be recorded. If, by chance, the deed should be recorded without an acknowledgement and remains so recorded for a period of ten years, the recording shall be valid as though it had been acknowledged.

Recording. (TC)

A deed need not be recorded to be valid between the parties. However, the prudent purchaser will immediately record the deed. Recording protects an innocent purchaser or encumbrancer that acts without knowledge of an unrecorded instrument and also provides a conclusive presumption that all persons have knowledge of the recorded instrument.

Dedication. (TC)

Occasionally, privately-owned land is transferred to the public without consideration, with the intent that the land will be accepted and used for public purposes. This is most common in real estate developments where the streets, water system and sewer lines have been constructed and paid for by the developer and subsequently dedicated to the public and given to the city for future maintenance.

Transfer at Death. (TC)

If one dies with a valid will (testate), the estate, consisting of all real and personal property (hereditaments), will be distributed to heirs and assigns according to the express intent of the decedent. A will handwritten by the testator is a holographic will. The gift of property by the last will and testament of the donor is a devise. The recipient of such property is the devisee. If one dies without a will (intestate), the estate will be distributed by succession, according to the descent and distribution statutes of the state.

In either case, the judicial process for disposition of the estate of the decedent will be the responsibility of the probate court acting through an executor or executrix named in the will or an administrator or administratrix who is appointed by the court in the event one dies without a will. In any case, the sale of real property after death cannot normally be consummated until the Oklahoma Tax Commission and the Federal Internal Revenue Service have given clearance.

Home Owners' Association (TC)

A homeowners' association is a nonprofit organization of homeowners for the purpose of maintaining and enforcing the restrictions, covenants and easements for the purpose of ensuring the orderly growth and maintenance of the neighborhood. These have members, not stockholders.

The Tax Reform Act of 1976 recognizes two types of HOA's. One is for condominiums and the other is for residential real estate management associations. The law protects the tax exempt status of the HOA only to the extent of their membership dues, fees and assessments from the member-owners.

In recent years, there have developed professional companies which manage HOA's.

Under some circumstances, HOA regulations may be enforced in court.

INVOLUNTARY TRANSFER (ALIENATION) (TC)

Rights to real property may be transferred through no voluntary act of the current owner. The most typical examples of involuntary alienation of rights include escheat, eminent domain, confiscation, accretion, and adverse possession.

Escheat. (TC)

The state is the potential heir of all owners of real estate. It takes their property unless someone else succeeds to its ownership either by virtue of disposition by a valid will or by the state rules of inheritance. The legal process of reversion of the ownership of property to the state is escheat. The most typical occasion giving rise to escheat is when the property owner dies intestate (no will) and without heirs capable of inheriting (no legal heirs).

Eminent Domain. (TC)

The power of eminent domain is an inherent right reserved by the government. It is the power of governmental units literally to take private property when it is concluded that such action is in the best interest of the general public. The method by which this power is exercised is called condemnation. Privately-owned property may be taken for public use by condemning it.

The taking or condemning of private property must be done in accordance with specific legislative authority and within the limitations of the owner's constitutional rights, both federal and state. Generally, payment must be made to the landowner based upon the fair value of the property taken and the landowner may also collect payments for damages (in terms of loss of value) to the property remaining.

Certain essential utilities such as gas companies, electric companies and railroads are frequently conferred the right of eminent domain. Once there has been a legitimate determination that private property is needed for a public purpose (that is, the taking is not arbitrary or capricious), the landowner can only dispute the value of the property taken, not the right to take.

Confiscation. (TC)

The government has the power to take property in time of emergency or war, without compensation. Such confiscation generally applies only to property of enemies of the government.

Section 881 of the *Federal Drug Enforcement Act of 1988* allows real property to be seized and forfeited if it is used to facilitate illegal drug traffic. Real property of owners and/or landlords may be confiscated due to the actions of others, including tenants. Those who can prove that they were "innocent owners," either by having no knowledge of the illegal activity or by making all reasonable effort to alleviate the activity, have some protection from "asset seizure."

Accretion and Erosion. (TC)

Accretion is the acquisition of land due to the gradual accumulation of soil (alluvion) by natural causes resulting in stream or river shoreline changes. Although usually beneficial for those landowners whose holdings are increased by the process, accretion may be detrimental to others who lose a portion of their holdings through erosion. The process of gradual recession of water from the usual watermark, thereby increasing land volume, is known as **reliction or dereliction**.

Avulsion is the loss of land due to the sudden removal of a considerable quantity of soil by an act of nature, such as a flash flood tearing away a sizeable portion of land. A riparian owner generally does not lose title to land by avulsion. The boundary lines stay the same no matter how much soil is lost.

Adverse Possession. (TC)

Adverse possession is a possession of private property which is inconsistent with and detrimental to the rights of the true owner. The title of private property may pass by prescription, against the will and desire of the owner, if the adverse claimant takes physical possession of the property for the statutory term of fifteen years. The justification for this "legalized stealing" of real estate is that if the true owners choose not to take action for such a long period of time, the law will not help them regain lost ownership. The public purpose of adverse possession is to prevent the abandonment of private property and to keep land productive for society.

To acquire legal title by adverse possession, the potential owner has to have been in actual possession that was open and notorious (obvious), exclusive (unshared), and continuous and uninterrupted, and with the claim of right of ownership for fifteen years in Oklahoma. A second or follow-up adverse claimant may "tack on" another period of continuous occupancy to that of the first adverse claimant who has sold or otherwise conveyed an interest in the property to the second claimant. By "tacking," the successive occupancies may total the necessary period of time.

Whenever title to real estate depends on a claim by virtue of adverse possession, it may be necessary to obtain a judicial determination that acquisition of the title has in fact occurred. The common name for such a proceeding is a quiet title suit. Those who claim title bring legal action in a local court against anyone and everyone who may have or may ever have had any claim against the property, no matter how remote, to prove the validity of their title. Such suits typically name everyone even remotely connected with the property and "the rest of the world" as defendants.

Title may also be acquired through adverse possession by a claimant who has only a color of title wherein the title may appear to be good, but, because of a certain defect, is in fact not valid. This commonly occurs in situations such as a forged deed where the occupant does not have title, but by fulfilling the requirements of adverse possession, good title may be acquired.

Adverse possession should not be confused with squatter's rights where in the claimant may not be seeking title. Although squatters may develop a "prescriptive claim" or title that can eventually ripen into good title, the process is much less certain than gaining title by adverse possession.

CONTRACT FOR DEED (TC)

A contract for deed, also known as an installment sales contract or as a land contract, is a conditional sales contract to purchase real property in which the buyer makes a down payment and where further payments are made in installments. In such contracts, the seller does not deliver the deed to the buyer until all, or a specified amount, has been paid on the price. In the event of default by the buyer, the seller is required by Section 11 A of Title 16 of *Oklahoma Statutes*, (*Constructive Mortgage Act*), to initiate a foreclosure action, even though the buyer does not have legal title to the real property. Duties of the buyer include paying taxes, insuring the property and maintaining the property.

The *Constructive Mortgage Act* also specifies that foreclosure cannot be attempted unless the mortgage tax is paid and it is recorded in the County Clerk's Office.

In a Contract for Deed, it may be months or years before the buyer receives a deed. It is common, therefore, to arrange for a third and neutral party to collect the buyer's payments and to assure that the contract terms are completed. This is referred to as a deed in escrow.

For deeds delivered in escrow, the deed must be delivered during the lifetime of the grantor and if he dies, title relates back to the date the deed was delivered to the escrow agent if all conditions of the escrow are met.

Ch. 6

TEST YOUR UNDERSTANDING

1. The initial conveyance of real property from the federal government to an individual is by
   1. an Act of congress.
   2. a deed from the Secretary of Interior.
   3. the U. S. Registrar of Deeds.
   4. **A patent.**

2. When the purchase contract has been properly executed by all the parties, there remains much to be done to effect a conveyance. During the interim, the interest of the purchaser would best be described as
   1. legal title.
   2. **equitable title.**
   3. ostensible title.
   4. purported title.

3. The main purpose of a deed is to
   1. evidence the terms of a real property transaction.
   2. **evidence the change in title or transfer of an interest in real estate.**
   3. identify the parties to a real property transfer.
   4. provide a written instrument suitable for recordation.

4. Involuntary alienation of an estate means
   1. the estate cannot be transferred without the consent of the owner.
   2. aliens are forbidden to own estates in fee simple n Oklahoma.
   3. **the ownership of estates may be transferred by operation of law.**
   4. no one can be compelled to transfer title without consent.

5. A executes a deed to B. After A records it, B moves into the property. Later, A seeks to set the conveyance aside, claiming that there had been no delivery of the deed. Why will A probably not succeed?
   1. B has already taken possession of the property.
   2. **Delivery is presumed by recording.**
   3. A deed is valid without recording.
   4. Recording established the priority of rights of the parties.

6. If a deed were made to Amy and she died prior to delivery, which of the following would be true?
   1. The property would revert to the government by escheat.
   2. The deed is not acceptable for recordation.
   3. **The deed would be invalid.**
   4. The deed would be valid.

7. Assume that a deed was signed by the grantor on Sunday and delivered to the grantee the next Tuesday. Which of the following statements is true?
   1. The deed is invalid.
   2. The deed is not acceptable for recordation.
   3. **Title will pass upon delivery and acceptance on Tuesday.**
   4. None of the above.

8. Eric Estoppel hands a deed made to Paul Pending with intent to pass title and with an oral request not to record it until after Estoppel dies. Which of the following is correct?
   1. Pending must comply or the deed will not be valid.
   2. **Valid delivery has occurred.**
   3. Delivery will not occur until Estoppel's death.
   4. Title does not pass until the deed is recorded.

74

9. **A general warranty deed**
   1. is also called a full covenant and warranty deed.
   2. protects the grantee "against the world".
   3. Both 1 and 2
   4. Neither 1 nor 2

10. **By means of a warranty deed, the grantor assures the grantee**
    1. that the property is free of structural defects.
    2. protects the grantee "against the world".
    3. Both 1 and 2
    4. Neither 1 nor 2

11. **The deed form that creates the greatest potential liability to the grantor is the**
    1. general warranty deed.
    2. administrator's deed.
    3. sheriff's deed.
    4. executor's deed.

12. **Sam Smooth conveyed a parcel of land by deed to Vera Slick, warranting only against defects in title occurring by, from, or under his ownership of the land. He conveyed by**
    1. general warranty deed.
    2. special warranty deed.
    3. sheriff's deed.
    4. quitclaim deed.

13. **A quitclaim deed conveys which of the following?**
    1. A property free of encumbrances.
    2. All future interest of a married couple.
    3. A grantor' interest, if any, in a property.
    4. A property guaranteed free of any flaws in the title.

14. **Betty Barstoule sold a parcel of to Eileen Slightly and gave a quitclaim deed. What is/are the warranty/warranties under such a deed?**
    1. Barstoule owned the property.
    2. That there are no encumbrances against the property.
    3. both A and B.
    4. Neither A nor B.

15. **A grantor has the least liability under a**
    1. general warranty deed.
    2. special warranty deed.
    3. quitclaim deed.
    4. bargain and sale deed.

16. **A quitclaim deed would always convey good legal title to real property in which of the following cases?**
    1. The grantor was living on the property at the time of the conveyance.
    2. The grantor had a good legal title to the real property.
    3. Both 1 and 2
    4. Neither 1 nor 2

17. **A quitclaim deed provides which of the following warranties?**
    1. Covenant of further assurance.
    2. Covenant of quiet enjoyment.
    3. Covenant of seizen.
    4. None of the above.

18. In order to be a valid and enforceable conveyance, there are certain things that must be contained in the deed. Which of the following would be needed?
    1. An acknowledgement.
    2. A granting clause.
    3. Signature of the grantor.
    4. Both 2 and 3

19. All of the following are essential elements in a valid deed EXCEPT the
    1. delivery and acceptance.
    2. grantor's signature.
    3. grantee's signature.
    4. property description.

20. A deed that is not in writing would be valid if
    1. al the other requirements of a deed are met.
    2. there are three or more witnesses to the conveyance.
    3. The parties to the conveyance have no intention of recording it.
    4. None of the above.

21. A valid deed must
    1. describe the property.
    2. name the grantor.
    3. name the grantee.
    4. all of the above.

22. The clause in a deed defining the interest or estate granted or the extent of the ownership granted is the
    1. habendum clause.
    2. testimonium clause.
    3. consideration clause.
    4. warranty clause.

23. Which of the following best describes the covenant of quiet assurance?
    1. The grantor promises to obtain and deliver any instrument needed to make the title good.
    2. The grantor guarantees that if the title fails in the future, the grantee will be compensated.
    3. The grantor warrants ownership with the right to convey title.
    4. The grantor assures that the title is good against the title claims of third parties.

24. Four warrants or covenants of the general warranty deed are as listed below. Which one is the covenant of seizen?
    1. Grantor owns the property and has good right and power to convey it.
    2. The property is free and clear of all liens and encumbrances.
    3. Grantor warrants quiet and peaceful possession of the property.
    4. Grantor will defend title against all persons who may lawfully claim the same.

25. The covenant whereby the grantor agrees to procure and deliver to the grantee any subsequent document necessary to make good the title being conveyed is the covenant of
    1. seizen.
    2. quiet enjoyment.
    3. encumbrance.
    4. further assurance.

26. The covenant against encumbrances in a deed of conveyance warrants against the existence of all of the following EXCEPT
    1. mortgages against the land.
    2. judgments against the land.
    3. easements that adversely affect the land.
    4. zoning ordinances that limit the use of the land.

27. A person who dies testate is said to have died
    1. leaving no heirs.
    2. indigent.
    3. without a will.
    4. leaving a will.

28. Clarence Cadaver, a single person, owned a parcel of land. Subsequent to Cadaver's death, the probate court determined the descent of the parcel of land in accordance with the state statutes. Cadaver, therefore, died
    1. testate.
    2. intestate.
    3. without a will.
    4. leaving a will.

29. Sam Francisco lived in California and died there. He owned some real property in Oklahoma. His heirs have become involved in a dispute regarding his Oklahoma real estate holdings. Which of the following is correct?
    1. The law of California where Francisco died will prevail.
    2. The law of Oklahoma where the property is located will prevail.
    3. Federal laws will prevail.
    4. County laws will have jurisdiction.

30. The supreme power inherent in the state to take land from the owner by due process of the law when necessary for the state's use in the public welfare is
    1. voluntary alienation.
    2. adverse conveyance.
    3. eminent domain.
    4. adverse possession.

31. The two requirements which must be met when government exercises its right under eminent domain are
    1. proposed use must be both practical and public.
    2. inconvenience of the owners must not be greater than the convenience of the public, and the government must justify its actions.
    3. proposed use must be practical and the owner must be compensated.
    4. proposed use must be public and the owner must be just compensated.

32. Molly, Polly and Dolly Parriott own a large home on a ten-acre parcel of land, all of which is needed by the state due to the creation of a new state highway. Regarding this case, all of the following statements are correct EXCEPT which one?
    1. The Parriott sisters may voluntarily agree to sell the land to the state.
    2. f the state can demonstrate the public need for the land, it may condemn the land and obtain title, even if the Parriotts will not sell voluntarily.
    3. If the state obtains the land, the Parriotts must be justly compensated for it.
    4. Severance damages may be awarded.

33. The reverting of property to the state when heirs capable of inheriting do not exist and there is no will is
    1. cheating.
    2. escheat.
    3. testating.
    4. unfair..

34. Title to land by accretion is acquired by
    1. the federal government.
    2. an owner of adjoining land as a result of natural causes.
    3. the state government.
    4. county through the process of escheat.

35. The sudden removal of land from one owner to another when a stream changes its channel is
    1. avulsion.
    2. accretion.
    3. erosion.
    4. dereliction.

36. A quick and violent change in the course of a stream will
    1. permanently change land boundaries.
    2. cause serious legal questions concerning property rights.
    3. Both 1 and 2
    4. Neither 1 nor 2

37. The right of an occupant of land to acquire title against the real owner, when the possession has been actual, continuous, hostile, visible, and exclusive for the legal period is
    1. adverse possession.
    2. confiscation.
    3. eminent domain.
    4. escheat.

38. A landowner can break an adverse claim by all of the following methods EXCEPT
    1. ousting the adverse occupant.
    2. giving the adverse occupant permission to stay.
    3. preventing trespassers from entering.
    4. observing the adverse occupant closely

39. In a sale by contract for deed, the buyer
    1. .has equitable title to the property.
    2. is entitled to a conveyance of the legal title when all payments have been made.
    3. Both 1 and 2
    4. Neither 1 nor 2

40. In the typical contract for deed, the buyer has which of the following duties?
    1. Payment of taxes.
    2. Insuring the property.
    3. Maintenance.
    4. All of these.

ANSWERS AND EXPLANATIONS

1. 4 The first entry in most abstracts is a patent. Most patents in Oklahoma are dated prior to the turn of the 20th century when the Territorial Lands were transferred to private ownership.

2. 2 Voluntary transfer of legal title is usually through a deed. A contract for sale acts to transfer equitable title to the buyer.

3. 2 Deeds are written instruments dated and signed by grantors creating or conveying interest in real property to named grantees.

4. 3 Involuntary alienation of property comes from such actions as adverse possession, by foreclosure, by tax sale, by eminent domain and escheat. Aliens have all rights of citizenship except for voting.

5. 2 The recording of a deed raises a presumption of delivery.

6. 3 To be valid, a deed must be delivered during the life time of the grantee by a competent living grantor.

7. 3 The day of the week has nothing to do with validity. A deed takes effect when delivered and accepted.

8. 2 Recording gives constructive notice to the world of the rights of the grantee in a particular parcel of real property and its constructive delivery. Personal (actual) delivery also validates the deed.

9. 3 A general warranty deed fully warranties good and clear title to the premises, with noted exceptions.

10. 2 A warranty deed warrants the title, not the fitness or quality of construction of real property.

11. 1 A warranty deed offers the grantee the greatest protection of any deed.
12. 2 A special warranty deed is one in which the grantors warrant or guarantee the title only against defects arising during the period of their tenure and ownership of the property and not against defects existing before that time.

13. 3 A quitclaim deed conveys the grantor's present interest, if any.

14. 4 A quitclaim deed carries no covenants or warranties.

15. 3 A quitclaim deed can be executed without subjecting the grantor to legal obligations.

16. 2 If a grantor has good legal title, a quitclaim deed will convey good legal title. Living on the property is irrelevant to title.

17. 4 A quitclaim deed provides no expressed or implied warranties. Its most common us is to clear title.

18. 4 A granting clause and the signature of the grantor are essential elements of a deed. A date is desirable but not absolutely necessary. Acknowledgement permits the instrument to be recorded.

19. 3 Legal description, signature of the grantor and delivery and acceptance are essential to a valid deed. The grantee does not sign the deed.

20. 4 No deed exists without being in writing.

21. 4 All are essential to a valid deed.

22. 1 The habendum clause is that part of the deed beginning with the words, "to have and to hold," following the granting clause and reaffirming the extent of ownership that the grantor is transferring.

23. 4 The Covenant of Quiet Enjoyment is the grantor's promise that the grantee's acquired title is good, not only against the grantor, but also against all third persons.

24. 1 The Covenant of Seizin promises that the grantor has title and the right of possession to the real property being conveyed.

25.4 The Covenant of Further Assurance means that the grantor will undertake whatever is necessary to perfect the title in favor of the grantee.

26. 4 The Covenant Against Encumbrances warrants that the real property is free of all liens and encumbrances except those specifically stated in the deed.

27. 4 The word "testate" means to die leaving a will.

28. 2 Persons who die without a will are said to have died intestate. Their property passes by intestate succession as determined through a court action.

29. 2 Laws of the state where the property is located will prevail. The domicile of the owner is irrelevant.

30. 3 A good definition of eminent domain.

31. 4 Acquisition of property by eminent domain must be for sufficient public use and just value must be paid.

32. 4 The price for land taken for public use is frequently negotiated between the owner and the government agency. If it cannot negotiate a satisfactory voluntary acquisition of the property, however, the government can initiate a condemnation action to take the property.

33. 2 A good definition of escheat.

34. 2 Accretion is the gradual an imperceptible addition of land by alluvial deposits of soil through natural causes. This added land becomes the property of the riparian or littoral owner.

35. 2 Avulsion is the loss of land when a sudden or violent action of nature results in its washing away.

36. 4 A riparian owner generally does not lose title to land by avulsion. The boundary lines stay the same no matter how much soil is lost.

37. 1 A good definition of adverse possession.

38. 4 Any of the first three will defeat an adverse possession claim.

39. 3 A contract for deed transfers equitable title like any other real estate sales contract. The contract buyer should receive a deed upon completion of the contract terms.

40. 4 A contract buyer has all the responsibilities of an owner.

COMMON LAW OF AGENCY (TC)

Special Note: The Oklahoma Brokerage Relationships Act of 2013 has abrogated the common law of agency as it relates to real estate licensees and their relation to members of the public. However, the relationship between the broker and the sales associate or broker associate remains the common law of agency. Additionally, agency law is practiced in many other states and is a part of the national portion of the state qualifying examination.

AGENCY (TC)

An agency is the legal relationship whereby one person, an agent, is authorized by another, a principal, to act on that person's behalf, and is empowered to do what the principal could lawfully do in person. The axiom of agency is, "He who acts through another acts himself." The principal thus assumes all the responsibilities of the acts of the agent in altering legal relationships with third parties on his behalf. In so dealing, an agency is formed and brings into effect the law of agency, which prescribes certain responsibilities and liabilities to the principal and the agent. These rules of law also delineate responsibilities, obligations, and duties with regard with dealing with third parties.

In the normal course of business, real estate licensees routinely create agency relationships. Most are intentional through an expressed agreement, either written or oral, while others are implied by the action of the parties. Still others may be inadvertent or accidental.

When property owners enter into listing agreements with real estate brokers to represent them in legal or business dealings with third parties, agencies are created. The agreement defines the terms of employment and outlines the duties and responsibilities of the agents (brokers) and the principals. At the same time, obligations to third parties (customers) are legally established.

The principal-agent relationship is generally created by an employment agreement between the parties in the form of a listing contract. A contract of employment is not necessary, however, for the creation of an agency. All that is required is mutual consent, the principal expressly or by implication indicating a willingness to be represented by another person, with the agent, either expressly of impliedly, indicating a willingness to act under the direction and control of the principal.

The Creation Process (TC)

Creation of an agency is easy. Therein lies the danger of creating responsibilities and duties accidentally, inadvertently, or unintentionally. An agency may subtly come into being when the conduct of the principal implies to a third party that a relationship is in effect, although neither the principal nor the agent may be aware of its existence.
The authorizing party in an agency relationship is the principal. Some action or conduct by a principal is necessary to create the relationship.

Seller of house (ex)

Anyone who can be a principal can be an agent. The requirements of an agency contract are the same as for any other contract. The parties must be legally competent, that is, they must have the legal capacity or power to enter into such a contract and commit themselves to the performance of its terms.

To qualify as legally competent, individuals must be of age and must be mentally competent. If an incompetent enters into an agency agreement, technically the agreement does not exist. It is void. Therefore, because minors and mental incompetents lack the capacity to contract, they cannot be principals except through guardians. While an agency contact entered into by a minor as agent is not enforceable by the principal against the minor, the minor as agent can bind the principal and third parties in unauthorized contracts. The capacity of the principal is at issue in this case.

A mentally incompetent person poses a special problem in agency. Some persons are actually incompetent at the time of an agency agreement but under the circumstances, it is difficult to recognize the affliction. The agency contract of one who has been adjudged incompetent is absolutely void and cannot be enforced. The only effective way to deal with a legally declared incompetent is through a guardian.

A person who has an interest adverse to a principal cannot serve as an agent without knowledge and consent of that party.

Corporations and partnerships may be agents for principals as they are legal entities which have the authority and capacity to act and contract. While unincorporated associations are not recognized as entities having legal capacity, members of the group may contract and be held legally responsible for actions of the association. Companies are licensed by the Oklahoma Real Estate Commission (or the regulating agency in other states), but in all instances, the responsibilities of agency fall on the principal broker.

It is a basic general principle of law that one cannot do indirectly what one cannot do directly. The reasoning behind this principle is the use of a subterfuge, undue or unfair advantage may be gained by one party in dealing with another.

Often, such attempts may be such a serious breach of acceptable conduct as to amount to fraud. In discussing capacity of minors to engage in agency relationships, note that while a minor may sometimes be the agent of an adult principal, a minor may not acquire the capacity to contract with others by engaging an adult agent to handle business transactions.

Agency Ratification (TC)

The agent is limited by the terms of the employment contract and the principal does not have to accept acts performed beyond the authority given the agent. However, an act that could have been authorized by the principal may be subsequently ratified. If an agent has secured an unauthorized offer, it may be concluded that the agency was created when the negotiations began. The subsequent adoption by the principal has authorized the act, ratifying the agency.

When real estate brokers work within the scope of their authority, they can legally bind their principals. It is important that all parties involved clearly be aware of the agent's authority and its source.

AGENCY AUTHORITY (TC)

There are several types of authority extended by a wide range of types of principals. For the purpose of real estate brokerage, two major types are identified: **actual** and **apparent**.

Actual Authority (TC)

Actual authority is by far the most common type. It is the authority specifically and clearly conferred by a principal. It consists of expressed authority and implied authority.

Expressed Authority (TC)

Expressed authority, commonly termed "express authority," is given to the agent in writing or orally, and sometimes by the conduct of the principal. The most obvious example of expressed authority is the written employment contract or listing agreement.

Implied Authority (TC)

Implied authority is that which the agent reasonably needs to perform expressed authority. For example, an administrative assistant is employed to manage a real estate brokerage office. The assistant is not expressly told to hire and fire custodial employees, but implied authority allows the assistant to do so.

Apparent Authority (TC)

Apparent authority, also known as "ostensible authority," is conferred on an agent by force of law to protect innocent third parties who rely on the impression created by the principal that appropriate authority has been conferred on a would-be agent. Such authority may be created by the "principal's silence" when there is a duty to speak. It results when the following conditions exist:
   1. One willfully or negligently conveys the impression that another is his agent.
   2. A third person, in reliance on the false impression, deals with the alleged agent and as a result of the dealing, adversely changes his legal position (some use the term "suffers damage").

TYPES OF AGENCIES (TC)

The type of agency created depends on the scope of responsibility given to the agent. Classification of agencies is based on the amount of authority given by the principal, ranging from very little to complete. There are many types of agencies and degrees of authority. Four basic categories are mentioned here, but only the first is normally applied to real estate brokerage relationships.

Special Agent (TC) ✓ *MOST IMPORTANT*

A special agent is one employed for the performance of a specific task. Once that is accomplished, the agency is extinguished. A real estate broker ordinarily is a special agent, one with limited authority, authorized to conduct a single transaction for a principal. The broker's principal is generally the owner of the real estate. Sometimes the principal is a buyer, commonly one seeking a special type of property. As a general rules, the broker's authority as a special agent is to find a purchaser who is ready, willing, and able to buy the property, either on the terms set out by the seller or on terms acceptable to the seller.

General Agent (TC) ✓

A general agent is one who has wide authority to conduct a series of transactions of a continuous nature on behalf of clients. With a general agency, a principal gives the agent the power to transact the affairs of the principal in a certain trade or business.

Universal Agent (TC) ✓

A universal agency empowers the agent to represent the principal in all matters that can be delegated. A universal agent literally has a power of attorney and can, without permission, enter into any contract for the principal. Such authority allows the agent to transact any and all business on behalf of the principal including the writing and endorsing of checks.

Ostensible or Apparent Agent (TC)

An ostensible or apparent agent is one who is considered by third persons to represent a principal whose words or conduct led the third party to believe that the agent had authority to act on behalf of the principal. Whether or not the agent has such authority, third parties who relied on the apparent authority may hold the principal liable for the acts for the purported agent.

Agency by Estoppel (TC)

Agency by estoppel is an implied agency or an ostensible agency. In this situation, an agency appears to exist because of the circumstances such as an agent acting as if he were the principal's agent. Unless the principal denies its existence, the agency may, in fact, exist, and the principal may be prevented from later denial by *estoppel*. Estoppel means that a person may not assert rights or facts which are inconsistent with a previously held position or conduct.

Agency Coupled with an Interest (TC)

An agency coupled with an interest is one in which the agent has an interest in the property, the subject of the agency. This agency can not be terminated by the principal and it is not terminated upon the death of the principal. The agent may have an ownership interest in the property or some other interest such as supplying the financing.

AGENCY RESPONSIBILITIES (TC)

The relationship of trust and confidence assumed by an agent is described as a fiduciary relationship in which the agent owes a duty of loyalty and trust to the client and has a duty of performance according to the terms of the employment contract. In turn, the principal has certain responsibilities toward the agent, while each has pre-established responsibility to third parties.

Court cases have established a specific set of common law duties in the usual agency situation. Federal statutes are also applicable in many cases, especially in labor law.

RESPONSIBILITIES OF AGENTS TO THEIR PRINCIPALS (TC)

Fiduciary duty requires that the agent always act in the best interest of the principal. The law implies certain responsibilities which hold in the normal real estate agency arrangement.

Performance (TC)

Agents cannot escape responsibility by assigning or delegating duties they have agreed to perform. Agency relationships are highly personal by nature, are non-delegable and, if the principal designates, cannot be performed by any other than the agent selected. In most real estate brokerage relationships, by custom, habit, and usage, sub-agents may be employed, particularly in showing properties and transmitting offers to owners. Utilization of sub-agents in any capacity, however, does not relieve the basic legal obligation of the agent. In short, an agent must perform the (contract) agency, and must do so in person.

Loyalty (TC)

By establishing an agency relationship, the agent is working for and is appointed by the principal. In this capacity, agents must be loyal, diligent, and faithful to their employers, and act in the most professional and ethical manner, putting forth their best efforts to further the interest of their principals.

To preclude unjust enrichment, agents may profit only by agreed upon compensation and must not have or represent any interest adverse or opposed to the principal. They may not accept secret gifts or fees from other parties without permission of their principals. Agents cannot use confidential information for their own personal benefit or gain. They may not later disclose to a third party secret information acquired as a result of the agency relationship.

Agents must not act as agents for both the principal and third parties (dual agency) without express permission of all parties. If such an occasion arises, each party must know the complete nature of the relationship existing between the agent and the other party, and understand the inability of the dual agent to adhere to the fiduciary duties of sale, loyalty and confidentiality. The agent must make a full disclosure of all pertinent facts before, during and after the transaction.

Agents may not compete with their principals in matters covered by the agency. Agents have the duty to keep; their principals fully informed at all times of all material facts or information obtained which could affect the subject matter of the agency. Agents must convey any information or notice from a third party intended to be transmitted to the principal. If agents neglect to communicate the information, the principals are as liable as though they had been informed or received notice directly. If agents fail to inform the principal, the principal can hold the agents liable for the resulting loss.

Although the requirement for loyalty is broad, it does not require an agent to cover dishonest acts of the principal which the agent may discover. The agent must act in a legal manner at all times or withdraw from the agency.

Obedience (TC)

An agent is obligated to perform the work assigned and to obey all reasonable, lawful, and moral instructions given by the principal in the performance of the agency. If losses to a principal are caused by acts committed by an agent acting beyond actual authority, the agent may be liable to the principal for those losses. An agent cannot justify actions by stating that they were done in good faith, or that the agent was really looking after the best interest of the client. The legal test is: Did the agent violate instructions?

In an emergency, however, when it is clearly in the best interest of the principal, the agent has the authority to disregard instructions.

Duty to Account (TC)

The agent has the duty to make an accounting to the principal for all property, money, or other valuable consideration received in the course of the agency. Accurate records and accounts of all transactions, whether or not consummated, must be kept on file for a minimum of five years.

All checks and monies rightfully belonging to others should be deposited promptly by the agent in a separate bank account called an escrow or trust account. Earnest deposit checks must be deposited before the end of the third banking day following acceptance of an offer by an offeree, unless otherwise agreed to in writing by all interested parties.

Escrow funds must be kept in a trust account until the transactions involved are consummated or terminated and a proper accounting is made. The commingling of the money held for others with the agent's general operating or personal accounts is prohibited.

Funds received by a sub-agent or an associate must be promptly turned over to the listing broker for deposit. If the seller should fail, refuse, or be unable to close a transaction through no fault of the purchaser, the earnest deposit must be returned to the purchaser.

Brokers and associates are responsible for furnishing duplicate originals of all material documents to the parties to the transaction. A duplicate copy is a document, no matter how prepared or reproduced, with original signatures placed on the document after reproduction or entry of all other information.

Brokers and associates are responsible for furnishing duplicate originals of all material documents to the parties to the transaction. A duplicate copy is a document, no matter how prepared or reproduced, with original signatures placed on the document after reproduction or entry of all other information.

Monies belonging to others cannot be converted to personal use. They are not available for other than intended use.

Care and Skill (TC)

The agent has the duty to act with reasonable care and to possess the skills exercised by persons in the community performing such skills. Reasonable judgment and care must be exercised in advertising and rendering service. Agents hold themselves out to the public as possessing certain abilities and skills have the duty to perform with competence. To the public, the licensee possesses knowledge, ability, and skill as represented. If a client suffers any loss due to the licensee's lack of care, knowledge or skill, the client can hold the licensee liable for such loss.

Because agents cannot escape responsibility for negligence or lack of ability by pleading ignorance, they should keep informed of social, economic, and legal developments in their fields of expertise.

RESPONSIBILITIES OF PRINCIPALS TO AGENTS (TC)

Although the realities of their normal functions do not fit neatly into this section of agency law, real estate agents should be aware of the following basic duties of principals.

Duty to Perform (TC)
The principal must abide by the terms of the agency contract and owes a duty of good faith and fair dealing to the agent. If the principal wrongfully breaks the contract, the agency is terminated, but the principal may be liable for damages to the broker. The principal must allow the agent a fair opportunity to perform the services and must not act in any manner which will harm the agent's reputation. Neither the principal nor the agent may interfere with the performance of the contract by the other and both must cooperate in the accomplishment of the objective.

Reimburse Expenses (TC)

If the agent incurs expenses in performing authorized acts for the principal, the principal has the duty to reimburse for all reasonable expenses so incurred.

Indemnify for Loss (TC)

The principal is responsible for making restitution to the agent who, without fault, sustains damages, losses, or injury as a result of the agency relationship.

Compensate for Services (TC)

When the agent has performed as agreed, the principal has the duty to pay the amount of commission agreed. If no amount of compensation is agreed upon or stated, the principal must pay the agent the current market rate of such services in that locality.

In some instances, the broker is not entitled to be paid for services rendered. No compensation is due if the:

    1. Objective of the agency is not legal.

2. Broker performs in a negligent manner resulting in loss or injury to the principal.

3. Broker makes misrepresentations or is guilty of fraudulent activity.

4. Broker represents others with interest adverse to the principal without knowledge and consent of the principal (undisclosed dual agency).

Respondent superior (TC) is a legal (Latin) term which relates to vicarious liability. It appears in the Oklahoma Brokerage Relationships Act as the vicarious liability provision between the single party broker and the party. In the common law of agency, so long as the agent is acting within the scope of the agency, the principal (party) may be held liable for the torts of the agent. In the Oklahoma Brokerage Relationships Act, the party (principal) may be held liable for the torts of the single party as long as the single party broker is acting within the scope of the brokerage relationship.

RESPONSIBILITIES OF PRINCIPALS TO THIRD PARTIES (TC)

The principal owes the duty to the third person to perform contracts negotiated by the authorized agent. If the contract is not performed, the third party may hold the principal
liable for breach of contract. Likewise, the third party is responsible to the principal for performing contracts made through the agent. The principal is personally liable for any tort (a civil wrong, such as fraud) of an agent if the principal authorized the agent to do the wrongful act, or if the act was within the scope of the agent's employment.

A seller of real estate is liable to the buyer for the representation as to a material defect in the property made by the broker or associate which induced the purchaser to buy, if such representation was made with either the knowledge of the seller or with express or implied consent.

RESPONSIBILITIES OF AGENTS AND THIRD PARTIES (TC)

While agents must be primarily loyal to principals, they must also be honest with third parties. Agents owe customers a duty of good faith.

If the agent has authority to negotiate a contract with a third party on behalf of the principal, the agent has no personal responsibility for performing the contract. If the principal whose identity is known (disclosed principal) fails or refuses to perform, the agent cannot be held liable for the non-performance of the principal.

If, however, the agent negotiates a contract for the principal without, in some way, revealing the existence of or the identity of the principal (undisclosed principal), the agent can be held personally liable for the performance of the contract by the third party. In this latter situation, the agent may also hold the third party responsible for performance.

An agent is personally responsible to the third party for any tort committed, with or without the permission of the principal.

If a person claims to be an agent for another, that person impliedly warrants or guarantees possession of such authority. One can be held liable to the third party for any loss caused by breach of such warranty even if there is no real authority to act as agent.

If a real estate broker or associate knowingly misrepresents a material fact concerning the property for the purpose of inducing the prospect to purchase, and the prospect buys relying on the misrepresentation, the agent is responsible for the tort of fraud or deceit. If the agent acted with the consent of the principal, or within the scope of authority given, the third party has a choice of recovering the loss from the agent or the principal. In turn, a third party is liable to the agent for any tort committed against the agent. In the usual real estate situation, the buyer and seller personally sign the contract. The question of liability on a contract made by a duly authorized agent does not normally arise.

Brokers or associates might be held liable for negligence if they fail to inform themselves of the facts which a reasonable inquiry might disclose. Prudent business practice requires the broker to make a careful investigation of the property before offering it for sale. In so doing, the broker can avoid the publicity of a lawsuit or the bad public relations of being suspected of fraud. The broker should never rely only on the word of the seller.

A real estate broker cannot sign a contract for the sale of real estate for a principal unless specifically authorized. The authority for a real estate agent is usually interpreted as being only to fid a ready, willing, and able purchaser to buy on the terms set forth by the seller and obtain an offer to purchase, If the owner fails or refuses to perform the contract of sale, the broker is not liable to the buyer.

Although agents could be held responsible for statements misrepresenting the property, they cannot be held liable for exaggerations that a prudent person would not normally construe as factual.

UNDISCLOSED DUAL AGENCY (TC)

It is both unethical and illegal for an agent to represent both parties without the consent of both. With the knowledge and consent of the parties, however, the agent may act for any or all and may receive compensation from each.

Deliberate creation of a dual agency, although legal, is considered a dangerous practice. The principal wants the broker to negotiate for the highest possible price; the third party wants the agent to arrange for the lowest price. In attempting to serve two masters, brokers may be sacrificing the interest of one to that of the other, or that of both to their own interest.

Dual agency, intended or not, can become the basis for lawsuits being brought against licensees by members of the public. These suits can result from confusion among buyers and sellers concerning the agency status of a broker and the broker not understanding the difference in the terms "clients" and "customers." Some prospective buyers (customers) are not aware that the agent who undertakes to show them properties or assists them in submitting offers to purchase traditionally does so as an agent of the owner (client). It is not clear to the buyer that the broker does not represent them and that they are without representation during the negotiations and consummation of the sale.

The ease with which an agency relationship can be created and the absence of any need for formalities or a writing make possible the so-called "inadvertent," "accidental" or unintended agency." Implied or inadvertent agencies have been determined to exist between agents and customers where the conduct of the agent was found to constitute the agent's consent to act on the customer's behalf in a particular transaction. Licensees often accidentally create dual agencies, being unaware that, by their action, an illegal undisclosed dual agency has come into being. Implied or inadvertent agencies can be created when agents lead customers to believe that they are acting in the customer's behalf or "doing the dealings" of the customers. Under the law of agency, such an inadvertent agency is a clear break of an agent's fiduciary obligation to the principal and generally is viewed to be an act of fraud. An undisclosed dual agent can be liable for damages and forfeiture of compensation as well as loss of a real estate license. Furthermore, any transaction procured by the dual agent can be rescinded without any showing of injury to the principal or bad faith by the agent.

In cases where the purchasers specifically enlist the aid of the licensee in identifying properties for inspection that meet their financial, locational, and spatial criteria, disclosure should take place at an early meeting between the broker or associate and the prospective purchaser. It should be explained to the "customers" that the broker is an agent of the seller, and they should be advised as to the kind of treatment, services, and loyalty they may expect from the agent.

The law is clear that an agent who shows a prospective purchaser certain properties offered for sale and transmits offers from the prospective purchaser to the owner does not become the agent of the prospective purchaser. An agency relationship with such a customer ordinarily does not result when the agent only shows available property, describing the amenities and attributes of the subject property. These activities are deemed to be ancillary to the broker's obligation to procure a ready, willing and able buyer.

BUYER BROKERAGE (TC)

It is also possible for an agent to be a "buyer representative," an agent who represents prospective purchasers rather than sellers. There are cases where customers specifically enlist the aid of an agent in identifying properties for inspection that met their locational, financial, and spatial criteria. Traditionally, such an agent is paid by the buyer to find an appropriate property.

In this arrangement the buyer representative actually represents the buyer while expecting the owner to pay the commission. Who pays the commission is not the determining factor in agency, although it is normal for agency to follow the money. The problem comes in determining who the agent actually represents and whether there is a conflict of interest.

In order to avoid creating dual agencies with their legal and economic consequences,
disclosure should take place at an early meeting between the agent and the prospective purchasers. It should be explained to the customers (prospective buyers) that the agent represents the principal, and they should be advised as to what kind of treatment, services, and loyalty may be expected from the agent.

Brokers may avoid dual agency by acting for one, and only one, principal in any particular transaction. Where an agent is a party to an employment agreement with an owner, the identity of the principal is clear; it is the owner. When not acting as an agent or sub-agent for the seller, the broker may act as an agent for the buyer, making the buyer the client. In so doing, commissions to be paid should be determined before property is shown, or certainly before negotiations begin.

Ch. 7

TEST YOUR UNDERSTANDING

1. Which of the following best defines the "Law of Agency?"
    1. The selling of another's property by an authorized agent.
    2. The rules that apply to the responsibilities and obligations of a person who acts for another.
    3. The principles that govern the conduct of business.
    4. The rules and regulations of OREC.

2. Persons who authorize others to act for them are
    1. employees.
    2. principals.
    3. authorities.
    4. third parties.

3. A person empowered to act on behalf of another is a/an
    1. middleman.
    2. agent.
    3. principal.
    4. third party.

4. Under the Law of Agency, licensees can be held liable if they fail to
    1. follow the legal instructions of their principals.
    2. possess and exercise the ability and skill of competent brokers or associates.
    3. use care in the performance of the agency.
    4. all of the above.

5. Real estate brokers authorized to conduct a single transaction for their principals are usually classified as
    1. general agents.
    2. universal agents.
    3. special agents.
    4. ostensible agents.

6. Agents having wide authority to conduct a series of transactions of a continuous nature on behalf of the clients are
    1. special agents.
    2. general agents.
    3. sub-agents.
    4. ostensible agents.

7. Associates owe all of the following duties except to
    1. obey all legitimate instructions from the broker concerning the transaction.
    2. be loyal to the interests of the principal.
    3. prepare the deed for the conveyance of title.
    4. disclose materials defect of the property to the broker and principal.

8. In an agency relationship with a principal, the broker must
    1. be loyal.
    2. obey reasonable instructions and not be negligent.
    3. account for all monies and property involved.
    4. all of these.

9. The broker must be loyal to the principal in which of the following ways?
    1. Profit only by agreed-upon commission and have no interests adverse or opposed to the principal.
    2. submit all offers to the principal until the principal accepts an offer.
    3. Both A and B.
    4. Neither A nor B.

10. A real estate broker acting as an agent of the seller
    1. must do as instructed.
    2. should do as instructed.
    3. should withdraw from the transaction.
    4. can ignore instructions.

11. A broker who acts as agent owes a fiduciary obligation to the seller. To the buyer of the property, the broker owes
    1. a duty of fairness and honesty.
    2. no duty because the sellers pays the commission.
    3. only the duty of honestly answering buyer questions.
    4. a duty to disclose only those items which the broker feels relate directly to the sale of the property.

12. Since employed by the principal, the broker
    1. may misrepresent the facts to the purchaser because the broker is not representing the purchaser.
    2. may misrepresent the facts to the purchaser if the principal so instructs.
    3. may not misrepresent the facts to a purchaser.
    4. none of the above.

13. A real estate broker, as agent for the owner, should
    1. submit only the most advantageous offers to the principal.
    2. make an honest profit on the sale in addition to the agreed-upon commission.
    3. be an agent for both the buyer and the seller.
    4. render faithful service to the principal, handling the sale of the property as if the broker owned it.

14. The fiduciary responsibility requires that the agent must always act in the best interest of the principal. As an example of this, a broker would have to disclose which, if any, of the following to the principal?
    1. The prospective buyer is a member of a minority group.
    2. The prospective buyer expressed an intent to violate restrictive covenants.
    3. The area that the seller is planning to move to has a very large minority population.
    4. The prospective buyer has indicated a willingness to pay more than now offering.

15. A broker owes certain fiduciary duties to the principal. Which of the following is not included in these duties?
    1. Loyalty to the principal.
    2. Obedience to the principal's instructions.
    3. Maintenance of the principal's property.
    4. Accountability for money and property entrusted to the agent.

16. A real estate professional expresses all of the following in a fiduciary relationship with the principal except
    1. loyalty.
    2. patriotism.
    3. honesty.
    4. professionalism.

17. When an agent has no authority but warrants to a third party that he does have authority as an agent, in the event of loss caused by breach of contract, the third party may
    1. hold the agent liable.
    2. has no recourse.
    3. hold the actual agent responsible.
    4. none of the above.

18. In the usual situation, a broker should
    1. represent everyone.
    2. make personal interest secondary to those of the buyer.
    3. make personal interest secondary to those of the seller.
    4. place personal interest first.

19. The creation of an agency relationship is usually the result of which of the following?
    1. Agency by estoppel.
    2. Agency by necessity.
    3. Implied agency agreements.
    4. Expressed agency agreements.

20. The broker's actual authority to sell a parcel of land is given in the
    1. contract of sale.
    2. listing contract.
    3. broker-associate agreement.
    4. Oklahoma Real Estate License Code.

21. The term "double agency" or "dual agency" applies to which of the following situations?
    1. The broker has a double escrow or double transaction on one property.
    2. The listing broker is cooperating with a selling broker.
    3. Two brokers have the same property listed.
    4. A broker is acting for both buyer and seller in the same transaction

22. Real estate agent may not legally represent all principals in the same transaction if.
    1. they have failed to inform all principals that they are the agent for each principal.
    2. they have not obtained consent of all to this agency relationship.
    3. they are collecting a commission from both principals without the knowledge of the other.
    4. any of the conditions exist.

23. Non-disclosure of dual agency can result in
    1. loss of license.
    2. contract rescission.
    3. Both 1 and 2
    4. Neither 1 nor 2

ANSWERS AND EXPLANATIONS

1. 2 A vast body of law, both common and statutory, controls the rights and duties of principals and agent. In addition to this general law of agency, which is applicable to all business transactions, state licensing laws also directly affect the agency relationship between real estate licensees, clients and the public.

2. 2 In a fiduciary relationship, principals are the persons who hire real estate brokers to represent them in the sale of property.

3. 2 Unlike an employee who merely works for a principal, an agent works in the place of the principal.

4. 4 Under common law principles, agents owe their principal personal performance, loyalty, obedience, disclosure of material facts (such as a proposed new school, highway relocation, or a new zoning ordinance that would tend to increase the property value over the agreed on listing price), to take reasonable care not to exceed the authority granted them or to misrepresent material facts to principals or to third parties, to keep proper accounts of all monies, and to place the interest of the principals above those of other persons (customers) involved in the transaction.

5. 3 In a standard listing contract, the broker is employed only to find a buyer who is ready, willing and able to make an offer acceptable to the principal. The broker is not authorized to sell the property nor to bind the principal to any contract for the sale of the property.

6. 2 A general agent is authorized to perform any and all acts associated with the continued operation of a particular job or a certain business. The essential feature of a general agency is the continuity of service.

7. 3 Preparation of a deed could be considered practicing law.

8. 4 the primary responsibilities of an agent to the principal.

9. 3 The agent must have the interest of the principal foremost and must keep the principal fully informed.

10. 1 A broker usually represents the seller and must perform the agency contract. As the fiduciary of the principal, the broker has certain duties, obligations, and high standards of good faith and loyalty. The other choices are unacceptable.

11. 1 In dealing with a third person, an agent must be fair, honest, and exercise care and diligence because the agent is liable for any material misrepresentations or negligent acts.

12. 3 If a real estate broker or associate knowingly misrepresents a material fact concerning the property for the purpose of inducing the prospect to purchase and the prospect purchases, relying on the misrepresentation, the agent is responsible for the tort or fraud or deceit.

13. 4 Faithful service is the fiduciary duty of an agent to the principal. All offers must be submitted to the principal, and only the agreed upon commission should be collected. The broker is normally the agent of the seller and cannot serve both buyer and seller without full knowledge and consent of both.

14. 4 Loyalty to the principal would require disclosure of such information.

15. 3 Maintaining the principal's property is not one of the fiduciary responsibilities. The others are fiduciary duties.

16. 1 Patriotism is not a fiduciary duty between agents and principals.

17. 1 A real estate broker is liable to a buyer if the agent acts in excess of the authority given by the seller.

18. 3 As fiduciaries, real estate brokers must handle the sale of properties of principals as though they were selling their own property.

19. 4 A listing is an expressed agency agreement.

20. 4 A listing contract is the means by which authority to act as an agent in a real estate transaction is usually given to the real estate broker.

21. 4 Dual agency can be defined as a situation where one broker or associate represents both parties to a transaction.

22. 4 All of these conditions must exist for an agent to legally represent all principals in the same transaction.

23. 3 The OREC can discipline an who is illegally involved in a dual agency by any disciplinary measure it has the power to effect. A conflict of interest exists when the agent represents both the seller and the buyer. This could lead to contract cancellation.

BROKER RELATIONSHIPS ACT, PRINCIPLES
(Any of this chapter could appear on the state portion of the test.)
NOTE: The following is the *Oklahoma Broker Relationships Act* as of 2013.

§858-351. Definitions: Unless the context clearly indicates otherwise, as used in Section 858-351 through 858-363 of The Oklahoma Real Estate License Code.:

1. "Broker" means a real estate broker, an associated broker associate, sales associate, or provisional sales associate authorized by a real estate broker to provide brokerage services;

2 "Brokerage Services" means those services provided by a broker to a consumer in a consumer transaction;

3. "Party" means a person who is a seller, buyer, landlord, or tenant or a person who is involved in an option or exchange;

4. "Transaction" means an activity or process to buy, sell, lease, rent, option or exchange real estate. Such activities or processes may include, without limitation, soliciting, advertising, showing or viewing real property, presenting offers or counteroffers, entering into agreements and closing such agreements; and

5. "Firm" means a sole proprietor, corporation, association or partnership.

§858-353. A. A broker shall have the following duties and responsibilities to a party, which are mandatory and may not be abrogated or waived by broker:

1. Treat all parties with honesty and exercise reasonable skill and care;
2. Unless specifically waived in writing by a party to a transaction:
    a. receive all written offers and counteroffers,
    b. reduce offers and counteroffers to a written form upon request of any party to a transaction, and
    c. present timely all written offers and counteroffers.
3. Inform in writing the party for whom the broker is providing brokerage services when an offer is made that the party will be expected to pay certain closing costs, brokerage service costs and approximate amount of the costs;
4. Keep the party for whom the broker is providing brokerage services informed regarding the transaction;
5. Timely account for all money and property received by the broker;
6. Keep confidential information received from a party or prospective party confidential. The confidential information shall not be disclosed by a broker without the consent of the party disclosing the information unless consent to the disclosure is granted in writing by the party or prospective party disclosing the information, the disclosure is required by law, or the information is made public or becomes public as the result of actions from a source other than the broker. The following information shall be considered confidential and shall be the only information considered confidential in a transaction:
    a. that a party or prospective party is willing to pay more or accept less than what is being offered;
    b. that a party or prospective party is willing to agree to financing terms that are different from those offered;
    c. the motivating factors of the party or prospective party purchasing, selling, leasing, optioning or exchanging the property, and
    d. information specifically designated as confidential by a party unless such information is public;
7. Disclose information pertaining to the property as required by the Residential Property condition Disclosure act; and.
8. Comply with all requirements of the Oklahoma Real Estate License Code and rules.

B. When working with both parties to a transaction, the duties and responsibilities set forth in this section shall remain in place for both parties.

SECTION 858-355.1

A. All brokerage agreements shall incorporate as material terms the duties and responsibilities set forth in Section 858-353 of The Oklahoma Real Estate License Code.
B. A broker may provide brokerage services to one or both parties in a transaction.

C. A broker who is providing brokerage services to one or both parties shall describe and disclose in writing to broker's duties and responsibilities set forth in Section 858-353 of The Oklahoma Real Estate License Code prior to the party or parties signing a contract to sell, purchase, lease, option, or exchange real estate.
D. A firm that provides brokerage services to both parties in a transaction shall provide written notice to both parties that the broker is providing services to both parties to a transaction prior to the parties signing a contract to purchase, lease option or exchange real estate.
E. If a broker intends to provide fewer brokerage services than those required to complete a transaction, the broker shall provide written disclosure to the party for whom the broker is providing brokerage services. Such disclosure shall include a description of those steps in the transaction for which the broker will not provide brokerage services, and also state that the broker assisting the other party in the transaction is not required to provide assistance with these steps in any manner.

SECTION 858-356

The written disclosures as required by subsection C of Section 3 of this act shall be confirmed by each party in writing in a separate provision, incorporated in or attached to the contract to purchase, lease, option, or exchange real estate. In those cases where a broker is involved in a transaction but does not prepare the contract to purchase, lease option, or exchange real estate, compliance with the disclosure requirements shall be documented by the broker.

SECTION 858-359 A. The payment or promise of payment or compensation by a party to a broker does not determine what relationship, if any, has been established between the broker and a party to a transaction.

B. In the event a broker receives a fee or compensation from any party to the transaction based on a selling price or lease cost of a transaction, such receipt does not constitute a breach of duty or obligation to any party to the transaction.

C. Nothing in this section requires a broker to charge, or prohibits a broker from charging, a separate fee or other compensation for each duty or other brokerage services provided during a transaction.

SECTION 858-350 A. The duties and responsibilities of a broker specified in Sections 858-351 through 858-363 of the Oklahoma Real Estate License Code shall replace and abrogate the fiduciary or other duties of a broker to a party based on common law principles of agency. The remedies at law and equity supplement the provisions of Sections 858-351 through 858-363 of the Oklahoma Real Estate License Code.

B. A broker may cooperate with other brokers in a transaction. Pursuant to Sections 858-351 through 858-363 of the Oklahoma Real Estate License Code, a broker shall not be an agent, subagent, or dual agent and an offer of sub-agency shall not be made to other brokers.

C. Nothing in this act shall prohibit a broker from entering into an agreement for brokerage services not enumerated herein so long as the agreement is in compliance with this act, the Oklahoma Real Estate License Code and the Oklahoma Real Estate Commission Administration Rules.

SECTION 858-362 A party to a real estate transaction shall not be vicariously liable for the acts or omissions of a real estate licensee who is providing brokerage services under Sections 858-351- through 858-363 of the Oklahoma Real Estate License Code.

SECTION 858-363 Each broker associate, sales associate, and provisional sales associate shall be associated with a real estate broker. Associates shall not enter into a brokerage agreement with a party in the associate's name and shall only be allowed to enter into the agreement in the name of the broker. A real estate broker may authorize associates to provide brokerage services in the name of the real estate broker as permitted under the Oklahoma Real Estate License Code, which may include the execution of written agreements.

Ch. 8

TEST YOUR UNDERSTANDING

1. After the transaction is closed, which of the following remains an obligation of the broker?
    1. Disclosure of the brokerage relationship.
    2. Disclosure of potential future vicarious liability.
    3. **Account for any money or property relating to the transaction.**
    4. Disclose any substantial misrepresentations relating to the transaction.

2. The Broker Relationships Act provides that, when the transaction is terminated, the broker must
    1. **keep confidential information confidential.**
    2. reveal all confidential information.
    3. disclose the exact terms of any commission splits between cooperating brokers.
    4. disclose any confidential information which pertains only to the opposite party in the transaction.

3. When a potential buyer asks questions about why the seller is selling the property, the broker
    1. may only have the buyer put his/her request in writing and submit it to the seller for response.
    2. **may explain the request involves confidential information which he/she has not been given permission to disclose.**
    3. may freely answer the question.
    4. may respond to such questions only if failure to do so will compromise the transaction.

4. In Oklahoma, the Common Law of Agency
    1. is still in full force and effect in brokerage relationships.
    2. relates only to relationships involving brokers.
    3. relates only to relationships involving cross sales.
    4. **has been abrogated by the Oklahoma Brokerage Relationships Act.**

5. Information concerning motivating factors, price and financing in relation to buyers and sellers, under the Broker Relationships Act is considered
    1. **confidential.**
    2. readily available under the Freedom of Information Act.
    3. at the discretion of the sales associate.
    4. All of the above.

6. Under the Oklahoma Broker Relationships Act, a broker shall not be
    1. an agent.
    2. a sub-agent'
    3. a dual agent.
    4. **All of the above**

7. In the event a broker receives a fee or compensation from any party to the transaction based on a selling price or lease cost in a transaction
    1. it is a violation of the Oklahoma Broker Relationships Act.
    2. **it does not constitute a breach of duty.**
    3. is a violation of Prohibited Dealings.
    4. is a violation of Substantial Misrepresentations.

8. If a firm provides brokerage services to both parties in a transaction
    1. **written notice to both parties shall be made in writing prior to the signing of a contract.**
    2. no such notice is required.
    3. if either party is informed, it shall be considered sufficient disclosure.
    4. a firm shall not provide services to both parties in a transaction under any circumstances.

9. A broker who is providing brokerage services to one or both parties shall
    1. inform at least one of the parties regarding the relationship.
    2. **describe and disclose in writing the broker's duties before the parties enter into a contract.**
    3. must disclose to at least one party the broker's duties and responsibilities.
    4. has no duty to disclose the broker's duties and responsibilities.

ANSWERS AND EXPLANATIONS

1. 3   All brokers must account for any money or property in his/her possession belonging to others when the transaction is terminated.

2. 1   A broker is required to keep all confidential information as confidential information even after the transaction is terminated.

3. 2   That a party is willing to pay more or accept less is confidential information.

4. 4   The Oklahoma Broker Relationships Act replaces and abrogates the Common Law of Agency.

5. 1   The obligation is to adhere to confidentiality so that neither party has an unfair advantage.

6. 4   The Oklahoma Broker Relationships Act replaces the Common Law of Agency.

7. 2   Such fees are considered acceptable.

8. 1   Such disclosure is required by the Oklahoma Broker Relationships Act.

9. 2   Such disclosure is required by the Oklahoma Broker Relationships Act.

SERVICE CONTRACTS

LISTING CONTRACTS AND PRICING

LISTING CONTRACT (TC)

The authority to act as a licensee is usually given to the real estate broker by means of a listing contract. This is the agreement of employment between the property owner and the broker whereby the owner lists property for sale with the broker. The listing may be either written or oral. While an oral listing is legal for the sale of real property, it is difficult to enforce should a conflict or dispute arise over the contract terms. The use of oral listings should not be considered by a real estate practitioner. All listings should be in writing and signed by both the owner and the broker, with copies given both parties. Such procedure will avoid possible misunderstandings that may arise regarding the listing and the exact terms thereof.

Unless brokers have listing contracts, oral or written, to support their claims of employment, they are not entitled to compensation, even though they may have procured the sale. The law will not assist "volunteers" in their claim of employment. Claims may arise out of the situation wherein two persons, having been introduced by the broker, at some later date consummate a deal for which the broker tries to collect a commission. Unless there were words or conduct on the part of the owner from which a brokerage contract could be implied, the broker cannot collect. Even if present, proof of the words or conduct or the intent or meaning thereof would be difficult to establish in court. The prudent and well-informed broker will be certain of the brokerage appointment and have it reduced to writing.

It is common for listings to provide, through a carry-over clause, that if the property is sold within a stated period of time after the expiration of the listing to any party with whom the listing broker negotiated and whose name was revealed in writing to the owner by the broker, the owner must pay the broker a commission.

In addition to multiple listings, there are four general types of listing contracts.

TYPES OF LISTINGS (TC)

Exclusive Right-to-Sell. (TC)

An exclusive right-to-sell listing gives the sole and exclusive right to sell the property during the listing period to the listing broker. Even if the owner should sell the property to a buyer procured by the owner, the broker is entitled to a commission. The best efforts of the broker can be applied with the broker being secure in the knowledge that the right of a commission and recovery of expenses to advertising and soliciting cannot be defeated by anyone during the listing period. This type of listing should be carefully drafted and clearly explained to the property owner.

Exclusive Brokerage/Agency. (TC) *[not used anymore]*

Under an exclusive brokerage listing, the owner agrees that the commission for the sale will be payable only to the broker named in the listing agreement. The owner also agrees that the property will not be listed with other brokers. However, if property is sold by the owner to a buyer found by the owner, the broker is not entitled to a commission. An exclusive brokerage listing permits application of the best efforts by the broker unhampered by possible interference from other brokers but still in direct competition with the seller.

Open Listings. (TC)

Under an open listing, the owner lists property with a broker at a specified price, agreeing to pay a commission on that price or any other price that may be accepted by the owner. The owner retains the right, however, to list the property with other brokers.

In an open listing, the owner pays a commission only to the broker who is the procuring cause of the sale. The owner, selling it to a buyer procured by the owner, is not obligated to pay compensation to any broker holding an open listing.

While not violating any laws nor being considered unethical by any professional standards, the open listing provides a less than desirable employment agreement between a broker and a seller. Open listing contracts are likely to produce quarrels over the commission when several brokers produce buyers ready, willing, and able to buy. Also, brokers are reluctant to make great effort or incur expenses when the owner or others may sell the property and without notice, dissolve the contractual responsibility of paying a commission to the broker.

Net Listings. (TC)

A net listing, which can occur in connection with any of the three types of listings specified above, is a contract to find a buyer or lessee for the property at a certain price to the owner. For example, the owner may give a net listing of $162,000 on the property to the broker. If the broker finds a buyer at $162,000 or less, no commission is payable. If the broker finds a buyer at $178,000, a commission of $16,000 is earned. In the latter case, the court will strictly interpret the listing contract, and, if the terms are not clear and definite, it may be held that the broker is entitled only to a fair commission and may not keep the full amount above the net listing price when it exceeds the usual commission.

Net listings are generally to be discouraged in the sale or development of real property. If the property sells for the net listed price or less, the broker receives nothing; if it sells for much more, the courts may not let the broker keep it all. In addition to no price being set, an open net listing does not oblige the owner to restrict the listing to one broker. On an open net listing given to three different brokers, the brokers could offer the property for sale to the same prospect at three different prices. Several brokers quoting different prices for the same property reflects adversely on the honesty and integrity of the real estate business.

Multiple Listings. (TC)

A multiple listing is not a separate kind of listing. Generally, it is an exclusive right-to-sell listing, with the additional feature that the other participating brokers may also sell the property as co-brokers of the listing broker. Brokers, usually members of a local real estate board, combine their interests through the facilities of a central listing bureau. Any broker who is a member of the multiple listing service may sell any property registered with the service. When the property is sold, the listing broker and the selling broker divide the commission according to pre-agreed terms between them. In order to implement his procedure, specific authority should be made in the listing agreement.

Of utmost importance in any listing is the broker's fiduciary duty of loyalty and fair play with the principal.

THE ANATOMY OF A LISTING CONTRACT

1. **Legal Description.**

    The legal description is a very necessary part of the listing contract. The address is also normally included for convenience in locating the property. The name of the addition is also usually included to help identify the property for cooperating real estate licensees. Additional descriptions may be used as may be necessary to aid in identifying the property.

2. **Date of Termination.**

    In compliance with Oklahoma Real Estate Commission Rule 605:10-17-4 (1) listing contracts must contain a date of termination. Listing contracts must provide a date of termination.

3. **Rate of Commission.**

    The listing contract must contain the rate of commission or fee which the licensee and seller have agreed upon through negotiations. Additional provisions may be included in this section which provide:

    A. In the case of an exclusive-right to-sell agreement, the commission will be paid when a ready, willing and able buyer is produced.
    B. The commission is earned when the licensee or anyone else produces a buyer ready, willing and able to purchase on terms acceptable to the seller.
    C. The usual listing contract will include a clause which provides that the licensee will be paid a commission, if a purchaser who was shown the property by the licensee and whose name is registered with the seller purchases the property within a specific time after the listing contract expires. This is often called the, "carry-over" clause.

D. Should the seller revoke the listing contract and then sell the property within a specified time to a prospect to that the licensee has shown the property, the seller owes a commission.

E. It is a customary practice for the above "carry-over" clause to be of no effect, if the seller lists the property with another license after termination.

4. **Duties of the Broker.**

The listing contract will customarily specify the duties of the licensee. This is frequently expressed as the "Broker's Authority." This is because, in order to carry out the broker's functions, the seller should give the broker the authority to do the following:

A. Advertise the property in a suitable way.
B. Use photographs of the property.
C. Place a yard sign on the property and remove any other such signs.
D. Keep utilities turned on at seller's expense.
E. Share information about the property with other brokers.
F. Have access to the property at reasonable times to show to prospective buyers.
G. Request financing information from current mortagagee or other lien holder(s).
H. Share sales information about the property with the Multiple Listing System (MLS).
I. Accept earnest money deposit(s) in connection with offers on the property.

5. **Duties of Owner(s).**

The seller(s) makes certain representations to the broker to facilitate the marketing of the property. These may include:

A. The seller(s) is the owner(s) of record of the property and has the right to sell it.
B. There are no options or first rights of refusal currently on the property.
C. Existence of Homeowner's Association and possible dues.
D. Presence of any special assessments.
E. Presence of any delinquencies or defaults.
F. The seller(s) has provided broker with current correct information and will notify broker of any change(s).
G. The seller(s) also agrees to cooperate with the broker to facilitate marketing of the property.
H. The seller(s) also agrees to not negotiate with any potential buyer, but will send such buyers to the broker.
I. The seller(s) agrees to give the broker copies of any leases which may be current on the property and keep broker informed of any tenant changes.

6. **Fair Housing Clause.**

By this clause the owner agrees to not discriminate in the sale of the property on the basis of age, race, color, religion, sex, national origin, handicaps or familial status.

7. **Broker Relationship.**

The broker will discuss the ***Oklahoma Broker Relationships Act*** with the seller(s). The seller(s) and the broker will mutually agree upon which legal relationship they will enter into.

TERMINATION OF THE BROKERAGE (AGENCY) (TC)

In order to end or release a brokerage agreement, the general rules of contracts apply. If a brokerage has not begun performance, the relationship may be terminated at will by either party without liability. A brokerage relationship can be terminated by acts of the parties or by operation of law.

ACTS OF THE PARTIES (TC)

Four standard ways exist by which the parties to a brokerage agreement, by either rightful or wrongful action, may voluntarily terminate a brokerage.

Revocation by the Principal/Party. (TC)

The principal has the power but not the right to revoke a brokerage agreement. Therefore, the principal may, at any time, revoke or cancel the listing contract. In so doing, however, unless the grounds are justified, the principal can be held liable for breach of contract if damages are suffered by the licensee/broker.

Renunciation by Licensee. (agent) (TC)

The licensee/broker also has the power to renounce or cancel the brokerage agreement at any time. In so doing, however, the licensee/broker may be held liable to the principal for breach of contract unless good reason can be shown to support the renunciation.

Mutual Consent. (TC)

By mutual agreement, the principal and the licensee/broker may agree to end the brokerage relationship at any time. Because many things can happen to cause one or the other to choose not to continue, it is not legal for either party to be bound by a listing agreement for an indefinite period.

Completion of the Contract. (TC)

The brokerage agreement itself usually sets the time of termination. If the agreement calls for the accomplishment of a particular objective, the licensee/broker ends when the objective has been reached. If the brokerage is for a definite period of time, such as ninety days or six months, the relationship terminates when the specified time has elapsed. In real estate, Commission Rule 605:10-17-4 (1) prohibits the making of a listing, brokerage or service contract without a date of termination. In other brokerage relationships, if no time is specified, it is generally implied that the relationship terminates after "reasonable" time lapses, considering the circumstances.

Failure to perform adequately or abandonment of the work may be grounds for ending a brokerage.

OPERATION OF LAW (TC)
Insanity. (TC)

The insanity (declared incompetency by the court) of either party to the brokerage generally will automatically terminate the listing. Notice to the principal or the licensee/broker of the insanity of the other is not required. In the event of the insanity of the licensee/broker, the licensee/broker may still be able to negotiate for the principal in deals with third parties who have no knowledge of the insanity or termination of a brokerage.

Bankruptcy. (TC)

By the general rule, the bankruptcy of either party will terminate the brokerage, except in the case where the bankruptcy has no effect upon the brokerage or its purpose.

Change in Law. (TC)

The title to the property involved in bankruptcy is usually transferred to a receiver, canceling the brokerage. A change of law making the purpose of the brokerage illegal will cancel the relationship.

Destruction. (TC)

The destruction or loss of the subject matter upon which the brokerage was created automatically ends the brokerage. The destruction of a house by fire terminates the broker's brokerage to sell the property. If a property has been condemned or declared uninhabitable, a listing contract is terminated. Loss of property through eminent domain ends the brokerage.

Death. (TC)

The death of the principal or the broker generally will automatically cancel the brokerage relationship, unless it is a brokerage coupled with an interest. Knowledge of the death of one party to the broker by the other party is not required.

PRICING REAL ESTATE

Price to be Offered.

In the listing process, perhaps the most important step is dealing with the sensitive subject of the worth of the home. Property must be viewed through the "eyes of the buyer." A well-priced home sells quickly for a good price. "Well-priced is half sold." The "right" price is the cornerstone of a successful sale.

Sellers usually have a certain net figure in mind as to what is expected from the sale. It may be based on the amount needed for the down payment on another home or perhaps on the amount they "have in it," including the improvements, taxes, and amortization payments made over a period of years. If that figure is beyond the reach of today's market, it will be futile to try to obtain such a price and they may have to be more realistic. What was paid for the property, its maintenance, and any improvements are irrelevant in the current market. Cost does not equal value. People, through demand, make value. Property is worth what an informed buyer will pay and that is determined through the tried and true basic laws of supply and demand.

Many sellers have a distorted concept of value and expect too much. They are optimists, tending to be over-impressed with the worth of their properties. People who have lived in a home for a long time and have raised a family there often have a tendency to inject a great deal of sentimentality into the selling price of their property, but unreasonable expectation is generally based on misinformation about property values in the area. Objective terms and specific figures must be used rather than subjective expressions.

A licensee must offer the property for sale only at the price the principal has agreed upon. A broker, however, should never be a party to any listing containing a figure substantially inflated or differing significantly from market value. Knowingly taking a listing that is grossly overpriced without proper counsel to the seller indicates that the licensee agrees with the misstated value and provides evidence of unethical practice.

Competitive Market Analysis. (TC)

Read on own....

To help in arriving at a salable price, some factual evidence as to the true market value of the property must be presented. A competitive market analysis (CMA) is a simplified version of the comparative market data approach used by appraisers and considered the logical approach to use in determining a price on single family residences. It provides an effective yardstick for measuring what buyers will pay and what the supply and demand is in an area.

Although developed in many forms, the CMA should include a list of properties "For Sale Now." These are the properties currently competing in the market.

A second set of properties are the "Sold Past 12 months" list. These are actual prices paid for the properties which have been definitely established and verified as being true data. This list should also note the original listed prices, the days the property was on the market, the date sold and the sales price. This is recorded history which cannot be changed no matter how much one would like to see it different.

The third list of properties will be those who listing expired during the past 12 months. This is what buyers would not pay. There is a price to pay for over pricing—a real financial risk by insisting on listing for too much. Sales people are turned off from such property after a couple of fruitless sales attempts and the price will ultimately have to be reduced. The "some fool" technique seldom works; that is, "Maybe some fool will come by and take it at that price." Most present-day buyers are well informed and careful in making such important financial commitments.

A balance will usually develop based on the asking price. Appropriate pricing will result in a reasonable amount of time required to find a qualified buyer and a satisfactory financing package. When the price is too high, market time is extended and financing arrangements become more difficult. If the price is too low, the property may sell immediately and financing will be readily available, but licensees have not lived up to their duty to the principal to obtain as high a price as reasonable.

Over-pricing adds to the time required to sell a home and may diminish the eventual selling price. When a house first comes on the market, prospects are eager to see it, creating a flurry of activity and interest. Most will likely be turned off by the price before making an offer.

The majority of qualified prospects will view the listing within the first two weeks followed by fewer and fewer as time goes on, and by the time the price is inevitably reduced, many of the original prospects will no longer be interested.

A relatively small variation from market value will have an impact on the number of typical buyers attracted to the property. Few prospects are interested in property listed well above market value. As the price asked approaches market value, interested buyers will increase substantially. At market value, it is estimated that 75% of typical buyers will be interested, while property listed below market value will bring out eager bargain hunters and opportunists.

To sum up the effect of over-pricing on showings, buyers qualified to buy at the overstated price will not be interested in the purchase because the value does not appear to be there. Those qualified to purchase the property at its market value will not even look if the price is set beyond their capacity.

It is essential that real estate licensees have a good working knowledge of the principles of establishing value of a given property. A recommendation of value too low will result in loss of money for the seller. Attempting to convince the owner that the property is worth more than its true value is misrepresentation.

Good Faith Estimate of Proceeds. (TC)

When a broker is unable to convince the property owner that the current market value is the price at which a property should be listed, the broker should diplomatically decline to accept the listing. A licensee is required to inform a buyer of anticipated closing based on the offered price and terms. If the offer accepted is different from that given at the time of listing, the net figure will be changed. The estimated net will help sellers determine whether or not they can financially accept the offer or will provide a basis for making a counteroffer.

Although a Competitive Market Analysis by the licensee should give a general indication of the value of the property, it may well be worth the cost to employ a professional appraiser to conduct a more thorough analysis of market conditions. Appraising is an art relying heavily on the effect of current economic conditions on value. The appraiser does not create value but rather interprets the factors which do and then reports a dollar estimate.

Market Value Estimation. (TC)

Market value, as defined by Fannie Mae (FNMA), is the most probable price which a property should bring in a competitive and open market under all conditions requisite to a fair sale, the buyer and seller, each acting prudently, knowledgeably and assuming the price is not affected by undue stimulus. Implicit in this definition is the consummation of a sale as of a specified date and the passing of title from seller to buyer under idealistic conditions whereby:

1. buyer and sellers are typically motivated;
2. both parties are well informed or well advised, and both are acting in what they consider their own best interest;
3. a reasonable time is allowed for exposure in the open market;
4. payment is made in terms of cash in U. S. dollars or in terms of financial arrangements comparable thereto; and
5. the price represents the normal consideration for the property sold unaffected by special or creative financing or sales concessions granted by anyone associated with the sale.

FORCES INFLUENCING VALUE (TC)

Appraisers also consider some or all of the forces that influence value before reaching a final value estimate.

Physical. (TC)

Physical characteristics, the site of the property, as well as the improvements, contribute to value. The general topography and location of land along with all improvements (buildings, sewer facilities, fencing) to the land are noted by the appraiser.

Economic. (TC)

Economic conditions which prevail at the time of valuation add to or detract from value. These include industrial and commercial trends, general price levels, interest rates, taxes, and the income level of the population in the area.

Social. (TC)

Social ideals and standards, such as population growth, marriage, birth, and death rates have changed greatly over the last several decades. Changes can cause rapid adjustment in value. In most large cities, people are found living in areas with persons of similar social and economic backgrounds. The appraiser is aware of social elements as well as outside pressures on the area which might affect value, such as urban renewal programs and the extent or absence of crime. In neighborhood areas, the family size and the age of the population should be investigated, as well as the quality of educational, medical, social, recreational, cultural, and commercial services available.

Political. (TC)

Political or governmental regulations, the rights and restrains associated with ownership of real estate, are considered by an appraiser. The value of a leasehold interest will be different from the value of a fee simple interest, for example. In periods of rising rents, a long-term lease may be more valuable than ownership. A clouded title may result in a lower valuation

An appraiser is also familiar with the general land-use plans, zoning, and subdivision regulations. Public services, such as fire protection, sewer and water, are important in the valuation process, as well as the laws, regulations and taxes impinging on property in a neighborhood.

Ch. 9

CHAPTER REVIEW

1. The usual listing contract authorizes a broker to
    1. find a purchaser and bind a principal to a contract.
    2. find a purchaser and accept a deposit with an offer to purchase.
    3. assure a prospective purchaser that an offer meeting the terms of the agreement will be accepted by the principal.
    4. cause to be conveyed that real property which is the subject of the listing.

2. Real estate listings, for the protection of all parties, should
    1. be prepared on proper listing forms.
    2. always be written.
    3. Both 1 and 2
    4. Neither 1 nor 2

3. Sally Seller and her friend, Bill Broker, met one evening at a cocktail party. When Sally told Bill that she had been appointed to a new job in another city, he asked whether she was going to sell her home. She said she was. Two weeks later Bill presented Sally with a Buyer, but she denied having hired Bill as a licensee. Which of the following is true?
    1. There can be no contract without a formal writing.
    2. Sally owes Bill a commission.
    3. When she said she was selling, Sally made a contract with Bill.
    4. To collect a commission, Bill will have to produce more convincing evidence that he was hired by Sally.

4. When Ellie Gant hires Bob Broker to sell her home, their listing contract gives Bob an exclusive-right-to-sell. Two weeks later, Ellie sells the home to a friend. Which of the following is true?
    1. Ellie will owe Bob one-half of the agreed upon commission.
    2. Ellie may not sell until the listing expires.
    3. Bob will receive no commission.
    4. Although Ellie has sold the house, Bob has earned a commission.

5. Under authority of a signed exclusive brokerage listing, Broker Hart diligently advertised to sell a home. Prior to the expiration date of the listing, the owners sold their home through their own efforts to friends and refused to pay Hart any commission whatsoever. The owners are legally obligated to pay Broker Hart
    1. no commission.
    2. one-half of a commission.
    3. all expenses incurred in advertising the home.
    4. a full commission.

6. A couple wants to sell their house. They want a broker to show the property, but they would like to be able to sell the house themselves without the obligation of paying a broker a commission. What form of listing would allow them to use the services of several brokers and not pay a commission should they sell the house themselves?
    1. Open listing.
    2. Exclusive brokerage.
    3. Exclusive right-to-sell.
    4. Multiple listing.

7. A couple enters into an open listing agreement with Snaildulst Realty. Later the sellers find a buyer themselves and notify the broker. Which would be true?
    1. The listing agreement is a voidable agreement at the option of the broker.
    2. The listing agreement remains in effect as a bilaterally enforceable agreement.
    3. The listing agreement is terminated.
    4. Half of the commission has been earned by Snaildust Realty.

8. A seller lists property for sale with a broker. In the listing contract, which is legal in Oklahoma, it is stipulated that the seller will receive $162,000 "net," with all proceeds over $162,000 being the broker's commission. This type listing would be a(n)
   1. open listing.
   2. exclusive brokerage listing.
   3. exclusive right-to-sell listing.
   4. net listing, considered dangerous for ethical reasons.

9. Multiple listing services are beneficial because they
   1. combine the best features of an open listing and an exclusive listing.
   2. expose properties to the prospects of many participating brokers.
   3. serves as a clearinghouse for salable property.
   4. do all of these.

10. Which is true concerning multiple listing services?
    1. Most are a function of the local board of REALTORS.
    2. All real estate licensees are members.
    3. They collaborate to set suggested commission rates for an area.
    4. All of the above.

11. The brokerage relationship will last until its purpose has been fulfilled or it is otherwise terminated. Which of the following would terminate the brokerage?
    1. Mutual consent.
    2. Death of the principal.
    3. Revocation by the broker.
    4. Any of these.

12. Which of the following would permit an owner to cancel a brokerage relationship?
    1. Death of the broker or destruction of the property.
    2. Lack of diligence by the broker in procuring a buyer.
    3. Refusal of the broker to reduce the listed price.
    4. All of the above.

13. Which of the following could terminate a brokerage relationship by operation of law?
    1. A change in law making the current use illegal.
    2. Bankruptcy of either the broker or the principal.
    3. Insanity of either the broker or the principal.
    4. Any of the above.

14. Smokey Seller owns a small restaurant she is anxious to sell. Shortly after she gives Broker Legg an exclusive right-to-sell listing, the restaurant is destroyed by fire. Which statement is true?
    1. The listing is terminated automatically by operation of law.
    2. The listing will terminate upon the expiration date.
    3. The contract will terminate only if Smokey and Legg agree.
    4. The listing will end at Legg's option.

15. You have been diligently working on a listing for many months. Before it expires, you find an excellent prospect who makes an offer for the listed price. Shortly after obtaining the offeror's signature, you discover that the owner was declared mentally incompetent a week before. You must now
    1. secure the signatures of the owner's children.
    2. sign the purchase offer for the principal.
    3. obtain the owner's signature.
    4. do nothing. Your authority ended a week ago.

16. Knowingly taking a listing that is grossly overpriced without proper counsel to the seller could be
    1. good business judgment.
    2. evidence of a violation of the *Brokerage Relationships Act.*
    3. a way to earn a larger commission.
    4. shrewd and acceptable business practice.

17. In setting a price on a house, the prudent broker will
   1. set an initial price considerably higher than the expected selling price to allow room for negotiations.
   2. start at a price below the market value as a come-on.
   3. advise the seller to set a price close to the market value.
   4. let the owners choose any price they think the property is worth.

18. Brokers may offer properties for sale at prices that
   1. they feel the properties are most likely to bring.
   2. their principals have agreed upon.
   3. equal to the price for which adjoining properties have been sold.
   4. none of these.

ANSWERS AND EXPLANATIONS

1. 2 A listing contract between a property owner and a real estate broker authorizes the broker to find a buyer or a tenant to certain real property.

2. 3 Oral listing contracts are legal and enforceable, but not recommended. Being employment contracts, they do not fall under the Statute of Frauds. Use of special written forms for each type of relationship is encouraged.

3. 4 There is no contract.

4. 4 In an exclusive right-to-sell listing, the listing broker is entitle to a commission if the property is sold by the broker or anyone else.

5. 1 With an exclusive brokerage listing the owner can sell without obligation to the broker for a commission.

6. 1 Under the terms and conditions of an open listing, the owner may sell the property without paying a commission to any of the brokers who may have listed the property.

7. 3 Under the terms and conditions of an open listing, the owner may sell the property without paying a commission to any of the brokers who may have listed the property.

8. 4 Because of the danger of unethical practices in net listings, their use is discouraged in Oklahoma and are illegal in some states.

9. 4 All are important features of multiple listings.

10. 1 In most instances, the broker securing the listing is not only authorized, but is obligated to turn the listing over to a multiple listing organization within a definite period of time so that it can be distributed to the other member brokers.

11. 4 A brokerage relationship between a principal/party and a licensee can be terminated at any time by any of these circumstances.

12. 4 Any of the three could cause the rescission of a listing contract.

13. 4 A change in law making the object of the relationship illegal or legal incapacity of either party will terminate a brokerage relationship. When bankruptcy has an effect on the relationship or its purpose by general rule, it will terminate the relationship.

14. 1 The law will act to terminate a brokerage relationship upon the destruction of the property.

15. 4 If the offeror or offeree should be declared incompetent before a contract is formed, there is no contract.

16. 3 Brokers should accept only those listings for which they feel they can perform a valuable service and can earn an honest commission.

17. 3 "Well priced is half sold."

18. 2 The only price to be quoted is the price shown on the listing.

VALUE AND APPRAISAL

VALUE (TC)

The determination of fair market value is central to every real estate transaction. The real estate broker and associate should be familiar with value and how it is estimated. The word value is subject to many interpretations and may mean different things to the same person at different times. To estimate the value of a specific parcel of real estate, it is necessary first to determine what type and for whom the value is to be measured.

Value may be qualified by a variety of specific adjectives which specify the type value being sought. The banker usually is looking for loan value. To the assessor, the value measure being sought is assessed value; the insurance agent seeks insured value. An accountant looks for book value. Potential buyers need to know value-in-use, value-in-exchange and investment values. To the seller, the value measures being sought are exchange value or market value.

ECONOMIC CONCEPTS OF VALUE (TC)

Value may be considered the present worth of future benefits. In the economic sense, value is the power of a good or service to command other goods or services in exchange. Value, however, is constantly changing, and must be defined by type and in light of current economic conditions. Price, on the other hand, is the number of dollars a person is willing to exchange for the value of a property. The "value" of money is influenced largely by the volume of money circulating in the economy. It may increase or decrease according to inflation or deflation rates. Value of a product tends to relate to the utility of the product. Economists use the term "utility" to mean what an item is good for.

Value-in-use is the ability of an economic good to produce income or amenities (non-monetary benefits) for the owner. Utility value is subjective in nature and may differ for individuals since everyone may not perceive the usefulness of an object in the same way. Utility value forms the basis for the market and income approaches in appraising.

Exchange value is determined in the marketplace, under purely competitive market conditions, and is the most probable price at which a willing buyer would buy and a willing seller would sell, neither being under no undue pressure, and both being fully informed about the various uses of the property. This value can be objectively estimated through observing both past and present actions of buyers and sellers in the marketplace. The market data direct sales comparison approach to appraising is derived from this concept.

Cost of production is the value, expressed as the cost in monetary terms, of the agents of production (land, labor, capital and entrepreneurship) required to produce an economic good. Economic theory holds that larger amounts of the agents in production produce greater net income up to certain point (the law of increasing returns). At this point, the maximum value is developed (the point of decreasing returns). Any additional expenditures do not produce a return commensurate with the additional investment (the law of diminishing returns). The cost of production can be objectively measured and forms the basis for the cost approach in appraising.

Supply and demand value is the price established in a competitive market. If supply exceeds demand, prices will fall and demand will be stimulated. Conversely, if demand for a product exceeds the available supply, prices will rise. Real estate markets are slow to adjust to changes in supply and demand because it takes a relatively long time to increase the supply through new construction, and, once built, these buildings remain on the market even when demand declines.

Value vs. price vs. cost value is a market concept and, therefore, reflects market conditions at a given time. In appraisal, it is the most probable selling price. Theoretically, value and price should be identical. However, a market price (actual selling price) may reflect financing terms or unusual conditions and not solely represent market value. Cost is the outlay of capital required. In most circumstances, cost will set an upper limit to value. Both price and cost are historical in nature while value is forward looking. None of these concepts equate to the other, but in combination and by comparison, a probable price can be estimated. **(TC)**

CHARACTERISTICS OF VALUE (TC)

Anything which has value possesses certain identifiable characteristics. These characteristics apply equally well to a loaf of bread, a gallon of gasoline, or to a parcel of real estate. Without any one of them, no value exists.

Utility. (TC)

To have value, real estate must be able to satisfy human needs or desires. The utility value varies from person to person since no two people have exactly the same needs. Utility is not inherent in the real estate itself, but appears when people realize and implement its uses.

Scarcity. (TC)

For anything to have value, it must be scarce. Real estate in urban areas is relatively more limited than land in rural areas. Therefore, the price per unit is higher and value is greater.

Demand. (TC)

The demand for real estate influences value. Demand is frequently measured in terms of the economic base of an area created by those industries which provide goods or services for export or consumption outside the area. These industries cause money to flow into an area which in turn creates a demand for real estate as well as other goods and services. Demand must be supported by purchasers able to buy or it is not effective demand.

Transferability. (TC)

While real estate is not portable as are most goods, the rights in real property are transferred from one to another. The ability of these rights in real property to command money or other goods in exchange is an important characteristic of value.

KINDS OF VALUE (TC)

Value may be divided into categories by type or purpose of the appraisal. In reality, all types of value have the marketplace as a reference point. In most cases, value, other than market value, has merely been adjusted to reflect the purpose of the value estimate.

Market Value. (TC)

The most common reason for an appraisal is to estimate market value. Market value is the same as value in exchange, being the most probable price which a property should bring in a competitive and open market under all conditions requisite to a fair sale, the buyer and seller, each acting prudently, knowledgeably and assuming the price is not affected by undue stimulus.

Assessed Value. (TC)

Assessed value is established for the purpose of distributing the cost of local government in some equitable fashion. It is usually expressed as a percentage of market value at a given time. In Oklahoma property assessment is limited to between 10% and 13-1/2% of fair cash value by the Oklahoma State Constitution.

Other Values. (TC)

Value that would be covered under insurance is the cost related to reproducing the structure only, since land value is not included.

Condemnation value is estimated in condemnation proceedings and is by legal definition the same as market value. In a partial taking, value may include damages to the remaining property.

The value of a lessee's interest in real property is the leasehold value. The rights valued would include use, duration of possession and enjoyment, but not disposition.

Retrospective value is the value of the property as of a previous date.

Going concern value which includes the value of goodwill, salvage value, and cash value are other common values that may be used.

BASIC PRINCIPLES OF VALUE (TC)

The following basic principles of value apply to every appraisal analysis. They apply whenever scarce resources must be allocated among competing, alternative uses. In a market economy, such as ours, price is the rationing mechanism for allocating the scarce resource, real property.

Highest and Best Use. (TC)

Highest and best use is the overriding principle for value. Only when property is developed at its highest and best use will value be at a maximum. Highest and best use is that which is possible under current regulations, reasonable use of the site and current or probable use in the near future. A site can have only one highest and best use at a given time. Improved property is assumed to be at its highest and best use until it can be shown that the site value without the improvement exceeds the combined value of the site and current improvement. Highest and best use can change over time. A lot with an old single family home in an area that has become commercial is probably no longer highest and best use as it may once have been.

Substitution. (TC)

The principle of substitution implies that a purchaser would pay no more for a parcel of real estate than the cost of acquiring a substitute. This substitute can be either a similar property or an investment which would provide a similar return. The return is usually measured in monetary terms. **For example**, an investor would be indifferent between investing in the stock market or real estate if both would provide the same dollar return and carried the same risk. One investment would substitute for the other. The return may also be measured in the form of amenities. A home buyer may perceive that a three bedroom house on one street is a substitute for a similar house on another street. However, if the first house was perceived to be more conveniently located, they would not be substitutes.

Change. (TC)

To estimate value, the appraiser must be able to identify current market conditions; that is, market conditions that prevail at a given moment. However, recognition must be given to the principle of change.

The physical, legal, social and economic forces comprising the environment within which real estate is located are constantly changing. Change may be occurring so slowly that to the inexperienced observer it is indiscernible, but the appraiser is trained to recognize not only the obvious but also the subtle indications which lead to change.

The appraiser views real property and its environment as though it is in a state of constant transition. He takes note of the past history of the property, its present state, and modifies the past trends and present statistics with analysis and judgment to forecast the property's value. For example, the appraiser observes and identifies the phase of development of the subject neighborhood life cycle, whether it is in the development state, stable stage, declining and deteriorating state, or a rehabilitation state. The appraiser then considers what these states mean to the value of the subject property.

Contribution. (TC)

The amount of value one component adds to total value is its contribution. The additional income generated by the component must exceed its cost or it will detract from, rather than contribute to, value. The appraiser uses the principle of contribution to estimate accrued depreciation under the cost approach to value.

Anticipation. (TC)

The value of income producing property is affected by the anticipated future income flows expected over time. This can be in the form of an annual yield on money invested or it may be in the form of income tax savings or capital gains when the property is sold. More than likely, the return will be measured by all three of the above or some combination of them. Returns may be magnified when investors use leverage (borrow) to finance property.

Balance. (TC)

Balance of uses is the combination of land uses in an area. Not all land in a city can be single family residential. There must also be apartments, businesses, schools, parks, and public uses.

The principle of balance is also referred to as the principle of conformity or the principle of homogeneity. This principle holds that maximum value is realized when a reasonable degree of similarity of property types and land usage is attained in an area or neighborhood as well as similar economic backgrounds for the inhabitants. Neighborhoods which have a similarity in terms of income levels and age composition of inhabitants tend to have higher real estate values than neighborhoods which have wide disparities in the make-up of inhabitant characteristics for these variables. Conformity does not necessarily imply monotony, however.

Areas which have land-uses that interact favorably and are compatible with one another have higher values than neighborhoods with incompatible land uses. For example, residential neighborhoods with appropriate recreational areas, adequate shopping, and proper street layouts providing accessibility and convenience to places of employment have higher values than residential neighborhoods encroached upon by industrial complexes which cause air pollution and noise, and create heavy traffic endangering the safety of children playing in the area.

Appropriate balance also refers to the proper combination of factors of production being assembled on a specific site. When an over improvement or super-adequacy is made to a site, the effect is to decrease the value of the subject site to the approximate level of surrounding properties. This is known as the concept of regression. For example, if a high quality $100,000 improvement is made in an area comprised predominately of $50,000 houses, the effect on value would be to decrease the value of the $100,000 unit.

In like manner, where an under improvement or deficiency exists on a site, the effect is to increase the value in a conforming neighborhood. Known as the concept of progression, it suggests low value property is positively affected by the proximity of more valuable properties while the concept of regression suggests expensive properties are affected adversely by the proximity of less expensive properties.

Externalities. (TC)

External economies or diseconomies over which a property owner has no control can have a positive or negative effect upon value. Real estate is especially subject to the effects of externalities ranging from population shifts to local government policies and administration, property taxes and social attitudes. Appraisers must be familiar with external conditions and events and be able to assess their impact on individual property values.

All real estate is immobile and fixed in its location and is a prisoner of its surroundings and the forces which affect and influence its environment. Therefore, the appraiser must observe changes which occur in their externalities and analyze their potential for creating, modifying, and destroying value. A change in zoning regulations, in the age composition of the inhabitants of a neighborhood, in income levels or in mortgage interest rates, all have the potential of affecting the value of real estate positively or adversely.

Competition. (TC)

Normal competition will preserve value. If there is little competition, excess profits will be made. Eventually others will be drawn into the market, wiping away the excess profit, sometimes causing ruinous competition.

Supply and Demand. (TC)

The principle of supply and demand is that price varies directly but not necessarily proportionately, with demand, and inversely, but not necessarily proportionately with supply.

The greater the supply of an item, the lower will be its value. The supply of homes in an area is affected by construction costs, supply of skilled labor, capital costs, land availability, and natural resources. A buyer's market exists when a buyer is in a more commanding position as to price and terms because real property offered for sale is in plentiful supply in relation to demand.

The demand side of the market can be influenced by the population's age, taste, income, numbers, composition, in-migration/emigration, and the availability and cost of housing and credit. A seller's market exists when a seller is in a more commanding position as to price and terms because demand exceeds supply.

ECONOMIC LIFE (TC)

The economic life of a property is the number of years over which the improvements are expected to or do render services exceeding the costs of operation. Theoretically, when property has been totally depreciated, it has no remaining value. Its economic life has been fulfilled. However, the economic life of a property is its useful life and not necessarily book value or the physical life of the improvements.

Depreciation, therefore, cannot be measured using the actual age of property. If property has been kept in good repair, the effective age may be less than chronological age. On the other hand, neglect and poor maintenance may contribute to a reduction in the estimated remaining life of the property. Therefore, the effective age may or may not be the same as chronological age. Effective age is how old the property appears to be in the eyes of the appraiser.

APPRAISAL

An appraiser's estimate of value should reflect the opinion of an average person reacting in the current market. The appraiser must be familiar with economic theory and prevailing economic conditions, as well as building construction, survey, and finance. Reaching a final value estimate is the product of the appraiser's research, skill, and judgment.

APPROACHES TO VALUE (TC)

In estimating property value, the appraiser would use one or more of the market, cost, or income approaches. Theoretically, all three should lead to the same value estimate. However, in practice they seldom produce the same estimate. Increasing emphasis is being placed on the market approach as the best indicator of value on residential property, but not necessarily on commercial or income producing property.

Market Data Approach. (TC)

The Market Data Approach is also referred to as the Direct Sales Comparison Approach. The rationale for the market data approach in appraising real property comes from the concept of value in exchange and substituting. The process used by the appraiser involves comparing the subject property, the property being appraised, with similar properties (comparables) that have sold recently. The market data approach is also referred to as the direct sales comparison approach. Basic to the use of the market data approach is a relatively active real estate market. This approach is most often used in appraising residential property as generally little difficulty is incurred in finding recent comparable sales. The market data approach becomes more difficult to apply in appraising commercial and special purpose properties. The market for commercial property may not be active enough to provide the appraiser with recent comparable sales or the property may be so specialized, like hospitals and churches, that no comparable sales are available.

The first step in using the market data approach is to identify the relevant market area. The appraiser moves from the general area, usually state and city to the more specific area, usually the neighborhood. The neighborhood is a complex socio-economic structure as well as a physical area and the value of property is affected by the size, condition and social environment of the neighborhood. The accessibility of the neighborhood to shopping, jobs and schools, legal restrictions, availability of public services, and natural terrain are all considered by the appraiser. Supply and demand factors at work in the area would be investigated to identify their impact on property value.

The second step is to collect information on the subject property and on comparable properties. The type of property data gathered by the appraiser includes date of sale, type of financing and pertinent physical factors as well as any unique characteristic that might affect value. The physical factors are size and location of the lot, size of the building, number and type of rooms, type of construction, and general condition and age of the improvements. A hundred percent location is the site best adapted to carrying on a given type of business.

The appraiser then analyzes recent sales of property similar to the subject property, compares them to the subject property, and makes adjustments for any differences found. The information on comparable sales can be taken from public records, real estate .licensees, or current owners. Many large cities have businesses which maintain data plants containing information on real estate sales. All data obtained by the appraiser should be carefully verified before it is used.

The adjustments in appraising are always made to the comparables to make them more similar to the subject property. Never adjust the subject property. The appraiser begins to make adjustments either in dollar amounts or percentage value to the comparable sales, if the comparables are poorer in some characteristic than the subject property, value is added. If they are better than the subject property, value is subtracted.

1. The first adjustment made is for date of sale. Value is affected by the passing of time. The farther removed the sale of a comparable is from the date of the appraisal, the more difficult it is to adjust for time.
2. The single factor that usually has the greatest bearing on the value of real estate is location. Properties, even though quite similar, may have different values, either because they are in different neighborhoods or because they are in a different part of the same neighborhood.
3. It may be necessary for the appraiser to adjust for physical characteristics such as square feet of living area, the presence or lack of heat and air, condition of the improvements, etc.
4. Since buyers are frequently willing to pay a higher price for a property in exchange for more favorable financing terms (an equity sale where the buyer can assume a low interest rate), the appraiser must investigate the type of financing to be used. Also, in order to be legitimate comparables, sales must be arms length transactions, not subject to the control or dominance of one of the parties. The sale between related persons or a forced sale would not be a valid comparable.
5. After the appraiser makes the adjustments, the adjusted sales price of the comparables provides a value range for the subject property. From this value range the appraiser would establish an indicated market value for the subject property. Usually the comparable requiring fewer adjustments is the most reliable indication or market value.

Direct Sales Comparison Example: The subject property is a nine year old brick veneer single family residence located in a middle class neighborhood of similar homes. The house contains 1993 square feet of living area and has a two car attached garage but no patio. It is in slightly less than average condition. The market in this area has been fairly stable over the last year. The appraiser was able to locate three similar homes that have recently sold and are in the same general area. All three are very similar to the subject except for some minor adjustments.

179,500

Comparable No. 1 is located one block away from the subject property. It is in average condition, is 218 square feet smaller than the subject and has an open patio. It sold six months prior to the effective date of the appraisal for $160,000.

Comparable No. 2 is located two blocks away from the subject. It is 171 square feet smaller than the subject, in about the same condition and it has a nice covered patio. It sold seven months ago for $158,000.

Comparable No. 3 is located three blocks away. It is 118 square feet smaller than the subject, is in about the same condition and has an open patio. It sold nine months ago for $154,000.

Cost Approach. (TC)

The cost approach is derived from the principle of substitution and contribution. A distinction must be made between reproduction cost and replacement cost. Reproduction cost is the cost to construct an exact duplicate of the building including any functional obsolescence which may be present. Replacement cost is the cost of constructing a substitute building with equal utility but without functional obsolescence or necessarily the same materials and construction techniques. The appraiser selects the replacement cost of a building as a guide in the cost approach.

Four steps are involved in the cost approach. (TC)

1. Determine the value of the land as if vacant and theoretically put it to its highest and best use. The direct sales comparison or market data approach is used to value the land.
2. Estimate the replacement cost new of the improvements as of the date of appraisal. Three alternative methods of estimating the replacement cost are: the quantity survey methods, the trade breakdown method, and the square foot or cubic foot method.
   A. In the quantity survey method, the different quantities of materials needed to replace the structure are calculated and multiplied by the price of each to estimate material cost. To this is added the number of hours of labor times the hourly wage, plus a necessary sum for overhead and profit.
   B. The trade breakdown method estimates replacement cost by breaking the building down into major functional parts or units. The cost of these units are developed from current market data and then multiplied by the appropriate measure. For example, if rough-in-framing costs $1 per linear foot installed (materials and labor), the 2000 linear feet of lumber were needed, the unit costs of each component are summed and added for indirect costs.
   C. The square foot/cubic foot methods are the easiest to use and the most common. To use the square foot or cubic foot method the cost of a new building, similar to the subject property, is averaged over the size of the building. The resulting factor can then be applied to the subject property and replacement estimated. If, for example, general office buildings are

estimated to cost $95 per cost square foot to construct and the subject property contains 5000 square feet of area, the replacement cost indicated would be $475,000. When figuring square footage of a house for appraisal purposes, outside measurement are used.

3. Estimate accrued depreciation from all sources and deduct it from replacement cost new. Depreciation is the loss in value from any and all causes while obsolescence is loss in value due to reduced desirability or usefulness. Accrued depreciation includes both and is the difference between replacement cost and market value, having nothing to do with the depreciation expense used on income statements for tax purposes. Usually accrued depreciation is broken down into physical deterioration, functional obsolescence and economic obsolescence.

A. Physical depreciation or physical deterioration is the loss in value resulting from normal wear and tear or from the action of the elements. Appraisers estimate this depreciation and classify it as curable depreciation or as incurable depreciation. If the cost to cure is less than or equal to value added, it is classed as curable physical depreciation. If the cost to cure is greater than value added, it is classed as incurable. Painting the trim or repairing window screens would probably be classed as curable, while structural decay too costly to repair, is incurable. Deferred maintenance is deterioration or loss of value resulting from postponed maintenance or neglect.

B. Functional obsolescence, the loss in value due to a change in technology, materials, or tastes, is also divided into curable and incurable forms. Small rooms, high ceilings, inadequate or outmoded plumbing, heating or air conditioning equipment would be classified as functionally obsolete, if their presence cause a decline in demand or utility.

C. External or economic obsolescence is a loss in value due to an influence external to the subject property. These influences can be a change in neighborhood, encroachment of nuisances, or other negative externalities which affect the subject property and which can be measured.

4. Add the estimated land value to the depreciated replacement cost to reach a value estimate. The value estimate resulting from the summation of these steps should reflect market value. However, in some cases market value may exceed replacement cost.

The cost approach depends heavily on the appraiser's ability to measure depreciation and the market response to it. The cost approach is most easily used in appraising new or nearly new buildings which have suffered very little depreciation. Depreciation cannot be measured using the actual age of the property. If property has been kept in good repair, the effective age may be less than chronological age.

Income Approach. (TC)

The economic concept of utility value and the principle of substitution provide the framework for the income approach to appraising. In this approach, emphasis is placed on the future stream of income that the property is expected to produce. It is an estimate of the value today of the ability to command money, either in the form of income or capital gains, or both, in the future.

Data Requirements.

The maximum gross possible income from all sources (rental income, parking, vending machines) that the property is expected to produce at 100% occupancy is first estimated. Current contract rent may not represent the maximum rent that could be produced if the property was operated under ideal management conditions.

An allowance for vacancy and collection losses is estimated and subtracted from gross possible income to arrive at effective gross income. Vacancy and collection losses are usually expressed as a percentage of rental income.

All annual operating expenses, those expenses necessary to keep the producing income, are subtracted from effective gross income to obtain the net operating income. Not included in operating expenses are any deductions for loan payments, depreciation, state and federal income taxes, or expenses of a personal nature. In addition, the operating statement must be treated to reflect annual expense even if actual payment is made on some basis other than an annual basis. Typical operating expenses are salaries, management fees, utilities, supplies, reserves for wasting parts, hazard insurance, ad valorem taxes, and accounting and legal fees.

Once net operating income has been determined, it is processed into a present value of land and buildings. The method for computing value based on anticipated net operating income is called capitalization. In applying the income approach, the appraiser usually bases the final value estimate on both the return over time and resale value at some future point in time.

Capitalization Rate. (TC)

The capitalization rate is the rate of return (yield) that an investor expects to earn on invested money. It is composed of the discount rate, which allows for return on investment or interest, and the recapture rate, which allows for return of investment during the period of ownership.

Gross Rent Multipliers. (TC)

A relationship between sales price and gross rent can be observed in the marketplace. Gross rent multipliers (GRM) provide a fairly reliable and easily calculated method of property valuation. The relationship is as follows:

Sales Price of Comparable = Gross Rent Multiplier
Gross Rent of Comparable

GRM X Gross Rent of Subject Property = Estimated Value

In order to use this method of valuation, the required information from a sufficient number of rental properties that have sold recently must be available. The gross rent at 100% occupancy is used and if the other properties are truly comparable to the subject property, it can be assumed that operating expenses and vacancy rates will also be similar. Adjustments are not usually made in using GRM.

EXAMPLE: Assume the subject property is a single family residence located in a neighborhood of similar homes, many of which are rentals rather than being owner occupied. The properties have sold within the last year. Their sales prices, monthly gross rents, and GRM are:

Sales Price	Monthly Gross Rent	GRM
$65,500	$570	$114.91
64,000	560	114.29
62,000	540	114.81
61,500	535	114.95
66,500	580	114.66

The subject property is currently being rented for $560 which multiplied by a gross rent multiplier of 114 indicates a market value of $63,840, rounded to $63,800. The GRM of 114 is probably the best estimate to use since it is most prevalent, the average GRM is 114.72 which produces a value of $63,899.

CORRELATION OF APPROACHES. (TC)

The final process concerning the value estimates provided by the three approaches is called correlation. In the correlation process, the appraiser weighs the relative importance of the results previously obtained and reaches a single, final, supportable estimate of market value. Correlation involves the application of judgment and analysis. The final reconciliation does not involve averaging the three indicators of value. It is highly unlikely that the three approaches to value will provide the appraiser with a single value estimate. The final value estimate is the opinion of the appraiser based on careful analysis and professional skill.

•TYPES OF APPRAISAL REPORTS

An appraisal report is basically a report to the client which is designed to convey the information gathered by the appraiser and the final value estimate. Regardless of form, all appraisals require the same analytical process. Three forms or types of reports are commonly used: the letter report, form report, and narrative report.

Letter.

A letter report is a written opinion of value. It does not include the amount of detail found in either the form report or the narrative report. The property description, purpose of appraisal, date of appraisal, estimate of value, and the signature of the appraiser are included.

Form.

Many mortgage lenders and insurers require the use of a form in appraisal reporting. The form used most frequently is the Fannie Mae (FNMA) No. 1004, a sample of which follows. The required information is supplied by checking boxes or filling in blanks. Form reports provide the client with a standardized method of obtaining information on property.

Narrative.

A narrative report is the most formal and extensive type of appraisal report. It provides the client with not only the salient facts related to the appraisal, but also the analytical procedure used by the appraiser. The supporting data on state, city, neighborhood, and comparables, together with all the information pertaining to the subject property (pictures, floor-plan, plot) are included in the narrative report. The approaches to the appraisal are explained as well as the reasoning process used by the appraiser in reaching the final value estimate.

THE APPRAISAL PROCESS

Every appraisal is a research problem and as such requires the appraiser to follow a definite process. The steps the appraiser goes through in reaching a final value estimate are as follows:

Define the Problem.

The first objective of the appraiser is to identify the property to be appraised, the rights or interests that are included, and the purpose of the appraisal. The effective date of the appraisal is established at this point.

Identify Data Requirements.

A well defined problem will lead the appraiser to the appropriate information needed. At this point the appraiser plans the research process to be followed and outlines the appraisal report.

Gather Data.

Once the type of data necessary to the problem has been identified, the appraiser can begin to gather it. Some information of a general nature applicable to the market area is probably contained in the appraiser's files and will be easy to gather. Information on specific market conditions that affect the property, data on comparables, and information concerning the property itself requires more effort on the part of the appraiser. In addition, all information which will be used in reaching the final estimate must be carefully verified and the sources noted.

Analyze Data.

The data analysis will lead to a determination of highest and best use. The highest and best use should coincide with the definition of the problem. If it is different, the appraiser must re-value the problem and the client's objective since obtaining the appraisal. The analysis will include adjusting comparables used in the market approach and reconciling their sales prices to an indicated market value of the subject property. In the cost approach, data analysis will lead to a depreciated reproduction or replacement cost new of the improvements to w which site value will be added to reach a value estimate. The income approach may not be appropriate on owner occupied residential properties. However, if the property is income producing, the analysis will provide a value based on capitalizing net income.

Reach Final Value Estimate.

Most appraisal problems require the appraiser to reach a single, final market value estimate. In reaching this conclusion, the appraiser reviews all of the information as well as the estimates provided by each approach. Each approach is viewed critically for appropriateness to the appraisal problem. More of than not, one approach will prove to be more appropriate than the others and is relied on more heavily by the appraiser. The final value reached by the appraiser is an estimate of value as of the date of the appraisal only, and as such, is usually rounded to the nearest hundred or even thousand dollars.

In some cases the appraiser may find it appropriate to indicate a range of value rather than a single estimate. Again, this depends on the nature of the problem and the objective of the client in obtaining the appraisal.

Write the Appraisal Report.

The final step in the appraisal process is to write the report to the client. It should be complete enough to convey to the reader the procedures used by the appraiser in reaching the final estimate. The information is presented in such a manner that the reader will come to the same conclusion of value as has the appraiser.

Every appraisal report, regardless of form will contain:

1. A description of property, including the legal description, a physical description, and a description of the rights involved.
2. The objective of the appraisal as stated by the client.
3. Effective date of the appraisal.
4. The supporting data and the analysis of the appraiser.
5. The final value estimate.
6. Statement of limiting conditions and the liability of the appraiser.
7. The certification of the appraiser attesting to the accuracy and reliability of the information contained in the report.
8. The signature of the appraiser, professional designation and qualifications.

DEPRECIATION FOR TAX PURPOSES (TC)

Real estate remains one of the businesses permitted to write off more money than that which is at risk in an investment. For income tax purposes, depreciation is an important area so far as investors in real estate are concerned. The following four techniques for calculation of depreciation are for tax purposes and result in book value. They are not generally useful in estimating current fair market value.

Straight-line depreciation is the reduction of value of a property in equal amounts during each year of its projected life. **(TC)**

The declining balance method is an accelerated depreciation format that can be applied to new rental residential property. Using the double declining balance method, the first year's depreciation is twice that of a normal year's depreciation under the straight-line approach. In the second year, it is calculated on the remaining undepreciated balance. It never gets to full depreciation but will reach scrap value. **(TC)**

The 150% declining balance works the same as the double declining balance except that it figures one and one half of the straight-line technique rather than double.

The sum of the year's digits method is useful for accelerated depreciation. It permits total depreciation of value over the life of the property. It works on the principle that the sum of the year digits for 10, for example, is 55. The first year the depreciation will be charged at 10/55, and the second year at 9/55. The tenth and last year will be 1/55. **(TC)**

ETHICS AND STANDARDS (TC)

Appraising real estate in Oklahoma does not require a real estate license. The State Insurance Department issues licenses and certifies appraisers. Federal law requires banking institutions to use state-licensed or state-certified appraisers in real estate transactions involving any federal agency. However, in order to appraise properties under $250,000, federal regulations do not require that the one doing the appraisal be a state licensed or state certified appraiser. This situation is referred to as the "**de minimus.**" **(TC)**

There are a number of professional organizations designed to promote high standards of professional skills and ethical behavior. A qualified appraiser will usually belong to one or more such organizations. The standards adhered to by appraisers affiliated with professional organizations cover the following points:

1. To abide by the code of ethics of the appraisal organization.
2. To report an unbiased and substantiated value estimate including all facts both helpful and detrimental to the client.
3. Maintain the confidentially of the appraisal.
4. To require a fee based on effort and time spent, not on obtaining some predetermined value estimate.

The appraiser is legally liable for intent to defraud and for giving false testimony in a court of law.

The **Uniform Standards of Professional Appraisal Practice** is commonly referred to as **USPAP. (TC)**

Ch-10

TEST YOUR UNDERSTANDING

1. The power of a good or service to command other goods or services in exchange is
   1. value.
   2. economic perfection.
   3. utility.
   4. need.

2. Market price is the
   1. true market value.
   2. price at public sale.
   3. price asked for the property on an open market.
   4. amount, in terms of money, paid for the property.

3. The value which represents the price that a property will bring if it is sold after being offered for a reasonable period of time, and the sale is completed between knowledgeable buyers and sellers, neither acting under duress, is the
   1. present value.
   2. current clause.
   3. market value.
   4. future value.

4. The elements necessary for property to possess value include
   1. demand.
   2. utility.
   3. transferability.
   4. all of the above.

5. The statement that no prudent person would pay more for a parcel of real property than the price of a reasonably close alternative which is available without undue delay, refers to the principle of
   1. balance.
   2. competition.
   3. conformity.
   4. substitution.

6. A neighborhood which maintains high property values because of its similar but not identical architectural styles is benefiting from the principle of
   1. change.
   2. conformity.
   3. substitution.
   4. progression.

7. An appraiser was hired to prepare a feasibility study for a 24-unit apartment building in which the owner was considering putting in a swimming pool. What basic principle of appraising would be used?
   1. Regression.
   2. Contribution.
   3. Competition.
   4. Substitution.

8. Joe Ego has his "dream house" constructed for $250,000 in an area where most new constructed homes are not as well equipped and typically sell for about $180,000. The value of Ego's house is likely to be affected by the principle of
   1. progression.
   2. assemblage.
   3. change.
   4. regression.

9. Highest and best use is
   1. single-family property zoned for industrial use.
   2. property purchased for owner use.
   3. the use which the purchaser intends when the property is purchased.
   4. the reasonable, possible, and probable use of the property that will yield the highest return on investment.

10. The principle of value that reflects the fact that the present use of a property may be different from its use ten years from now is the principle of
    1. competition.
    2. substitution.
    3. change.
    4. conformity.

11. The first thing appraisers should know in undertaking an appraisal assignment is
    1. how they are to be paid.
    2. the selling price of the property.
    3. the purpose of the appraisal.
    4. what property has sold for recently in the area.

12. When figuring square footage of a house for appraisal purposes, use
    1. outside measurements.
    2. inside measurements.
    3. Both 1 and 2.
    4. Neither 1 nor 2.

13. Which of the following should have no influence on an appraisal compensation?
    1. The complexity of the appraisal.
    2. The time required to make the appraisal.
    3. The value estimated in the appraisal.
    4. The expenses of the appraiser.

14. In the comparison approach to appraisal, after adjustments are made for each comparable, the result is
    1. the adjusted market value.
    2. an absolute value.
    3. a SWAG.
    4. the market price.

15. An appraiser who is using the comparison method to appraise a single-family residence would never use the selling price of which of the following?
    1. A similar home that sold over six month ago.
    2. A similar home that sold recently but is located in another neighborhood.
    3. A similar home that was sold by owners who were forced to sell at any price because of financial difficulties.
    4. A home of similar size situated on a corner lot.

16. The principle factors for which adjustment must be made in using the market data approach include
    1. location and physical features.
    2. date of sale.
    3. terms and conditions of sale.
    4. all of the above.

17. In appraising a single-purpose building, such as a church, the most reliable approach to an indication of its value would generally be the
    1. cost approach.
    2. market data approach.
    3. income approach.
    4. both 1 and 2.

18. The rate of return that an investor expects to earn on invested money is the
    1. effective gross income.
    2. **capitalization rate.**
    3. quantity return.
    4. net operating income.

19. If you were to calculate the cost of rebuilding a structure using exactly the same material used in the original construction, you would determine the cost of
    1. **reproduction.**
    2. replacement.
    3. Both 1 and 2.
    4. Neither 1 nor 2.

20. Which of the following items would not be relevant in the appraisal of an older property?
    1. **The original cost.**
    2. Current reproduction cost.
    3. An estimate of accrued depreciation.
    4. Recent selling prices of comparable properties in the neighborhood.

21. All of the following are correct statements concerning depreciation, EXCEPT
    1. a loss of value from any cause.
    2. the subject of wear and tear on investment property or property used in a trade of business.
    3. includes all of the influences that reduce the value of a property below its replacement cost new.
    4. **always concerned with intrinsic value and not concerned with factors outside.**

22. Physical deterioration results from
    1. action of the elements.
    2. normal wear and tear.
    3. **both 1 and 2.**
    4. neither 1 nor 2.

23. When changing tastes and standards cause an existing house to lose value, there is
    1. physical deterioration.
    2. economic obsolescence.
    3. **functional obsolescence.**
    4. sociological deterioration.

24. You are appraising a 20 year old apartment house. When this building was constructed, the neighborhood was exclusively residential. Today, scattered industrial uses are found in the area. This is an example of
    1. functional obsolescence.
    2. **economic obsolescence.**
    3. physical deterioration.
    4. psychological obsolescence.

25. Quality appraisals require expertise and experience. Anyone who works as an appraiser is required to
    1. hold an active Oklahoma real estate broker's license.
    2. have a minimum of six month training under a recognized senior appraiser.
    3. be an active and certain member of any one of the recognized appraisal societies.
    4. **do none of the above.**

ANSWERS AND EXPLANATIONS

1. 1 A standard definition of value.

2. 4 Market price is the actual amount of money paid.

3. 3 A standard definition of market value.

4. 4 All of these elements must be present.

5. 4 The value of real property is generally influenced by the cost of acquiring a substitute (comparable) property. When two or more commodities of similar utility are available, the one with he lower price generally will receive the greater demand. People generally do not pay more for a property than the cost of buying land and building a similar residence.

6. 2 Residences that do not conform to the design, type of construction, conditions and maintenance, etc. of other homes in the neighborhood generally suffer some degree of loss in value. An over-improvement or under-improvement indicates lack of conformity and usually suffers some degree of loss in value.

7. 2 The effect of value of one component is dependent on its contribution to the sale.

8. 4 A property may decrease in value by being in a neighborhood with properties of lesser value.

9. 4 Highest and best use of the land is that which, at the date of appraisal, is legal (zoning) and will yield the highest net return (money) in the foreseeable future.

10. 3 Nothing remains static. Changes in physical and economic conditions as well as the actions of buyers and sellers generally continue.

11. 3 The purpose of the appraisal is significant because it affects the choice of method and selection of data. For instance, an appraisal of the same property for the fire insurance and one for investment purposes will result in different estimates of value.

12. 1 The buildings inside measurements are used for determining room size, but the building's outside measurements are used to calculate square footage.

13. 3 The time spent, the complexity of the appraisal and expenses incurred, are legitimate factors in determining an appraisal fee.

14. 1 After making adjustments to each comparable property, the appraiser arrives at an adjusted market value.

15. 3 The price of a home sold under pressure is not a valid comparison factor. Adjustments can be made for time lapses, for another neighborhood and to the quality of lots with reasonable accuracy.

16. 4 Adjustments to the comparable should be made to each of these factors.

17. 4 A church is one kind of property which is appraised frequently with the cost method because few properties of this sort change hands on the open market.

18. 2 The capitalization rate ratio is: Net Operating Income over Sales Price.

19. 1 Reproduction cost is the present cost of reproducing the improvement with an exact replica, not one with just similar utility, as in the replacement cost.

20. 1 The original cost has virtually nothing to do with the current value of older properties. The market data approach usually accurately reflects the value of older properties.

21. 4 An appraisal must always be objective.

22. 3 The most common cause of physical depreciation, usually curable.

23. 3 A typical cause of incurable loss in value due to external causes outside the property itself, usually incurable.

24. 2 Economic obsolescence is loss in value due to external causes outside the property itself, usually incurable.

25. 4 The Oklahoma Real Estate License Code does not cover appraising. State licensing or certification is required for real estate transactions involving federal agencies.

MARKETING AND SELLING REAL PROPERTY

The Marketing Function.

The marketing function, finding a buyer, begins when the broker has listed a property for sale. Listing contracts are the inventory of the real estate store. The key to a successful business in real estate centers around those functions related to the listing.

There are many excellent sources for obtaining listings, including canvassing, referrals, vital records information, newspapers, homes for sale by owner (FSBOS) and expired listings. Listing opportunities often come from floor time, a designated time for a sales associate to answer the telephone and talk to walk-in prospects. It is the individual choice of each .licensee as to the method most effective for use in soliciting listings. Therefore, no effort will be made to enumerate the advantages and disadvantages of the various techniques.

Misrepresentation. (TC)

Brokers should accept only those listings on which they feel they can perform a valuable service and earn an honest commission. In securing listings, .licensees should be aware that they must abide by the *Oklahoma Real Estate License Code* and *Oklahoma Real Estate Commission Rules*. In particular, each .licensee should be mindful of Section 858-312 (2) of the Code which prohibits the "making of substantial misrepresentation or false promises in the conduct of business or through licensees, associates or advertising, which are intended to influence, persuade or induce others."

An innocent statement of fact may be termed misrepresentation, commonly defined as a false or misleading statement. If a broker or associate relies upon facts given by a seller or other real estate licensees and repeats those facts which are later proven untrue, the broker is responsible for misrepresentation. This places a burden on the selling broker or licensee, but one that must be assumed in a climate of consumerism.

Intentional misrepresentation occurs when the person making the statement knows it to be false. Negligent misrepresentation occurs when the person making the representation should have known it was false. The law places a duty on real estate licensees to discover and reveal material facts because of the licensee's expert training and the reliance of the public on the licensee. A fact is material if a contract would not have been consummated or would not have been made on the same terms if the fact were known by the parties.

Misrepresentation does not require intent. An innocent misstatement is actionable and could place a broker or associate in double jeopardy. First, the broker could be liable in a civil court for damages in a lawsuit, and secondly, under provision of the *Oklahoma Real Estate License Code*, Paragraph 605:10-17-4 (3), could have a suspension or revocation of the real estate license or other penalties. Any representations to a prospective purchaser should also include a source of those representations, whether they be from a seller or other documents.

Misstatements based on opinion cannot be construed as fraudulent acts. Opinion is an expression of what one believes to be true, may be positive or negative, and is not fact. Exaggerated or superlative comments not made as representations of fact, such as "this house is the best buy on the market," are "sales talk" or "puff," not fraudulent and the doctrine of caveat emptor applies. However, in oral or written communication, remarks should clearly be prefaced with, "in my opinion," "I believe that" or "I think that," to avoid misrepresentation. In law, potential buyers must not rely on opinions. They must discover facts for themselves. Since they may not rely on opinions, there is no misrepresentation. One test of "harmless trade puffery" is whether a reasonable person would have relied on the statement.

Licensees deal daily with situations ripe for misrepresentation. Areas where misrepresentation may occur include statements about value of property, conditions of property, title, boundaries, zoning, covenants, expenses related to the property, facts relevant to the transaction, and market conditions.

Code and Rules Affecting Marketing. (TC)

The marketing of real property is divided into two primary activities, advertising and showing. Many proven methods of advertising and showing the property may be utilized by the individual brokers or associates. The methods are left to the discretion of licensees as long as such methods do not conflict with good ethics or the *Oklahoma Real Estate License Code* and *Oklahoma Real Estate Commission Rules*. Specific acts which are prohibited by law or rule are:

1. The making of substantial misrepresentation or false promises in the conduct of business, or through licensees, real estate associates or advertising, which are intended to influence, persuade or induce others. [858-312 (2)]
2. Treat all parties with honesty and exercise reasonable skill and care. [858-353.1 and 858-354.B.1]
3. Guaranteeing or having authorized or permitted any real estate broker or real estate associate to guarantee future profits which may result from the sale of real estate. [858-312 (10)]
4. Advertising or offering for sale, rent or lease any real estate, or placing a sign on any real estate offering it for sale, rent or lease without the consent of the owner or authorized agent. [858-312 (11)]
5. Soliciting, selling, or offering for sale by offering prizes for the purpose of influencing a purchaser or prospective purchaser of real estate. [858-312-12]
6. Advertising to buy, sell, rent or exchange any real estate without disclosing that they are real estate brokers or associates. [858-312 (20)]
7. Repeated misrepresentations, even though not fraudulent, which occur as a result of the failure by the brokers or associates to be informed of pertinent facts concerning property as to which they are performing services. [605: 10-17-4 (3)]
8. Failure to make known to any prospective purchaser any interest the licensee has in the property being sold. [605:10-17-4 (7)]
9. Failure to reduce a bona fide offer to writing when a proposed purchaser requests such offer to be submitted. [605:10-17-4 (10)]
10. Failure to disclose to a buyer a known material defect regarding the condition of a parcel of real estate of which a broker or associate has knowledge. [605:10-17-5 (2)]

Caveat Emptor.

Caveat emptor was a by-word for the conduct of business in decades past. To some degree, this legal maxim still remains, in that the courts charge the buyer with the responsibility of inspecting the property and searching the public records to determine the interest of other parties. The current thrust of consumer rights and the abilities for instant communication have cast much more responsibility on the owner and the .licensee in revealing facts or defects which might cause the prospective purchaser to make an offer different from one proffered without the knowledge. Few, if any, real estate brokers or associates would knowingly conceal information regarding a material defect in property being sold. The consumerism movement, however, means that those involved in real estate must protect the buyer by advising of such defects, as well as material facts that might affect property value.

Psychologically Impacted Property/Stigmatized Property. (TC)

In psychologically impacted or stigmatized real estate, it is sometimes difficult to determine what is a material fact. Section 858-513 specifically exempts the requirement for disclosing that the property was the site of a suicide, homicide or other felony. Also the failure to disclose to the prospective purchaser that a former occupant was suspected to be infected or was in fact infected with a communicable disease not likely to be transmitted through occupancy is not misrepresentation. If, however, a bona fide buyer requests such information in writing the .licensee is required to inquire of the seller and must reveal the findings. Such findings, however, must be disclosed in accordance with the state privacy act. For guidance, the real estate licensee should see Rule 605:10-15-3.

NEGOTIATING FUNCTIONS

A purchase contract as relates to real estate is a written agreement with a deposit receipt whereby the purchaser agrees to buy certain property and the seller agrees to sell upon terms and conditions set forth therein. The real estate licensee must see that an agreement is formed by maintaining a close vigil from initial point of indication of interest in a property on the part of a prospect, to final acceptance of an offer and communication of the acceptance back to the purchaser.

Qualifying Buyers and Preparing Offers. (TC)

The real estate licensee needs to find qualified buyers and determine their desire, financial capacity, and special needs. By qualifying the buyer, the licensee is able to make an estimate of the amount of money that a prospective purchaser has available to enable that individual to successfully complete a real estate transaction. Such information would include the amount available for down payment and closing costs as well as expected monthly income to be able to afford a mortgage that might be created by the purchase of the property.

If statements are made to the effect that "you will not qualify or cannot qualify for a mortgage," the broker may be in violation of the *Federal Equal Credit Opportunity Act* as well as effectively violating fiduciary responsibilities by not preparing and showing an offer to the principal. The licensee is only able to use general qualifying rules that lenders tend to apply in the area and can make statements only to the effect that it will be difficult to qualify for a loan under such conditions.

When financing a real estate transaction, the prudent lender examines the past financial history of the borrower, seeking assurance that the borrower has a satisfactory credit rating (evidence of willingness to pay) and has adequate financial ability to repay the anticipated loan. The lending institutions normally consider the borrower's total income and stability of the borrower's business position along with outstanding liabilities. Although they consider the income of a spouse, lenders are little influenced by occasional overtime earning or the need for financial assistance. In summary, all lenders look to the traditional three C's: Capacity (current income), ability of the appliance to repay the debt; Character (credit), applicant's history of debt repayment; and Capital (collateral), sources other than income from which to pay the debt.

If the transaction involves no lending institution and involves a private mortgage agreement between a seller and buyer, the .licensee should apply very specific qualifying terms to protect the principal in the transaction. Once the general ability of an individual to be able to afford down payments and future flows required of a mortgage are satisfied, the .licensee is able to prepare an offer for a specified piece of property.

Presentation of Offers.

An offer to purchase is merely a specific price and set of conditions proposed by an offeror to a seller for a piece of property. The licensee presents the offer to the principal along with the estimate of the net proceeds to the seller based upon the presumption that the offer will be accepted. The licensee should explain at this time to the seller exactly what the price, conditions, and ramifications of accepting the offer would be. It is imperative that the .licensee make as close an estimate as possible since much animosity can be created when either the seller or buyer receives substantially less or is charged substantially more than the estimate presented during the time of offer or acceptance. In the event counteroffers occur, the broker should revise the net statements each time a different price and/or term appears.

The licensee normally is representing the seller. The preparation of the estimated net to the seller will indicate financially whether or not the seller will possibly accept this offer or give a basis for making a counteroffer. Offers coming from cooperating brokers will come to the listing broker so that they can be presented and the seller advised as to ramifications. Relative to offers pending, *Oklahoma Real Estate Commission Rule* 605:10-17-4 (11) requires that a broker submit all written bona fide offers to an owner when such offers are received prior to a seller accepting an offer in writing.

BROKERAGE COMPENSATION (TC)

To be entitled to compensation, the real estate broker, in addition to being licensed, must:

1. Establish employment with a principal;
2. Be the procuring cause of producing a final buyer who is ready, willing, and able to purchase the property on the terms set forth by the owner or on other terms acceptable to the owner;
3. The sale must be consummated or defeated by the refusal or neglect of the owner to consummate the sale as agreed upon. In the occasional case where the broker represented the buyer, the terms of 2 and 3 above are changed to fit that situation.

The compensation of brokers is customarily a commission fee paid by the seller from the seller's proceeds, determined as a certain percentage of the selling price of the property. The rate of commission is established by agreement of the parties, not by law. The rate of the commission should be stipulated in the listing agreement since this is a negotiable item between principal and broker.

By Oklahoma law, the broker is entitled to a commission if the sale is not consummated due to a defect in the title which the owner refuses or neglects to correct, provided the broker has obtained an enforceable contract which binds the purchaser to complete the sale when any such defect is corrected.

If the buyer wrongfully refuses to complete the sale, the broker may look to the seller for reimbursement of expenses not to exceed the amount of the agreed upon commission. Frequently the contract to purchase or the listing agreement will provide that, in case of forfeiture of the earnest deposit by the purchaser, the amount will be divided between the broker and seller fulfilling the broker's claim to compensation.

Only the seller may assert a forfeiture of earnest money. It is the prerogative of the seller to decide whether to insist on forfeiture or seek, or example, the remedy of specific performance. The broker cannot make this election for the seller, nor take any action which might impair the rights of the seller. The licensee usually has no right to the purchaser's money as such, but at most, is only entitled to share in the proceeds forfeited in favor of the seller.

If the purchaser makes an offer to buy conditioned on some event, such as the ability to secure a loan, the buyer may rightfully cancel the contract of purchase and is entitled to a refund of the earnest deposit if the condition does not occur. In such event, the broker is not entitled to a commission.

If the broker finds a buyer for the property who offers a lower price or different terms from that agreed to by the owner in the listing and the owner accepts these changed terms, the broker is entitled to a commission. The principal has impliedly agreed to, or has ratified, variations in the terms of the original brokerage contract. The real estate purchase contract often states which party (usually the seller) is to pay the broker commission. The contract is valid without such a provision, but it serves the purpose of removing all doubt as to w ho is responsible for paying the commission.

RECORD KEEPING (TC)

A broker is required by Commission Rule to maintain a bookkeeping system that accurately and clearly discloses information relating to trust accounts. Further, by Rule 605:10-13-1 (1), all records and files must be maintained for a minimum of five years after consummation of a transaction. In case of trust account records, the five years commences with the date of disbursal of funds. Files and records are interpreted to include listings, purchases, contracts, trust account records, correspondence with the Commission, as well as general ledgers, files and correspondence relating to listings and sales. In the event that a principal broker, for any reason, ceases to be a principal broker, the files and records are to be transferred to the person who secures the broker business by purchase or other means. If no succession of business occurs, the broker shall maintain the files and records personally.

In addition, the broker or associate is required to furnish any party or parties in a transaction copies of all documents that pertain to that transaction, including sales contracts and closing statements.

While the maintenance of records on a trust account covers all monies that the broker handles on behalf of others, the provision of copies of instruments relating to a transaction and the five-year maintenance rule typically refer only to those transactions that have been consummated. For record keeping purposes as well as for the broker's protection, copies of documents relating to offers on properties should be maintained regardless of whether or not a transaction occurs. If the Commission should request information for the investigation of a complaint, maintenance of these records will provide evidence that may be supportive of the broker's position.

INSPECTION FOR THE BUYER AND WARRANTIES (TC)

In conjunction with the full disclosure and misrepresentation problems experienced by brokers, there are two devices available for the protection of all parties involved in a transaction. It is good practice for the broker or associate to suggest that inspections for the buyer be obtained prior to the closing of any transaction. Who bears the cost of the inspections, payable at closing, is negotiable in the contract. These inspections are for such items as termites and mechanical items including plumbing, heating, and electrical equipment.

A second device available for the protection of all undisclosed dual agency parties in the transaction is a home warranty program, which is basically a warranty that covers defects in certain items of a building. Depending upon the type of warranty program, the coverage could extend from structural defects, such as roofing, electrical or plumbing, to include regular household appliances, such as stoves or dishwashers. the warranty is usually for a specified period of time and will differ for used and new homes. If a defect occurs, the warranty agreement will correct this defect subject to any deductible amounts in the policy. The cost of the warranty program normally will be borne by either the buyer or seller, depending upon the particular program utilized.

FEDERAL CONSUMER CREDIT PROTECTION ACTS

TRUTH-IN-LENDING ACT (TC)

Popularly known as the *Federal Truth-in-Lending Act*, this legislation went into effect in 1969. It was subsequently amended to be known as the *Truth-in-Lending Simplification and Reform Act (TILSRA) of 1980*. Implemented by Federal Reserve

Board *Regulation Z*, the act requires that a borrower be clearly shown how much is being paid for credit in both dollar terms and percentage terms before being committed. This enables the borrower to compare the costs among various lending agencies and to make a more informed borrowing decision. The borrower in also given the right to rescind (cancel) the transaction in certain instances. The key provision of the act was to devise a standardized yardstick by which prospective borrowers could measure and compare the various credit terms available to them. Those transactions with individuals for personal, family, and household uses, not exceeding $25,000, fall under the Act. All real estate transactions, regardless of the amount, are covered.

Those who must comply with the Truth-in-Lending Act are: (TC)

1. Persons who extend credit in the ordinary course of their business.
2. Persons who arrange for credit on behalf of another.
3. Advertisers of products or items being sold on credit.

Financing subject to the act includes: (TC)

1. All consumer credit to natural persons.
2. Assumptions of notes accompanying mortgages and deeds of trust and contracts from creditors.

Exempt from the act are: (TC)

1. Business and commercial loans.
2. Personal property loans in excess of $25,000.
3. Loans repayable with four or less installments that do not carry a finance charge.
4. Financing extended to corporations, partnerships, associations, and agencies.

The *Truth-in-Lending Act* requires that the terms and conditions of the loan be disclosed in writing to the borrower before a permanent contractual relationship is made between the borrower and the lender. To give the borrower a clear picture of the annual rate cost of credit, the act requires that lenders use a uniform measure called the annual percentage rate (APR). This combines the interest rate, loan fees, discount points and other costs of obtaining the loan into a single figure that also shows the borrower:

1. The date the finance charge will begin.
2. The number of monthly payments.
3. The due dates of payments.
4. Any default or delinquency charges.
5. Any payoff penalties.
6. Any balloon payments.
7. The total amount of credit that will be made available to the borrower.
8. The method of computing credits for early payment.
9. The composition of finance charges.
10. The total finance charge.
11. The total of all payments including principal.
12. A description of the property used as collateral for the loan.

Additionally, if the loan is connected with a sale, the cash price, down payment, and unpaid balance must also be stated in writing.

The advertising of credit terms is permitted under the *Truth-in-Lending Act* provided certain rules are followed. Real estate licensees who write advertisements for property they have listed may advertise the cash price and the APR, if it is identified as such. If any other credit terms are added, then full disclosure must be made in the advertisement. This means that the ad must state the cash price, APR, down payment, monthly payment, loan fees, terms of the loan, number of payments (except for first liens on homes), finance charge, and total charge.

Under *Truth-in-Lending*, those transactions where liens will be placed on real estate, the right of rescission is available. This right must be exercised within three (3) days following the date of the transactions or on the date that the lender disclosed the amount and rate of finance charges, whichever is later. However, the right of rescission does not apply to mortgages to finance the initial purchase nor the construction of a dwelling. The act of rescission does not allow the lender to charge penalties or additional charges. As relates to real estate licensees, the advertising of credit is strictly regulated by *Regulation Z*. If specific terms are given, they must include cash price, required down payment, number and amount of all payments, and the annual percentage rate which includes all charges, rather than the effective interest rate alone.

Generally speaking, if there is an institutional lender making a loan as part of the sale, the lender will handle the truth-in-lending details. In that event, the primary responsibility of the real estate to the *Truth-in-Lending Act* is to make certain that any advertisements are written to conform to the law.

The penalties for noncompliance under *Regulation Z* are twice the amount of the finance charge or a minimum of $100 up to a maximum of $500 plus court costs, attorney's fees, and any actual damages. A fine of up to $5,000 or one year imprisonment, or both, can be imposed for willful violation of *Regulation Z*. Although this Act primarily applies to lenders, real estate licensees are subject to it, if they in fact become arrangers of financing as such. **(TC)**

EQUAL CREDIT OPPORTUNITY ACT (TC)

The *Equal Credit Opportunity Act* was passed in 1974 with the purpose of encouraging extension of credit with impartiality and without regard to race, color, religion, national origin, sex or marital status, age, source of income or any right under the Consumer Credit Protection Act.

The Federal Trade Commission is charged with enforcement.

The major provisions of the act include:
Lenders may not make discriminatory statements.

Lenders may not ask about marital status for an applicant applying for an unsecured loan.

Sex and marital status may not be used as factors in credit scoring.

Lenders may not ask about child-bearing intentions.

Lender may not ask about spouse's bad credit if borrower is applying independently.

Lender may not discount part time income.

Lender may not ask about how child support or alimony payments may affect borrower's income.

Lender may not ask about how much the borrower depends upon child support or alimony income.

Lender must tell borrower why any loan was turned down.

Lender must tell borrowers of their right to know about their credit reports.

Lender must make the following disclosure: "The Federal Equal Credit Opportunity Act prohibits creditors from discriminating against credit applicants. The federal agency that administers compliance with this law concerning this (insert name of lender) is (name of appropriate regulatory agency)."

The civil liability for violations of the act include:

Lender may be liable for actual damages.

Lender may be liable for punitive damages not to exceed $10,000.

In a class action suit, the lender may be liable for the lesser of $500,000 or 1 % of the lender's net worth.

Ch. 11

TEST YOUR UNDERSTANDING

1. Which of the following advertising practices is allowed by law in Oklahoma?
    1. Placing a "for sale" sign on property without the owner's permission.
    2. Offering free lots or prizes for the purpose of influencing a purchaser or prospective purchaser of real estate.
    3. Placing an ad using a franchised logo, but not the name of the broker.
    4. **None of the above.**

2. Brokers and associates may advertise their own property
    1. as private owners.
    2. any way they wish.
    3. by post office box or telephone number.
    4. **only as licensees marketing their own property.**

3. A real estate licensee placed a "blind ad" in a local newspaper. The distinction of a "blind ad" is that it does not properly
    1. give the address of the licensee.
    2. **identify the licensee.**
    3. give the selling price of the property.
    4. show the address of the property.

4. When licensees personally buy properties which they have listed, they
    1. **must disclose their true position to the owner.**
    2. are under no obligation to advise the vendor of the status.
    3. Both 1 and 2.
    4. Neither 1 nor 2.

5. The primary purpose of the Truth-in-Lending Act is to
    1. save the general public money in their installment purchasers.
    2. establish a more uniform set of charges.
    3. **disclose to the consumer the cost and conditions of the installment purchase.**
    4. assist the federal government in controlling "shady" lending practices.

6. Truth-in-Lending statutes require disclosure of
    1. the finance charge as an annual percentage.
    2. the number, amount and due date of all payments.
    3. the method of computing unearned finance charges.
    4. **all of the above.**

7. The Taters apply for a $250,000 loan to buy a small business. Is this transaction covered by Regulation Z?
    1. No, because only transactions of $25,000 or less are covered.
    2. **No, because business loans are not covered.**
    3. Yes, because all real estate credit transactions are covered.
    4. Yes, because the purchase of commercial property by individuals, but not firms, is covered.

8. According to the guidelines in the Truth-in-Lending Act (Regulation Z), it is required that the interest charged on a loan be expressed as an
    1. approximate percentage rate.
    2. **annual percentage rate.**
    3. average percentage rate.
    4. estimated percentage rate.

9. Under the truth-in-Lending Act, which of the following items could not be stated in the advertisement unless a full disclosure was made regarding finance charges?
　　1. Excellent loan for assumption.
　　2. FHA financing available.
　　3. Reasonable monthly payments.
　　4. Interest at 10%

ANSWERS AND EXPLANATIONS

1. 4   All are causes for suspension or revocation of a real estate license.

2. 4   When advertising real property a licensee's professional status must be revealed in every instance.

3. 2   Licensed brokers are prohibited by the state license law from using "blind ads."

4. 1   Licensees are required to disclose the fact they have a license in all circumstances related to real estate transactions.

5. 3   Regulation Z was created to obligate credit institutions to inform borrowers of the true cost of obtaining credit so that costs among various lending agencies can be compared and more informed borrowing decisions may be made.

6. 4   If any credit terms other than the APR and the cash price are added, full disclosure must be made in an advertisement.

7. 2   Exemptions from Regulation Z include business and commercial loans, personal property loans in excess of $25,000, loans repayable with four or less installments that do not carry finance charges, and financing extended to corporations, partnerships, associations, and agencies.

8. 2   This gives the borrower a clear picture of the annual cost of credit.

9. 4   "Interest at 10%" triggers the requirement of full disclosure. If any specific credit terms are stated, then the price, down payment, and the amount of the mortgage must be disclosed together with the due dates, the number of payments, and the annual percentage rate (APR). An advertisement that mentions price alone does not "trigger" additional disclosures.

FAIR HOUSING

CIVIL RIGHTS ACTS

FAIR HOUSING LAW (TC)

The Fair Housing Laws have as their primary purpose the creation and assurance of fair housing opportunity for everyone. ***The Civil Rights Act of 1866*** provides: "All citizens of the United States shall have the same right, in every state and territory, as is enjoyed by white citizens thereof to inherit, purchase, lease, sell, hold, and convey real and personal property." ***The Civil Rights Act of 1964*** expanded and reinforced the federal government's fair housing regulations and prohibited the discrimination in any housing project or program that received federal funding. This included a small percentage of the total housing activity of the United States and did not have a great deal of impact.

The Federal Fair Housing Law of 1968, as amended, also known as the ***Open Housing Law***, contained in Title VIII of the ***Civil Rights Act of 1968*** provided that it is unlawful to discriminate on the basis of race, color, religion, sex, or national origin when selling or leasing residential property. The 1968 act expressly prohibited discriminatory acts including:

1. Refusing to sell or rent to, deal or negotiate with any person.

2. Discriminating in terms or conditions for buying or renting housing.

3. Discriminating by advertising that housing is available only to persons of a certain race, color, religion, sex, or national origin.

4. Denying that housing available for inspection, sale, or rent when it is really available.

5. Blockbusting, commonly known as "panic selling" or "panic peddling," defined as persuading owners to sell or rent housing because minority groups are moving into the neighborhood and property values will be affected.

6. Denying or making different terms or conditions for home loans by commercial lenders, such as banks, savings and loan associations, and insurance companies.

7. Denying to anyone the use or participation in any real estate services such as brokers' organizations, multiple-listing services, or other facilities related to the selling or renting of housing.

8. Steering prospects to or from certain geographic areas based on race.

9. Redlining, the practice of restricting the number of loans or the loan-to-value ratio is certain areas of community based on the fact that the area is becoming racially integrated.

The Federal Fair Housing Law applies to single family as well as multi-family housing. Single-family housing owned by private individuals is covered when a broker or other person in the business of selling or renting units is used and discriminatory advertising is used. Single-family houses owned by other than private individuals or a private individual who owns more than three houses or who in any two-year period sells more than one in which he is not a most recent resident are also covered under the act. Those multi-family structures of five or more units or the multi-family structures containing four or fewer units, if the owner does not reside in one of those units, are covered under the act.

Certain acts are not covered by the ***Federal Fair Housing Law***. **(TC)**

1. Single-family units owned by a private individual owner of three or fewer units if:

    a. a broker is not used,

    b. discriminatory advertising is not used, and

    c. no more than one house in which the owner was not the most recent resident is sold during any two-year period.

2. Rental of units or rooms in an owner-occupied multi-family structure of two to four families and discriminatory advertising is not used.

3. Limiting the sale, rental or occupancy of dwelling which a religious organization owns or operates for other than commercial purposes to persons of the same religion, if membership in that religion is not restricted on the basis of race, color, or national origin.

4. Limiting to its own members the rental or occupancy of lodgings that a private club owns or operates for other than a commercial purpose.

The above acts are covered, however, under the ***Civil Rights Act of 1866*** by the interpretation of the United State Supreme Court as indicated in the landmark case of ***Jones vs. Mayer***. The distinction between the ***Federal Fair Housing Law*** exempting certain owners or groups and the ***Civil Rights Act of 1866*** is that the 1866 law prohibits all racial discrimination without exception or exemption. **(TC)**

The 1968 act provides three ways of obtaining compliance: **(TC)**

1. Complaints can be sent to the U. S. Department of Housing and Urban Development in Washington, D.C. or any Regional Housing and Urban Development Office within one year of the alleged grievance.

2. Any individual may take a complaint directly to the United States District Court or State or local county court within two years of the alleged discriminatory act, whether or not a complaint has been filed with HUD. In some cases, an attorney may be appointed for the complainant and the payment of fees, costs of security can be waived.

3. The Attorney General of the United States may file a court action when information about possible discrimination comes to the attention of the office. Complaints that are brought under the ***Civil Rights Act of 1866***, however, must be taken directly to a federal court.

OKLAHOMA FAIR HOUSING LAW, 1985. (TC)

The Oklahoma Fair Housing Law of 1985, covers essentially the same ground as the previous federal law except that it prohibits discrimination based on age and handicap. The Oklahoma act also makes it illegal to:

1. Refuse to consider any public assistance, alimony, or child support, awarded by a court that can be verified as to the amount regularity and length of time to be received as a valid source of income.

2. Refuse to rent or lease to a handicapped person based on the person's use of a bona fide, properly trained guide, signal or service dog.

3. Demand an additional non-refundable fee or an unreasonable deposit for rent from a handicapped person for such a guide, signal or service dog. However, the handicapped person may still be liable for damage done to the dwelling by such a dog.

The act specifically directs the Oklahoma Real Estate Commission to review the cases of licensees convicted of discrimination in housing and to take appropriate action, such as suspending or revoking licenses. The same exemptions to the original federal act are found in the Oklahoma act with the addition of the following exemptions:

1. The act does not prohibit any person from refusing to sell or rent any housing which has been planned exclusively for elderly persons and occupied exclusively by elderly persons.
2. Ordering punitive damages in an amount not to exceed $5,000.
3. Ordering a person to rehire, reinstate, and/or provide back pay to any employee or licensees discriminated against because of obedience to the fair housing laws of the state.

Fair Housing Amendments Acts, 1988. **(TC)**

The 1988 amendment to the *Civil Rights Act* adds familial status (families with children) and handicapped as bases on which discrimination is illegal. The law affects sales and rentals as well as protective covenants banning children in condominiums, subdivisions and planned communities. Exemptions include owners (not licensees) who own three or fewer houses, owners who have four or fewer units and who occupy one unit, and certain types of housing occupied by the elderly.

Rental or financing of housing and buildings that were previously "adult only" can exclude children only if the managers or owners have adopted a policy to rent or sell to the elderly only. Housing for the elderly is defined as a community where at least 80 percent of the dwellings are occupied by at least one person age 55 or older, and significant facilities and services are provided; or those occupied solely by people age 62 and older. **(TC)**

The definition of "handicapped" includes mentally and physically handicapped, alcoholics and persons with communicable diseases not transferable through occupancy. It does not include current drug abusers, persons who have one or more prior felony drug convictions, or sexual preference. A landlord is not required to rent to a person who poses a direct threat to the health, safety or property of others. **(TC)**

Disabled tenants have the right to make modifications to a dwelling at their own expense. The tenants have to agree to restore the property to its original condition when they leave. Landlords will be held in violation if they refuse to make reasonable modifications in the premises to accommodate the handicapped. **(TC)**

AMERICANS WITH DISABILITIES ACT

New construction of multi-family housing units in buildings of four or more units with an elevator, or first floor units in other buildings consisting of four or more units, must contain certain features of accessibility for the handicapped. These features are: **(TC)**

1. An accessible route into and through the dwelling;
2. Light switches, electrical outlets, thermostats and other environmental controls in accessible locations;
3. Reinforcements in bathroom walls to allow later installation of grab bars; and
4. Usable kitchen and bathrooms such that an individual in a wheelchair can maneuver about the space.

In addition to these features in each unit, all multi-family dwellings are required to have their public and common use portions readily accessible to and usable by handicapped persons, and all doors will be designed to allow passage into and within multi-family dwellings by handicapped persons in wheelchairs. **(TC)**

COMPLIANCE TESTING

From time to time, real estate offices are visited by individuals or organizations testing or checking compliance with fair housing laws. The "testers" or "auditors" play the role of persons looking for housing to buy or rent. They observe whether fair housing laws are being followed, and if not, they lodge complaints with appropriate fair housing agencies.

The following steps are usually involved in the testing procedure following a complaint that a particular broker has been acting in a discriminatory manner:

1. A Caucasian couple of certain socio-economic status is sent to the suspected broker and shows interest in the property in question.
2. Soon after, a minority couple of the same socio-economic background will come to the same real estate broker. They will answer the same essential questions with the same essential answers as did the earlier couple.
3. After the minority couple has finished, a different Caucasian couple will come in and repeat the same procedure.
4. The attitudes and representations of the broker to all three couples would now be compared and these findings will all be admissible in court procedures.

The testing for fair housing compliance is a recognized investigative technique and has been held legal by the Supreme Court. The argument that it is an unconstitutional appropriation of a real estate salesperson's time or an interference with free speech has been rejected. It must, therefore, be recognized as a risk and a cost of business.

Ch. 12

TEST YOUR UNDERSTANDING

1. Under Title VIII of the Civil Rights Act of 1988, as amended, discrimination is in place when individuals are denied housing on the basis of
    1. race, religion, creed or age.
    2. sex, national origin, handicap or familial status.
    3. Both 1 and 2.
    4. Neither 1 nor 2.

2. Which of the following is permitted under the Federal Fair housing Act?
    1. Advertising property for sale only to special groups.
    2. Altering the terms of a loan for a member of a minority.
    3. Refusing to sell a home to a member of a minority because of poor credit history.
    4. Telling an individual that an apartment has been rented when, in fact, it has not.

3. Any restrictive covenant which prohibits transfer of a property to persons of a particular race
    1. invalidates the conveyance.
    2. has no effect on the conveyance; the covenant is unconstitutional and unenforceable.
    3. creates a power in the grantee to avoid in the conveyance.
    4. retains in the grantor power to enforce the covenant.

4. The Supreme court case most cited for prohibiting "racial discrimination" in the sale or rental of housing is styled
    1. Kramer vs. Kramer.
    2. Randle vs. Norick.
    3. Masters vs. Johnson.
    4. Jones vs. Mayer.

5. A broker obtained a ready, willing and able buyer who signed an offer to buy a house on the listed price and terms. Because of the buyer's race, the seller refused the offer. The broker may
    1. sue the seller for a commission.
    2. advise the prospect of the right to complain to the U.S. Department of Housing and Urban Development.
    3. warn the seller that refusal is a violation of the Fair Housing act.
    4. do any of the above.

6. The Catholic Church owns an apartment building. It leases the apartments to elderly church members at cost and makes no profit from the rental. A non-Catholic wishes to rent a vacant unit
    1. The church must rent the unit to the non-Catholic of be in violation of the 1968 Fair Housing Law.
    2. The church can give preference to a member of the church.
    3. The church may not limit the occupancy to church members under the 1968 law, but can give preference.
    4. The church is exempt totally from the 1968 law and need not worry about rental policy.

7. The agency responsible for the administration and enforcement of the 1968 Civil Rights Act is the
    1. Internal Revenue Service.
    2. Federal Housing Administration.
    3. Department of Housing and Urban Development.
    4. Federal Attorney General's Office.

8. You are a homeowner who is concerned that your neighborhood may be entering a racially transitional state. A broker whom you have contacted informs you that Haitian refugees are purchasing a home in your neighborhood. The broker indicates also that prices will decline because of this influx of refugees. The broker has
    1. violated the Civil Rights Act of 1968 through redlining.
    2. violated the Civil Rights Act of 1968 through racial steering.
    3. violated the Civil Rights Act of 1968 through panic selling.
    4. not violated the Civil Rights Act of 1968 in any sense.

9. Discrimination in housing may occur when
   1. a broker refuses to serve someone of Chinese descent.
   2. an owner refuses to discuss possible terms of a sale with a Catholic.
   3. a protestant landlord charges Jewish people a higher rent than Protestant renters.
   4. All of the above.

10. The 1988 amendment to the Civil Rights Act adds all of the following to the "protected classification list" except
   1. families with children.
   2. the mentally incapacitated.
   3. those with communicable diseases not transferable through occupancy.
   4. sexual preference.

11. All of the following are examples of steering except
   1. attempt on the part of a community to exclude Chicano buyers from the neighborhood.
   2. concentrated effort to attract black clients to a neighborhood that is already 90% black.
   3. effort to encourage whites in a neighborhood to sell because of the recent purchase of a home in that area by a black family.
   4. attempt to block an Oriental couple from moving into a community that is 90% white.

12. The practice of redlining
   1. is a legitimate lawful and often beneficial lending policy, sanctioned by the entire free enterprise system.
   2. is a policy of systematic discrimination against an area or neighborhood by refusing to make loans there for home improvement and purchase, regardless or the borrower's ability to repay.
   3. is nothing more than loan underwriting.
   4. refers to investors' rapid withdrawal of funds from the savings and loan or commercial bank, resulting in disintermediation.

ANSWERS AND EXPLANATIONS

1. 2 Title VIII, as amended, addresses race, color, religion, sex, national origin, handicap and familial handicap but not age.

2. 3 While discriminatory financial practices are unlawful, it is lawful to refuse to loan money if based solely on sound business practice. A poor credit rating is justification for denying real estate service.

3. 2 The U. S. Supreme Court has declared that restrictive covenants attached to deeds and plats based on race are unconstitutional and unenforceable (Shelly vs. Kramer, 1948).

4. 4 Jones vs Meyer was a landmark civil rights case which reinforced the Civil Rights Act of 1866 in declaring all discriminatory acts relating to race in real estate illegal, without exception.

5. 4 All are appropriate if the discrimination is based on race.

6. 2 An exception to the Federal fair Housing Act is the sale, rental, or occupancy of dwellings owned and operated by a religious organization for other than commercial purposes to persons of the same religion, if membership in that religion is not restricted on account of race, color, sex, national origin, handicap or familial status.

7. 3 The Department of Housing and Urban Development, commonly known as HUD, is a federal cabinet department responsible to the administration of fair housing laws and other housing programs.

8. 3 Panic selling (panic peddling) is the aggressive form of "blockbusting". It is defined as the soliciting of sales or listings, making written or oral statements which create fear or alarm,, transmitting written oral warnings or threats, soliciting prospective minority renters or buyers, or acting n any other manner so as to induce or attempt to induce the sale or lease of residential property, either

   a. through representation regarding the present or prospective entry of one or more minority residents into an arca, or

   b. through representations that would convey to a reasonable person under the circumstances, regardless whether or not overt reference to minority status is made, that one or more minority residents are or may be entering the area

9. 4 Refusing to sell or rent to, deal or negotiate with any person is contrary to public policy when based on Race and ethnic background.

10. 4 Sexual preference remains an unprotected class in housing discrimination. Familial status was added with certain limitations while "handicapped person" was redefined to include the mentally incapacitated and those with communicable diseases not transferable through occupancy. Alcoholism is also included in the definition of handicapped.

11. 3 Steering is often difficult to detect because the steering tactics can be so subtle that the home seeker is unaware that a choice has been limited.

12. 2 A redlining policy may be so sever that the lending institution has a strict prohibition against lending any money in certain areas. The usual justification for "redlining" is that the lender wants to limit the risks in an area that is deteriorating. A redlining policy based on the fact that a certain area of a community is becoming racially integrated is illegal and is in violation of Title VIII of the Federal Civil Rights Act and the Federal Home Loan Bank Board (FHLBB) anti-redlining regulations.

CONTRACT LAW OVERVIEW

The major purpose of contract law is to assure that a contract is properly formed and is binding on and enforceable by the parties. Contracts constitute "binding arrangements for the future," and may be either written or oral. The existence of a contract imposes obligations on the parties, and as a result, creates certain rights and/or limitations for those parties.

Real estate brokers and associates live and operate in a world of contracts, an integral part of their normal course of business. During the workday life of the licensee, contracts come early, often, and with great rapidity in even a simple sale of real estate. First, of course, is the listing agreement. When an offer is made, the intricacies of the contract of sale must be dealt with. At the same time, various contracts with abstractors, attorneys, consulting inspectors, and other support services enter the picture. Finally, closing brings more contracts to consider.

Contract law is often complicated for even the most competent specialist and situations arise where the legal aspects of a contract are not clear. It is imperative that each element of every contract be understood by all parties. If there is any question, the advice of an attorney should be sought. Real estate licensees should never risk loss by giving legal advice beyond their competence.

Defining a Contract. (TC)

A contract may be defined as an agreement between two or more competent persons, having for its purpose a legal objective wherein the parties agree to act in a certain manner. A contract may also be defined as a voluntary agreement supported by legal consideration between legally competent parties to do or refrain from doing some legal act. In essence, a contract is a set of promises that courts can enforce.

In real estate practice there are many different types of contracts, each of which must meet certain minimum requirements for enforcement. The most commonly encountered contracts used in professional real estate brokerages are listing contracts and contracts for sale.

RECOGNIZED CLASSIFICATIONS OF CONTRACTS (TC)

In the discussion and study of contract law, reference is often made to different kinds of contracts and their various characteristics. These classifications are not all inclusive nor all exclusive. Any given contract may be classified in more than one category at the same time.

A formal contract depends upon a particular form or mode of expression for its legal status based on statutory requirements. With certain exceptions, such as contracts under seal, negotiable instruments, and recognizance, formal contracts no longer are used. An informal contract is one for which the law does not require a particular set of formalities. Virtually all contracts used in real estate transactions are considered informal or ordinary agreements which may use any style of language as long as they meet the basic common law requirements for a valid contract. Although they may in fact be very complicated, real estate contracts are usually considered "simple" contracts.

Unilateral. (TC)

A unilateral contract is one in which only one party makes a promise which may be accepted upon the act of another. It is generally considered to be a promise in exchange for performance. A unilateral contract is "one-sided" because only the offeror, who makes this promise, will be legally bound.

Bilateral. (TC)

In a bilateral contract, both parties make promises. It is a two-sided agreement wherein each party is both a promisor and a promisee and is under duty to render a performance and enjoys the right to receive a performance. This is the more common type of contract in real estate. A sales contract whereby the owner agrees to transfer title in exchange for the buyer's agreement to pay cash is a clear example of a bilateral contract, the exchange of a promise for a promise.

145

Executory and Executed. (TC)

A contract which is in the process of being carried out is an executory contract. When both parties have rendered their promised performance, the contract may be considered fully executed (performed). A contract may be wholly performed on one side, but unperformed on the other, or unperformed on both sides in whole or in part (partially executed). A real estate sales contract is executory until closed.

A contract for sale of real estate does not transfer legal title, but during the time a real estate contract is executory, signed by both parties, the purchaser has equitable title. If the seller refuses to sell, the purchaser after tendering performance can sue for specific performance and has the right to demand that legal title be transferred upon payment of the full purchase price.

Express. (TC)

Contractual liability may be developed in several different ways. Where language is used to indicate an agreement in words (as in a written contract for sale of real estate) or where words are not used but actions manifest an assent to contract, the contract is referred to as an express contract.

Implied. (TC)

Implied contracts are distinguishable from express contracts only in that the offer and/or acceptance are found from conduct rather than expressed words. The law will imply a contract where neither words nor actions expressed an agreement but where a person accepts and retains the beneficial results of another's services which were rendered at their own request and which they had no reason to suppose were gratuitous. Implied contracts for the sale of real estate cannot be enforced.

LEGAL EFFECT OF CONTRACTS (TC)

[handwritten note: legal but not enforced]

The legal effect of express and implied contracts is the same. The only difference is the manner in which assent is manifested. Both are consensual in that there is a voluntary acceptance of benefits by one or both parties resulting in the creation of a contractual obligation. Real estate brokers are well advised, however, to assure that all contracts are expressed in writing in order to ensure enforceability.

Valid. (TC)

A valid contract contains all the essential elements of a contract and is legally binding on all parties.

Void. (TC)

A void contract is one that has no legal effect. It is no contract at all. It is actually inaccurate to call such an agreement a contract since a contract by definition is a legally enforceable agreement. A void contract usually comes about as a result of the absence of one or more essential elements of a contract. A contract entered into to burn down a building, for example, is a void contract as the objective is illegal.

Voidable. (TC)

A voidable contract is one that is valid and enforceable on its face but may be properly rejected by one of the parties. The aggrieved party, however, must take action to have the contract voided.

Unenforceable. (TC)

An unenforceable contract may satisfy all the basic requirements for a valid contract, but cannot be enforced in the courts because of some statutory requirement or some rule of law.

Quasi Contracts. (TC)

Some contracts are "implied in law," not to be confused with "implied contracts" discussed above. Quasi contracts are non-consensual obligations imposed by law to prevent unjust enrichment of one person at the expense of another. A quasi contract is not a contract as such, as it is not based on expressed or implied promises.

Quasi contracts are obligations created by law (in the absence of any agreement between the parties) as a method of giving a remedy in the nature of contract relief. A quasi contract might be imposed in a circumstance in which one has received and retains money or goods which in fairness and justice belongs to another. They are used to fill the void where no consensual contract liability exists.

FOR EXAMPLE: A broker ordered ten lock boxes for securing homes listed for sale. The vendor, through an honest mistake, shipped 100 units which the broker used. Although no contract existed for the excess items, the broker would be expected to pay for them if they are kept.

The law reasonably protects against improper suits resulting from quasi contracts. These may be applied in a wide variety of situations, but in general, the following hold.

1. The amount recovered must be the reasonable value of the goods or services rendered.
2. An opportunist or an intermeddler who tries to force benefits upon another cannot recover.
3. The provider of the benefits must have expected to be paid. It must not have been intended to be gratuitous.

Contract Form.

No "one absolute correct form" is required for a valid contract. Any form used, however, should specify all the terms and conditions of the agreement between the parties and must be signed by those to be legally bound by the document.

Seven essential elements are necessary in a real estate sales contract, the absence of any one of which will make a contract void, voidable, or unenforceable. **(TC)**
1. There must be an offer and an acceptance.
2. There must be reality of consent.
3. There must be legal consideration.
4. The parties must have legal capacity to contract.
5. The object of the contract must be legal.
6. The document must be in writing.
7. The property must have a legal description.

In examining an agreement to determine whether or not a valid contract has in fact been created, contract attorneys scrutinize each element. The failure of any one results in a decision of "no contract."

In addition to the above, other provisions are usually included in a contract. Among these are:

1. Date of the agreement.
2. Terms of payment.
3 Special agreements or contingencies between the parties.

OFFERS. (TC)

The first element of any contract is an offer, that is, a promise by one party, the offeror, to act or perform in a specified manner provided the other party acts or performs in a manner requested. An offer confers upon the offeree a legal power to accept. Upon acceptance, a contract is created.

The agreement process begins when the offeror makes an offer to another, the offeree. The offer may be accepted as presented or a counter proposal may be made. Often there is negotiating back and forth over the terms of the proposed contract before a firm agreement is concluded, particularly in the sale of real estate.

If an offeree creates any variance from the terms proposed in the offer in accepting it, the initial offer has been turned down and a counteroffer is being made. With each subsequent counteroffer, the offeree switches legal position to offeror while the offeror becomes the offeree. If a seller does not want to risk the loss of a sale, acceptance of an offer to purchase must be unequivocal.

Requirements of an Offer. (TC)

For an offer to be considered legally sufficient it must meet three requirements:

1. The offer must be serious (bona fide).

2. It must be reasonably complete and unambiguous.
3. It must be appropriately communicated to the offeree.

Serious Intent. (TC)

The offeror must intend that an offer become a contract. Acts, words, and behavior should lead a reasonable person familiar with the business being transacted into believing that a bona fide offer has been seriously and voluntarily proffered. Statements made in jest, under great stress, or through bluffing, are not tenders of offers.

Reasonably Definite and Complete Terms. (TC)

When an offer is incomplete or vague and the terms are unclear and uncertain, it cannot serve as the basis for a contract. In law, the words did not rise to the status of an offer. The requirements are not absolute certainty, however, but only a reasonable definiteness and sometimes the terms are only implied. If the offer includes the usual essential terms which are e the names of the parties, the subject matter involved, the price, and the time and place for performance, It will usually be considered as having met the requirement. The requirement of definiteness dictates the use of a legal description in a contract for sale of real estate.

Communicating the Offer. (TC)

An offer is not legally effective until the party to whom it is directed has received it. If an offeree has no knowledge of an offer, it has not been properly communicated and is therefore not in effect. The requirement of communication of offers goes further in that it must be communicated by the offeror personally or by an authorized representative. A buyer who has learned that a property owner "will sell his house for $75,000" cannot create a contract by saying to the owner, "I'll take it."

Estimation of Seller's Net and Buyer's Cost. (TC)

When an offer is presented, real estate brokers are required by Rule 605:10-17-4 (8) to inform the buyer and seller as to the anticipated costs at closing. They must prepare a good faith estimate of the seller's net proceeds and the buyer's net costs based on the offered price and terms. Sample forms appear at end of chapter. If an offer is less than the listing price, the seller's net figure will have changed from that as given at the time of the listing.

Counteroffers. (TC)

A counteroffer is a response to an offer which relates to the same subject matter as the original offer but differs from it in one or more particulars. A counteroffer operates as a rejection of the offer. In effect, it amounts to a conditional acceptance which the original offeror, now the offeree, must agree to for a contract to be formed.

Any attempt on the part of an offeree to change the terms proposed by the offeror creates a counteroffer. It has the effect of a new offer, rejecting the original. The original offer cannot be accepted thereafter by the offeree unless the offeror revives it by repeating it.

TERMINATION OF OFFERS (TC)

Although there are exceptions, as a general rule, offers may be withdrawn at any time and for any reason prior to acceptance. This is so even if the offeror says the offer will be kept open for a specified period of time. The power to accept continues until the offer is terminated by some legally recognized method.

Lapse of Time. (TC)

An offer may contain wording indicating the time limit for remaining open. The offer is revoked if the offeree fails to accept it within the prescribed time. In the absence of specifically stated time, a reasonable period of time will be adjudged. After the time has expired, any attempt on the part of the offeree to accept the offer simply constitutes a new offer.

Revocation by the Offeror. (TC)

An offeror may withdraw a simple offer for any reason (or without stating or having a reason) at any time prior to acceptance by the offeree. Even if an offeror agrees to hold an offer open to acceptance for a certain time, the offeror is generally not bound to do so.

If an offeree wants to be certain that an offer will be h held open for a certain period, the offeree must contract with the offeror. In other words, the offeree must "buy" the time needed by entering into an option contract. Options are often simply part of another agreement, such as options negotiated by lessees to buy leased premises. In these cases, the options are part of the basic contract, and are supported by the consideration of the basic contract. No additional or express consideration is necessary for them to be binding.

Rejection by the Offeree. (TC)

The offer is terminated when the offeree expressly states that the offer will not be accepted or if the offeree fails to fulfill a condition prescribed by the offeror. Most frequently, however, rejection comes in the form of a counteroffer which is a conditional acceptance based on certain changes made in the terms. The original offer is rejected in either case and is no longer operative. The original offer is dead and cannot be accepted later unless revived by the offeror repeating it.

Death or Insanity of Either Party. (TC)

Although neither death nor insanity of either party will terminate an executed contract, an offer will end upon the occurrence of death or upon declaration of insanity of either party, regardless of notice thereof.

Destruction of Subject Matter. (TC)

Should the property subject to the offer be destroyed or lost at no known fault of either party, the offer is terminated.

Supervening Illegality. (TC)

The offer is void if legislation is enacted subsequent to the offer making it illegal. This is true even if the offer has been accepted and a contract has come into effect. The executory portion of such a contract cannot be enforced.

ACCEPTANCE (TC)

For a contract to be binding, it must have a genuine acceptance as well as a bona fide offer. Acceptance of an offer is essential to the creation of contract. The offeree must meet exactly all the terms and conditions set forth by the offeror. No mutual consent is present if negotiations are merely conditional.

When a valid offer has been properly accepted, there is a "meeting of the minds." No contract exists unless there is mutual consent or assent. Acceptance is both a matter of intention and an over act of manifestation. An acceptance must be both positive and unequivocal. It may not change any of the terms of the offer, add to, remove from, nor modify in any way the provisions of the offer.

In the case of a bilateral contract, acceptance is some overt act by the offeree indicating an acceptance of the terms of the offer, such as written or spoken words, or other action communicated to the offeror.

Where an offer contemplates the formation of a bilateral contract, the offeree must communicate an acceptance to the offeror or at least place the acceptance in the ordinary channel of communication in order to form a contract.

Where the offer consists of a promise in exchange for an act, the formation and existence of the contract does not depend upon notice being given to the offeror of the acceptance. Compliance by performance of the requested act is sufficient. Performing the requested act (or forbearance) with the intention of accepting the offer is acceptance for a unilateral contract.

Once an acceptance has been communicated, the contract is completely formed and subsequent communications do not affect it except for a mutual agreement to rescind or modify.

REALITY OF CONSENT (TC)

The consent of the parties to the contract must be real before there is a contract. The terms of the contract must reflect the true intention of the parties, i.e., what the parties have reasonably indicated outwardly – not their secret intent. In order to be recognized as a valid contract, the assent of the parties must be genuine and free from mistake, misrepresentation, fraud, duress, menace or undue influence.

Mistakes. (TC)

Depending upon the nature of the mistake, the effect of a mistake on the validity of a contract varies. Innocent mistakes serve to cancel agreements. Mistakes based on ignorance or poor judgment or the fact that the contract had not been read before signing cannot be claimed as material mistakes sufficient to terminate a contract. If a mistake is made in the preparation of the offer, it is probably curable and will not affect the contract. If the identity of one of the parties to the contract or the identity of the subject matter is incorrect, the contract may not be void, but may be voidable. A court may reform the contract. If, however, there is ambiguous language which does not express the meaning or intentions of the parties, there is no contract.

Should the contract be in violation of law, it is void. However, if it is in the interpretation of the law and the contract is based on an erroneous conclusion, the contract cannot be disavowed. It has been generally assumed that everyone knows the law and failure to understand the legal consequence of signing a contract will not bring relief. In more recent times, however, the presumption that everyone knows the law is being given less weight.

When both parties contract in the belief that certain conditions exist when in fact they do not, the contract is voidable.

Misrepresentation. (TC)

An unknowing or innocent misstatement of a material fact, without intention of deceit, can make a contract voidable at the option of the party to whom the misrepresentation was made.

Fraud. (TC)

Any attempt to gain some unfair or dishonest advantage over another will defeat the reality of consent and cause the contract to be voidable, if not void. A defrauded party has the right to collect damages or have contract rescinded. Contracts based on substantial misrepresentation, the knowing and deliberate misrepresentation of material facts, and done with the intent to deceive and possibly cause harm and injury, are usually voidable at the option of the injured party. Failure to disclose known defects ("remaining silent") can be considered fraud. If altered after acceptance, the contract is voidable by the purchaser.

Misstatements based on opinion cannot be construed as fraudulent acts. Exaggerated or superlative comments not made as representations of fact, such as "this is a real good buy," are not fraudulent. One test of "harmless trade puffery" is whether a reasonable person would have relied on the statement.

Duress. (TC)

Since the bargain theory of contracts is fundamental to the free enterprise system, the law will not permit one party to coerce another into an assent to an agreement. Duress is the use of force or restraint to cause others to do something they would not do otherwise. Under these conditions, there can be no genuine meeting of minds and such a contract is not enforceable against the forced party.

Menace. (TC)

Although menace is a mild form of duress, by Oklahoma Statute (Title 15, Sec. 53), it is one of the bases for avoiding an agreement on grounds of defective assent. Menace is compelling a person by wrongful threat of force to do or agree to do an act. It includes the use of fear or threat of unlawful or violent injury to any person, or threat of injury to the character of any such person.

Undue Influence. (TC)

Overcoming freedom of will through unfair persuasion is undue influence. It usually involves transactions resulting in unnatural enrichment of someone because of their domination of another person. Such unfair persuasion is usually an exploitation of such weakness as mental infirmity, ignorance, lack of experience, old age, poor health, physical handicap, emotional strain, or financial distress.

Undue influence most often results from a relationship of trust and confidence between two persons wherein one is justified in assuming that the other will be looking after the former's best interest when the latter is actually violating the fiduciary relationship.

LEGAL CONSIDERATION (TC)

A contract may meet all other requirements to make it valid and yet fail because of lack of the technical requirement of sufficient legal consideration. The concept of consideration is not only difficult to define, it is also one of the most difficult concepts to justify. Its roots go back to the beginning era of development of modern contract law.

Consideration is something of value which is committed by each of the parties to an agreement and without which the parties cannot be held to their promise. Unless a bargain is reached in exchanging something for something, a contract cannot be legally enforced. For a contract to be formed, something must be given in an exchange. Our legal system will not enforce a contract based on purely gratuitous promises.

Valuable Consideration. (TC)

Valuable consideration may be a mutual exchange of promises by which the parties obligate themselves to do something they were not legally required to do before. Consideration must have value. There must be a reciprocal relationship between the offeror's promise and the offeree's performance or return promise. Valuable consideration may be property, time, service, the payment of money, other things of value measurable in dollars, or simply a legal right.

Consideration may also be defined as a legal detriment to the promisee bargained for by the promisor. Legal detriment means that the promisee gives up or promises to give up a legal right, or assumes or promises to assume a legal burden. In the normal course of business, both parties suffer legal detriments and both enjoy legal benefits from entering into a contract. In bilateral contracts, both parties incur legal detriment.

The general trend in contract law is to place more emphasis on the intent of the parties. Intent will determine whether a detriment or benefit has resulted from the bargain, and whether consideration is created, binding the parties to keep their promises. The determination of intent is through the same objective standard applied to making and accepting an offer.

Good Consideration. (TC)

Most contracts are supported by valuable consideration, distinguishing them from gifts. Good consideration (love and affection, with no pecuniary measure of value) is sufficient to support a gift deed, but is insufficient for most other contracts.

Love and affection may be compelling motives for making a promise, but they are not words of bargaining. Because such a contract is not supported by present consideration, courts may not specifically enforce such a promise should the grantor have a change of mind before performing. A completed gift is irrevocable while a gratuitous promise is generally unenforceable. The grantee cannot enforce any covenants supported only by good consideration against the grantor.

If the transfer was done to avoid creditors, a contract supported only by good consideration can be set aside because no money actually changed hands.

Nominal Consideration. (TC)

Nominal consideration is consideration in name only bearing no relation to market value. It may be used to disguise the true value of the exchange, or may be as stated. A recital of obvious nominal consideration would be: "$10.00 and other valuable consideration."

Adequacy of Consideration. (TC)

The law does not require adequacy of consideration to find a contract enforceable. The value given to constitute legally adequate consideration has no relationship to actual value. Once consideration is found in a contract, courts seldom will inquire into its adequacy or sufficiency. The law usually is not concerned whether the value of one of the promises is equal in value to the other.

151

As a general rule, the recital of a promise for a promise is sufficient consideration to create a binding mutual obligation. Because the value of the exchange is involved, the fact that some duty was exchanged for a relatively small amount or that one party got the better of a bargain does not usually concern the courts. As long as the parties to the contract appear to have equal bargaining capabilities, the value of mutual consideration is not important. The law requires only that consideration exchanged meet the definition.

A written agreement that states consideration has been given is not conclusive proof that consideration has been bargained and paid. Consideration must have some value and must actually be given. Earnest money deposits are not intended to make a purchase contract binding; they serve only as a source of payment for damages in the event the prospective purchasers do not keep their promises and breach the contract.

A nominal sum written into a contract will not always suffice as legal consideration. The amount is not the issue but whether or not actual consideration was given. In some states, "One dollar in hand paid in consideration of X's promises to. .." will not make the promise enforceable. In Oklahoma, however, the recital of any payment may be interpreted as a promise to pay and a binding contract is thereby created. Proof of legal consideration in addition to that recited, such as forbearance of a right to bring a justifiable law suit, would be sufficient even though the Statutes, Title 15, Section 114, states that a written instrument expressing consideration is presumptive of consideration. Section 115 places the burden of proof of lack consideration on the party seeking to invalidate or void the contract (instrument).

Past Consideration No Consideration.

Because consideration is something given in exchange for a promise and to induce it, there must be present consideration to support a contract. Past consideration is an attempt to support present promises with a previously conferred benefit. A past event given as consideration makes a contract unenforceable because the object of the contract was not something bargained for. Anything that has occurred prior to the promise cannot be consideration.

Illusory Promise Not Consideration.

The content of the promise may determine whether a bargained for promise constitutes adequate consideration. A promise may be so worded that it is left up to the promisor to decide whether or not to perform. It may be worded so that the promisor has an unrestricted right to cancel the contract. Because such words in the promise do not obligate the promisor, it is an illusory promise. There being no legal detriment to the promise, such consideration is legally insufficient. For example: "I will sell you a corner lot when I plat my next subdivision" is, without more, an illusory promise.

Illegal Consideration.

A promise which requires the commission of a crime or which violates basic public policy is obviously illegal and will void a contract. It is not always clear what does or does not violate statutes designed to protect the public health and morals. A court decision may be necessary to determine whether consideration given is legal.

Options and Consideration.

An option is a right given for a consideration to purchase or lease a property upon specified terms within a specific time, without obligating the party who received the right to exercise the right. It must be supported by consideration and, to be enforceable, must have all the elements of a contract. A promise to pay a mere recital of consideration alone is not sufficient consideration to exercise an option.

CONTRACTUAL CAPACITY OF PARTIES (TC)

All persons are presumed to have the legal capacity to enter into contracts.
Some, however, do not have the full understanding of their rights nor the capacity to understand the nature, purpose, and effect of a contract. These are considered in law not to have full contractual capacity and are afforded some degree of special protection under the law. Among them are minors, mental defectives and intoxicated persons.

Minors. (TC)

Oklahoma Statutes define a minor as a person under the age of eighteen (Title 15, Sec. 13). The courts recognize that persons of immature years lack capacity to compete on an equal basis with other persons, so they have given minors the right to protect themselves against their own lack of experience, judgment and ability. Although some minors have the intelligence to comprehend the most complex of transactions, they need to be protected from their immaturity, inexperience and tendency to buy impulsively.

The general rule of law is that any time prior to attaining the age of majority and within a reasonable period thereafter, nearly all contracts entered into by the minor may be avoided with no liability. After reaching legal age, minors may ratify or approve their previous contracts and will then be bound by them. A "reasonable time" for affirming or disavowing a contract depends on conditions surrounding the situation. In Oklahoma, for most situations, the time period is one year beyond achieving majority.

Adults are in the perilous legal position of being liable for contracts which can be disaffirmed or canceled by a party who is a minor. Since a contract with a minor binds both the minor and the adult unless the minor elects to disaffirm it, a contract with a minor is not void on its face, but is voidable. The burden is upon adults to ascertain that the persons with whom they deal are of legal age.

RATIFICATION

Ratification is a manifestation of an intention to be bound by a contract entered into during the period of minority. Minors cannot ratify a real estate contract until they come of age, at which time there are several ways to manifest ratification.

No Action.

If the minor does nothing to disaffirm the contract within a reasonable period of time after attaining majority, the contract will be considered affirmed. Reasonableness of time will depend on the situation. If the contract is executory, more time may be allowed than if the contract is completed.

Express Ratification.

Upon reaching the age of majority, persons may expressly declare their intention in words to be bound by a contract entered into as a minor. The means of expression is not important. It can be written or it may be made orally and no particular form of expression is required. It must be more than a mere acknowledgement of the existence of the agreement. It must be an indication of an intent to be bound by the contract.

Implied Ratification.

The conduct of a person may imply an intention to continue the responsibility attendant to the contract. For example, if a minor purchases a home three months before reaching majority and continues to meet monthly payments and reside therein after reaching majority, the action would constitute ratification.

DISAFFIRMANCE

The major objective of the law in giving a minor the right to avoid contracts was to protect the minor's estate from dissipation during minority and did not include the requirement that the minor return to the adult the consideration received. In more recent times, the tendency of courts has been to have the minor place the adult in status quo, that is, restored to the legal position prior to the contract. Upon rescission of a voidable contract, the parties must return any consideration that was exchanged. The minor owes the duty to return to the other party of the contract any payment received and which he still has at the time of disaffirmance. The minor is also entitled to recover all the payments made as well as the return of any property still in the possession of the other contracting party.

There are several exceptions to the general rule that minors may avoid their contracts. One is that contracts made by minors to obtain necessaries are not voidable by minors and will be enforced against them. Necessaries are those things personal to the minor, such as food, clothing, shelter, medical care, elemental education, training for a trade, and the tools of a trade, suitable for the minor's station in life.

In matters related to housing, minors who are married have rights different from those of unmarried minors. Anyone who is legally married and otherwise qualified may dispose of and make contracts relating to real estate, regardless of age.

A minor cannot be held liable for damages for loss of rent caused by the breach of a lease, but can be held liable for the reasonable rental value of the premises during the time occupied, provided it would be classed as a necessary and suitable to the minor's station in life.

Period of Minority.

The age at which the period of minority ends is calculated from the first minute of the day on which a person is born to the same minute of the corresponding day completing the period of minority (Title 15, Sec. 13, O.S.). In other words, majority begins on a person's eighteenth birthday.

Legal procedures have been established to provide "judicial emancipation" of minors. Upon petition by or on behalf of a minor and a court hearing, a judge may find that removal of the disabilities of minority is in the best interest of the minor and may declare the minor capable of tending to affairs of business and competent to enter into contracts.

MENTALLY INCAPACITATED (TC)

Mentally incapacitated persons are given the same protection as that given to minors. Many incompetent persons have never been adjudged as such and continue to function in business, freely entering into contracts. Contracts of incompetents are voidable, not void. Should the person be determined to have been incompetent at the time the contract was entered into, affirmative action on the part of the incompetent will be necessary to set it aside later. Since it is difficult to recognize the affliction of incompetence, there is no effective way to avoid the problem except through the exercise of good judgment.

The contracts of persons judicially declared insane are void and can never have any effect. Because the proceedings by which guardians and conservators are appointed are a matter of public record, all those dealing with an insane person or an adjudged incompetent are presumed to know of that person's inability to enter into contracts.

INTOXICATED PERSONS (TC)

The rules regarding the contracts of persons under the influence of alcohol or other drugs are similar to those of other persons lacking the capacity to understand the nature of a transaction. The contract of an intoxicated person is usually binding, except where that person is so intoxicated as to be incapable of understanding the consequences of the transaction. In that case, the intoxicated person, upon regaining sobriety, may ratify the contract or may disaffirm the contract and recover the consideration given. In the case of disaffirmance, the other party must also be returned to the same legal position as before the contract.

CORPORATIONS AND OTHER FORMS OF ORGANIZATIONS (TC)

Legal counsel should always be sought when entering into contracts involving any type or organization.

The contractual ability of a corporation is usually determined by its charter and by-laws. Its capacity to contract may be related only to specific matters or it may be related to broad areas of business transactions. It is usually necessary to obtain copies of minutes of corporate meetings showing that the transaction is authorized and indicating who is empowered to sign for matters involving real property on behalf of the corporate contractor.

A partnership cannot contract except through a general partner. Each general partner has the authority to bind the firm. Third parties dealing with a partner are entitled to rely on the partner's representations of having authority even when a partner is exceeding authority.

Unincorporated associations cannot contract in the name of the association as they do not have a clearly recognized legal status. They must be treated as a group of individuals with each member of the association (or syndicate, or other designation) having the legal capacity to contract. A contract entered into in the name of an unincorporated association will bind the members who authorized the contract or ratified it after it was negotiated.

Governmental units have no capacity to conduct business of any kind unless they are specifically authorized by statute to do so. They are strictly controlled by statutes and ordinances, so it is important in dealing with any governmental unit to verify its authority to contract.

ILLITERATES

Illiterate persons are considered competent to contract. A contract signed by an illiterate is presumed valid unless fraud or undue influence can be proved.

FELONS

Legal rights of persons convicted of felonies are suspended upon a sentence of imprisonment in a state penitentiary for any term less than life. If sentenced to life imprisonment or death, rights are completely taken away and they cannot enter into valid contracts, except for the sale of their interest in real property. Parole restores a limited series of civil rights, including the right to contract. All rights may be regained when a full pardon is granted.

Ch. 13

TEST YOUR UNDERSTANDING

1. A contract may be an agreement
   1. to do a certain thing.
   2. not to do a certain thing.
   3. **Both 1 and 2.**
   4. Nether 1 nor 2.

2. A real estate sales contract, unless otherwise provided,
   1. vests equitable title in the buyer at the time the contract is ratified.
   2. is merged into the deed at settlement.
   3. **Both 1 and 2.**
   4. Neither 1 nor 2.

3. A bilateral contract is one in which the
   1. promise of one party is given in exchange for the performance of an act by another.
   2. consideration is always money.
   3. acceptance is presumed if the contract is beneficial to the offeree.
   4. **promise of one party is given in exchange for the promise of another.**

4. A written contract would be best described as a(n)
   1. implied contract.
   2. **expressed contract.**
   3. ostensible contract.
   4. negotiated contract.

5. A seller gave an open listing to several brokers specifically promising that if one of the brokers found a buyer for the seller's real estate, the seller would then be obligated to pay a commission to that broker. This offer by the seller is a(n)
   1. executed agreement.
   2. discharged agreement.
   3. implied agreement.
   4. **unilateral agreement.**

6. When a licensee accepts a listing on real property and promises to advertise and promote its sale in exchange for the promise of a commission, if successful, there is
   1. a binary contract.
   2. no contract until the property is sold.
   3. an implied contract.
   4. **a bilateral contract.**

7. A contract between a seller and a buyer is a(n)
   1. general contract.
   2. unilateral contract.
   3. implied contract.
   4. **bilateral contract.**

8. Before communication to the prospective purchaser of the seller's acceptance of an offer, the prospective purchaser may withdraw the offer at any time
   1. unless the offer states it is irrevocable.
   2. provided the offer is not supported by a deposit.
   3. provided the offeree has breached the offer.
   4. **for any reason.**

9. Broker Sal Manella has found a buyer for Phil Anderer's home. The buyer has entered into a real estate sales contract for the property for $1,000 less than the asking price and has deposited $5,000 earnest money with Broker Manella. Anderer is out of town for the weekend and Manella has been unable to inform him of the signed agreement. At this point, the real estate sales contract is a(n)
    1. voidable contract.
    2. offer.
    3. executory contract
    4. implied contract.

10. If a seller makes any alteration in an offer before accepting it, the buyer
    1. is still bound by the original offer.
    2. may withdraw the offer within the time specified in the offer.
    3. is relieved of the original offer.
    4. must forfeit the earnest money if the counter is not accepted.

11. The signing of a purchase contract by a buyer sets in motion a series of events leading, normally, to a binding contract of sale. Which of the following is NOT true?
    1. An offer may be accepted.
    2. An offer may lapse through passage of the time period.
    3. An offer may be withdrawn at any time before acceptance.
    4. A counteroffer is only a temporary rejection and does not destroy the offer.

12. A valid contract is binding upon all parties
    1. and cannot be nullified by any of the parties.
    2. but can be nullified by any of the parties with proper notice.
    3. Both 1 and 2.
    4. Neither 1 nor 2.

13. A contract that has no legal effect because it does NOT contain all the essential requirements is
    1. voidable.
    2. unenforceable.
    3. void.
    4. canceled.

14. A void contract
    1. has never been a contract at all.
    2. entails no obligation by either party.
    3. Both 1 and 2.
    4. Neither 1 nor 2.

15. A voidable contract is one which
    1. was valid at the time it was executed but for some reason cannot be proved or judgment obtained by either or both parties.
    2. has no legal effect since it is really not a contract.
    3. contain all legal elements essential to its existence.
    4. is valid and enforceable on it face but may be properly rejected by one of the parties.

16. An oral contract for real estate is generally
    1. void.
    2. unenforceable.
    3. illegal.
    4. caveat stupidity.

17. To be binding on the buyer and seller, an agreement for transfer of real property must
    1. be recorded.
    2. contain an offer and acceptance.
    3. be acknowledged.
    4. satisfy all of the above.

18. Simon Simpleton signs a real estate contract without first reading it. This allows him to later break the contract on the basis of
    1. mistake.
    2. ignorance.
    3. Both 1 and 2.
    4. Neither 1 nor 2.

19. The absence of duress, menace, and undue influence is a requirement of
    1. reality of consent.
    2. lawful objective.
    3. competent parties.
    4. sufficient consideration.

20. An owner gave an option on the property for 90 days for a cash consideration of $1,000. The optionee later assigned the option to another party for a valuable consideration. Before expiration of the option, the owner decided not to sell the property and to take it off the market. Which of the following is correct?
    1. The option is void. An option cannot be assigned.
    2. The owner can refuse to sell as the consideration paid by he assignee was not in cash.
    3. The assignee would have a good chance in civil court to compel the optionor to sell if the option is exercised before its expiration date.
    4. The option is not binding on the optionor as $1,000 is not sufficient consideration.

21. The term "consideration" as applied to real estate contracts includes which of the following?
    1. Values given, rendering of services, or money.
    2. Acts done, forbearance of acts, of favors granted.
    3. Mutual promises.
    4. All of the above.

22. The term "valuable consideration" as used in a contact can include which of the following?
    1. Anything movable of monetary value.
    2. Expert services for which a fee could be charged.
    3. Both 1 and 2.
    4. Neither 1 nor 2.

23. A consideration for a legal contract may take the form of a
    1. promise not to marry.
    2. promissory note with interest.
    3. promise to build a fence.
    4. All of the above.

24. When the consideration in a contract takes the form of money, it is
    1. valuable consideration.
    2. good consideration.
    3. Both 1 and 2.
    4. Neither 1 nor 2.

25. When a parent conveys property to a child as a gift out of love for the child, the consideration in the deed is
    1. valuable.
    2. good.
    3. excellent.
    4. intrinsic.

26. A contract secured after deliberate misrepresentation by the seller
    1. is void at the outset.
    2. is voidable by the buyer.
    3. violates the Statutes of Frauds.
    4. is completely unenforceable.

27. Generally, if a purchaser has signed a contract under duress, the contract is
   1. void.
   2. voidable by the seller.
   3. voidable by the buyer.
   4. a unilateral contract.

28. The term "contractual ability" means which of the following?
   1. The parties to the contract are competent to enter into a valid agreement.
   2. The contract is drawn up by a person legally qualified to do so.
   3. The agreement contemplates a purpose that is legal.
   4. The contract contains all the clauses and covenants necessary to be valid.

29. In order to possess the full capacity to contract, one must
   1. be of sound mind.
   2. have reached the age of majority.
   3. Both 1 and 2.
   4. Neither 1 nor 2.

30. Which of the following is not fully competent to contract?
   1. A minor.
   2. An incompetent.
   3. An inebriate.
   4. All of these.

31. If a minor becomes a party to a contract, the contract is usually
   1. void on its face.
   2. voidable by the minor.
   3. both 1 and 2.
   4. neither 1 nor 2.

32. A twelve-year old boy or girl cannot enter into a valid contract because by law a twelve-year old is
   1. a minor.
   2. legally incompetent.
   3. both 1 and 2.
   4. neither 1 nor 2.

33. Maudie buys ten acres of land from Peggy, who is a minor. Maudie hires an architect and builds an expensive home on the land. When Peggy achieves her majority, she disaffirms the sale, tenders the full purchase price for the land back to Maudie. Who receives the home and the land?
   1. While some courts may be sympathetic toward Maudie's plight, the general rule is the Peggy would win because the contract for sale of land with a minor is voidable on the part of the minor.
   2. Maudie would win because after Peggy, a minor, attains adulthood, she may ratify to disaffirm the contract.
   3. The contract is binding on Maudie so she will retain the home and the land.
   4. Maudie was obviously insane to enter into the contract in the first place. She can plead insanity and void the contract.

34. Snow, a broker, sells a parcel of real estate for Flake, a minor, age 17 years and 10 months. When Flake becomes of age, he disaffirms the contract of sale. The broker demands that Flake pay the commission and, upon Flake's refusal, begins suit for payment. Which of the following is correct?
   1. The validity of the contract will be upheld because Flake is now over eighteen years of age.
   2. may be forced through a suit for specific performance.
   3. is the basis for the recovery of a commission of the broker produces a buyer ready, willing and able to purchase.
   4. is of no value and is void.

35. A contract entered into by a competent and an incompetent may be disaffirmed by which of the following?
   1. A competent party.
   2. The incompetent party.
   3. Both 1 and 2.
   4. Nether 1 nor 2.

ANSWERS AND EXPLANATIONS

1. 3 By definition, contracts are agreements to do certain things or to refrain from certain action.

2. 3 Sales contracts transfer equitable title only. They are not instruments of conveyance. Upon settlement, the contract ceases to exist as it is merged into the deed. However, if a sales contract calls for something to be done after closing and delivery of the deed, such as the installation of a sewer system, this requirement will usually survive the deed and be enforceable.

3. 4 A good definition of a bilateral contract.

4. 2 A contract in writing in which the parties have stated their intentions fully and in explicit terms is an expressed contract.

5. 4 Since there is no obligation on the part of the broker to perform, there is a unilateral contract.

6. 4 When there is a promise from one party given in exchange for the promise of another, a bilateral contract exists.

7. 4 When a seller promises to sell certain property to a buyer for a given price and the buyer promises to purchase that real property for that price, a bilateral contract is created.

8. 4 A prospective buyer need have no reason for withdrawal of an offer and may do so without legal liability at any time before acceptance. The offeror reserves the right to withdraw an offer at any time until an acceptance is received.

9. 2 A presentation or proposal for acceptance remains an offer until accepted. An indication, signed by all parties, of willingness to be bound by the terms of an offer establishes the "meeting of the minds".

10. 3 If, upon receipt of the offer to purchase, the seller insists upon some modification in the terms or conditions, the purchaser is relieved of the original offer.

11. 4 A counteroffer is a rejection of the original offer. Once rejected, an offer cannot be accepted later.

12. 1 By definition, a valid contract is enforceable in every respect and is binding upon all parties.

13. 3 A real estate contract cannot exist without all of the essential elements.

14. 3 A void contract has no legal force or binding effect. It is a nullity, not enforceable. A void agreement is no contract at all. A contract for an illegal purpose (i.e. gambling) is void.

15. 4 A voidable contract is subject to rescission by one of the parties who acted under disability.

16. 2 Unless required by law, oral contracts can be just as valid as written contracts. Generally, however, real estate contracts, except those for leases of one year or less, must be in writing to be enforceable. All essential terms of the contract must complete and certain so that the entire agreement is set forth in writing, and nothing material is left to be agreed upon in the future.

17. 2 A binding agreement need not be acknowledged or recorded.

18. 4 Signing a contract binds one to it whether or not the contents were known or the soignée was mistaken.

19. 1 A meeting of the minds cannot exist under any of these conditions.

20. 3 This is a valid contract and may be exercised by the optionee.

21. 4 These identify the standard forms of legal consideration in a real estate contract rendered.

22. 3 Valuable consideration can only be something of monetary value or services rendered.

23. 4 All are acceptable items of legal consideration.

24. 1   Money identifies the consideration as valuable consideration.

25. 2   A good consideration does not require anything of monetary value. However, it may be insufficient in some cases to cause the transfer of title. One giving good consideration cannot enforce a contract if the grantors change their minds.

26. 2   Deliberate misrepresentation in a contract can result in rescission by the innocent party who relied on false statements.

27. 3   Duress consists of compelling a person, through force or fear, to agree to a contract. The aggrieved party, the purchaser may rescind the contract.

28. 1   Most adults, including those who are illiterate, have full capacity to enter into a legally binding contract.

29. 3   Both of these are requirements for the unlimited ability of a person to enter into a legally binding contract.

30. 4   Anyone adjudicated insane or an officer of a corporation who is not authorized to execute a contract on behalf of the corporation has no capacity to contract under any circumstances. The contract of an intoxicated person is usually binding, except where that person is so intoxicated that he is incapable of understanding the nature of the transaction. In that case, the intoxicated person may subsequently cancel or ratify the contract. A minor has limited ability to contract, which means that the contract of a minor is valid only if the minor does not disaffirm such a contract during minority or shortly after reaching majority. Contracts made by minors to obtain such necessities as food, clothing, and shelter, however, are not voidable by minors and will be enforced against them.

31. 2   Most contracts entered into by a minor are generally voidable at the minor's option. A contract with a minor is valid on its face pending affirmation or disaffirmation on the part of the minor.

32. 3   A minor is legally incompetent and does not have the legal capacity to transfer title to property.

33. 1   Since the grantor of a deed must be competent, a deed by a minor is voidable. Even if a minor misrepresents age, the minor can disaffirm a contract, subject to action in damages for fraud.

34. 3   If a minor lists property with a broker, the broker would not be able to collect an earned commission if, upon finding a ready, willing, and able buyer, the minor decides to repudiate the listing contract.

35. 2   Minors and inebriates are incompetents but have limited capacity to contract and, under certain conditions, can disaffirm their contracts.

CONTRACT LAW AND PERFORAMNCE

Legality of Object, Written Document, Performance

LEGALITY OF OBJECTIVE (TC)

The objective of a contract refers to the action the contract requires the parties to take or not to take. Legality of objective implies that a contract must contemplate a legitimate purpose and must not be contrary to law. Since all contracts must have a legal purpose, any contract formed to accomplish an illegal end was never a contract and is void from its inception.

The general rule is that a contract must be legal in its formation and operation. Any contract requiring the violation of a statute, the commission of a crime, or which is contrary to accepted standards of morality, is illegal and void. There are, however, exceptions to the rules and each case must be decided according to the facts. What in fact constitutes illegality does not lend itself to a neat statement of legal principles and may or may not be illegal depending on the circumstances.

Another general rule is that if part of a contract is illegal, the illegal part taints the whole agreement and causes it to be void. However, depending upon the seriousness of the illegality, the courts may not require dismissal, especially if it causes severe penalty to an innocent party. If an agreement is "divisible," the legal part can be enforced concurrently with the voidance of the illegal part.

An infinite variety of situations give rise to illegal objectives. In general, a contract will be illegal if prohibited by statute, is in violation of the common law, or is contrary to public policy. By necessity, these are addressed here in general classifications, are not inclusive of all, and represent only a few of the possibilities within categories.

Agreements illegal by Statute. (TC)

An agreement is illegal if it comes within a class of agreements made illegal by statutory law. Some statutes expressly state that certain types of agreements are "illegal," "unlawful," or "void." This clearly indicates the intention of the legislative body to make such agreements illegal. However, where the intention is not expressed, it is not always clear whether the agreement should be held legal or not.

Statutes in all states regulate or prohibit wagering. A contract to lease a building for an illegal gambling casino would not be enforceable. To create speculative risks where no risk previously existed (wagering) is usually prohibited by statute, whereas a good faith transaction of the commodity market is legal. Regulatory agencies are established in all states to protect the public and to require licenses for the practice of professions. Any contract in which a person bargains to perform services requiring a license or engages in a regulated business without first having obtained a license for that purpose is illegal.

Anti-trust laws are designed to maintain and preserve business competition. The *Sherman Anti-Trust Act* specifically provides that "every contract…or conspiracy in restraint of trade...is declared illegal." Price fixing occurs when parties conspire to set prices for rentals rather than let those prices be established though competition on the open market. If a group of real estate brokers creates a "fee schedule" of commission rates to which all must adhere, there is a violation of the anti-trust laws. Agreements to allocate the sales market and/or set commission rates are direct illegal restrains of trade.

Other types of trade restraint are not covered by anti-trust legislation. A reasonable amount of restraint of trade is acceptable under common law.

1. It is not unusual for a seller of a business to enter into a contract agreeing not to compete with the buyer for a given period of time.
2. Partnerships are sometimes dissolved under the condition that the withdrawing partner is not allowed to start a business in competition within a given time or distance from the established business.
3. Employees are often required, as a condition of employment, to enter into an agreement with the employer that upon termination the employee will not compete by setting up a similar business or go to work for a competitor.
4. Employees may agree not to reveal trade secrets after leaving he company.

These provisions are valid provided they are reasonable. As long as the public is not deprived of a benefit which could result from the competition, the courts will usually enforce such restriction.

AGREEMENTS CONTRARY TO PUBLIC POLICY (TC)

Although there is no rigid definition of unconscionability, it is a legal doctrine whereby a court will refuse to enforce a contract that is grossly unfair or unscrupulous at the time it was made. Even though an unconscionable agreement does not constitute fraud or some other traditional variety of illegal conduct, if it is offensive to the public conscience, it may be held illegal.

Courts may refuse to enforce a contract when there is evidence of undue influence exerted upon the principal or the beneficiary on the part of the licensee. When the personal interests of the licensee are enhanced in the transaction, it is considered immoral or unethical and against public policy. In general, such agreements involving conflict of interest are illegal unless there is full disclosure and the other parties effectively consent.

An agreement to commit a crime or tort is obviously illegal. A crime is a wrong to the public, whereas a tort is a wrong or injury to an individual or individuals. A contract to induce someone to commit a criminal or tortuous act is illegal and unenforceable. But a contract which may indirectly aid or contribute to an illegal activity is not automatically rendered illegal.

Provisions of a lease exonerating a landlord from liability for injuries caused to the tenant by the landlord's own negligence are known as exculpatory clauses and are contrary to public policy. In Oklahoma, they are prohibited by statute in residential lease agreements.

Dual Contracts. (TC)

It is illegal [Commission Rule 605-10-17-5 (1)(4)] to have two contracts between the buyer and the seller for the same property with each contract containing different terms, with the intention of submitting a fraudulent contract to a lending institution to induce a larger loan. Such dual contracts make the licensee participant a party to fraudulent collusion and subject to censure as well as to civil damages.

A licensee cannot declare to the lender that the earnest deposit was greater than it truly was, or delay in depositing the earnest payment so that the assets of the purchaser will be inflated. A broker cannot be a party to naming a false consideration by accepting an earnest deposit in the form of a check while agreeing not to deposit it in an attempt to mislead the mortgage company as to the financial resources of the buyer.

STATUTE OF FRAUDS (TC)

Good business practice calls for all important and complicated business transactions to be reduced to writing. An oral contract is as enforceable as a written one, except for those classes of contracts thought to affect such vital interest that a writing should be required as evidence of contractual intent.

When parties to an oral contract are in full agreement on all terms, the contract is binding and enforceable in the courts. Oral contracts, however, are subject to misunderstanding of the rights and obligations of the parties and may be difficult to prove in a court proceeding should a dispute arise. The terms are more easily forgotten than the terms of a written contract, and are thereby more susceptible to the perpetration of fraud by one seeking enforcement of a contract or terms that never in fact existed. This was recognized centuries ago in English Law and has evolved into "statutes of frauds" being adopted with minor variations in all states. These laws are based on the general pattern of the 1677 English statute called the ***Statute for the Prevention of Frauds and Perjuries***.

The general thrust of the ***Oklahoma Statute of Frauds*** (Title 15, Sec. 136.5, O.S.) is that certain contracts must be in writing to be enforceable.

> The following contracts are invalid, unless the same, or some note or memorandum, therefore be in:
>
> Writing and subscribed by the party to be charged, or by his agent,
>
> An agreement for the leasing for a longer period than one (1) year, or for the sale of real property,
>
> Or of an interest therein; and such agreement, if made by a licensee of the party sought to be charged,

Is invalid, unless the authority of the agent be in writing, subscribed by the party sought to be charged.

The primary purpose of the *Oklahoma Statute of Frauds* is to require reliable evidence that an alleged contract was indeed entered into. A principle it serves is to minimize the possibility of a court being tricked into improperly ruling on matters involving real estate and certain other special situations. To accomplish this purpose, the statute requires that an agreement covered by the statute, or some note or memorandum thereof, must be in writing and signed by the party against whom enforcement is sought. Otherwise, the agreement is not enforceable in court.

The Statute of Frauds can itself be used as an instrument of fraud for oppression against persons ignorant of the writing requirement or lacking in bargaining power to complete a writing. To prevent injustice which can arise from the misuse of the writing requirement and to avoid unjust enrichment in statute of frauds cases, an executed (performed) contract cannot be re-opened because it failed to comply with all provisions of the statute. If an oral contract is fully executed, both parties having completed their required performances, the contract may not be set aside. It is a closed deal.

So far as real estate licensees are concerned, the two main classes of contracts covered by the statute are contracts for the sale of an interest in land and leases not performable within a year.

CONTRACT FOR SALE OF INTEREST IN LAND (TC)

Under *Statutes of Frauds*, an oral contract for sale of real estate falling within the scope of its provisions is unenforceable, not void or voidable. A contract for the sale of real property, or which will affect any ownership rights or interest therein, must be evidenced by a writing to be enforceable. Such contracts provide evidence of an intention to enter a contract but are not the instruments which actually convey title. Examples of instruments conveying an "interest in land" are mortgages, easements, contracts to purchase or to sell, contracts or the exchange of real estate, contracts for deed, options, and leases (unless the lease is within a statutory exception for short-term leases).

A deed transferring title from a grantor to a specified grantee must be in writing, not as a requirement of the *Statute of Frauds*, but for another reason. A deed, although a contract, is not making a promise. It actually transfers the interest and when recorded in the public land records, gives constructive notice of ownership.

CONTRACTS NOT TO BE PERFORMED WITHIN ONE YEAR

The dividing line between long-term and short-term contracts is one year. Except for contracts for the transfer of interest in real estate, executory bilateral contracts which can be performed within one year are excluded from the *Oklahoma Statute of Frauds*. If the performance of the contract cannot conceivably occur within one year, the contract is long-term, covered by the statute, and needs to be evidenced by a writing to be enforceable.

Contracts for the lease of real estate for periods of more than one year fall within the *Statute of Frauds*. If a tenant has signed a lease, and has been accepted by the landlord, the landlord may enforce the document even though the landlord may not have actually signed the lease. The tenant in this case is the party the landlord is "charging with performance."

The one-year period begins with the time the contract is made, not the time it becomes effective. A lease entered into on July 1 for one year, beginning July 3, is a long-term contract as it cannot be performed within a year of its making. Since the law does not usually count fractions of days, a one-year lease entered into on January 1 would begin on January 2 and run through January 1 of the following year is still a short-term contract.

Writing Over Oral or Printed Form.

Where there was an intention to reduce a contract to writing, the written contract will supersede all prior negotiations and conversations relative to the agreement. Words hand written on a printed form will prevail over contradictions in the printed matter.

Any modifications of contracts falling under the provisions of the *Statute of Frauds* must meet the requirement of the statute to be enforceable. If the parties mutually wish to cancel an enforceable contract in whole or in part, however, an oral agreement can rescind any written contract. **(TC)**

Parol Evidence Rule.

The courts in general look solely to the writing in determining the contents of a contract. Since all preliminary negotiations are merged with a final unambiguous contract, the last writing best expresses the intent of the parties. Oral evidence is not admissible to add to, alter, vary, or contradict the terms of a written contract. However, when one of the parties contends that part of the writing has been omitted or that part of the agreement has been stated incorrectly, the court will look to the principle of law known as the parol evidence rule.

Parol evidence, or oral evidence, applies only to writings. There can be no application of the parol evidence rule unless there is a written contract in which the parties intended to integrate all the terms of their agreement. The purpose of parol evidence is to assure the certainty and security of transactions by giving binding effect to a final expression of an agreement. It is used to determine whether the writing was the complete and intended statement of the contract.

It is determined by a judge after oral testimony whether the contract properly reflects the agreement or should be added to or modified per the intentions of the parties.

CONTRACT PERFORMANCE

PERFORMANCE OF CONTRACTS (TC)

Performance of contracts means that the parties have carried out the obligations imposed upon them. In general, an executed contract is valid and binding upon the parties, their heirs and assigns. Those entering into contract usually expect to render a performance as agreed. In fact, the whole system of the business world depends upon contracting parties abiding by the contracts they make.

The most common means of termination of contracts is complete and literal performance of the contractual duty in full. However, circumstance may vary from that originally contemplated. Performance as first agreed may have to be superseded by a subsequent agreement or an alternation in the initial contract.

Substantial Performance. (TC)

Even if the contract is not fulfilled in every particular, the full or literal performance of all conditions may not be required. If the portion unfulfilled was a promised performance, there can be damages for its partial breach. Justice does not demand complete, literal fulfillment of all conditions, only substantial fulfillment.

Satisfactory Performance. (TC)

If the contract is required to be completed "to the satisfaction" of the other party and the "satisfaction" can be measured objectively, a contract may be considered performed when performance meets the objective standard.

Timely Performance. (TC)

Many contracts will specify a time for completion of their terms. Many contract forms will include the words "time is of essence" which means legally that strict adherence to the time provision of the contract can be, but not necessarily will be, enforced.

Merger. (TC)

Unless otherwise provided in a real estate contract, all of the contract terms are merged into and superseded by the deed. In effect, a contract merges into the deed and ceases to exist. If the seller wants any of the terms of the contract to continue and survive the deed, a special survival clause must be inserted in the deed. If the sales contract, however, calls for something to be done after the closing, such as roof repair, the requirement would usually survive the deed and be enforceable.

DISCHARGE BY ACTION OF THE PARTIES (TC)

As applied to contracts, discharge means the termination of a contractual obligation prior to completion of performance according to its terms. When the parties to a contract wish to put an end to the contract without performance, or with a view to performance in a different manner, they may alter the performance obligations in some way.

Waiver. (TC)

If one party voluntarily relinquishes a right under contract to require complete performance, strict performance has been waived, relieving the obligor of the waived obligation.

Mutual Rescission. (TC)

Both parties may agree to cancel the contract. The agreement of rescission is in effect a new contract with both parties agreeing to surrender the rights which were established by the old contract. The consideration for the new contract is the surrendering the rights of the old one.

Accord and Satisfaction. (TC)

When both parties desire to alter or amend the original contract rather than put an end to it, they may resort to an "accord and satisfaction" which is similar to creating a substitute contract. If the new agreement is reached after the original contract has matured or after breach of the original contract, the new agreement is called an accord. The acceptance by both parties of a new contract in place of the old is called a satisfaction.

Substitute Contract. (TC)

A breaching party may be willing to complete the contract if more favorable terms can be negotiated. If the other party will agree to voluntarily make certain changes in the contract, a substitute contract will replace the old one. The contract should be re-drafted and signed by the parties involved.

    FOR EXAMPLE: A signs a 5-year lease to pay $900 per month for an office. Three years later he finds another location and wants to move. In the meantime, rents for similar offices in the building decline to $600 per month. In order to keep A, the landlord may be willing to reduce the rent to a price more in line with the market value, on the condition A signs a new year lease.

    Or perhaps the rent for comparable office space has increased to $1,000 per month. The landlord may be happy to cancel A's lease in favor of one to B for current market value.

Novation. (TC)

An alternative to mutual rescission is novation. A novation is the substitution of a new party who assumes the responsibilities of the old party releasing the other from the obligation.

Abandonment. (TC)

When a tenant has an unexplained absence from a leased space for a reasonable period of time after default in the payment of rent, the lease may be presumed abandoned and the terms of the contract breached. The leasehold contract has been terminated. In some jurisdictions, in the case of residential space, statutes prescribe a specific time period. In Oklahoma, whether or not there has been an abandonment is a question of fact determined by the circumstances in each case.

Impossibility. (TC)

A contract originally contemplated cannot be performed when the promised performance is literally no longer possible. Should the contractor delivering personal services die or have an incapacitating illness before the performance was due or completed, the contract could be discharged on the grounds of impossibility. Other circumstances relating to this category would be destruction of the property or the source of supply essentials to the performance, or changes in the law (intervening illegality) declaring the performance illegal.

Uniform Vendor and Purchaser Risk Act.

Oklahoma statutes provide, in the absence of contractual agreement, for placing the burden of loss when a building under contract of sale is destroyed. ***The Uniform Vendor and Purchaser Risk Act*** (Title 16, Sec. 201) provides that, in the absence of an agreement otherwise, the risk of loss does not pass from the seller to the buyer until either legal title or possession has passed to the buyer. Once title or possession has passed, the buyer is responsible for subsequent losses. The act covers situations in which all or a material part of the property is destroyed or is taken by eminent domain. If the property is destroyed through the fault of one or the other of the parties, the party at fault must bear the loss.

Unforeseeable Difficulties. (TC)

When one of the parties encounters exceptional circumstances considered substantial, unforeseen, and unforeseeable, the contract cannot be enforced. If the problem could have been anticipated, the obligation is legally enforceable. For instance, bad weather, excavation problems, and rising prices can be expected, while an unprecedented flood or a terrorist's bombing cannot be foreseen.

Frustration of Purpose. (TC)

When performance once sought by an obligee is no longer of value to the obligee, cancellation of the contract may be sought. Even though the performance is possible and legal, changed circumstances no longer provide the purpose intended causing frustration of purpose.

   FOR EXAMPLE: A party rents an apartment along Park Avenue because it provides an excellent view of a ticker tape parade for the returning football team victorious in a bowl game. The apartment had been advertised and offered for one day for that purpose by the apartment owner. However, a blizzard of unusual proportions strikes the state and the parade is cancelled. The purpose in contracting for the use of the apartment is frustrated and the contract may be terminated.

Impracticability. (TC)

Performance may also be excused where the fulfillment of the contract has become impractical. Unforeseen developments, such as great expense, injury or loss for the promisor can lead to cancellation, as well as when the benefits of the promise have little or no further value.

DISCHARGE BY OPERATION OF LAW (TC)

Sometimes contracts are discharged by law without regard to the will of the parties. Due process is always provided, but circumstances surrounding the contract may result in its cancellation by operation of law. Such discharges include, but are not limited to, the following examples:

   Contracts merged or fused into subsequent agreements are discharged by superseding contracts.
   The time limit for bringing suit for breach of contract may expire under the statute of limitations, barring the right of action to enforce contractual obligations due to unreasonable delay in seeding action.

   Unknown and unauthorized alterations made in a written, signed contract can result in its termination.

   A discharge of responsibility may result from bankruptcy when the court releases the debtor from contractual obligations.

Statutes of Limitation. (TC)

The statute of limitations provides that, after a statutory number of years, a definite cutoff point is reached in bringing certain legal actions. The law is intended to aid the vigilant. In theory, if the true owners of property are not interested in protecting their property, neither are the courts. In these times of rapid transportation and instant communication, property owners do not need an extended period of time to know what is happening to their property in order to take legal action to protect their rights.

Doctrine of Laches. (TC)

The doctrine of laches does not provide a statutory period of time but recognizes an unreasonable delay in bringing action. It will not permit the enforcement of certain legal rights beyond a time determined to be reasonable by reasonable persons in the business. A common sense way to express it is, "You cannot sit (or sleep) on your rights.

REMEDIES FOR BREACH (TC)

Both the promisor and the promisee have a number of remedies in the event of an unexcused failure of the other party to perform a required contractual obligation. The most commonly sought remedies in lawsuits for breach of contracts are legal remedies (damages) and equitable remedies (specific performance and rescission). The circumstances and law of each transaction determine the best legal action.

The law requires the court to examine four areas before a plaintiff may successfully collect for a breach of contract. The first test is cause; the damage must be caused by the breach. The second is that the amount of damages must be reasonably ascertainable. Thirdly, the damages must have been reasonably foreseeable when the contract was performed. Finally, the injured party must mitigate the damages to reduce loss. The requirement of mitigation, for example, requires a landlord to make a reasonable good faith effort to lease space when a tenant has moved out in violation of a lease.

Legal Remedies. (TC)

The rationale for contract damage awards is that parties are entitled to damages for their loss of expectancies. An injured party is entitled to be placed, as nearly as practicable, in the position which would have been achieved if the contract had been performed as agreed.

The broad classes of damages awarded by courts as remedies for breach of contract injuries are compensatory, consequential (or special), liquidated, punitive, and nominal.

Compensatory Damages. (TC)

Plaintiffs usually seek money to compensate for harm sustained as a result of a breach of contract. Where the payment of money is an adequate substitute for the performance promised by a breaching party, a judgment for damages is the sole remedy. The amount of damages sustained from a breach of contract must be proven within a reasonable degree of certainty, as noted above.

Consequential (Special) Damages. (TC)

Consequential or special damages are damages which a plaintiff seeks in order to recover loss indirectly caused by the breach of contract. Most real estate sales contracts include a liquidated damages clause which allows the contracting parties to receive a stipulated amount to be paid as the sole remedy in case of breach by the other. If the sum agreed upon (usually the amount of the earnest deposit) was reasonably proportionate to the probably damages which would result from the anticipated breach, such a clause is valid and enforceable by the injured party.

Liquidated Damages. (TC)

It is difficult and impractical to accurately predetermine liquidated damages. If the damages agreed to in the contract are excessive, the liquidated damages clause is unenforceable. Oklahoma Statute, Title 15, Sec. 215B, provides, however, that liquidated provisions in real estate contracts are valid if the damage penalty does not exceed 5% of the purchase price. If 5% of the purchase price is not sufficient to cover the loss, courts may award damages in excess of the contracted settlement.

Punitive Damages. (TC)

Where extreme circumstances justify penalizing the defendant, courts sometimes award damages to an injured person which are vindictive and exemplary. The award is not intended to repay the injured party for actual losses suffered but is designed to punish the perpetrator. Punitive damages may be statutory in nature. For example, treble damages are authorized by federal law in restraint of trade cases.

Nominal Damages. (TC)

When a court or jury finds that there was technically a breach of contract in which no significant pecuniary loss was sustained, damages may be awarded in a token amount, such as one dollar. In some situations, courts will conclude that money is insufficient to make all parties "whole" again. Typical equitable remedies include specific performance and rescission of agreements.

EQUITABLE REMEDIES (TC)

Specific Performance. (TC)

As land is a unique item, when parties bargain for a specific piece of property, they are not required to substitute another. Based on the premise that no two pieces of real estate are exactly alike, the doctrine of specific performance requires performance in strict accordance with the terms of the contract. Money is not an adequate substitute for land as money cannot replace a piece of land identical to the parcel under contract. As damages cannot therefore be established in terms of mere money, the promised act must be completed as promised and the contract specifically performed. To use specific performance as a remedy, the plaintiff must show that the contract as to the defendant is just and reasonable.

Rescission of Contract. (TC)

Innocent parties are allowed to withdraw from contracts if induced to enter into a contract by fraud or misrepresentation. By rescinding such contracts, parties may legally withhold the performance of an obligation. Those legally incompetent to contract may rescind their agreements.

Ch. 14

TEST YOUR UNDERSTANDING

1. It is said that a valid contract must have legality of object. Which of the following best describes "legality of object"?
    1. All parties are of legal age and agree upon the legal consideration to be paid.
    2. The contract must not be for an illegal purpose or against public policy.
    3. Either party has the legal right to cancel the contract, provided legal notice is given.
    4. An agreement between competent parties that is legally enforceable.

2. The Statute of Frauds, as applied to real estate sales contracts, requires that
    1. all contracts for the sale of real property, in order to be enforceable, must be in writing.
    2. such contracts must be signed by the party to be charged thereby.
    3. Both 1 and 2.
    4. neither 1 nor 2.

3. Under the Statute of Frauds all contracts for the sale of real estate must be in writing to be enforceable in court. The principle reason for this statute is to
    1. prevent the buyer from defrauding the seller.
    2. prevent perjury and fraudulent proof of a fictitious oral contract.
    3. protect the buyer from the broker.
    4. protect the general protect from fraud due to unrecorded deeds.

4. The Statute of Frauds
    1. requires all real estate contracts to be in writing. → not all
    2. prohibits oral real estate purchase contracts.
    3. Both 1 and 2.
    4. Neither 1 nor 2.

5. The Statute of Frauds involves contracts which must be in writing to be enforceable. Which of the following falls within the Statute of Frauds?
    1. A contract for the sale of real property.
    2. A contract for the sale of an interest in real estate.
    3. A contract for the leasing of real property for two years.
    4. All of these.

6. A valid and binding contract for sale of real estate must
    1. be entered into by competent parties.
    2. be bound by a consideration.
    3. cover a legal and moral act.
    4. all of the above..

7. For a real estate contract to be binding and enforceable, it must be
    1. entered into by competent parties and bound by consideration.
    2. for a legal or moral act, in writing, and have an offer and acceptance.
    3. Both 1 and 2.
    4. Neither 1 nor 2.

8. In which of the following circumstances would a contract be terminated by acts of the parties?
    1. Death of either party.
    2. Financial impossibility.
    3. Completion of the objective of the contract.
    4. Bankruptcy of either party.

9. The withdrawal of an offer before acceptance is a
    1. reversion.
    2. rescission.
    3. rejection.
    4. revocation.

171

10. Which of the following does not terminate an offer to sell real estate?
   1. Lapse of reasonable time.
   2. Rejection of the offer by the offeree.
   3. Death of the sale associate.
   4. A revocation of the offer.

11. Mr. Weak made a bona fide offer to buy property listed with you. As the licensee, you present the offer the next morning and leave your principal a signed copy of the acceptance. That afternoon you are shocked to learn that Mr. Weak died the previous night. Based on this information, which of the following would best describe this situation?
   1. Weak's death terminated the offer.
   2. The contract would be binding on Weak's heirs, assigns and successors.
   3. While the contract would be binding, it would be difficult to enforce.
   4. Both B and C.

12. Mr. Ree is a trustee of the estate of a minor, Miss Young. He persuades her by threats to sell her land to a dummy corporation that he has formed. Unfortunately, unknown to him, the land floods each spring when the snow thaws and remains under water for months. When he discovers this fact, Mr. Ree asks the court to void the sale because of his mistake. The court should
   1. void the contract because of duress.
   2. void the contract because of the mistake.
   3. not void the contract because only he had made a mistake.
   4. not void the contract because he is not the innocent party.

13. Competent parties are essential for the validity of a contract. In addition, which of the following is (are) required?
   1. Legality of objective.
   2. Recording.
   3. Acknowledgement.
   4. All of theses.

14. A broker, if involved in the utilization of dual contracts is
   1. justified in the action as long as no one gets hurt.
   2. a party to a fraud.
   3. well within the limits of the law.
   4. functioning legally as long as everyone involved knows of the arrangement.

15. The following people participated in the preparation of a false, fictitious real estate contract which was submitted to a lending agency. Which ones are guilty of substantial misrepresentation?
   1. Buyer and real estate broker.
   2. Seller and sales associate.
   3. Both 1 and 2.
   4. Neither 1 nor 2.

16. The Uniform Vendor and Purchaser Risk Act provides that when property under contract of sale is destroyed by fire prior to the transaction being closed, at no fault of the purchaser who is not in possession. The assumption of risk falls upon the
   1. buyer.
   2. seller.
   3. lender.
   4. insurance company.

17. In anticipation of a breach of contract, the parties may specify in the contract the amount of damages to be paid in case of a breach. This is known as the
   1. collectable damages clause.
   2. liquidated damages clause.
   3. the habendum clause.
   4. declaratory evidence clause.

18. **Noah Count, buyer, defaulted on his sales contract with Don Trodden, the seller. Trodden may**
    1. cancel and declare the contract forfeited.
    2. sue for specific performance.
    3. sue Count for damages.
    4. Do any of these.

19. **What is a rescission of a contract?**
    1. A ratification of a contract by all parties.
    2. A return to the situation as it was before the contract was executed.
    3. A revision in the terms of a contract.
    4. A transfer of responsibility from one of the parties to the contract to an interested third party.

20. **A contract may be discharged by**
    1. performance of the parties.
    2. mutual assent of the parties.
    3. Both 1 or 2.
    4. Neither 1 nor 2.

21. **The substitution of a new contract and/or party for an existing one is a(n)**
    1. breach.
    2. option.
    3. novation.
    4. subterfuge.

ANSWERS AND EXPLANATIONS

1. 2 Legality of objective implies that a contract must contemplate a legitimate purpose, not to be contrary to law.

2. 3 Both are provisions of the Statute of Frauds.

3. 2 The purpose of the Statute of Frauds is to prevent the perpetration of fraud by one seeking enforcement of a contract that was never in fact made. It is not designed to prevent the performance of oral contracts.

4. 4 Oral contracts are legal. However, all enforceable contracts for the transfer of real property must be evidenced by a written agreement.

5. 4 Under the Statute of Frauds, these contracts must be in writing to be enforceable:
    1. A contract for the sale of real property or any interest therein.
    2. A contract which by its terms cannot be performed within one year from the date of the contract.
    3. An agreement to answer for the debt(s) of another.
    4. An agreement in consideration of marriage.
    5. The Uniform Commercial Code requires a written contract for the sale of goods (tangible personal property other than money or investment securities) where the contract price is $500 or more.

6. 4 All are essential to a valid real estate contract.

7. 3 A summary of the essential elements of a real estate contract.

8. 3 Death, bankruptcy and financial impossibility are operations of law.

9. 4 The seller can revoke an offer at any time prior to the broker's producing a ready, willing, and able buyer at the listing terms.

10. 3 A sales associate is a licensee of the principal and, therefore, is not a party to the contract. The others are standard means of offer termination by acts of the parties.

11. 1 When death occurs prior to acceptance of an offer, the offer is automatically terminated. There is no contract.

12. 4 A contract resulting from undue influence is rescindable only by the aggrieved party.

13. 1 Legality of objective is an essential element of a valid contract. For validity, a contract need not be acknowledged or recorded.

14. 2 Substantial misrepresentation is fraudulent activity.

15. 3 Anyone involved in fraudulent contracts in real estate is guilty of substantial misrepresentation.

16. 2 Unless the purchase agreement provides otherwise, the risk of loss does not pass to the vendor to vendee until either legal title or possession has passed to the vendee.

17. 2 Often the seller in a real estate contract retains the buyer's deposit money as damages when the buyer decides not to perform the contract to purchase the property. Additional damages may be recovered if unilateral rescission of the contract by the buyer results additional financial loss to the seller.

18. 4 All are possible remedies for breach of contract.

19. 2 A rescission is the legal remedy of canceling, terminating or annulling a contract and restoring the parties to their original positions.

20. 3 Sales contracts may be terminated by mutual agreement or by full performance by all parties.

21. 3 A definition of novation.

FINANCING REAL ESTATE

ECONOMIC BASE

Base Industry.

For a community to prosper and possibly grow in population, it must be able to sell what it produces to other communities. This economic activity produces a flow of income which enables its citizens to buy those things or services they are unable to produce. An agricultural area, for example, may produce a variety of farm products which it "exports" or sells for cash. Obviously, it then uses the cash to purchase items which are not manufactured in the community. A community's ability to export its products in return for cash or goods is its economic base.

Service Industry.

Service industries produce goods or services which do not leave the community. Real estate companies, for example, perform the majority of their functions within the local community for the local community. Teachers, doctors and dentists, grocery stores, restaurants, etc. provide services for the community and not for "export." These may be called secondary industries or service industries.

Effects on Value.

A community's base industry is essential for its survival. The exportation of locally produced goods causes an inflow of cash. The greater the exports, generally, the greater the availability of cash. If a community has a variety of items to sell outside (or export), its economy will expand increasing the availability of jobs, thereby increasing the demand for real estate, thereby increasing its value.

FEDERAL GOVERNMENT INFLUENCE (TC)

Money is a commodity and responds to the laws of supply and demand in similar ways. However, if the supply of money is too great, the result is inflation and its value is decreased. On the other hand, if there is not enough money in the economy, the result is an increase in the price of money and the interest rates increase. In the United States, the Federal Reserve Bank and the U. S. Treasury work together to keep the supply (and demand) for money within reasonable levels.

Fiscal Policy and the U. S. Treasury. (TC)

The supply and demand for money determine the basic mortgage interest rate at lending institutions. General economic conditions and the degree of risk involved, added to the basic rate, determine the actual interest rate that will be charged for a particular mortgage loan. The supply of mortgage funds depends to a large extent on the level of savings in financial institutions, but it is influenced as well by government policies.

Fiscal policy is the management of government programs, and spending for those programs allowed in the federal budget. The agency that manages the government's fiscal activities is the U. S. Treasury. These activities are financed by the issuance of treasury bills, treasury certificates, and treasury notes. The sale of these instruments constitutes borrowing by the federal government and must be repaid from budget surpluses or refinanced by the issuance of new debt instruments.

The U. S. Congress, in its function, normally passes legislation requiring the government to spend money. The government gets its money from taxes. In those circumstances when it cannot acquire enough money through taxation, it requires the U. S. Treasury to borrow the money. This process of borrowing money to fund its budget is called fiscal policy. The U. S. Treasury borrows money to fund government expenses through the sale of government bonds.

Bonds are certificates of indebtedness, or "I.O.U.s". In other words, the U. S. Government, through selling bonds (Savings Bonds, T-bills, treasury certificates, etc.), competes in the money market for the supply of money. This is called the fiscal policy of the government. Generally, we refer to the amount of money the government borrows as "the deficit."

Monetary Policy and the Federal Reserve Board. (TC)

The federal government, in the form of the Federal Reserve System, exercises monetary controls regulating the ways in which the money markets operate. There are three specific policy actions available to the Federal Reserve System to regulate the money supply and, therefore, the price of money (the interest rate). These three are (1) open market operations, (2) discount rates, and (3) changes in legal reserve requirements. These policies have an impact on the member banks of the Federal Reserve System.

Open Market Operations. (TC)

Open market operations are part of the main tools used by the Federal Reserve System to adjust the money supply. When Treasury-issued securities are bought in the open market by the Federal Reserve, more money is available for the banking system which will then expand the overall economy. The sale of Treasury-issued securities removes money from the marketplace, which then tends to reduce the expansion and growth of the economy. The price at which these securities are either bought or sold sets the daily or weekly interest rate quotations available.

Discount Rates. (TC)

When member banks need to borrow, they are able to obtain funds from the Federal Reserve System. The cost of funds to the member bank is referred to as the <u>discount rate</u> and is, in fact, an interest rate. From an economic point of view, as the discount rate increases, the economic incentive to borrow by the member bank system should be reduced. Thus, less money will be available to expand the money supply. Conversely, a reduction of the discount rate, making credit easier, would lead to more funds borrowed (demanded) and an increase in the money supply by the banking system.

Reserve Requirements. (TC)

The Federal Reserve System requires member banks to maintain a certain percentage of time and demand deposits on hand as cash or its equivalent. These reserves provide a degree of liquidity and safety and a way the Federal Reserve controls the supply of money. However, the ability to get deposits and, in turn, loan these deposits to consumers who, in turn, deposit a portion of the loan means that the banking system ultimately has the ability to expand the money supply. Therefore, an increase in the reserve requirements will reduce the ability of the banking system to expand the money supply. More money can be made available by reducing the reserve requirements.

SECONDARY MORTGAGE MARKET (TC)

The Secondary Mortgage Market is made up of three organizations whose function it is to see that the availability of money for mortgages is kept available and secure. These three organizations are Fannie Mae, the Government National Mortgage Association, called Ginnie Mae, and the Federal Home Loan Association, called Freddie Mac.

Fannie Mae. (TC)

Fannie Mae was created to provide liquidity in the mortgage market through the purchase or sale of FHA or VA loans. Until 1968 Fannie was a federal agency, but became a privately-owned corporation which is now traded on the New York Stock Exchange and deals in the purchase and sale of conventional, FHA and VA loans. Fannie Mae can raise funds by going to the capital market and bidding for funds successfully against other borrowers, or by selling mortgages which it currently holds in its portfolio.

Freddie Mac. (TC)

Freddie Mac, the common name for the Federal Home Loan Mortgage Corporation (FHLMC), is the secondary market mechanism for the savings and loan associations, operating similarly to Fannie Mae and the Government National Mortgage Association. Freddie Mac can purchase pools of conventional mortgages as well as FHA and VA mortgage loans. Freddie Mac has forced a degree of standardization on the savings and loan associations' mortgage lending practices since they will only purchase loans which are prepared using a standardized loan application, credit report, and appraisal form as published by Freddie Mac. The function of the agency is to buy mortgages in the secondary market when money is tight, thus providing more funds to the member associations for lending in the local areas; and absorbing excess funds from member associations when money is less tight by the sale of mortgages to those member institutions.

Ginnie Mae.

Ginnie Mae, the popular name for the Government National Mortgage Association (GNMA), was created to replace Fannie Mae when it became a private corporation. Ginnie Mae is a corporation under the control of the Department of Housing and Urban Development. The direct charges of Ginnie Mae are to administer special assistance programs, usually aimed at low income housing, and to work with Fannie Mae in secondary market activities.

Mortgage Pools. (TC)

Fannie Mae is the largest of the "pass through mortgage pools." That is, Fannie Mae guarantees to "pass through" the interest, principal and any prepayments on principal to a pool of investors. Fannie Mae is a "mortgage-backed security" operation. Fannie Mae issues securities which are backed by mortgages. The money investors invest with Fannie Mae is in turn invested by Fannie Mae in mortgages. Fannie Mae issues a certificate of guarantee of return to investors.

As an oversimplification, this system allows lenders in the primary mortgage market to lend money to home buyers then sell millions of dollars worth of notes to Fannie Mae and her investors, get money in return and keep the mortgage money market turning.

Participation Certificates. (TC)

Participation certificates are a system used by Freddie Mac to allow mortgage lenders in the primary mortgage market to sell mortgages to Freddie Mac. When the lender delivers mortgages to Freddie Mac, Freddie Mac gives the lender an undivided interest in a pool of conventional mortgages. Freddie Mac then guarantees to the primary mortgage market lender that the principal and interest will be repaid. Freddie Mac sets very strict requirements on these loans by requiring a very high loan to value ratio.

These participation certificates may be used as collateral for loans by the primary lender or sold for cash. They have become desirable investments for institutionalized investors who want high quality, high yield investments. Individuals may also invest in participation certificates if they can afford to purchase them in $25,000 blocks.

Usury. (TC)

The maximum interest that may be charged on mortgage loans is set by state law. Interest in excess of this rate is called usury and lenders are subject to penalties for charging usurious rates. The penalties for usurious loans range from loss of right to collect any interest, loss of the entire amount loaned in addition to the interest, or only being able to collect the amount borrowed plus interest at the legal rate.

TYPES OF INFLATION

Cost-Push Inflation.

When the cost of the raw materials involved in the production of a product increase causing the price of the end product to increase, it is inflation pushed by increasing manufacturing costs-cost-push inflation.

Demand-Pull Inflation.

When there are a lot of buyers demanding a product, the competition among them for the product will result in an escalation of the price bid for the item(s) resulting in a kind of auction wherein the price increases-demand-pull inflation.

Monetary Inflation.

When the government prints more money than the marketplace demands, the value of each dollar decreases resulting in more dollars being required to purchase an item-monetary inflation.

Real Cost Inflation.

When it becomes more and more difficult to produce a product of the same quality, the cost of production will increase causing real-cost inflation.

THE MORTGAGE AND NOTE (TC)

In any mortgage there are two distinct documents. The promissory note is the promise to repay a debt under specific terms which the mortgage gives the lender added ability to collect the debt in case of default. The mortgage creates a lien that can be exercised if the terms of the note are not met. The pledge of property as security for debt without delivering possession is called **hypothecation**. In order to have an enforceable mortgage loan, both the note and the mortgage must be executed.

The terms of the note specify the amount of the debt, method of payment, rate of simple interest, recourse on behalf of the mortgagee (lender) in the event of default, and other clauses such as prepayment penalties.

The note is in writing, is an unconditional promise to pay, and is paid either to order or to the bearer. Instruments payable to bearer can be transferred to a third party by delivery. Those documents payable to order can be transferred by endorsement to a third party.

The note specifies where payment shall occur as well as how the payment shall be computed. In a straight note, the borrower repays the principal in a lump sum at maturity with interest being paid in installments or at maturity. The most common payment plan requires the mortgagor (borrower) to pay a constant amount each payment period. The application of the payment is first to interest and then to the reduction of the amount borrower (principal). This is known as interest payable in arrears.

VA and FHA loans permit prepayment without special fees. When other loans are paid ahead of the term specified in their notes, however, borrowers may be assessed prepayment penalties based on the amount of the loans paid off. The typical payment premiums are specified so that the penalty is highest in the early years and declines over subsequent years. Further, the penalty will sometimes be applied if the borrower pays off more than twenty percent of the loan in any one year. The real estate licensee, when listing a property, should ascertain if any existing mortgage notes have pay-off penalties so that such will be addressed in net-to-seller estimate statements.

In the event that the borrower does not pay within typically fifteen days of the installment due date, the lender can assess a monthly late charge. The late charge is usually a percentage of the monthly payment not received, and will vary from locality to locality. The last clause typically referred to in a note is a cross-reference that this instrument or note is secured by a mortgage. The cross-reference then constitutes an enforceable mortgage loan.

Obligor-Obligee. (TC)

The items of the mortgage refer directly back to the terms of the note and establish that the subject property is security for the debt. The lender and the borrower are both identified, the amount of the debt is indicated, and the legal description is also stipulated.

The borrower becomes the obligor and the lender the obligee. The following are usually listed among the obligations of the borrower:

1. Payment of debt service, the principal and interest according to the terms of the note;
2. Payment of ad valorem taxes which can be on the basis of an escrow account held by the lender or can be made directly by the borrowers;
3. Maintenance of adequate hazard insurance to protect the interest of the lender; and
4. Maintenance of the property in good condition at all times. The lender reserves the right to inspect the property to ensure this maintenance.

Mortgagee and Mortgagor. (TC)

These are terms with which many people have some difficulty understanding. Simply defined, the mortgagee is the lender and the mortgagor is the borrower/home buyer.

The mortgage. (TC)

If a borrower defaults on the loan by failing to perform any of the above four requirements of the obligor, the mortgage contains several clauses which may be begun by the lender to take the property back in a foreclosure process. The most common cause of default is the failure of the borrower to meet the monthly payments. There is also usually a stipulation for a grace period during which the borrower can cure the default and resume meeting the obligation contained in the mortgage.

Acceleration Clause. (TC)

If a borrower defaults, the lender has a most important provision in the mortgage to allow him/her to collect the remaining debt called the acceleration clause. The acceleration clause allows the lender to declare the entire amount due and payable immediately. The acceleration clause can also indicate the grace period, the notification to the borrower that action will be undertaken, and the allowance of additional expenses involved in the foreclosure process to be charged to the borrower.

Waiver of Homestead. (TC)

Another important clause is the waiver of homestead. The homestead laws apply as exempting a borrower's principal residence (homestead) from being taken to satisfy a debt. Taking of the homestead can occur only where the homestead itself is pledged as collateral for the debt.

Defeasance Clause. (TC)

The defeasance clause in a mortgage states that when the debt is paid in full the mortgage is "null and void." In other words, when the debt is paid, the mortgage is defeated or ceases.

Alienation Clause/Due-on-Sale Clause. (TC)

Typical mortgages currently being written contain transfer clauses which will cover the interest in the property, if it is sold or transferred without the existing debt being paid off. The lender reserves the option under this type clause to: (1) call the entire loan due and payable under a due-on-sale or alienation clause; (2) have the purchaser of the property assume the mortgage, at which time the lender maintains the right to reset the interest rate on the mortgagee; and (3) release the original borrower from the obligations of the mortgage and note, if the purchaser is acceptable to the lender and the loan is assumed. This process is referred to as an assumption of mortgage.

If the purchaser is not acceptable to the lender, the transfer could occur, but would be referred to as "subject to the mortgage," and the original borrower is still liable under the original terms of the mortgage and note. The original borrower is not released from liability. The original borrower remains liable on the assumption arrangement unless the mortgagee has issued a release of liability. Many lenders do not like this kind of assumption of mortgage, called "non-qualifying" assumption. They frequently include a clause in the mortgage preventing a "non-qualifying assumption."

Condemnation Clause. (TC)

Many mortgages contain a condemnation clause which states that if any branch of government takes the property or any part of it, the money paid by the government for the taking will be applied to the note/mortgage.

Satisfaction of Mortgage. (TC)

The satisfaction of mortgage is a document provided to the borrower by the lender when the debt is satisfied. It is sometime called a release of mortgage. Either of these documents is commonly recorded in the county clerk's office to give constructive notice of the satisfaction of the debt.

Estoppel. (TC)

If the mortgagee decides to sell the mortgage in order to raise capital for further investment, the estoppel clause in the mortgage provides that upon the request of the mortgagee, the mortgagor will furnish an estoppel certificate indicating the present value of the mortgage. Also known as the "certificate of no defense," this document precludes the mortgagors from claiming that they did not owe that amount in case of subsequent foreclosure.

First Mortgage/Second Mortgage. (TC)

The first mortgage is a legal document pledging collateral for a loan that has first priority over all other claims against the property except taxes and bonded indebtedness. The first mortgage will be superior to all subsequent mortgages in a foreclosure action.

A second mortgage is one which has a second place of priority behind the first mortgage. Any other mortgage after the second is also known as a junior mortgage.

Subordination. (TC)

Subordination refers to position of priority among mortgages. Sometimes a lender will voluntarily take a lower position in the positions of priority to gain some other favorable condition or position.

Chattle Liens or Mortgages.

Chattle is personal property. A chattle lien is a lien or mortgage on personal property.

Personalty.

Personalty is another word used to indicate personal property.

DEED OF TRUST (Title Theory-not used in Oklahoma) (TC)

A deed of trust is an instrument which conveys ownership rights to a third party, usually a trust company, as security for a debt. Essentially, a deed of trust is a mortgage. The parties involved in a deed of trust are the **TRUSTOR** (borrower), the **BENEFICIARY** (lender), and the **TRUSTEE** (the neutral third party).

In the deed of trust arrangement, the borrower gives the lender a note (the instrument of indebtedness) and the deed (of trust) is conveyed to a third party (trustee) where it is held until the note is paid off.

Of course, the deed of trust is recorded in the county where the property is located for the purpose of constructive notice.

In the deed of trust situation, the owner is said to have **NAKED** or **BARE** title because the purchaser has the usual rights of ownership such as possession, use and the right to sell. When the purchaser pays off the debt, the lender will authorize request of re-conveyance and the trustee will cancel the note and issue a re-conveyance or release deed which conveys the deed to the borrower. This document is then recorded by the borrower.

LENDING PRACTICES AND LENDER REQUIREMENTS (TC)

REDLINING (TC)

Redlining is a violation of the *Federal Fair Housing Law of 1968*. It is the practice of restricting the number of loans or the loan-to-value ratio in certain areas of a community based on the fact that the area is or is becoming racially integrated. Redlining may be done by insurance companies who refuse to sell insurance in an area because of race. It can also be done by a real estate company which refuses to list or sell houses in an area because of race.
The term "redlining" stems from the practice in former years of lending institutions drawing a red line around a neighborhood and indicating a refusal to make loans in the area because of race.

PREDATORY LENDING (TC)

Predatory lending practices are illegal. They are lending practices wherein the lender charges unsophisticated borrowers excessive charges for the loan. These charges are usually far in excess of customary practices. The penalty for such illegal lending practices is frequently a term in a federal penitentiary.

PRIMARY MORTGAGE MARKETS (TC)

Most real estate financing is provided by private lenders. The ability and authority to finance such activity may vary according to regulations imposed by the various governmental agencies. Regulated lending practices are those which conform to the regulations of FHA and VA and Rural Development. These federal agencies have been developed for the purpose of making housing more readily and easily affordable. Each has a set of regulations with which lenders and borrowers must conform in order to obtain the support of the federal agency.

Conventional mortgages are those that do not involve governmentally insured or guaranteed type programs. Payment of the debt is the responsibility of the borrower. Conventional loans typically involve large down payments, usually in the range of twenty percent or more. However, the advent of private mortgage insurance has made conventional lending competitive with other types by reducing down payment requirements.

Savings and Loan Associations.

Historically, savings and loan associations were the major source of residential loans. However, during the economic stress of the early 1980's many converted to other types of operations such as mortgage banking, commercial banking or simply closed. The main function of savings and loan associations, for the few which still exist, is to attract savings from a local area for investment back into that area in the form of mortgages. Savings and loans attract money from local savers and have an advantage over local banks in that they are able to pay slightly higher interest rates on accounts.

Savings and loan associations are either formed as stock companies or mutual companies, chartered either by the state in which they are located or by the federal government. *The Financial Institutions Reform, Recovery* and *Enforcement Act of 1989* provided for the dismantling of the Federal Home Loan Bank Board. The legislation also abolished the Federal Savings and Loan Insurance Corporation.

In the place of the FSLIC, the new law set up the Federal Deposit Insurance Corporation as the primary federal agency responsible for insuring the deposits of savings associations as well as banks.

The Office of Thrift Supervision has been created to replace the Federal Home Loan Bank Board. The OTS is under the supervision of the Treasury Department.

The type of loans in which the savings and loan associations specialize are primarily one to four units in size of properties located within one hundred miles of the main office for persons relying on non-governmental or conventional loans. The normal loan to value ratio is approximately 80%. However, higher percentage loans may be made if the borrower will purchase private mortgage insurance (PMI). The associations can make loans on other types of property as well as construction loans. However, the operation and activities, as well as regulations, governing associations may differ from area to area.

Disintermediation. (TC)

Disintermediation happens when depositors in Savings and Loan Associations take their money out of Savings and Loan accounts and arrange for the money to be deposited in such things as money market funds, bonds or government securities rather than in the Certificates of Deposit in the Savings and Loans. This practice in the 1980 was a serious difficulty for the Associations.

The Primary Mortgage Market system was restructured by two significant pieces of federal legislation. The first of these was the *Depository Institutions Deregulation and Monetary Control Act.* It was signed into law by President Carter. The act made commercial banks more competitive in the mortgage lending market. It also allowed Savings and Loan Associations to enter into higher risk loans such as business ventures and raw land. They suffered as a result of some bad lending practices in these new areas of lending.

Then, in 1989, President Bush signed the *Financial Institutions Reform, Recovery, and Enforcement Act* known as FIRREA. This resulted in the licensing and regulating of real estate appraisers and the closing of many existing Savings and Loan Associations.

Commercial Banks. (TC)

Commercial banks are depository institutions which are able to make loans for many reasons for many different activities. The majority of the funds under the control of or available for investment by commercial banks are demand deposits, short-term in nature. Therefore, the predominant type of loans by banks has been short term in nature. However, due to FIRREA and the *Depository Institutions Deregulation and Monetary Control Act*, banks are sources of long-term loans for real estate mortgage lending.

One lending activity of commercial banks for real estate has been and continues to be construction loans or interim financing for development purposes. In this activity, banks provide a scheduled, periodic and partial advance of funds to a builder as progress payments as each construction stage is completed. The lending area tends to be local in nature. Interest rates for construction loans are normally higher than long-term rates available on permanent loans.

Life Insurance Companies.

Life insurance companies generate large insurance reserves which are in fact savings, and are held for policy holders. The source of these funds is regional or national in nature and the sums of money are quite large. The investment of these funds is limited to some degree by the states in which companies are incorporated or licensed. Since the policy reserves are long-term in nature, insurance companies desire to invest in long-term assets that require a minimum of administration.

The placement of large sums of money with minimum administrative cost requires that insurance companies specialize in one or two types of lending activities. The minimum amount of loans with the maximum of dollars involved would be for large commercial projects such as shopping centers, apartment complexes, etc. The lending activities for these types of loans are also on a wide geographic basis.

A second type of lending activity would be the purchase in the secondary market of large blocks of existing mortgages from other lending agencies. The purchases would come from wide geographic areas, and thus, the insurance company would like to purchase loans which have either governmental insurance or governmental guarantees attached to them, or seasoned conventional loans where the down payments are substantial and/or private mortgage insurance exists for a part of the loan. The major objective of insurance companies is to deal with as few borrowers as possible, thus collections will be from large borrowers or from other lenders who service (collect the payments) the mortgages purchased in the secondary market.

Mortgage Companies. (TC)

Local lending activities are enhanced by mortgage banking companies which are in effect money brokers. The mortgage banker represents other institutional investors such as pension funds, insurance companies, savings banks, and the like. The company originates mortgages in the primary market for sale to these other institutional lenders in the secondary market, thus the control on the mortgage banking firm comes from the lenders to whom they are trying to sell loans.

The characteristics of the loans are determined by the type of purchaser in the secondary market. The mortgage banking firm does not lend its own money, but uses interim financing, typically from a commercial bank. As loans are originated, they are pledged as collateral for the interim financing and then the interim financing is paid off when the entire portfolio of loans is sold. This process is known as "warehousing" loans.

Mortgage bankers make their profits from two sources. First, loan origination fees are charged along with normal closing costs which generate income; and secondly, the function of servicing loans is performed by the local firm. Service consists of collecting monthly payments and arranging for their proper distribution; i.e. a portion is allocated to escrow or to an impound account for the payment of taxes and insurance, with the principal and interest passed on the institutional lender. For making the collections on the mortgage package, and forwarding only one payment to the owner of the package of mortgages, the mortgage banking firm collects a service fee. Mortgage banking companies serve as correspondent or intermediary position between the borrower and the final lender in the marketplace.

Mortgage Brokers. (TC)

A broker is defined as a person or organization who finds someone who wants to buy something and someone who wants to sell it and gets the two together for the transaction and collects a Commission for facilitating the transaction. Mortgage brokers are individuals or companies who are licensed by the state and find persons who wish to borrow money to purchase a house and persons or institutions who wish to lend money on real estate and facilitate the transaction. Of course, they expect to collect a Commission on the transaction. In Oklahoma, mortgage brokers are licensed by the Department of Consumer Credit.

Mortgage brokers do not have money of their own for lending. They facilitate the transactions for investors of various kinds. They may do FHA, VA or conventional loans.

ROLE OF GOVERNMENTAL AGENCIES IN MORTGAGE LENDING (TC)

Federal Housing Administration. (TC)

One of the purposes of the *National Housing Act of 1934*, which established the Federal Housing Administration, was to provide long-term loans with higher loan to value ratios. The FHA operates and administers many lending programs for which it will underwrite mortgage insurance. The FHA programs are not direct lending programs, but only provide insurance on qualified properties and individuals. The list of various FHA programs is long and changes from time to time.

The four major functions of FHA are to:

1. Provide insurance for mortgages;
2. Provide stability in the buying and selling of mortgages in the secondary mortgage market;
3. Raise building standards; and
4. Facilitate and encourage home ownership.

Veterans Administration (VA). (TC)

Another prominent government agency involved in the mortgage market is the Veteran's Administration. While not a direct lender, the VA guarantees loans made to eligible veterans. The definition of eligibility varies from time to time. The current definition may be obtained from the Veteran's Administration. Eligible veterans may secure certificates of eligibility from the Veteran's Administration which outlines their benefits. They may then apply to any designated VA lender for a loan under the program.

The Veteran's Administration is authorized to guarantee loans for the eligible veteran. The distinction between the VA and the FHA loan is that, while the FHA is insured and a premium is required for that insurance, the Veteran's Administration loan is a guarantee program and involves no cost to the veteran. However, in recent years the VA has established a funding fee which it charges veterans for making the guarantee available. Congress passed increases in the fee in 1982, 1991 and 1993. This fee is charged for interest rate buy downs, manufactured housing loans, and for assumptions by other veterans.

Conventional Financing. (TC)

Conventional mortgages are those that do not involve governmentally insured or guaranteed type programs. Payment of the debt is the responsibility of the borrower. Conventional loans typically involve large down payments, usually in the range of twenty percent. In recent years conventional loans are available as conventional insured or conventional uninsured. Conventional insured loans involve private mortgage insurance which allows for a lower down payment. Conventional uninsured typically require a twenty percent down payment and are not insured.

Loan to Value Ratio. (TC)

The loan to value ratio is the relationship between the amount of the loan and the appraised value of the security, the property, expressed as a percentage of the appraised value. A loan with a twenty percent down payment would be expressed as an 80% loan to value ratio. A loan with a three percent down payment would be expressed as a 97% loan to value ratio.

Amortized Loan. (TC)

An amortizing loan is one in which a portion of each payment goes to reduce the amount of outstanding principal and another portion goes to pay the interest due on the loan. The amortizing mortgage is popular in America because by the end of the loan term all of the interest and principal is paid and the borrower owes no more money.

Origination Fee. (TC)

The origination fee is a price charged by the lender for doing all the work necessary for the borrower to get the loan. It includes the overhead of the lender, the loan officer's salary, etc. It is usually a percentage of the loan amount. Frequently it is one percent of the loan amount.

Mortgage Insurance. (TC)

Lenders have historically considered a loan in which the borrower has 20% of his or her own money invested to be "safe." That is to say, the borrower is less likely to default on a loan in which he has a significant amount of money invested. However, it became apparent that with a lower down payment requirement than 20%, more loans could be made. Therefore, mortgage insurance was created for the purpose of insuring the first 20% of the loan in favor of the lender so the borrower could purchase a property with a lower down payment. With mortgage insurance, if the borrower defaulted, the lender's interest was insured.

Private mortgage insurance is available for conventional loans. This means that a borrower has the option of borrowing money from a conventional lender with a lower down payment (say 5%) and paying an insurance premium to insure the balance.

Another option a borrower on a conventional loan has is to make a 20% down payment and have no mortgage insurance.

There are several different types of mortgage insurance and it is wise to read the exclusions section of these policies just as you would for any other insurance.

Up-Front Mortgage Insurance Premium. (TC)

FHA is a government program which sells insurance for mortgages. They do not lend money. They simply sell insurance on the mortgage to make it a little easier for the borrower to produce the down payment funds. The Up Front Mortgage Insurance is a premium which is paid by the borrower "up front" when the loan is made. The amount of this insurance is 1.5% of the loan amount. This UFMIP is a one time payment. In addition, the FHA also charges an annual premium which is one half of one percent of the loan balance. In other words, 1/12 of the annual premium is added to the monthly payment.

TYPES OF MORTGAGES (TC)

The types of mortgages can be discussed in two different ways. First, mortgages can be typified by the payment structure which is associated with a specific mortgage, and secondly, mortgages can be identified by the source of funds. Prior to the 1930's most mortgages were term mortgages which were interest only loans for a stipulated time period. None of the principal was reduced, and therefore the mortgages had to be renewed or refinanced at stipulated time periods. Another type was the interest extra loan in which a fixed amount of principal was repaid in installments along with accrued interest on the declining principal balance.

BUDGET MORTGAGE (TC)

After the impact of the depression, the creation of the Federal Housing Administration (FHA) resulted in the creation of a budget mortgage. This new mortgage was an installment note, a fully amortizing mortgage, which means the principal would be fully paid off over the life of the mortgage. Each payment contained both principal and interest, and at the end of the mortgage period, the debt would have been fully satisfied. This is probably the most commonly used type of mortgage in residential loans. It is sometimes called a PITI mortgage; the letters representing Principal, Interest, Taxes and Insurance.

BLANKET MORTGAGE (TC)

A blanket mortgage is one which includes more than one parcel of real estate under a single mortgage. A blanket mortgage covers more than one parcel of piece of property and is relatively common in the development of property. The difference between a blanket mortgage and a regular mortgage is that a release clause will be included, stipulating the terms by which the borrower can remove one of the parcels as security for the debt.

PACKAGE MORTGAGE (TC)

A package mortgage includes both real property as well as fixtures and appliances, normally thought of as personal property, which are located on the premises. These types of loans have become more common as apartment complexes are bought and sold with furnishings and fixtures included in the price.

OPEN-END MORTGAGE (TC)

An open end mortgage permits the mortgagor to borrower additional money after the loan has been reduced without rewriting the mortgage.

PURCHASE MONEY MORTGAGE (TC)

Real estate licensees sometimes call a loan which the seller is carrying a purchase money mortgage. It is also sometimes called a seller carry back which is used to finance the purchase.

WRAP-AROUND MORTGAGE (TC)

A wrap-around mortgage is a form of seller financing typically used when interest rates are higher. A warp-around mortgage is placed "around" an existing mortgage but remains subordinate to the mortgage it "wraps."

An example of a wrap-around mortgage is as follows. There is an existing mortgage of $60,000 at 6% with fifteen years remaining on the loan. For this example, the available interest rate is 9%. The sales price of the subject property is $120,000 as negotiated between the seller and the buyer. The seller and the buyer agree to allow the buyer to "wrap" the existing mortgage of $60,000 at 6% with a new junior mortgage for $50,000 at 9% with the buyer giving the seller $10,000 down payment.

The advantage to the seller is that the property is sold for $120,000 with the first mortgage still in place. The seller remains responsible for this mortgage and makes payments. The seller is then in possession of the $10,000 down payment and a junior mortgage for $50,000 at 9% interest. Over time, this may become a suitable profit for the seller. The caveat is that the first mortgagee on the original mortgage must be informed of this change in ownership and approve of it.

The advantage to the buyer is the bulk of the purchase price is at the lower interest rate and is able to purchase the property at a lower net interest rate and payment.

REVERSE ANNUITY MORTGAGE (TC)

A reverse annuity mortgage is a mortgage in reverse. It is a way for a homeowner, frequently a senior citizen, who wants to continue living in his home but has a need for additional income. The homeowner sells the house but remains in it. He gets either a lump sum payment or a monthly payment. He does not repay the loan until he dies, in which case the buyer gets the house. If he sells the house, he must pay off the loan.

CONTRACT FOR DEED (TC)

A contract for deed, also known as an installment sales contract or as a land contract, is a conditional sales contract to purchase real property in which the buyer makes a down payment and where further payments are made in installments. In such contracts, the seller does not deliver the deed to the buyer until all, or a specified amount, has been paid on the price. In the event of default by the buyer, the seller is required by Section 11A of Title 16 Oklahoma Statutes (***Constructive Mortgage Statute of 1976***), to initiate a foreclosure action, even though the buyer does not have legal title to the real property. Duties of the buyer include paying taxes, insuring the property and maintaining the property. In a contract for deed, it may be months or years before the buyer receives a deed. It is common, therefore, to arrange for a third and neutral party to collect the buyer's payments and to assure that the contract terms are completed. This is referred to as a deed in escrow.

For deeds delivered in escrow, the deed must be delivered during the lifetime of the grantor, and, if he dies, title relates back to the date the deed was delivered to the escrow agent if all conditions of the escrow are met.

OPTION TO PURCHASE (TC)

An option is an executed unilateral contract. A person who is interested in purchasing a particular property may ask the seller to not sell the property for a specific time. This is a circumstance for which the buyer is willing to pay. Therefore, the buyer offers the seller a suitable amount of money and the seller agrees to not sell the property for a specific agreed upon time. The buyer may then use the time to assemble funds of do inspections, etc. and "exercise" the option to purchase, or not, as is deemed expedient by the buyer. During this "option period" the seller cannot sell to any one other than the potential buyer.

ADJUSTABLE RATE MORTGAGE (TC)

An adjustable rate mortgage is one in which the interest rate paid by the borrower is not fixed. Rather, it "adjusts" according to changes in the market's interest rate. Often the initial interest rate on an adjustable rate mortgage is lower than that available on a fixed rate mortgage.

Interest Rate. (TC)

The interest rate on an adjustable rate mortgage is arranged to go up or down according to some kind of interest rate sensitive instrument which changes with the demands of the marketplace. These "indexes" may be treasury bills or securities or bonds.

Margin. (TC)

Margin has to do with profit for the lender. It may be two or three percent depending on the particular loan. Generally, the margin rate stays the same during the loan. It may be, however, a good measure of ARMs for consumers. A lower margin rate may mean a lower payment for the borrower.

Interest Rate Cap. (TC)

Federal law requires lenders to disclose to borrowers on ARMs the interest rate cap on the loan. Frequently, the terms of the ARM are that the interest rate may increase only a certain amount per year. The rate of increase may be as low as one half of one percent or as high as two percent, perhaps more. Many lenders impose a total ceiling of as much as eighteen percent over the life of the loan.

Payment Cap. (TC)

A payment cap places a limit on how much increase can be made on a monthly payment in one year. A payment cap often used is around seven and one half percent. This means that no matter how much the margin rate and the interest rate increase, the total monthly payment can not increase more than the payment cap.

Negative Amortization. (TC)

Amortization is a process of making payments which "kill off" the remaining amount of principal borrowed. In a negative amortization situation, the amount of the monthly payment is insufficient to reduce the unpaid loan amount balance. In fact, in some cases, the monthly payment may be insufficient to even stay even resulting in the amount of outstanding principal increasing because unpaid interest is added to the outstanding balance. In some cases, a limit may be set on the level to which the unpaid accumulating principal may increase. This is often set at 125%.

AUTOMATED UNDERWRITING SYSTEM

Automated underwriting systems are computer software systems which make the loan application process very quick. The originator is able to enter information about the potential borrower into the computer where is it analyzed, verifying the borrower's income employment and assets. The software contains a uniform loan application. Once the information is analyzed the buyer is either accepted or not. If not, the borrower is classified as either "refer" or "caution". If the borrower is listed as refer, the application is sent to the underwriting department with four or more reasons why the application has been referred. If the application is listed as "caution," there are serious problems which prevent the loan from being made to the borrower.

Automated underwriting systems can speed up lending process and, under some circumstances, get an applicant approved in a matter of minutes.

GRADUATED PAYMENT MORTGAGE

A graduated payment mortgage has a fixed interest rate and maturity date but the monthly payments increase gradually as the mortgage matures. Generally the earlier payments are lower and may not be sufficient to pay principal and interest. Later, the monthly payment increases until, eventually, it begins to reduce the principal amount. The advantage of this type loan is to allow borrowers who are younger to purchase a house with lower payments, and, as their income may increase, their ability to reduce the principal may also increase.

CONSTRUCTION LOAN

A construction loan is also called an interim loan. It is obtained usually by a builder to finance the construction of the house. Generally, this loan is obtained from a bank and an account is set up for the builder. When each phase of the construction is reached, the builder is able to draw the necessary funds to pay for the construction. The lender usually does not want to lend the total amount of funds because the level of construction does not collateralize the full amount. These are generally balloon loans with interest only payments.

FORECLOSURES (TC)

When a borrower defaults on payments or fails to fulfill any of the other obligations set forth in the mortgage, the lender's rights can be enforced through foreclosure. Foreclosure is a legal procedure in which the property pledged as security is sold to satisfy the debt. The foreclosure procedure brings the rights of the parties and all junior lien holders to a conclusion. It passes title to either the person holding the mortgage document to a third party who purchases the realty at a foreclosure sale. The purchaser could be the mortagee. The property is sold free of the foreclosing mortgage and all junior liens.

DEED IN LIEU OF FORECLOSURE (TC)

An alternative to foreclosure is a deed in lieu of foreclosure. A lender may accept a deed from the borrower in lieu of proceeding with a foreclosure action. This is often known as a "friendly foreclosure" because it is done through mutual agreement of the borrower and the lender rather than by a foreclosure lawsuit. A major disadvantage of a deed in lieu of foreclosure is that the mortagee accepts the deed subject to any existing junior liens. In a foreclosure action, all junior liens are generally eliminated. Also by accepting a deed in lieu of foreclosure, the lender normally gives up any rights to FHA mutual mortgage insurance or private mortgage insurance or VA guarantees. Another disadvantage is that the lender gives up the right to obtain a deficiency judgment in the event he is unable to sell the property for enough to recover his investment. In addition, a deed in lieu of foreclosure generally results in a negative entry on the borrower's credit report.

EQUITY OF REDEMPTION (TC)

Most states give defaulting borrowers a change to redeem their property through an equitable right of redemption. After default but before the foreclosure sale, the borrower pays the amount in default, plus administrative costs and fees, the debt will usually be reinstated. In some instances the person who repays the loan may be required to pay the full outstanding amount. If a person other than the mortgagor pays the outstanding debt, the mortgagor becomes liable to that person.

Some states allow borrowers who are in default a period of time in which to redeem their property after the foreclosure sale. This period varies from states to state and may be as long as three years. The mortgagor who can raise the funds to redeem the property will pay the money into the court. In Oklahoma, the period of redemption is relatively brief. At the foreclosure sales, the purchaser is generally required to pay 10% of the purchase price at the time of purchase and the balance within thirty days. At that point, in Oklahoma, the borrower has no further right of redemption.

JUDICIAL FORECLOSURE (TC)

Judicial foreclosure allows the property to be sold by a court order after the mortgagee has given sufficient notice. When a borrower defaults, the lender may accelerate the due date of all remaining monthly payments. The lender's attorney can then file a suit to foreclose the lien. After presentation of the facts in court, the property is ordered sold. A public sale is advertised and held, and the real estate is sold to the highest bidder.

POWER OF SALE FORECLOSURE (TC)

Non-judicial foreclosure is allowed in some states including Oklahoma. When the security instrument, the mortgage, contains a Power-of-Sale clause, in non-judicial foreclosure, no court action is required.

To institute a non-judicial foreclosure, the mortgagee may be required to record a notice of default at the county clerk's office. The default must be recorded within a designated time to give adequate notice to the public of the intended auction. This official notice is generally accompanied by advertisements that state the amount due and the date of the public sale. After the property is sold, the mortgagee may be required to file a copy of a notice of sale or an affidavit of foreclosure. In Oklahoma, the mortgagee often may elect judicial foreclosure rather than non-judicial foreclosure or power of sale foreclosure.

STRICT FORECLOSURE (TC)

Although judicial foreclosure is the prevalent practice, it is still possible in some states for a lender to acquire mortgaged property through a strict foreclosure process.

First, appropriate notice must be given to the delinquent borrower. Once the proper papers have been prepared and recorded, the court establishes a deadline by which time the balance of the defaulted debt must be paid in full. If the borrower does not pay off the loan by that date, the court simply awards full legal title to the lender. No sale takes place.

DEFICIENCY JUDGMENT (TC)

The foreclosure sale may not produce enough cash to pay the loan balance in full after deducting expenses and accrued unpaid interest. In this case, the mortgagee may be entitled to a personal judgment against the borrower for the unpaid balance. Such judgment is a deficiency judgment. It may also be obtained against any endorsers or guarantors of the note and against any owners of the mortgaged property who assumed the debt by written agreement. However, if any money remains from the foreclosure sale after paying the debt and any other lines such as a second mortgage of a mechanic's lien, expenses and interest, these proceeds are paid to the borrower.

SHORT SALE (TC)

A short sale occurs when a foreclosure is in process. The foreclosure sale has not yet taken place and the home owner is still in possession of the property. Some lenders will negotiate with a potential purchaser in order the "cut" the losses which will inevitably accompany a foreclosure. This is a part of a loss mitigation program for lenders. Please, note, however, not all lenders will entertain an offer in short sale (sometimes called a "short pay") situation.

Ch. 15

TEST YOUR UNDERSTANDING

1. The availability of real property loans may be affected importantly by which of the following actions of the Federal Reserve Bank?
    1. Increasing he reserve requirement of member banks of the Federal Reserve Bank System.
    2. Selling government securities in the open market.
    3. Increasing the discount rate charged member banks of the Federal Reserve Bank.
    4. All of the above.

2. Real estate loans are relatively liquid and market able because of the
    1. great value of the securities.
    2. size and number of lenders involved in originating them.
    3. primary mortgage market.
    4. secondary mortgage market.

3. A buyer is qualified to obtain an FHA loan for the purchase of a new home. From which of the following may a loan be obtained?
    1. Federal Housing Administration.
    2. Federal National Mortgage Association.
    3. A qualified lending institution.
    4. Federal Home Loan Bank System.

4. Sources of funds for mortgages would include
    1. savings and loan associations.
    2. commercial banks and private parties.
    3. pension funds and credit unions.
    4. All of the above.

5. The factor which generally exerts the greatest influence on mortgage interest rates is the
    1. condition of the money market.
    2. value of mortgaged properties.
    3. terms of loans secured by mortgaged properties.
    4. stabilizing result of offsetting ultra-conservative and over-optimistic practices of mortgage lenders.

6. Interest on a real estate mortgage loan is usually paid
    1. in arrears.
    2. in advance.
    3. as the borrower is able to pay.
    4. when the loan is due.

7. The practice of charging points in connection with mortgage loans is because of the lender's desire to
    1. increase the effective yield.
    2. obtain the market yield.
    3. close the gap between market rates and fixed rates.
    4.. All of the above.

8. A mortgage that covers a number of parcels of real property and that may provide for the release of each parcel as certain payments are made to reduce the loan is a(n)
    1. blanket mortgage.
    2. open-end mortgage.
    3. balloon mortgage.
    4. partially amortized mortgage.

9. A balloon mortgage
    1. has a final payment significantly larger than all the others.
    2. can be increased by borrowing additional funds at a later date.
    3. expands principal balance as payments are applied.
    4. is a mortgage taken back from the purchaser, by the seller, as part of the purchase price.

10. The Veterans Administration
    1. guarantees lenders against the loss caused by the borrower's default on a loan.
    2. insures loans.
    3. normally provides money to eligible veterans for the purchase of homes.
    4. pays all closing costs.

11. When the FHA insures a lender against default, the insurance
    1. carries the full faith and credit of the United States Government.
    2. is backed by the insurance fund established by the Federal Housing Administration.
    3. doesn't mean a thing.
    4. guarantees that no foreclosure action will ever be necessary.

12. On an FHA loan, the buyer would NOT
    1. be required to pay a 20% down payment.
    2. need to find an approved lender willing to make the loan.
    3. have to buy a house that meets minimum FHA construction standards.
    4. be charged for mortgage insurance to protect the lender, the premium for which could be paid by the seller.

13. The acceleration clause in a note is
    1. the holder's right to call all the balance due in event of default.
    2. the right of the mortgagor to make advance payments without penalty.
    3. a provision used to protect the mortgagor's interest.
    4. Both 2 and 3.

14. A clause making the entire balance of a loan due if property is sold and/or title transferred is a(n)
    1. subordination clause.
    2. alienation or "due on sale" clause.
    3. "dead end" clause.
    4. escalator clause.

15. An alienation clause, if the mortgaged property is sold
    1. allows a lender the opportunity to accept or reject the purchaser as a substitute.
    2. gives the lender an opportunity to eliminate low interest rate loans.
    3. Both 1 and 2.
    4. Neither 1 nor 2.

16. A mortgage contained a clause making the entire debt due if the mortgagor conveyed title to the property to a third person. The property was conveyed. The mortgagee brought an action to accelerate the debt.
    1. The mortgagee will win.
    2. The purchaser will be held liable.
    3. The acceleration clause is void.
    4. The mortgagor will win.

17. When financing a real estate transaction, the prudent lender usually seeks assurance that
    1. the borrower's credit is satisfactory and they have adequate ability to repay the loan.
    2. the market value of the real property used as security for the loan is more than the amount borrowed.
    3. title to the real property used as security for the loan is good.
    4. All of the above.

18. Mortgage lending policies of typical financial institutions are LEAST influenced by which of the following?
    1. The relative attractiveness of other forms of investment.
    2. The present and potential value of a property.
    3. The borrower's need for financial assistance.
    4. The location of the property.

19. A mortgagee is a person who
    1. lends money to a mortgagor.
    2. borrows money and puts property up as loan security.
    3. leases real property.
    4. purchase land on the installment plan.

20. The written instrument, known as the "debt instrument," that usually accompanies the mortgage is the
    1. deed.
    2. abstract of title.
    3. contract of sale.
    4. promissory note.

21. When property fails to sell at a court foreclosure for an amount sufficient to satisfy the mortgage debt, the mortgagee may sue for which of the following?
    1. A judgment by default.
    2. A deficiency judgment.
    3. A satisfaction of mortgage.
    4. A deed in lieu of foreclosure.

22. In the event of a sheriff's sale after foreclosure where the net amount received is greater than the indebtedness, the excess would belong to the
    1. mortgagor.
    2. mortgagee.
    3. Sheriff's office.
    4. purchaser.

23. A mortgage is
    1. a signed document acknowledging he existence of a debt.
    2. a pledge of security for repayment of a debt.
    3. the same as a promissory note.
    4. always signed by the mortgagee.

24. An instrument executed by the mortgagor showing the amount of unpaid balance due on the mortgage, and that the mortgagor admits is owed on the debt and must pay in full at maturity, is a(n)

    1. estoppel certificate.
    2. subrogation certificate.
    3. certificate of full release.
    4. default disclaimer.

25. A release clause in a mortgage
    1. provides for an option to extend its due date.
    2. releases a guarantor from further liability under specified conditions.
    3. when a part of a document creates a lien second only to the lien of taxes and assessments.
    4. Allows portions of the property given as security to be released from the mortgage lien upon performance of specified acts.

26. A mortgagee may include in a mortgage items which, when they occur, are considered default by the mortgagor and grounds for a foreclosure action. Such items include all of the following EXCEPT
    1. non-payment of real property taxes.
    2. negligence in caring for the property.
    3. illegal use of the property.
    4. detrimental zoning by a city or county.

27. When title to real estate is taken "subject to" an existing mortgage, the
1. buyer does not become liable for repayment of the loan.
2. seller remains responsible for the repayment of the loan.
3. Both 1 and 2.
4. Nether 1 nor 2.

ANSWERS AND EXPLANATIONS

1. 4 Traditional means of government regulation of the money market.

2. 4 By buying mortgages after they have been originated, the secondary mortgage market returns money to the primary money market for more new loans.

3. 3 Only qualified lending institutions provide money for the purchase of FHA homes. Neither FHA nor secondary mortgage agencies normally make loans.

4. 4 The major source of primary mortgage funds.

5. 1 Availability of money ant its cost are the primary factors in determining interest rates.

6. 1 Interest on a mortgage is simple interest, usually calculated and paid at the end of each month.

7. 4 The three basic reasons for charging discount points.

8. 1 The description of a blanket mortgage.

9. 1 The distinguishing feature of a balloon mortgage.

10. 1 The function of the VA in the mortgage market is to guarantee mortgage loans made for qualified veterans. It neither lends money nor insures loans.

11. 2 Losses are paid from insurance funded by premium paid by borrowers.

12. 1 FHA down payments may be as low as 3%.

13. 1 The acceleration clause is triggered by failure to conform to covenants in the note or mortgage, such as failure to make payments, pay taxes, pay insurance, etc.

14. 2 The due-on-sale clause effectively eliminates the possibility of the new buyer's assuming the mortgage unless the mortgagee permits the assumption.

15. 3 The lender's primary concern with a due-on-sale clause is to renegotiate interest rates if they have increased significantly since the loan's origination date.

16. 1 Violation of the due-on-sale clause causes the entire debt to become due and payable.

17. 4 Lending institutions take all of these items into account when making a loan.

18. 3 Unfortunately, it is not how bad a person needs financial assistance buy rather an ability to repay which influences whether money can be borrowed or not.

19. 1 Remember, "ee" is for receive. The mortgagee receives a mortgage. The mortgagee is also the lender while the mortgagor is the lendee.

20. 4 The first instrument signed at a financial closing is the promissory note acknowledging the debt and promising to repay.

21. 2 This is the procedure for a deficiency judgment which, if obtained, is levied against the borrower personally for the balance of a mortgage debt when a foreclosure sale fails to generate funds sufficient to satisfy the debt's outstanding balance.

22. 1 Under judicial foreclosing proceedings, if the foreclosure sale generates more money than is required to satisfy the indebtedness and expenses, the excess funds are paid to the borrower.

23. 2 While the note is the debt instrument, the mortgage is the security instrument pledging the property in case of default.,

24. 1 The estoppel certificate is provided by the mortgagor confirming the unpaid balance of the debt.

25. 4. The release clause typically used in a blanket mortgage, enables the mortgagor to obtain partial releases of specified parcels from the mortgage upon the payment of a larger than pro rata portion of the loan.

26. 4 The first three are items which would trigger the acceleration clause, causing the note and mortgage to be in default and bringing about a foreclosure action.

27. 3 When a purchaser acquires a property "subject to" an existing mortgage, the purchaser is placed under no personal obligation to repay the note and the seller is not relieved of repayment responsibilities.

CLOSING A TRANSACTION

PRE-CLOSING PROCEDURES (TC)

The full complexity of the real estate transaction becomes obvious in the closing process. All the details of the purchase contract must be handled or prepared for between the time of signing by the
parties and the actual closing meeting. The details of title search and the curing of any problems, decisions as to how the buyer may take title, loan arrangements, check of property tax records, inspections, and reports must all be accomplished to complete a closing.

Many real estate brokerage firms rely on professional closing agencies to accomplish closing. Since closing is a complex process involving multiple details that vary with each transaction, the assistance of a closing specialist may be a good idea. However, the fact remains that, no matter who closes the transaction, the listing broker generally retains responsibility. Therefore, the broker and associates must be highly knowledgeable and adept in understanding the closing process and all of its details and accounting procedures.

BUYER'S FINAL INSPECTION WALK-THROUGH (TC)

It is a generally accepted good practice for the buyer to inspect the property just prior to the closing meeting. In most circumstances, it may have been several days or even weeks since the buyer made the initial inspection and looking at the property just prior to closing is for the purpose of allowing the buyer to make certain that any agreements in the contract were accomplished. Should the buyer discover that the seller has damaged the property or appliances do not work, a list of these should be made and funds withheld or escrowed at closing to pay for any necessary repairs or replacements.

SELLER'S ISSUES AND RESPONSIBILITIES AT CLOSING (TC)

The seller is generally responsible for performing certain contract terms such as providing compliance with inspections and repair requirements and title in such condition as is acceptable to the buyer.

The seller should also bring garage door remote controls, door keys, access Codes to any security system, etc. If the property is part of a home owner's association or condominium, a copy of the bylaws and fees may be helpful. Additionally, any conditions, covenants and restrictions (Car's) affecting the property should be disclosed to the buyer.

If income is generated by the property, a rent statement and expenditures should also be made available to the buyer. Also, a letter to the tenants about the change in the ownership should be furnished.

BUYER'S ISSUES AND RESPONSIBILITIES AT CLOSING (TC)

The buyer's responsibility relates to the performance of his/her side of the contract. Generally, in a real estate purchase contract, the buyer promises to exchange money (or something of value acceptable to the seller) for the deed (ownership rights). Therefore, the primary responsibility of the buyer is to bring money to the closing. This may be in the form of "cash" (check) or funding through a lending institution. When the funds are exchanged for the deed, the contract is performed. However, the real estate transaction may prove to be one of the most complex transactions on the planet. The following will build upon that premise.

REAL ESTATE BROKER'S ROLE AT CLOSING (TC)

It is generally accepted that the listing broker is responsible for the closing. This is because of regional custom and the fact that the broker was hired through the listing agreement to market the property and, possibly, advocate for the seller until the transaction is "closed." As the "professional" associated with the transaction, the broker is responsible for attending to the administrative tasks during the executory period of the contract which allow for the parties to perform their side of the contract.

The buyer is interested in receiving a deed without unacceptable flaws. The seller is interested in receiving the bargained for value in exchange for the deed. The broker is responsible for guiding and educating the parties to the contract so they may adequately perform.

"DRY" OR "TENDER" CLOSING

There are occasions when the buyer (or possibly the seller) illegally refuses to close. In this case, the first step for the broker is to contact his/her attorney because an illegal refusal to close constitutes a breach of the contract. No broker should attempt to take care of a breach or potential breach without advice from an attorney.

In the case of a potential breach, an attorney may advise a "dry" or "tender" closing. A dry closing is one that is complete in all of the contract requirements except for the final acts of fund disbursements and delivery of documents. In law, the word "tender" means an offer. In the case of a "dry" closing, the seller is offering the deed in exchange for the agreed upon terms.

In the case where the seller illegally refuses to close, a buyer could hold a "dry" closing, tendering the agreed upon price. This would likely be conducted by the buyer's representative.

The broker will schedule the closing. All documents including the earnest money from the trust account will be prepared. The seller and the broker will meet for the closing at the appointed time prepared for disbursement and document delivery.

If the buyer attends the closing and participates as called for in the contract, there is no breach. If, however, the buyer does not attend, the seller and the broker have demonstrated their willingness to close according to the contract terms and are in a better position in the event of a suit. Obviously, the reverse is true in the case of buyer brokerage.

CLOSER'S RESPONSIBILITY (TC)

Frequently, a professional closing company is hired to handle all of the process of the closing. This does not relieve the broker of the responsibility for the closing, but does provide the parties and the broker(s) with a professional who is accustomed to performing the closing function as a part of his daily business.

The closer needs the buyer's name(s) exactly how he/she wants to take title on the deed. The closer will also require the buyer's social security account number. This will be required by the lending institution.

The closer will need the correct address and legal description of the property that is being sold. It is essential the legal description be correct in order to prevent errors in conveyancing.

It will be necessary to have the seller's full name(s) and a copy of the title policy the seller received when he/she bought the property, or possibly help in locating the abstract of title.

The next thing the closer will do is order a survey or check to see if one is being ordered. Then the closer will order loan payoff on the existing loan making sure it is good at time of closing. Then the closer will contact licensees, buyer, seller or whomever might have the following information:

      a. termite certificate.
      b. plumbing inspection and any other inspections.
      c. lender repairs.
      d. well and septic inspection of required.
      e. plumbing repairs.
      f. home owner warranty program, if any.
      g. any repairs that need to be made and bills that need to be added to the settlement statement.

Following this, the closer will read the contract to determine what its terms are and who has agreed to pay for what service(s), etc.

The closing package is required to be obtained from the lender 24 hours before closing.

Next, the closer will calculate the closing statement figuring in taxes and other pro-rations.

The closer will then verify funds and, if at all possible, get the figures to the buyer ahead of time.

The closer will prepare the documents necessary for the closing including a 1099 for reporting the transaction to the Internal Revenue Service.

As a final preparation, the closer will check all the documents and figures for accuracy.

At the closing the closer will verify the identities of the buyer(s) and seller(s) normally by checking drivers' licenses.

Then the closing is conducted during which the closer explains the documents to the buyer and seller and obtains signatures on appropriate documents.

After the closing, the closer will make sure all documents are filed, packages are delivered to the lender, title policies are issued and sent to respective parties in a timely manner and also ensure the recording of all necessary documents.

IRS REPORTING REQUIREMENTS (TC)

Sale of all real estate is reported to the Internal Revenue Service on a Form 1099. When the closing is completed, the following people are responsible, in priority order, to complete the Form 1099 and send it to the IRS:

>First: the closer.
>Second: the lender.
>Third: the selling broker.
>Fourth: the buying broker.
>Fifth: any one designated by the U. S. Treasury.

The 1099 form is filed as a part of the closing process and no charge is made to a taxpayer for the service.

THE CLOSING (TC)

The way in which a real estate firm handles the process of closing is important to the future success of the firm. If the closing is handled poorly, it is likely the buyer and seller will not wish to repeat the experience with that company. However, the reverse is also true. If there are no surprises at closing and all the parties to the transaction are satisfied, the buyers and seller may become "repeat business" at some time in the future. This is one salient reason brokers use professional closing companies when possible.

It is obvious the degree of quality in which the company handles this phase of the transaction will contribute to both "word of mouth" advertising and future business. Therefore, the work of a broker or associates have only just begun with the signing of the contract.

The closing function of the firm is to ensure a "good" closing for all parties involved. A closing involves not only the buyer, seller, and broker(s), but includes the lending institution, the title insurance company, the attorney, inspector(s), etc. All these have input and may create or solve problems.

Step one is for the real estate company to assume responsibility for the closing. The custom, practice and presidence have indicated the listing broker is generally responsible for the closing, among other things. Included in this responsibility may be the broker helping the parties to the contract select a closing company.

The next step is to see that all the closing documents are prepared in advance and, when possible, submitted to the appropriate party(ies). Procrastination in document preparation, presentation and review is the source of trouble. Timely preparation helps to prevent errors. The parties to the closing have the opportunity to review the documents to find and correct errors and resolve objections.

An area of the closing costs is where the broker has a teaching job to do. There are perceptions in the minds of the buyer and seller with which to deal. Frequently, the buyer and the seller view "closing costs" as a lump sum which is to be "taken care of" at the closing table. Experienced real estate brokers and associates realize there may be items of expense that are not part of "closing costs" which must be satisfied. For example, some utility bills may be paid in advance. The buyer must purchase the unused portion of the bills. These expenses may not be considered "closing costs," depending on the customs of the area.

Typical closing costs may include:

>Taxes and insurance premiums for escrow.
>Any special assessments.
>Documentary (or conveyance) stamps.

Broker's Commission.
Termite or pest inspection.
Environmental audit or inspection.
Recording fees.
Closing company's fee.
Electrical/mechanical inspection.
Loan origination.
Attorney fee.
Survey fee.
Credit report.
Transfer fee.
Title insurance premium.
Mortgage insurance premium.

(**NOTE**: This is not a complete list as there may be other fees depending on the terms of the loan and the contract).

Closers frequently prepare a checklist of items which must be accomplished prior to closing and another check list of items to be done at the closing meeting.

It is the custom in Oklahoma and other areas of the West and Southwest for closing companies to handle the closing. The documents are delivered to the closing company which holds them until all are complete. The function of the broker (real estate firm) will be to work with the closing company to see that all documents are prepared, complete and correct. This business practice helps to eliminate procrastination and "surprises."

When all the documents are prepared and reviewed, the closing company will have a "closing meeting" for the purpose of completing the transaction. The seller "delivers" title (deed) to the buyer in exchange for the agreed upon price. In Oklahoma, transfer of title takes place upon delivery of the deed to the grantee/buyer.

DELIVERY OF THE DEED

When the deed is delivered and accepted by the buyer/grantee, title has transferred. Delivery and acceptance must occur during the lifetime of the grantor. The deed must be signed by the grantor, be in writing, contain the names of the grantor and the grantee, contain the words of conveyance, and contain a correct legal description. While it is not a legal requirement that a deed be recorded in the County Clerk's office, failure to record avoids the legal presumption of delivery and acceptance.

REAL ESTATE SETTLEMENT AND PROCEDURES ACT (TC)

The Real Estate Settlement Procedures Act (RESPA) requirements apply when the purchase of residential real estate is financed by a federally related mortgage loan. By definition, a federally related loan includes any loans made by banks, savings and loan associations, or other lenders who are covered by either the Federal Deposit Insurance Corporation, those insured by FHA or guaranteed by the Veterans Administration, those loans to be sold to Fannie Mae, GNMA, or FHLMC or any loans administered by the Department of Housing and Urban Development.

The requirement under RESPA requires a lender to:

1. Provide a copy of the booklet *"Settlement Costs and You"* to every person making a loan application.

2. At the time a loan application is taken, or within three (3) business days, provide the borrower with a good faith estimate of the cost to close the loan;

3. Provide the loan closing information on a Uniform Settlement Statement which details all financial particulars in the transaction. The borrower may, upon request, inspect the settlement statement one day prior to the closing, to the extent that the figures are available.

The requirements under RESPA explicitly disallow the payment of kickbacks in any form. Kickbacks may be considered mortgage fraud and may carry fines and/or prison penalties.

TITLE 24, CODE OF FEDERAL REGULATIONS, PART 3500, APPENDIX A (TC)

"The following are instructions for completing sections A through L of the *Uniform Settlement Statement*, **HUD-1**, required under Section 4 of RESPA and called *Regulation X*. This form is to be used as a uniform settlement statement of actual costs and adjustments to be given to the parties in connection with the settlement. The instructions for completion of the form are primarily for the benefit of the persons who prepare the statements and need not be transmitted to the parties as an integral part of the form. There is no objection to the use of the form in transactions in which its use is not legally required."

RESTRICTIONS-KICKBACKS, EXCESS AMOUNTS IN ESCROW (AGGREGATE ADJUSTMENT) (TC)

Compliance with *the Real Estate Settlement Procedures Act* is mandatory for all persons involved in the real estate business. Persons who have violated RESPA have received penalties including triple damages, fines and imprisonment.

Specifically, RESPA covers real estate licensees, mortgage lenders, title companies, home owner warranty companies, hazard insurance companies, appraisers, flood and tax service providers, and inspection services. Moving companies, gardeners, painters, etc. are not covered.

Specifically, RESPA makes it illegal for a real estate broker or associate to receive "a thing of value" for referring business to a closing company or a mortgage banker, mortgage broker, title company, etc. RESPA also makes it illegal for the service provider to split fees for settlement services unless there is an actual service performed.

Affiliated Business Arrangements. (TC)

Some real estate firms own an interest in a closing company or mortgage brokerage operation. This is legal and the licensee must disclose the relationship with the joint venture company when it refers a customer and does not require the customer to use the joint venture operation as a condition of the sale or purchase.

Additionally, RESPA requires that the real estate firm which is owner or part owner of such an affiliated business arrangement does not receive any payment(s) from the affiliated business arrangement other than a return on its ownership interest in the company. RESPA also requires that these payments can not vary according to the volume of referrals the real estate firm makes to the affiliated business arrangement.

Aggregate adjustment. (TC)

The aggregate adjustment (or aggregate analysis) is an accounting method a service uses in conducting an account analysis of an escrow account by computing the sufficiency of an escrow account's funds by analyzing the account as a whole. Basically, what this means is the government will only allow the lender to keep a certain amount in an escrow account for a given time period. The lender can no longer keep excessive funds in an escrow account to make money (interest). This is the monthly escrow prepaid deposits.

Generally, the aggregate adjustment is a credit to the borrower and reduces the amount for all combined escrow items such as hazard insurance premiums, private mortgage insurance and taxes. The adjustment is an attempt to ensure that the escrow account, when reaching its lowest level during a given year, contains more than the allowable cushion selected by the lender, usually two months. However, the intent is to ensure the lender does not keep an excessive amount of the borrower's money in escrow.

REGULATIONS AFFECTING REAL ESTATE

The Oklahoma Real Estate License Code

§59-858-101. Title and construction.

This Code shall be known and cited as "The Oklahoma Real Estate License Code". Laws 1974, c. 121, § 101, operative July 1, 1974.

§59-858-102. Definitions.

When used in this Code, unless the context clearly indicates otherwise, the following words and terms shall be construed as having the meanings ascribed to them in this section:

1. The term "real estate" shall include any interest or estate in real property, within or without the State of Oklahoma, whether vested, contingent or future, corporeal or incorporeal, freehold or nonfreehold, and including leaseholds, options and unit ownership estates to include condominiums, time-shared ownerships and cooperatives; provided, however, that the term "real estate" shall not include oil, gas or other mineral interests, or oil, gas or other mineral leases; and provided further, that the provisions of this Code shall not apply to any oil, gas, or mineral interest or lease or the sale, purchase or exchange thereof;

2. The term "real estate broker" shall include any person, partnership, association or corporation, foreign or domestic, who for a fee, commission or other valuable consideration, or who with the intention or expectation of receiving or collecting a fee, commission or other valuable consideration, lists, sells or offers to sell, buys or offers to buy, exchanges, rents or leases any real estate, or who negotiates or attempts to negotiate any such activity, or solicits listings of places for rent or lease, or solicits for prospective tenants, purchasers or sellers, or who advertises or holds himself out as engaged in such activities;

3. The term "broker associate" shall include any person who has qualified for a license as a broker and who is employed or engaged by, associated as an independent contractor with, or on behalf of, a broker to do or deal in any act, acts or transaction set out in the definition of a broker;

4. The term "real estate sales associate" shall include any person having a renewable license and employed or engaged by, or associated as an independent contractor with, or on behalf of, a real estate broker to do or deal in any act, acts or transactions set out in the definition of a real estate broker;

5. "Provisional sales associate" shall include any person who has been licensed after June 30, 1993, employed or engaged by, or associated as an independent contractor with, or on behalf of, a real estate broker to do or deal in any act, acts or transactions set out in the definition of a real estate broker and subject to an additional forty-five-clock-hour postlicensing educational requirement to be completed within the first twelve-month license term. However, the Oklahoma Real Estate Commission shall promulgate rules for those persons called into active military service for purposes of satisfying the postlicensing educational requirement. The license of a provisional sales associate shall be nonrenewable unless the postlicensing requirement is satisfied prior to the expiration date of the license. Further, the term sales associate and provisional sales associate shall be synonymous in meaning except where specific exceptions are addressed in the Oklahoma Real Estate License Code;

6. The term "successful completion" shall include prelicense, postlicense, and distance education courses in which an approved public or private school entity has examined the individual, to the satisfaction of the entity and standards as established by the Commission, in relation to the course material presented during the offering;
7. The term "renewable license" shall refer to a sales associate who is a holder of such license or to a provisional sales associate who has completed both the prelicense and postlicense educational requirements within the required time period as stated in the Code;
8. The term "nonrenewable license" shall refer to a provisional sales associate who is the holder of such license and who has not completed the postlicense educational requirement;
9. The term "surrendered license" shall refer to a real estate license which is surrendered, upon the request of the licensee, due to a pending investigation or disciplinary proceedings;
10. The term "canceled license" shall refer to a real estate license which is canceled, upon the request of the licensee and approval of the Commission, due to a personal reason or conflict;
11. "Licensee" shall include any person who performs any act, acts or transactions set out in the definition of a broker and licensed under the Oklahoma Real Estate License Code;
12. The word "Commission" shall mean the Oklahoma Real Estate Commission;
13. The word "person" shall include and mean every individual, partnership, association or corporation, foreign or domestic;
14. Masculine words shall include the feminine and neuter, and the singular includes the plural; and
15. The word "associate" shall mean a broker associate, sales associate or provisional sales associate.

§59-858-201. Oklahoma Real Estate Commission.
A. There is hereby re-created, to continue until July 1, 2017, in accordance with the provisions of the Oklahoma Sunset Law, the Oklahoma Real Estate Commission, which shall consist of seven (7) members. The Commission shall be the sole governmental entity, state, county or municipal, which shall have the authority to regulate and issue real estate licenses in the State of Oklahoma.
B. All members of the Commission shall be citizens of the United States and shall have been residents of the State of Oklahoma for at least three (3) years prior to their appointment.
C. Five members shall be licensed real estate brokers and shall have had at least five (5) years' active experience as real estate brokers prior to their appointment and be engaged full time in the real estate brokerage business. One member shall be a lay person not in the real estate business, and one member shall be an active representative of a school of real estate located within the State of Oklahoma and approved by the Oklahoma Real Estate Commission.
D. No more than two members shall be appointed from the same congressional district according to the latest congressional redistricting act. However, when congressional districts are redrawn, each member appointed prior to July 1 of the year in which such modification becomes effective shall complete the current term of office and appointments made after July 1 of the year in which such modification becomes effective shall be based on the redrawn districts. No appointments may be made after July 1 of the year in which such modification becomes effective if such appointment would result in more than two members serving from the same modified district.

§59-858-202. Appointment - Tenure - Vacancies - Removal.
A. Members of the Oklahoma Real Estate Commission shall be appointed by the Governor with the advice and consent of the Senate.
B. Members of the Commission shall serve until their terms expire. The terms of the Commission members shall be for four (4) years and until their successors are appointed and qualified.

C. Each successor member and any vacancy which may occur in the membership of the Commission shall be filled by appointment of the Governor with the advice and consent of the Senate.
D. The Governor may select appointees from a list of at least three qualified persons submitted by the Oklahoma Association of Realtors, Incorporated.
E. Each person who shall have been appointed to fill a vacancy shall serve for the remainder of the term for which the member whom he will succeed was appointed and until his successor, in turn, shall have been appointed and shall have qualified.
F. Members of the Commission may be removed from office by the Governor for inefficiency, neglect of duty or malfeasance in office in the manner provided by law for the removal of officers not subject to impeachment.

§59-858-204. Officers - Employees - Duties and compensation - Meetings.
A. The members of the Commission, within thirty (30) days after their appointment, shall organize and elect a chairman and vice-chairman. Annually thereafter the offices of chairman and vice-chairman shall be attained through election by Commission members.
B. The Commission, as soon after the election of the chairman and vice-chairman as practicable, shall employ a secretary-treasurer and such clerks and assistants as shall be deemed necessary to discharge the duties imposed by the provisions of this Code, and shall determine their duties and fix their compensation subject to the general laws of this state.
C. The chairman of the Commission, and in his absence the vice-chairman, shall preside at all meetings of the Commission and shall execute such duties as the Commission, by its rules, shall prescribe.
D. The secretary-treasurer shall keep a complete and permanent record of all proceedings of the Commission and perform such other duties as the Commission shall prescribe.

§59-858-205. Oklahoma Real Estate Commission Revolving Fund.
A. There is hereby created in the State Treasury a revolving fund for the Oklahoma Real Estate Commission, to be designated the "Oklahoma Real Estate Commission Revolving Fund". The fund shall consist of all monies received by the Oklahoma Real Estate Commission other than the Oklahoma Real Estate Education and Recovery Fund fees or appropriated funds. The revolving fund shall be a continuing fund not subject to fiscal year limitations and shall be under the control and management of the Oklahoma Real Estate Commission.
B. The Oklahoma Real Estate Commission may invest all or part of the monies of the fund in securities offered through the "Oklahoma State Treasurer's Cash Management Program". Any interest or dividends accruing from the securities and any monies generated at the time of redemption of the securities shall be deposited in the General Operating Fund of the Oklahoma Real Estate Commission. All monies accruing to the credit of the fund are hereby appropriated and may be budgeted and expended by the Oklahoma Real Estate Commission.
C. Expenditures from this fund shall be made pursuant to the purposes of this Code and without legislative appropriation. Warrants for expenditures shall be drawn by the State Treasurer based on claims signed by an authorized employee or employees of the Oklahoma Real Estate Commission and approved for payment by the Director of the Office of Management and Enterprise Services.

§59-858-206. Suits - Service - Seal - Certified copies - Location of office.
A. The Commission may sue and be sued in its official name, and service of summons upon the secretary-treasurer of the Commission shall constitute lawful service upon the Commission.

B. The Commission shall have a seal which shall be affixed to all licenses, certified copies of records and papers on file, and to such other instruments as the Commission may direct, and all courts shall take judicial notice of such seal.
C. Copies of records and proceedings of the Commission and all papers on file in the office, certified under the seal, shall be received as evidence in all courts of record.
D. The office of the Commission shall be at Oklahoma City, Oklahoma.

§59-858-207. Annual report of fees.

The Commission shall at the close of each fiscal year file with the Governor and State Auditor and Inspector a true and correct report of all fees charged, collected and received during the previous fiscal year, and shall pay into the General Revenue Fund of the State Treasury ten percent (10%) of the license fees collected and received during the fiscal year.

§59-858-208. Powers and duties of Commission.

The Oklahoma Real Estate Commission shall have the following powers and duties:
1. To promulgate rules, prescribe administrative fees by rule, and make orders as it may deem necessary or expedient in the performance of its duties;
2. To administer examinations to persons who apply for the issuance of licenses;
3. To sell to other entities or governmental bodies, not limited to the State of Oklahoma, computer testing and license applications to recover expended research and development costs;
4. To issue licenses in the form the Commission may prescribe to persons who have passed examinations or who otherwise are entitled to such licenses;
5. To issue licenses to and regulate the activities of real estate brokers, provisional sales associates, sales associates, branch offices, nonresidents, associations, corporations, and partnerships;
6. Upon showing good cause as provided for in The Oklahoma Real Estate License Code, to discipline licensees, instructors and real estate school entities by:
    a. reprimand,
    b. probation for a specified period of time,
    c. requiring education in addition to the educational requirements provided by Section 858-307.2 of this title,
    d. suspending real estate licenses and approvals for specified periods of time,
    e. revoking real estate licenses and approvals,
    f. imposing administrative fines pursuant to Section 858-402 of this title, or
    g. any combination of discipline as provided by subparagraphs a through f of this paragraph;
7. Upon showing good cause, to modify any sanction imposed pursuant to the provisions of this section and to reinstate licenses;
8. To conduct, for cause, disciplinary proceedings;
9. To prescribe penalties as it may deem proper to be assessed against licensees for the failure to pay the license renewal fees as provided for in this Code;
10. To initiate the prosecution of any person who violates any of the provisions of this Code;
11. To approve instructors and organizations offering courses of study in real estate and to further require them to meet standards to remain qualified as is necessary for the administration of this Code;
12. To contract with attorneys and other professionals to carry out the functions and purposes of this Code;

13. To apply for injunctions and restraining orders for violations of the Code or the rules of the Commission;
14. To create an Oklahoma Real Estate Contract Form Committee by rule that will be required to draft and revise real estate purchase and/or lease contracts and any related addenda for voluntary use by real estate licensees;
15. To enter into contracts and agreements for the payment of food and other reasonable expenses as authorized in the State Travel Reimbursement Act necessary to host, conduct, or participate in meetings or training sessions as is reasonable for the administration of this Code;
16. To conduct an annual performance review of the Executive Director and submit the report to the Legislature; and
17. To enter into reciprocal agreements with other real estate licensing regulatory jurisdictions with equivalent licensing, education and examination requirements.

§59-858-209. Compliance with the Administrative Procedures Act.
A. In the exercise of all powers and the performance of all duties provided in this Code, the Commission shall comply with the procedures provided in the Administrative Procedures Act. Appeals shall be taken as provided in said act.
B. The Commission may designate and employ a hearing examiner or examiners who shall have the power and authority to conduct such hearings in the name of the Commission at any time and place subject to the provisions of this section and any applicable rules or orders of the Commission. No person shall serve as a hearing examiner in any proceeding in which any party to the proceeding is, or at any time has been, a client of the hearing examiner or of any firm, partnership or corporation with which the hearing examiner is, or at any time has been, associated. No person who acts as a hearing examiner shall act as attorney for the Commission in any court proceeding arising out of any hearing in which he acted as hearing examiner.
C. In any hearing before the Commission, the burden of proof shall be upon the moving party.

§59-858-301. License required – Exceptions.
It shall be unlawful for any person to act as a real estate licensee, or to hold himself or herself out as such, unless the person shall have been licensed to do so under the Oklahoma Real Estate License Code. However, nothing in this section shall:
1. Prevent any person, partnership, trust, association or corporation, or the partners, officers or employees of any partnership, trustees or beneficiaries of any trust, association or corporation, from acquiring real estate for its own use, nor shall anything in this section prevent any person, partnership, trust, association or corporation, or the partners, officers or employees of any partnership, trustees or beneficiaries of any trust, association or corporation, as owner, lessor or lessee of real estate, from selling, renting, leasing, exchanging, or offering to sell, rent, lease or exchange, any real estate so owned or leased, or from performing any acts with respect to such real estate when such acts are performed in the regular course of, or as an incident to, the management, ownership or sales of such real estate and the investment therein;
2. Apply to persons acting as the attorney-in-fact for the owner of any real estate authorizing the final consummation by performance of any contract for the sale, lease or exchange of such real estate;

3. In any way prohibit any attorney-at-law from performing the duties of the attorney as such, nor shall this Code prohibit a receiver, trustee in bankruptcy, administrator, executor, or his or her attorney, from performing his or her duties, or any person from performing any acts under the order of any court, or acting as a trustee under the terms of any trust, will, agreement or deed of trust;
4. Apply to any person acting as the resident manager for the owner or an employee acting as the resident manager for a licensed real estate broker managing an apartment building, duplex, apartment complex or court, when such resident manager resides on the premises and is engaged in the leasing of property in connection with the employment of the resident manager;
5. Apply to any person who engages in such activity on behalf of a corporation or governmental body, to acquire easements, rights-of-way, leases, permits and licenses, including any and all amendments thereto, and other similar interests in real estate, for the purpose of, or facilities related to, transportation, communication services, cable lines, utilities, pipelines, or oil, gas, and petroleum products;
6. Apply to any person who engages in such activity in connection with the acquisition of real estate on behalf of an entity, public or private, which has the right to acquire the real estate by eminent domain;
7. Apply to any person who is a resident of an apartment building, duplex, or apartment complex or court, when the person receives a resident referral fee. As used in this paragraph, a "resident referral fee" means a nominal fee not to exceed One Hundred Dollars ($100.00), offered to a resident for the act of recommending the property for lease to a family member, friend, or coworker;
8. Apply to any person or entity managing a transient lodging facility. For purposes of this paragraph, "transient lodging facility" means a furnished room or furnished suite of rooms which is rented to a person on a daily basis, not as a principal residence, for a period less than thirty (30) days; or
9. Apply to employees of a licensed real estate broker who lease residential housing units only to eligible persons who qualify through a state or federal housing subsidized program to lease the property in an affordable housing development project. "Affordable housing development project" means a housing development of four or more units constructed for lease to specifically eligible persons as required by the particular federal or state housing program, including, but not limited to, the U.S. Department of Housing and Urban Development, the U.S. Department Agriculture Rural Development, the U.S. Department of Treasury Internal Revenue Service, or the Oklahoma Housing Finance Agency.

§59-858-301.1. Eligibility for license - Applicants convicted of criminal offenses - Time periods for disqualification - Procedure.
  A. Any applicant convicted of any crimes defined in Section 13.1 of Title 21 of the Oklahoma Statutes shall not be eligible to obtain a real estate license within twenty (20) years of the completion of any criminal sentence, including parole and probation.
  B. Any applicant convicted of a felony involving forgery, embezzlement, obtaining money under false pretense, extortion, conspiracy to defraud, fraud, or any other similar offense or offenses shall not be eligible to obtain a real estate license within ten (10) years of the completion of any criminal sentence, including parole and probation.
  C. Any applicant convicted of any other felony shall not be allowed to obtain a real estate license within five (5) years of the completion of any criminal sentence, including parole and probation.

D. For the purposes of this section, the term "applicant" shall mean any person making an application for original licensure as a provisional sales associate, sales associate, broker associate, or broker, and shall not apply to any licensee seeking renewal of a current license.

E. Any applicant with a felony conviction shall not automatically receive a license after the timelines set forth in this section, but may be licensed in accordance with the licensing provisions set forth in the Oklahoma Real Estate License Code and Rules.

§59-858-301.2. Notification of Commission of conviction or plea of guilty or nolo contendere to felony offense.

Every licensed person pursuant to the provisions of the Oklahoma Real Estate License Code shall notify the Commission in writing of the conviction or plea of guilty or nolo contendere to any felony offense within thirty (30) days after the plea is taken and also within thirty (30) days of the entering of an order of judgment and sentencing.
Added by Laws 2009, c. 133, § 2, eff. Nov. 1, 2009.

§59-858-302. Eligibility for license as provisional sales associate - Qualifications - Examination - Posteducation requirement.

A. Any person of good moral character, eighteen (18) years of age or older, and who shall submit to the Commission evidence of successful completion of ninety (90) clock hours or its equivalent as determined by the Commission of basic real estate instruction in a course of study approved by the Commission, may apply to the Commission to take an examination for the purpose of securing a license as a provisional sales associate. The education required in this subsection shall only be valid for a period of three (3) years from the date the school certified successful completion of the course; thereafter, the applicant shall be required to successfully complete an additional ninety (90) clock hours or its equivalent in basic real estate instruction.

B. Application shall be made upon forms prescribed by the Commission and shall be accompanied by an examination fee as provided for in this Code and all information and documents the Commission may require.

C. The applicant shall appear in person before the Commission for an examination which shall be in the form and inquire into the subjects the Commission shall prescribe.

D. If it shall be determined that the applicant shall have passed the examination, received final approval of the application, and paid the appropriate license fee provided for in this Code along with the Oklahoma Real Estate Education and Recovery Fund fee, the Commission shall issue to the applicant a provisional sales associate license.

E. Following the issuance of a provisional sales associate license, the licensee shall then submit to the Commission, prior to the expiration of the provisional license, evidence of successful completion of forty-five (45) clock hours or its equivalent as determined by the Commission of postlicense education real estate instruction in a course(s) of study approved by the Commission. A provisional sales associate who fails to submit evidence of compliance with the postlicense education requirement pursuant to this section, prior to the first expiration date of the provisional sales associate license, shall not be entitled to renew such license for another license term. However, the Commission shall promulgate rules for those persons called into active military service for purposes of satisfying the postlicense education requirement.

§59-858-303. Eligibility for license as real estate broker or broker associate - Examination.

A. Any person of good moral character, who holds a renewable sales associate license and who shall have had two (2) years' experience, within the previous five (5) years, as a licensed real estate sales associate or provisional sales associate, or its equivalent, and who shall submit to the Commission evidence of successful completion of ninety (90) clock hours or its equivalent as determined by the Commission of advanced real estate instruction in a course of study approved by the Commission, which instruction shall be in addition to any instruction required for securing a license as a real estate sales associate, may apply to the Commission to take an examination for the purpose of securing a license as a real estate broker or broker associate. The education required in this subsection shall only be valid for a period of three (3) years from the date the school certified successful completion of the course; thereafter, the applicant shall be required to successfully complete an additional ninety (90) clock hours or its equivalent in advanced real estate instruction.
B. Application shall be made upon forms prescribed by the Commission and shall be accompanied by an examination fee as provided for in this Code and all information and documents the Commission may require.
C. The applicant shall appear in person before the Commission for an examination which shall be in the form and shall inquire into the subjects which the Commission shall prescribe.
D. If it shall be determined that the applicant shall have passed the examination, received final approval of the application, and paid the appropriate license fee provided for in this Code along with the Oklahoma Real Estate Education and Recovery Fund fee, the Commission shall issue to the applicant a broker or broker associate license.

§59-858-303B. Accounting of expenditure for services.

Any real estate broker who charges and collects any fees in advance of the services provided by the broker shall provide a detailed accounting of expenditures to the person such services are performed for within ten (10) days after the time specified to perform such services or upon written request from person for whom services are performed for, but no longer than one (1) year from date of contract for such services.
Added by Laws 1985, c. 231, § 6, operative July 1, 1985.

§59-858-304. Evidence of successful completion of basic or advanced real estate instruction - Syllabus of instruction.
A. A certified transcript from an institution of higher education, accredited by the Oklahoma State Regents for Higher Education or the corresponding accrediting agency of another state, certifying to the successful completion of a six-academic-hour basic course of real estate instruction, or its equivalent, for which college credit was given, shall be prima facie evidence of successful completion of the clock hours of basic real estate instruction for a provisional sales associate applicant as required in Section 858-302 of this Code. The education required in this subsection shall only be valid for a period of three (3) years from the date the school certified successful completion of the course; thereafter, the applicant shall be required to successfully complete an additional six-academic-hour basic course of real estate instruction, or its equivalent.
B. A certified transcript from an institution of higher education, accredited by the Oklahoma State Regents for Higher Education or the corresponding accrediting agency of another state, certifying to the successful completion of a three-academic-hour course of real estate instruction, or its equivalent, consisting of the provisional sales associate postlicense education requirements for which college credit was given, shall be prima facie evidence of successful completion of the clock hours of real estate instruction for the postlicense education requirement as required in Section 858-302 of this title.

C. A certified transcript from an institution of higher education, accredited by the Oklahoma State Regents for Higher Education or the corresponding agency of another state, certifying to the successful completion of a six-academic-hour advanced course of real estate instruction, or its equivalent, for which college credit was given, shall be prima facie evidence of successful completion of the clock hours of advanced real estate instruction, or its equivalent, as required in Section 858-303 of this Code for a broker applicant.
D. Each school, whether public or private other than institutions of higher education, must present to the Commission its syllabus of instruction, prior to approval of such school.

§59-858-305. Licensing of associations, corporations and partnerships.
A. The Oklahoma Real Estate Commission may license as a real estate broker any association or corporation in which the managing member or managing officer holds a license as a real estate broker, as defined in this Code, and in which every member, officer or employee who acts as a real estate broker or real estate sales associate holds a license for that purpose, as defined in this Code. The Commission may license as a real estate broker any partnership in which each partner holds a license as a real estate broker, as defined in this Code.
B. Application for licenses described in this section shall be made on forms prescribed by the Commission and shall be issued pursuant to rules promulgated by the Commission.

§59-858-306. Licensing of nonresidents.
A. Any person who desires to perform licensed activities in Oklahoma but maintains a place of business outside of Oklahoma may obtain an Oklahoma nonresident license by complying with all applicable provisions of this Code including the successful completion of the applicable Oklahoma state portion of the real estate examination.
B. The nonresident shall give written consent that actions and suits at law may be commenced against the nonresident licensee in any county in this state wherein any cause of action may arise or be claimed to have arisen out of any transaction occurring in the county because of any transactions commenced or conducted by the nonresident or the nonresident's associates or employees in such county. The nonresident shall further, in writing, appoint the secretary-treasurer of said Commission as service agent to receive service of summons for the nonresident in all of such actions and service upon the secretary-treasurer of such Commission shall be held to be sufficient to give the court jurisdiction over the nonresident in all such actions.
C. A broker who is duly licensed in another state and who has not obtained an Oklahoma nonresident license may enter a cooperative brokerage agreement with a licensed real estate broker in this state. If, however, the broker desires to perform licensed activities in this state, the broker must obtain an Oklahoma nonresident license.

§59-858-307.1. Issuance of license - Term - Fees.
A. The Oklahoma Real Estate Commission shall issue every real estate license for a term of thirty-six (36) months with the exception of a provisional sales associate license whose license term shall be for twelve (12) months. License terms shall not be altered except for the purpose of general reassignment of the terms which might be necessitated for maintaining an equitable staggered license term system. The expiration date of the license shall be the end of the twelfth or thirty-sixth month, whichever is applicable, including the month of issuance. Fees shall be promulgated by rule, payable in advance, and nonrefundable.

B. If a license is issued for a period of less than thirty-six (36) months, the license fee shall be prorated to the nearest dollar and month. If a real estate sales associate or a provisional sales associate shall qualify for a license as a real estate broker, then the real estate provisional sales associate's or sales associate's license fee for the remainder of the license term shall be prorated to the nearest dollar and month and credited to such person's real estate broker's license fee.

§59-858-307.2. Renewal of license - Continuing education requirement.
 A. Beginning November 1, 2004, as a condition of renewal or reactivation of the license, each licensee with the exception of those exempt as set out in this section shall submit to the Oklahoma Real Estate Commission evidence of completion of a specified number of hours of continuing education courses approved by the Commission, within the thirty-six (36) months immediately preceding the term for which the license is to be issued. The number of hours, or its equivalent, required for each licensed term shall be determined by the Commission and promulgated by rule. Each licensee shall be required to complete and include as part of said continuing education a certain number of required subjects as prescribed by rule.
 B. The continuing education courses required by this section shall be satisfied by courses approved by the Commission and offered by:
    1. The Commission;
    2. A technology center school;
    3. A college or university;
    4. A private school;
    5. The Oklahoma Association of Realtors, the National Association of Realtors, or any affiliate thereof;
    6. The Oklahoma Bar Association, American Bar Association, or any affiliate thereof; or
    7. An education provider.
 C. The Commission shall maintain a list of courses which are approved by the Commission.
 D. The Commission shall not issue an active renewal license or reactivate a license unless the continuing education requirement set forth in this section is satisfied within the prescribed time period.
 E. The provisions of this section do not apply:
    1. During the period a license is on inactive status;
    2. To a licensee who holds a provisional sales associate license;
    3. To a nonresident licensee licensed in this state if the licensee maintains a current license in another state or states and has satisfied the continuing education requirement for license renewal in that state or states. If the nonresident licensee is exempt from the continuing education requirements in all states where the nonresident holds a license, the nonresident licensee shall successfully complete this state's continuing education requirement for license renewal or reactivation; or
    4. To a corporation, association, partnership or branch office.

§59-858-307.3. Application for reissuance of license after revocation.
 A person shall not be permitted to file an application for reissuance of a license after revocation of the license within three (3) years of the effective date of revocation.

§59-858-307.4. Criminal history record - Investigation - Costs.
 A. Prior to the issuance of a license pursuant to this Code, each applicant shall submit to a national criminal history record check, as defined by Section 150.9 of Title 74 of the Oklahoma Statutes.
 B. Upon receipt by the Commission of criminal history, the Commission shall conduct an investigation in accordance with rules promulgated by the Commission.
 C. The costs associated with the national criminal history record check shall be paid by the applicant.

§59-858-308. Current list of licensees.
 In the interest of the public, the Commission shall keep a current list of the names and addresses of all licensees, and of all persons whose licenses have been suspended or revoked, together with such

other information relative to the enforcement of the provisions of this Code as it may deem advisable and desirable. Such listings and information shall be a matter of public record.

§59-858-309. Inactive status for licensees.
- A. The Commission may place a license on inactive status when the request therefor is accompanied by sufficient reason; however, said status shall not relieve the licensee from paying the required fees. The request for inactive status shall be in writing on forms furnished by the Commission.
- B. During active military service, any licensee shall not be required to pay the fees but shall request the inactive status prior to each term for which the license is to be issued.

§59-858-310. Location of office - Licenses for branch offices.
- A. A real estate broker shall maintain a specific place of business. Such place of business shall comply with all local laws and shall be available to the public during reasonable business hours.
- B. If a real estate broker maintains more than one place of business and the additional location is an extension of the main office, a branch office license must be obtained for each additional location. Each branch office shall be under the direction and supervision of a separate broker and shall be considered a managing broker of the branch office. Application shall be made upon forms as prescribed by the Commission.

§59-858-311. Action not maintainable without allegation and proof of license.

No person, partnership, association or corporation acting as a real estate licensee shall bring or maintain an action in any court in this state for the recovery of a money judgment as compensation for services rendered in listing, buying, selling, renting, leasing or exchanging of any real estate without alleging and proving that such person, partnership, association or corporation was licensed when the alleged cause of action arose.
Added by Laws 1974, c. 121, § 311, operative July 1, 1974. Amended by Laws 1998, c. 60, § 17, eff. Jan. 1, 1999.

§59-858-312. Investigations - Cause for suspension or revocation of license.

The Oklahoma Real Estate Commission may, upon its own motion, and shall, upon written complaint filed by any person, investigate the business transactions of any real estate licensee, and may, upon showing good cause, impose sanctions as provided for in Section 858-208 of this title. Cause shall be established upon the showing that any licensee has performed, is performing, has attempted to perform, or is attempting to perform any of the following acts:
1. Making a materially false or fraudulent statement in an application for a license;
2. Making substantial misrepresentations or false promises in the conduct of business, or through real estate licensees, or advertising, which are intended to influence, persuade, or induce others;
3. Failing to comply with the requirements of Sections 858-351 through 858-363 of this title;
4. Accepting a commission or other valuable consideration as a real estate associate for the performance of any acts as an associate, except from the real estate broker with whom the associate is associated;
5. Representing or attempting to represent a real estate broker other than the broker with whom the associate is associated without the express knowledge and consent of the broker with whom the associate is associated;
6. Failing, within a reasonable time, to account for or to remit any monies, documents, or other property coming into possession of the licensee which belong to others;
7. Paying a commission or valuable consideration to any person for acts or services performed in violation of the Oklahoma Real Estate License Code;

8. Any other conduct which constitutes untrustworthy, improper, fraudulent, or dishonest dealings;
9. Disregarding or violating any provision of the Oklahoma Real Estate License Code or rules promulgated by the Commission;
10. Guaranteeing or having authorized or permitted any real estate licensee to guarantee future profits which may result from the resale of real estate;
11. Advertising or offering for sale, rent or lease any real estate, or placing a sign on any real estate offering it for sale, rent or lease without the consent of the owner or the owner's authorized representative;
12. Soliciting, selling, or offering for sale real estate by offering "free lots", conducting lotteries or contests, or offering prizes for the purpose of influencing a purchaser or prospective purchaser of real estate;
13. Accepting employment or compensation for appraising real estate contingent upon the reporting of a predetermined value or issuing any appraisal report on real estate in which the licensee has an interest unless the licensee's interest is disclosed in the report. All appraisals shall be in compliance with the Oklahoma real estate appraisal law, and the person performing the appraisal or report shall disclose to the employer whether the person performing the appraisal or report is licensed or certified by the Oklahoma Real Estate Appraiser Board;
14. Paying a commission or any other valuable consideration to any person for performing the services of a real estate licensee as defined in the Oklahoma Real Estate License Code who has not first secured a real estate license pursuant to the Oklahoma Real Estate License Code;
15. Unworthiness to act as a real estate licensee, whether of the same or of a different character as specified in this section, or because the real estate licensee has been convicted of, or pleaded guilty or nolo contendere to, a crime involving moral turpitude;
16. Commingling with the licensee's own money or property the money or property of others which is received and held by the licensee, unless the money or property of others is received by the licensee and held in an escrow account that contains only money or property of others;
17. Conviction in a court of competent jurisdiction of having violated any provision of the federal fair housing laws, 42 U.S.C. Section 3601 et seq.;
18. Failure by a real estate broker, after the receipt of a commission, to render an accounting to and pay to a real estate licensee the licensee's earned share of the commission received;
19. Conviction in a court of competent jurisdiction in this or any other state of the crime of forgery, embezzlement, obtaining money under false pretenses, extortion, conspiracy to defraud, fraud, or any similar offense or offenses, or pleading guilty or nolo contendere to any such offense or offenses;
20. Advertising to buy, sell, rent, or exchange any real estate without disclosing that the licensee is a real estate licensee;
21. Paying any part of a fee, commission, or other valuable consideration received by a real estate licensee to any person not licensed;
22. Offering, loaning, paying, or making to appear to have been paid, a down payment or earnest money deposit for a purchaser or seller in connection with a real estate transaction; and
23. Violation of the Residential Property Condition Disclosure Act.

§59-858-312.1. Certain persons prohibited from participation in real estate business.
A. No person whose license is revoked or suspended shall operate directly or indirectly or have a participating interest, or act as a member, partner or officer, in any real estate business, corporation, association or partnership that is required to be licensed pursuant to this Code.

B. No person whose license is cancelled, surrendered or lapsed pending investigation or disciplinary proceedings shall operate directly or indirectly or have a participating interest, or act as a member, partner or officer, in any real estate business, corporation, association or partnership that is required to be licensed pursuant to this Code until such time as the Commission makes a determination on the pending investigation or disciplinary proceedings and approves an application for license.

§59-858-313. Confidential materials of the Commission.
The following materials of the Commission are confidential and not public records:
1. Examinations conducted by the Commission and materials related to the examinations; and
2. Educational materials submitted to the Commission by a person or entity seeking approval and/or acceptance of a course of study.

§59-858-351. Definitions.
Unless the context clearly indicates otherwise, as used in Sections 858-351 through 858-363 of The Oklahoma Real Estate License Code:
1. "Broker" means a real estate broker, an associated broker associate, sales associate, or provisional sales associate authorized by a real estate broker to provide brokerage services;
2. "Brokerage services" means those services provided by a broker to a party in a transaction;
3. "Party" means a person who is a seller, buyer, landlord, or tenant or a person who is involved in an option or exchange;
4. "Transaction" means an activity or process to buy, sell, lease, rent, option or exchange real estate. Such activities or processes may include, without limitation, soliciting, advertising, showing or viewing real property, presenting offers or counteroffers, entering into agreements and closing such agreements; and
5. "Firm" means a sole proprietor, corporation, association or partnership.

§59-858-352. Repealed by Laws 2012, c. 251, § 9, eff. Nov. 1, 2013.

§59-858-353. Broker duties and responsibilities.
A. A broker shall have the following duties and responsibilities to all parties in a transaction, which are mandatory and may not be abrogated or waived by a broker:
1. Treat all parties with honesty and exercise reasonable skill and care;
2. Unless specifically waived in writing by a party to the transaction:
   a. receive all written offers and counteroffers,
   b. reduce offers or counteroffers to a written form upon request of any party to a transaction, and
   c. present timely all written offers and counteroffers;
3. Timely account for all money and property received by the broker;
4. Keep confidential information received from a party or prospective party confidential. The confidential information shall not be disclosed by a firm without the consent of the party disclosing the information unless consent to the disclosure is granted in writing by the party or prospective party disclosing the information, the disclosure is required by law, or the information is made public or becomes public as the result of actions from a source other than the firm. The following information shall be considered confidential and shall be the only information considered confidential in a transaction:
   a. that a party or prospective party is willing to pay more or accept less than what is being offered,

- b. that a party or prospective party is willing to agree to financing terms that are different from those offered,
- c. the motivating factors of the party or prospective party purchasing, selling, leasing, optioning or exchanging the property, and
- d. information specifically designated as confidential by a party unless such information is public;
5. Disclose information pertaining to the property as required by the Residential Property Condition Disclosure Act; and
6. Comply with all requirements of The Oklahoma Real Estate License Code and all applicable statutes and rules.

B. A broker shall have the following duties and responsibilities only to a party for whom the broker is providing brokerage services in a transaction which are mandatory and may not be abrogated or waived by a broker:
1. Inform the party in writing when an offer is made that the party will be expected to pay certain costs, brokerage service costs and approximate amount of the costs; and
2. Keep the party informed regarding the transaction.

C. When working with both parties to a transaction, the duties and responsibilities set forth in this section shall remain in place for both parties.

§59-858-354. Repealed by Laws 2012, c. 251, § 9, eff. Nov. 1, 2013.

§59-858-355. Repealed by Laws 2012, c. 251, § 9, eff. Nov. 1, 2013.

§59-858-355.1. Brokerage services to both parties in transaction - Disclosure.
A. All brokerage agreements shall incorporate as material terms the duties and responsibilities set forth in Section 858-353 of The Oklahoma Real Estate License Code.
B. A broker may provide brokerage services to one or both parties in a transaction.
C. A broker who is providing brokerage services to one or both parties shall describe and disclose in writing the broker's duties and responsibilities set forth in Section 858-353 of The Oklahoma Real Estate License Code prior to the party or parties signing a contract to sell, purchase, lease, option, or exchange real estate.
D. A firm that provides brokerage services to both parties in a transaction shall provide written notice to both parties that the firm is providing brokerage services to both parties to a transaction prior to the parties signing a contract to purchase, lease, option or exchange real estate.
E. If a broker intends to provide fewer brokerage services than those required to complete a transaction, the broker shall provide written disclosure to the party for whom the broker is providing brokerage services. Such disclosure shall include a description of those steps in the transaction for which the broker will not provide brokerage services, and also state that the broker assisting the other party in the transaction is not required to provide assistance with these steps in any manner.

§59-858-356. Disclosures – Confirmation in writing.
The written disclosures as required by subsection C of Section 858-355.1 of this title shall be confirmed by each party in writing in a separate provision, incorporated in or attached to the contract to purchase, lease, option, or exchange real estate. In those cases where a broker is involved in a transaction but does not prepare the contract to purchase, lease, option, or exchange real estate, compliance with the disclosure requirements shall be documented by the broker.

§59-858-357. Repealed by Laws 2012, c. 251, § 9, eff. Nov. 1, 2013.

§59-858-358. Duties of broker following termination, expiration or completion of performance.
Except as may be provided in a written brokerage agreement between the broker and a party to a transaction, the broker owes no further duties or responsibilities to the party after termination, expiration, or completion of performance of the transaction, except:
1. To account for all monies and property relating to the transaction; and
2. To keep confidential all confidential information received by the broker during the broker's relationship with a party.

§59-858-359. Payment to broker not determinative of relationship.
A. The payment or promise of payment or compensation by a party to a broker does not determine what relationship, if any, has been established between the broker and a party to a transaction.
B. In the event a broker receives a fee or compensation from any party to the transaction based on a selling price or lease cost of a transaction, such receipt does not constitute a breach of duty or obligation to any party to the transaction.
C. Nothing in this section requires a broker to charge, or prohibits a broker from charging, a separate fee or other compensation for each duty or other brokerage services provided during a transaction.

§59-858-360. Abrogation of common law principles of agency – Remedies cumulative.
A. The duties and responsibilities of a broker specified in Sections 858-351 through 858-363 of The Oklahoma Real Estate License Code shall replace and abrogate the fiduciary or other duties of a broker to a party based on common law principles of agency. The remedies at law and equity supplement the provisions of Sections 858-351 through 858-363 of The Oklahoma Real Estate License Code.
B. A broker may cooperate with other brokers in a transaction. Pursuant to Sections 858-351 through 858-363 of The Oklahoma Real Estate License Code, a broker shall not be an agent, subagent, or dual agent and an offer of subagency shall not be made to other brokers.
C. Nothing in this act shall prohibit a broker from entering into an agreement for brokerage services not enumerated herein so long as the agreement is in compliance with this act, the Oklahoma Real Estate Code and the Oklahoma Real Estate Commission Administration Rules.

§59-858-361. Use of word "agent" in trade name and as general reference.
A real estate broker and the associates of a real estate broker are permitted under the provisions of Sections 858-351 through 858-363 of this title to use the word "agent" in a trade name and as a general reference for designating themselves as real estate licensees.

§59-858-362. Vicarious liability for acts or omissions of real estate licensee.
A party to a real estate transaction shall not be vicariously liable for the acts or omissions of a real estate licensee who is providing brokerage services under Sections 858-351 through 858-363 of The Oklahoma Real Estate License Code.

§59-858-363. Associates of real estate broker - Authority.
Each broker associate, sales associate, and provisional sales associate shall be associated with a real estate broker. Associates shall not enter into a brokerage agreement with a party in the associate's name and shall only be allowed to enter into the agreement in the name of the broker. A real estate broker may authorize associates to provide brokerage services in the name of the real estate broker as permitted under The Oklahoma Real Estate License Code, which may include the execution of written agreements.

§59-858-401. Penalties - Fines - Injunctions and restraining orders - Appeals.
- A. In addition to any other penalties provided by law, any person unlicensed pursuant to The Oklahoma Real Estate License Code who shall willingly and knowingly violate any provision of this Code, upon conviction, shall be guilty of a misdemeanor punishable by a fine of not more than One Thousand Dollars ($1,000.00), or by imprisonment in the county jail for not more than six (6) months, or by both such fine and imprisonment.
- B. In addition to any civil or criminal actions authorized by law, whenever, in the judgment of the Oklahoma Real Estate Commission, any unlicensed person has engaged in any acts or practices which constitute a violation of the Oklahoma Real Estate License Code, the Commission may:
    1. After notice and hearing, and upon finding a violation of the Code, impose a fine of not more than Five Thousand Dollars ($5,000.00) or the amount of the commission or commissions earned, whichever is greater for each violation of the Code for unlicensed activity;
    2. Make application to the appropriate court for an order enjoining such acts or practices, and upon a showing by the Commission that such person has engaged in any such acts or practices, an injunction, restraining order, or such other order as may be appropriate shall be granted by such court, without bond; or
    3. Impose administrative fines pursuant to this subsection which shall be enforceable in the district courts of this state. The order of the Commission shall become final and binding on all parties unless appealed to the district court as provided in the Administrative Procedures Act. If an appeal is not made, such order may be entered on the judgment docket of the district court in a county in which the debtor has property and thereafter enforced in the same manner as an order of the district court for collection actions.
- C. Notices and hearings required by this section and any appeals from orders entered pursuant to this section shall be in accordance with the Administrative Procedures Act.
- D. Such funds as collected pursuant to this section shall be deposited in the Oklahoma Real Estate Education and Recovery Fund.

§59-858-402. Administrative fines.
- A. The Oklahoma Real Estate Commission may impose administrative fines on any licensee licensed pursuant to The Oklahoma Real Estate License Code as follows:
    1. Any administrative fine imposed as a result of a violation of this Code or the rules of the Commission shall not:
        a. be less than One Hundred Dollars ($100.00) and shall not exceed Two Thousand Dollars ($2,000.00) for each violation of this Code or the rules of the Commission, or
        b. exceed Five Thousand Dollars ($5,000.00) for all violations resulting from a single incident or transaction;
    2. All administrative fines shall be paid within thirty (30) days of notification of the licensee by the Commission of the order of the Commission imposing the administrative fine;
    3. The license may be suspended until any fine imposed upon the licensee by the Commission is paid;
    4. If fines are not paid in full by the licensee within thirty (30) days of the notification by the Commission of the order, the fines shall double and the licensee shall have an additional thirty- day period. If the doubled fine is not paid within the additional thirty-day period, the license shall automatically be revoked; and
    5. All monies received by the Commission as a result of the imposition of the administrative fine provided for in this section shall be deposited in the Oklahoma Real Estate Education and Recovery Fund, created pursuant to Section 858-601 of this title.

B. The administrative fines authorized by this section may be in addition to any other criminal penalties or civil actions provided for by law.

§59-858-503. Headings.
Article and section headings contained in this Code shall not affect the interpretation of the meaning or intent of any provision of this Code.

§59-858-513. Psychologically impacted real estate - Factors included - Nondisclosure of facts - Certain actions prohibited - Disclosure in certain circumstances.
   A. The fact or suspicion that real estate might be or is psychologically impacted, such impact being the result of facts or suspicions, including but not limited to:
      1. That an occupant of the real estate is, or was at any time suspected to be infected, or has been infected, with Human Immunodeficiency Virus or diagnosed with Acquired Immune Deficiency Syndrome, or other disease which has been determined by medical evidence to be highly unlikely to be transmitted through the occupancy of a dwelling place; or
      2. That the real estate was, or was at any time suspected to have been the site of a suicide, homicide or other felony, is not a material fact that must be disclosed in a real estate transaction.
   B. No cause of action shall arise against an owner of real estate or any licensee assisting the owner for the failure to disclose to the purchaser or lessee of such real estate or any licensee assisting the purchaser or lessee that such real estate was psychologically impacted as provided for in subsection A of this section.
   C. Notwithstanding the fact that this information is not a material defect or fact, in the event that a purchaser or lessee, who is in the process of making a bona fide offer, advises the licensee assisting the owner, in writing, that knowledge of such factor is important to the person's decision to purchase or lease the property, the licensee shall make inquiry of the owner and report any findings to the purchaser or lessee with the consent of the owner and subject to and consistent with applicable laws of privacy; provided further, if the owner refuses to disclose, the licensee assisting the owner shall so advise the purchaser or lessee.

§59-858-514. Registered sex offenders or violent crime offenders - No duty to provide notice regarding.
The provisions of the Sex Offenders Registration Act and the Mary Rippy Violent Crime Offenders Registration Act shall not be construed as imposing a duty upon a person licensed under the Oklahoma Real Estate License Code to disclose any information regarding an offender required to register under such provision.

§59-858-515.1. Size of property for sale.
   A. In connection with any real estate transaction, the size or area, in square footage or otherwise, of the subject property shall not be required to be provided by any real estate licensee, and if provided, shall not be considered any warranty or guarantee of the size or area information, in square footage or otherwise, of the subject property.
   B. 1. If a real estate licensee provides any party to a real estate transaction with third-party information concerning the size or area, in square footage or otherwise, of the subject property involved in the transaction, the licensee shall identify the source of the information.
      2. For the purposes of this subsection, "third-party information" means:
         a. an appraisal or any measurement information prepared by a licensed appraiser,
         b. a survey or developer's plan prepared by a licensed surveyor,
         c. a tax assessor's public record,
         d. a builder's plan used to construct or market the property, or

- e. a plan, drawing or stated square footage provided by the owner or agent of the owner, as it relates to commercial buildings or structures for sale or for lease only. Commercial land shall be verified by one of the methods provided for in subparagraphs a through d of this paragraph.
- C. A real estate licensee has no duty to the seller or purchaser of real property to conduct an independent investigation of the size or area, in square footage or otherwise, of a subject property, or to independently verify the accuracy of any third-party information as such term is defined in paragraph 2 of subsection B of this section.
- D. A real estate licensee who has complied with the requirements of this section, as applicable, shall have no further duties to the seller or purchaser of real property regarding disclosed or undisclosed property size or area information, and shall not be subject to liability to any party for any damages sustained with regard to any conflicting measurements or opinions of size or area, including exemplary or punitive damages.

§59-858-515.2. Violation of duty to disclose source of information - Damages.
- A. If a real estate licensee has provided any third-party information, as defined in paragraph 2 of subsection B of Section 1 of this act, to any party to a real estate transaction concerning size or area of the subject real property, a party to the real estate transaction may recover damages from the licensee in a civil action only when a licensee knowingly violates the duty to disclose the source of the information, as required in paragraph 1 of subsection B of Section 1 of this act.
- B. The sole and exclusive civil remedy at common law or otherwise for a violation of paragraph 1 of subsection B of Section 1 of this act by a real estate licensee shall be an action for actual damages suffered by the party as a result of such violation and shall not include exemplary or punitive damages.
- C. For any real estate transaction commenced after the effective date of this act, any civil action brought pursuant to this section shall be commenced within two (2) years after the date of transfer of the subject real property.
- D. In any civil action brought pursuant to this section, the prevailing party shall be allowed court costs and reasonable attorney fees to be set by the court and collected as costs of the action.
- E. A transfer of a possessory interest in real property subject to the provisions of this act may not be invalidated solely because of the failure of any person to comply with the provisions of this act.
- F. The provisions of this act shall apply to, regulate and determine the rights, duties, obligations and remedies, at common law or otherwise, of the seller marketing his or her real property for sale through a real estate licensee, and of the purchaser of real property offered for sale through a real estate licensee, with respect to disclosure of third-party information concerning the subject real property's size or area, in square footage or otherwise, and this act hereby supplants and abrogates all common law liability, rights, duties, obligations and remedies of all parties therefor.

§59-858-601. Creation - Status - Appropriation - Expenditures - Use of funds - Eligibility to recover.

A. There is hereby created in the State Treasury a revolving fund for the Oklahoma Real Estate Commission to be designated "Oklahoma Real Estate Education and Recovery Fund". The fund shall consist of monies received by the Oklahoma Real Estate Commission as fees assessed for the Oklahoma Real Estate Education and Recovery Fund under the provisions of this act. The revolving fund shall be a continuing fund not subject to fiscal year limitations and shall be under the administrative direction of the Oklahoma Real Estate Commission. The Oklahoma Real Estate Commission may invest all or part of the monies of the fund in securities offered through the "Oklahoma State Treasurer's Cash Management Program". Any interest or dividends accruing from the securities and any monies generated at the time of redemption of the securities shall be deposited in the Oklahoma Real Estate Education and Recovery Fund. All monies accruing to the credit of the fund are hereby appropriated and may be budgeted and expended by the Oklahoma Real Estate Commission for the purposes specified in Section 858-605 of this title. Expenditures from said fund shall be made pursuant to the laws of this state and the statutes relating to the said Commission, and without legislative appropriation. Warrants for expenditures from said fund shall be drawn by the State Treasurer, based on claims signed by an authorized employee or employees of the said Commission and approved for payment by the Director of the Office of Management and Enterprise Services.
B. Monies in the fund shall be used to reimburse any claimant who has been awarded a judgment, subject to subsection C of this section, by a court of competent jurisdiction to have suffered monetary damages by an Oklahoma real estate licensee in any transaction for which a license is required under The Oklahoma Real Estate License Code because of an act constituting a violation of The Oklahoma Real Estate License Code.
C. In determining a claimant's eligibility to recover from the fund, the Commission may conduct an independent review of the merits, findings and damages involved in the underlying action and may conduct an evidentiary hearing to determine if a claim is eligible for recovery from the fund and the amount of damages awarded are due an act constituting a violation of The Oklahoma Real Estate License Code.

§59-858-602. Additional fee - Disposition.
A. An additional, nonrefundable fee as promulgated by rule by the Commission shall be added to and payable with the license fee for both new licenses and renewals of licenses for each licensee as provided in Section 858-307.1 of this title. Such additional fee shall be deposited in the Oklahoma Real Estate Education and Recovery Fund.
B. If a license is issued for a period of less than thirty-six (36) months, such additional fee shall be prorated to the nearest dollar and month.
C. If a real estate sales associate or provisional sales associate shall qualify for a license as a real estate broker, the additional fee for the remainder of the term shall be prorated to the nearest dollar and month and credited to the additional fee added to and payable with the real estate broker license fee.
D. At the close of each fiscal year, the Commission shall transfer into the Oklahoma Real Estate Commission Revolving Fund any money in excess of that amount required to be retained in the Oklahoma Real Estate Education and Recovery Fund and that amount authorized to be expended as provided within this Code that is remaining in the Oklahoma Education and Recovery Fund and unexpended.

§59-858-603. Eligibility to recover from fund - Ineligibility.
A. Any claimant shall be eligible to seek recovery from the Oklahoma Real Estate Education and Recovery Fund if the following conditions have been met:

1. An action has been filed in district court based upon a violation specified in the Oklahoma Real Estate License Code;
2. The cause of action accrued not more than two (2) years prior to the filing of the action;
3. At the commencement of an action, the party filing the action shall immediately notify the Commission to this effect in writing and provide the Commission with a file-stamped copy of the petition or affidavit. Said Commission shall have the right to enter an appearance, intervene in, defend, or take any action it may deem appropriate to protect the integrity of the Fund. The Commission may waive the notification requirement if it determines that the public interest is best served by the waiver, that is to best meet the ends of justice and that the claimant making application made a good faith effort to comply with the notification requirements;
4. Final judgment is received by the claimant upon such action;
5. The final judgment is enforced as provided by statute for enforcement of judgments in other civil actions and that the amount realized was insufficient to satisfy the judgment; and
6. Any compensation recovered by the claimant from the judgment debtor, or from any other source for any monetary loss arising out of the cause of action, has been applied to the judgment awarded by the court.

B. A claimant shall not be qualified to make a claim for recovery from the Oklahoma Real Estate Education and Recovery Fund, if:
1. The claimant is the spouse of the judgment debtor or a personal representative of such spouse;
2. The claimant is a licensee who acted in their own behalf in the transaction which is the subject of the claim; or
3. The claimant's claim is based upon a real estate transaction in which the claimant is, through their own action, jointly responsible for any resulting monetary loss with respect to the property owned or controlled by the claimant.

§59-858-604. Application for payment - Amount - Assignment of rights, etc. - Insufficient funds - Revocation of licenses.

A. Any claimant who meets all of the conditions prescribed by this act may apply to the Commission for payment from the Oklahoma Real Estate Education and Recovery Fund, in an amount equal to the unsatisfied portion of the claimant's judgment, which is actual or compensatory damages, or Twenty-five Thousand Dollars ($25,000.00), whichever is less. The claimant is entitled to reimbursement for attorney fees reasonably incurred in the litigation not to exceed twenty-five percent (25%) of the claimant's amount approved by the Commission. Attorney fees charged and received shall be documented, verified, and submitted with the claim. Court costs and other expenses shall not be recoverable from the fund.

B. Upon receipt by the claimant of the payment from the Oklahoma Real Estate Education and Recovery Fund, the claimant assigns the claimant's right, title and interest in that portion of the judgment to the Commission which shall be subrogated up to the amount actually paid by the fund to the claimant or to the claimant and the claimant's attorney. Upon suit to collect upon a judgment, the claimant shall have priority over the fund. Any amount subsequently recovered on the judgment by the Commission, to the extent of the Commission's right, title and interest therein, shall be used to reimburse the Oklahoma Real Estate Education and Recovery Fund.

C. Payments for claims arising out of the same transaction which constitutes a claimant's cause of action based upon a violation of the Oklahoma Real Estate License Code shall be limited in the aggregate of Fifty Thousand Dollars ($50,000.00) irrespective of the number of claimants or parcels of real estate involved in the transaction.

D. Payments for claims based upon judgments against any one licensee shall not exceed in the aggregate Fifty Thousand Dollars ($50,000.00).
E. If at any time the monies in the Oklahoma Real Estate Education and Recovery Fund are insufficient to satisfy any valid claim, or portion thereof, the Commission shall satisfy such unpaid claim or portion thereof as soon as a sufficient amount of money has been deposited in the fund by collecting a special levy from members of the fund of an amount not to exceed Five Dollars ($5.00) each fiscal year. If the additional levy is not sufficient to pay all outstanding claims against the fund, the claims shall be paid as the money becomes available. Where there is more than one claim outstanding, the claims shall be paid in the order that they were approved.
F. Any claim against a corporation, association or partnership would be imputed to the managing broker(s) at the time the cause of action arose.
G. The license of said licensee shall be automatically revoked upon the payment of any amount from the Oklahoma Real Estate Education and Recovery Fund on a judgment against a licensee. The license shall not be considered for reinstatement until the licensee has repaid in full, plus interest at the rate of seven percent (7%) a year, the amount paid from the Oklahoma Real Estate Education and Recovery Fund on the judgment against the licensee.

§59-858-605. Expenditure of funds.

At any time when the total amount of monies deposited in the Oklahoma Real Estate Education and Recovery Fund exceeds Two Hundred Fifty Thousand Dollars ($250,000.00), the Commission in its discretion may expend such excess funds each fiscal year for the following purposes:

1. To promote the advancement of education in the field of real estate for the benefit of the general public and those licensed under the Oklahoma Real Estate License Code, but such promotion shall not be construed to allow advertising of this profession;
2. To underwrite educational seminars and other forms of educational projects for the benefit of real estate licensees;
3. To establish real estate courses at institutions of higher learning located in the state and accredited by the State Regents for Higher Education for the purpose of making such courses available to licensees and the general public; and
4. To contract for a particular educational project in the field of real estate to further the purposes of the Oklahoma Real Estate License Code.

Oklahoma Real Estate Commission Rules

Title 605 - Oklahoma Real Estate Commission

Chapter 1 - Administrative Operations

Subchapter 1 – General Provisions

605:1-1-1. Statement of purpose
The fundamental and primary purpose of the Real Estate Commission is to safeguard public interest and provide quality services by assisting and providing resources; encouraging and requiring high standards of knowledge and ethical practices of licensees; investigating and sanctioning licensed activities; and through the prosecution of any unlicensed person who violates the "Oklahoma Real Estate License Code and Rules."

605:1-1-2. Authority
The rules of this Title are hereby adopted in accordance with the provisions of Title 59, Section 858-101 et seq. and the provisions of Sections 301-327 of Title 75, Oklahoma Statutes, 1971.

605:1-1-3. Title and construction
The rules of this Title shall be known as the "Oklahoma Real Estate Commission Rules."

605:1-1-4. Operational procedures
(a) **Organization.** The organization of the Commission is declared to be that as enumerated in Sections 858-201 through 858-204 of the heretofore described Code.
(b) **Operational procedures.** The general course and method of operation shall be as hereinafter specified in overall provisions of the rules of this Title.
(c) **Open Records Act.** In conformance with Title 51, Section 24 A.1., et seq, Oklahoma Statutes, 1985, titled "Oklahoma Open Records Act" all open records of the Real Estate Commission may be inspected and copied in accordance with procedures, policies, and fee as required by the Commission. The Commission shall charge the following:
  (1) A fee of $.25 for each xerographic copy or micrographic image.
  (2) A fee of $1.00 for each copy to be certified.
  (3) A fee of $10.00 per hour for a record or file search.
  (4) A fee of Forty Dollars ($40.00) per extract for License Data extract.
  (5) A fee of Fifty Dollars ($50.00) every three (3) months for an Examinee Data extract.
  (6) A fee of no more than Seven Dollars and Fifty Cents ($7.50) for a convenience fee for any electronic/on-line transaction.
(d) **Petition for promulgation, amendment or repeal of any rule.** Any person may petition the Commission in writing requesting a promulgation, amendment or repeal of any rule.
  (1) The petition must be in writing in business letter form or in the form of petitions used in civil cases in this State, and shall contain an explanation and the implications of the request and shall be:
    (A) Signed by the person filing the petition and be filed with the Secretary-Treasurer of the Commission.
    (B) Submitted to the Commission at least thirty (30) days prior to a regular meeting.
    (C) Considered by the Commission at its first meeting following such thirty (30) days.
    (D) Scheduled for a public hearing before the Commission within sixty (60) days after being considered by the Commission in a regular meeting.
  (2) Within sixty (60) days after the public hearing, the Commission shall either grant or deny the petition. If the petition is granted, the Commission shall immediately begin the procedure for the promulgation, amendment or repeal of any rule pursuant to Title 75 O.S. 303.
  (3) If the petition is denied the parties retain their rights under 75 O.S. Sec. 318, to proper Judicial Review.
(e) **Petition for declaratory ruling of any rule or order.**
  (1) Any person may petition the Commission for a declaratory ruling as authorized by Section 307 of Title 75 of the Oklahoma Statutes as to the applicability of any rule or order of the Commission. Such petition shall:

(A) be in writing;
(B) be signed by the person seeking the ruling;
(C) state the rule or order involved;
(D) contain a brief statement of facts to which the ruling shall apply; and
(E) if known and available to petitioner, include citations of legal authority in support of such views.
(2) The Commission shall have at least thirty (30) days to review the petition. Following the review period, the Commission shall consider the petition at its next meeting.
(3) The Commission may compel the production of testimony and evidence necessary to make its declaratory ruling.
(4) Declaratory rulings shall be available for review by the public at the Commission office.
(f) **Contract Forms Committee.**
(1) The contract forms committee is required to draft and revise real estate purchase and/or lease contracts and any related addenda for standardization and use by real estate licensees (Title 59 O.S. 858-208 (14).
(2) The committee shall consist of eleven (11) members. Three (3) members shall be appointed by the Oklahoma Real Estate Commission; three (3) members shall be appointed by the Oklahoma Bar Association; and five (5) members shall be appointed by the Oklahoma Association of Realtors, Incorporated.
(3) The initial members' terms shall begin upon development of the forms and each member shall serve through the effective date of implementation of form(s) plus one (1) year. Thereafter, the Oklahoma Real Estate Commission shall appoint one (1) member for one (1) year, one (1) member for two (2) years, and one (1) member for three (3) years; the Oklahoma Bar Association shall appoint one (1) member for one (1) year, one (1) member for two (2) years, and one (1) member for three (3) years and; the Oklahoma Association of Realtors, Incorporated shall appoint two (2) members for one (1) year, two (2) members for two (2) years, and one (1) member for three (3) years. Thereafter, terms shall be for three (3) years and each member shall serve until their term expires and their successor has been appointed. Any vacancy which may occur in the membership of the committee shall be filled by the appropriate appointing entity.
(4) A member can be removed for just cause by the committee.
(5) Each member of the committee shall be entitled to receive travel expenses essential to the performance of the duties of his appointment, as provided in the State Travel Reimbursement Act.

Title 605 - Oklahoma Real Estate Commission

Chapter 10 - Requirements, Standards and Procedures

Subchapter 1 – General Provisions
Subchapter 3 – Education and Examination Requirements
Subchapter 5 – Education and Examination Requirements
Subchapter 7 – Licensing Procedures and Options
Subchapter 9 – Broker's Operational Procedures
Subchapter 11 – Associate's Licensing Procedures
Subchapter 13 – Trust Account Procedures
Subchapter 15 – Disclosures, Brokerage Services and Statute of Frauds
Subchapter 17 – Causes for Investigation; Hearing Process; Prohibited Acts; Discipline

Appendix A – Residential Property Disclosure Statement
Appendix B – Residential Property Condition Disclaimer Statement Form

605:10-1-1. Purpose
The rules of this Chapter establish procedures and standards that apply to real estate licensees, real estate schools and instructors, and which must be complied with as authorized under the provisions of the Oklahoma Real Estate License Code, Title 59, O.S., Sections 858-101 through 858-605.

605:10-1-2. Definitions
When used in this Chapter, masculine words shall include the feminine and neuter, and the singular includes the plural. The following words or terms, when used in this Chapter, shall have the following meaning, unless the context clearly indicates otherwise:

"Advertising" means all forms of representation, promotion and solicitation disseminated in any manner and by any means of communication, to include social networking, to consumers for any purpose related to licensed real estate activity.

"Bona fide offer" means an offer in writing.

"Branch office" means an extension of a broker's main office location and normally is located at a different location than the main office. A branch office shall not be independently owned by any person other than the applicable broker or entity.

"Branch office broker" means a person who qualified for a broker license and who is designated by a broker to direct and supervise a branch office on behalf of the broker in conformance with Section 858-310 of the Code. A branch office broker is considered an associate of the broker.

"Broker" means a sole proprietor, corporation, managing corporate broker of a corporation, association, managing broker member or manager of an association, partnership, or managing partners of a partnership and shall be one and the same as defined as a broker in Section 858-102 of the Code and whom the Commission shall hold responsible for all actions of associates who are assigned to said broker.

"Code" when used in the rules of this Chapter, means Title 59, Section 858-101 et seq, Oklahoma Statutes as adopted 1974 and amended.

"Entity" means association, corporation and partnership.

"Filed" means the date of the United States postal service postmark or the date personal delivery is made to the Commission office.

"Firm" means a sole proprietor, corporation, association or partnership.

"Inactive status" means a period in which a licensee is prohibited from performing activities which require an active license.

"Nonresident" means a person who is licensed to practice in this state, however, does not maintain a place of business in this state but maintains a place of business in another state and who periodically comes to this state to operate and perform real estate activities.

"Previously licensed applicant" means a person who has been licensed in another state and desires to obtain a resident license in this state.

"Provisional sales associate" shall be synonymous in meaning with sales associate except where it is specifically addressed in Subchapters 3, 5 and 7 of this Chapter.

"Rents or leases real estate" as referenced in Title 59, Section 858-101, subparagraph 2, means the licensed activities provided by a broker through a property management agreement with a party for a fee, commission or other valuable consideration, or with the intention or expectation of receiving or collecting a fee, commission or other valuable consideration. Licensed property management activities may include, but shall not be limited to, showing real property for rent or lease; soliciting tenants and landlords; negotiating on behalf of the tenant or landlord; and complying with and maintaining the property in accordance with Title 41, Oklahoma Statutes, Non-Residential/Residential Landlord and Tenant Acts.

"Resident" means a person who is licensed in this state and operates from a place of business in this state.

"Sole proprietor" means a broker who is the sole owner of a real estate business.

"Trade name" means the name a firm is to be known as and which is used in advertising by the firm to promote and generate publicity for the firm. A firm may or may not do business in the name under which their license is issued but must register with the Commission all trade names used by the firm.

605:10-1-3. Appeal of administrative decisions; procedures
(a) Unless specifically provided for elsewhere in this Chapter, any adverse administrative action or decision rendered by the Commission, its staff on behalf of the Commissionor a third party contract vendor, may be appealed by the adversely affected party filing within thirty (30) days of notice of such action or decision, a written request for a hearing.
(b) Upon receipt of a request for any non-disciplinary hearing provided for in this Section, or any other rule of this Chapter, the Secretary-Treasurer shall schedule an administrative decision hearing before a Hearing Examiner, a selected panel of the Commission, or the Commission as a whole giving at least fifteen (15) days notice of such

hearing. Such hearing shall be public except that upon motion, witnesses, other than the adversely affected appealing party, may be excluded from the hearing room when such witnesses are not testifying. A court reporter shall be present to record the proceedings in behalf of the Commission. Any person desiring a copy of the transcript of the proceedings may purchase such from the reporter.

(c) In the case of a proceeding conducted by the Commission as a whole or a panel of the Commission, the Chairman or his designee shall preside. Designated counsel shall advise the chair as to rulings upon the questions of admissibility of evidence, competence of witnesses and any other question of law where such ruling is required or requested.

(d) The appealing party may present his or her own evidence or may present such through his or her counsel. In order that the hearing will not be encumbered by evidence having no bearing on the issues, testimony by all witnesses will be limited to matters relevant to the issues involved.

(e) The order of procedure shall be as follows:
   (1) Recitation of the administrative action or decision.
   (2) Presentation of the adversely affected party's appeal.
   (3) Questioning of the appealing party by the hearing panel or Hearing Examiner.
   (4) Response by the Commission or Commission representatives detailing grounds for and basis for the administrative decision or action.
   (5) Examination of witnesses by appealing party with cross-examination of such witnesses.
   (6) Closing statements by the appealing party.

(f) If the case is heard by the Commission as a whole, the Commission shall deliberate and render its decision with confirmation of such decision in writing in the form of an Order distributed to all parties by mail.

(g) In the case of a hearing conducted by a Hearing Examiner or a panel of the Commission, following the hearing, the Hearing Examiner or attorney sitting as counsel to the panel of the Commission shall prepare a recommended Order to be considered by the Real Estate Commission as a whole at a future meeting. All parties will be furnished copies of the recommended Order and notified as to the date the recommendations will be considered by the Commission for adoption. At the same time, notice will be given also to the parties that written exceptions or requests to present oral exceptions or arguments, if any, should be submitted on or before a designated date pursuant to Section 311, Title 75, Oklahoma Statutes. Upon adoption of the recommended Order by the Commission as a whole, such Order shall be distributed to all parties.

605:10-1-4. Returned checks - disposition

(a) All fees are received subject to collection. Payment of a fee to the Commission with a dishonored check may be prima facie evidence of a violation of Title 59, Section 858-312.

(b) If the Commission receives a check that is dishonored upon presentation to the bank on which the check is drawn, a returned check fee of Thirty-five Dollars ($35.00) will be charged. If such payment is for fees, or other amounts due the Commission, and the check is not replaced within the specified time frame as determined by the Commission, such request shall be deemed incomplete and the transaction null and void.

(c) Other services may be delayed or denied if a check is dishonored upon presentation to the bank on which the check is drawn.

605:10-3-1. Prelicense education requirements

(a) On and after July 1, 1993, as evidence of an applicant's having satisfactorily completed those education requirements as set forth in Sections 858-302 and 858-303 of the Code, each applicant for licensure shall present with his or her application a certification showing successful completion of the applicable course of study approved by the Commission as follows:
   (1) To qualify an applicant for examination and licensure as a provisional sales associate, the course shall consist of at least ninety (90) clock hours of instruction or its equivalent as determined by the Commission. In order for a provisional sales associate to obtain a sales associate license, the provisional sales associate must, following issuance of a provisional license, complete additional education as required in Section 858-302 of the Code. The prelicense course of study shall be referred to as the Basic Course of Real Estate, Part I of II and shall encompass the following areas of study:
      (A) Real Estate Economics and Marketing
      (B) Nature of Real Estate

(C) Rights and Interest in Real Estate
(D) Legal Descriptions
(E) Title Search, Encumbrances, and Land Use Control
(F) Transfer of Rights
(G) Service Contracts
(H) Estimating Transaction Expenses
(I) Value and Appraisal
(J) Marketing Activities
(K) Fair Housing
(L) Contract Law Overview
(M) Contract Law and Performance
(N) Offers and Purchase Contracts
(O) Financing Real Estate
(P) Closing a Transaction
(Q) Regulations Affecting Real Estate
(R) Disclosures and Environmental Issues
(S) Property Management and Leasing
(T) Risk Management
(U) Professional Standards of Conduct
(V) Law of Agency

(2) To qualify an applicant for examination and licensure as a broker, the course shall consist of at least ninety (90) clock hours of instruction or its equivalent as determined by the Commission. Such course of study shall be referred to as the Advanced Course in Real Estate and shall encompass the following areas of study:

(A) Laws and Rules Affecting Real Estate Practice
(B) Broker Supervision
(C) Establishing a Real Estate Office
(D) Professional Development
(E) Business, Financial, and Brokerage Management
(F) Oklahoma Broker Relationships
(G) Anti-Trust and Deceptive Trade
(H) Risk Management and Insurance
(I) Mandated Disclosures, Hazards, and Zoning
(J) Real Estate Financing
(K) Specialized Property Operations and Specialty Areas
(L) Trust Accounts and Trust Funds
(M) Closing a Real Estate Transaction
(N) Closing Statements
(O) Professional Standards of Conduct
(P) Property Ownership
(Q) Land Use Controls and Regulations
(R) Valuation and Market Analysis
(S) Law of Agency
(T) Contracts
(U) Transfer of Property
(V) Practice of Real Estate
(W) Real Estate Calculations

(b) As evidence of an applicant's having successfully completed those education requirements as set forth in Section 858-304 of the Code, each applicant shall present a certified transcript from an institution of higher education, accredited by the Oklahoma State Regents for Higher Education or the corresponding accrediting agency of another jurisdiction.

(1) The basic course of real estate shall be limited to Basic Real Estate Principles and Practices; provided, however, that a course or combination of courses not so titled may be accepted if the course content has been determined by the Commission to be equivalent as one and the same as enumerated in this Section.

(2) The advanced course of real estate shall be limited to Advanced Real Estate Principles and Practices; provided that a course or combination of courses not so titled may be accepted if the course content has been determined by the Commission to be equivalent as one and the same as that enumerated in this Section.

(3) The Commission shall accept in lieu of a certified transcript a course completion certificate as prescribed by the Commission.

(c) **Entities allowed to seek approval.** The education courses required of this Section shall be satisfied by courses approved by the Commission and offered by:
  (1) The Commission
  (2) An area vocational-technical school
  (3) A college or university
  (4) A private school
  (5) The Oklahoma Association of Realtors, the National Association of Realtors, or any affiliate thereof,
  (6) The Oklahoma Bar Association, American Bar Association, or any affiliate thereof; or
  (7) An education provider.

(d) **Attendance and successful completion required for in-class credit.** To complete any in-class offering, a person must physically be present during all of the offering time and successfully complete all course requirements to include an examination.

(e) **Successful completion of materials and examination required for distance education credit.** To complete a distance education course offering, a person must successfully complete all course requirements to include all modules and an examination.

605:10-3-2. Application for license

(a) **Requirements for completing application.**
  (1) Any person seeking a real estate license shall make application for such license on a form provided by the Commission. The form shall contain, but not be limited to, the following:
    (A) Legal name to include first, middle and last name.
    (B) Routine biographical information.
    (C) License history in Oklahoma and other states.
    (D) Criminal and/or civil charges or convictions, including bankruptcy and judgments.
    (E) Compliance with Title 59 O.S. 858.301.1 regarding felony convictions.
    (F) Recent photograph.
    (G) Birth date.
    (H) Evidence of successful completion of course requirement as specified in the "Code".
    (I) A sworn statement as to accuracy of the application information.
    (J) Documentation required for compliance necessary to verify citizenship, qualified alien status, and eligibility under the Personal Responsibility and Work Opportunity Reconciliation Act of 1996.
    (K) Social security number, pursuant to Title 56, Oklahoma Statutes, Section 240.21A.
    (L) Submit to a national criminal history record check, as defined by Section 150.9 of Title 74 of the Oklahoma Statutes. A fee amount, not to exceed sixty dollars ($60.00), shall be sent to the Commission to begin the process of the national criminal history check.
    (M) A completed national criminal history record check, completed for the Commission, shall be valid for six (6) months from the date of issuance from the issuing authority.
    (N) In the event an applicant is not physically able to submit to finger printing, other applicant identifiers shall be utilized, i.e., name, birth date and social security number.
  (2) An applicant indicating a bankruptcy or judgment, criminal and/or civil charges or convictions on the application, must submit with the application official documents to the Commission which pertain to the disposition of the matter. If official documents are unable to be obtained, a detailed letter explaining the matter(s) must be attached to the application.

(b) **Applicant shall appear for examination.** Each applicant shall appear for an examination as soon as possible subsequent to the filing of an approved application or the signing of a form as required in 605:10-3-3.

(c) **Applicant must be of good moral character.** The application submitted by an individual seeking a license must indicate that the applicant possesses a reputation for honesty, truthfulness, trustworthiness, good moral character, and that he or she bears a good reputation for fair dealing.

(d) **Determining good moral character.** In determining whether or not an applicant meets the definition of good moral character, the Commission will consider, but not be limited to, the following:
  (1) Whether the probation period given in a conviction or deferred sentence has been completed and fully satisfied to include fines, court costs, etc.
  (2) Whether the restitution ordered by a court in a criminal conviction or civil judgement has been fully satisfied.
  (3) Whether a bankruptcy that is real estate related has been discharged.
  (4) Whether an applicant has been denied licensure or a license has been suspended or revoked by this or any other state or jurisdiction to practice or conduct any regulated profession, business or vocation because of any conduct or practices which would have warranted a like result under the Oklahoma "Code".
  (5) Whether an applicant has been guilty of conduct or practices in this state or elsewhere which would have been grounds for revocation or suspension under the current Oklahoma "Code" had the applicant been licensed.
(e) **Subsequent good conduct.** If, because of lapse of time and subsequent good conduct and reputation or other reason deemed sufficient, it shall appear to the Commission that the interest of the public will not likely be in danger by the granting of such license, the Commission may approve the applicant as relates to good moral character.

605:10-3-3. Proceedings upon application for a license
(a) **Qualified application.**
  (1) **Approved application.** If the Commission is of the opinion that an applicant for license is qualified, the application shall be approved. An approved application shall be valid for ninety (90) days.
  (2) **Denial of application.** If, from the application filed, or from answers to inquiries, or from complaints or information received, or from investigation, it shall appear to the Commission the applicant is not qualified at any time before the initial license is issued, the Commission shall refuse to approve the application and shall give notice of that fact to the applicant within fifteen (15) days after its ruling, order or decision.
(b) **Appeal of denial of application.** Upon written request from the applicant, filed within thirty (30) days after receipt of such notice of denial, the Commission shall set the matter for hearing to be conducted within sixty (60) days after receipt of the applicant's request.
(c) **Applicant hearing.** The hearing shall be at the time and place as prescribed by the Commission. At least ten (10) days prior to the date set for hearing the Commission shall notify the applicant and other persons protesting, and shall set forth in a notice the reason or reasons why the Commission refused to accept or approve the application. The written notice of the hearing may be served by personal delivery to the applicant and protesters, or by mailing the same by registered or certified mail to the last known address of the applicant and/or protesters.
(d) **Hearing procedures.** The hearing procedure shall be that as outlined in 605:10-1-3 titled "Appeal of administrative decisions; procedures."

605:10-3-4. Broker applicant; experience
(a) No individual shall be licensed as a real estate broker unless in addition to the other requirements in the Code, he or she has served two (2) years, or its equivalent, as a licensed real estate provisional sales associate and\or sales associate, with and under the instructions and guidance of a licensed real estate broker of this state or any other state at least twenty-four (24) months within the five (5) year period immediately prior to the filing of his or her application for license as a real estate broker in Oklahoma.
(b) An application submitted for the purpose of seeking a license to function as a real estate broker shall not be accepted for filing by the Commission unless such applicant has completed the two (2) year apprenticeship requirement on or before the date such application is submitted.

605:10-3-5. Examinations
(a) **Applicant must appear in person.** When an application for examination has been submitted to the Commission, the applicant shall be required to appear in person, at a time and place to be designated by the Commission, and answer questions based on the required subject matter as prescribed elsewhere in the rules of this Chapter. On and after August 1, 2001, each broker examination fee shall be Seventy-five Dollars ($75.00) and each provisional sales associate/sales associate examination fee shall be Sixty Dollars ($60.00.)

(b) **Special accommodations.** In cases where special accommodations are necessary under the requirements of the Americans with Disabilities Act, applicants must notify the examination supplier in advance by submitting a written request, on a form prescribed by the Commission, describing the disability and necessary accommodations.

(c) **Failure to pass examination.** If an applicant fails to pass the examination prescribed by the Commission, the Commission may permit subsequent examinations upon receipt of a new examination fee for each examination to be attempted.

(d) **Applicant request to view failed examination.** An applicant who fails the examination has the option of reviewing their missed questions at the end of their examination. An applicant may challenge the validity of any question(s) they identify as incorrectly graded. A challenge to a question that pertains to the Oklahoma law portion of the examination will be sent to the Commission by the examination supplier. A challenge to a question that pertains to the national portion will fall under the review policy of the examination supplier. In either case, both the examination supplier and/or the Commission shall have five (5) business days in which to review and issue a response to the applicant. Applicants will be allowed up to one (1) hour to review their exam and the applicant will not be allowed to test on the same day they review a failed examination. No notes, pencils or electronic devices will be allowed during review nor will they be allowed to leave the examination area with the examination questions.

(e) **Application valid for one year.** The original examination application shall be valid for one (1) year from date of filing. After such date, an applicant must complete a new original application form.

(f) **Passing percentile of examination.** A score of seventy-five percent (75%) or more shall be considered a passing grade on the broker or provisional sales associate/sales associate examination.

(g) **Validity period of examination results.** The results of an examination wherein an applicant scored a passing grade shall be valid for one (1) year from the date of such examination.

(h) **Disciplinary examination fee.** A fee shall be charged for an examination which is directed by Order of the Commission as disciplinary action.

(i) **Examination voided.** A licensee or instructor applicant caught cheating during the course of a real estate examination shall:
  (1) immediately forfeit the examination,
  (2) be given a failing score,
  (3) be disqualified from retaking the examination for one year, and
  (4) be allowed to file an appeal with the Commission under Rule 605:10-1-3.

605:10-3-6. Continuing education requirements

(a) **Definition.** Continuing education shall be defined as any real estate oriented education course or equivalent, hereinafter called offering(s) intended:
  (1) To improve the knowledge of licensees.
  (2) To keep licensees abreast of changing real estate practices and laws.
  (3) To help licensees meet the statutory requirements for license renewal.

(b) **Purpose.** The purpose of continuing education is to provide an educational program through which real estate licensees can continually become more competent and remain qualified to engage in real estate activities for which they are licensed. Such activities involve facts and concepts about which licensees must be knowledgeable in order to safely and confidently conduct real estate negotiations and transactions in the public's best interest.

(c) **Goals.** The goals of continuing education are:
  (1) To provide licensees with opportunity for obtaining necessary current information and knowledge which will enable them to conduct real estate negotiations and transactions in a legal and professional manner in order to better protect public interest.
  (2) To assure that the licensees are provided with current information regarding new and/or changing laws and regulations which affect the real estate business.
  (3) To ensure that the consumers interest is protected from unknowledgeable licensees.

(d) **Objectives.** The objectives of continued education are as follows:
  (1) For licensees to expand and enhance their knowledge and expertise so as to be continually effective, competent, and ethical as they practice real estate.
  (2) For licensees to review and update their knowledge of federal, state and local laws and regulations which affect real estate practices.

(e) **Entities allowed to seek approval.** The Commission may approve and/or accept any offering provided by an entity which meets the purposes, goals, and objectives of the continuing education requirement. The Commission may accept the following offerings as proof of meeting the continuing education requirement:
   (1) Any offering which is approved and presented by those entities enumerated in paragraph B, of 858- 307.2 of the "Code".
   (2) Any offering in real estate, or directly related area, approved and/or accepted by the real estate regulatory agency in another state; provided such offering is not excluded elsewhere in this Chapter.
   (3) Any offering in real estate, or directly related area, not accepted in paragraphs (1) or (2) of this subsection, which can be determined by the Commission to be in compliance with the intent of the rules of this Chapter.
   (4) Completion of an approved ninety (90) hour prelicense broker course or an approved forty-five (45) hour provisional sales associate postlicense course, or its respective equivalent as determined by the Commission shall suffice for 21-hours of continuing education credit for a licensee. An individual segment of an approved prelicense broker course or an approved provisional sales associate postlicense course shall suffice for continuing education credit provided such individual segment has also been separately approved for continuing education credit.
(f) **Ineligible courses.**
   (1) The following offerings will not be considered by the Commission to meet continuing education requirements:
      (A) General training or education not directly related to real estate or real estate practices.
      (B) Offerings in mechanical office and business skills such as typing, speed reading, memory improvement, report writing, and personal motivation that is not directly related to real estate.
      (C) Sales promotion or other meetings held in conjunction with the general real estate brokerage business.
      (D) Meetings which are a normal part of in-house training.
      (E) That portion of any offering devoted to breakfast, luncheon, dinner, or other refreshments.
      (F) Prelicense general training and education to obtain a provisional sales associate or sales associate license or license examination refresher courses for provisional sales associate/sales associate or broker.
   (2) The list in (1) of this subsection does not limit the Commission's authority to disapprove any offering which fails to meet the adopted purposes, goals and objectives.
(g) **List of approved entities.** The Commission shall maintain a list of approved entities.
(h) **Licensee responsible for notification to Commission.** Each licensee shall be ultimately responsible to the Commission to furnish evidence of having successfully completed the continuing education requirements for license renewal, activation, or reinstatement, as set forth elsewhere in this Chapter. Each licensee shall present to the Commission evidence of completion of a minimum of twenty-one (21) clock hours of continuing education offerings acceptable by the Commission. As evidence of having completed the requirement each licensee shall present:
   (1) A certificate, and/or documents, statements and forms, as may reasonably be required by the Commission, or
   (2) A certified transcript; provided, however, if such offering is taken as an accredited C.E.U. (Continuing Education Unit) a certificate may be accepted in lieu of the transcript.
(i) **Attendance and successful completion required for in-class credit.** To complete any in-class offering, a person must physically be present during all of the offering time and successfully complete all course requirements.
(j) **Successful completion of materials and examination required for distance education credit.** To complete a distance education course offering, a person must successfully complete all course requirements to include all modules and an examination.
(k) **Course limitations.**
   (1) A particular course offering may not be taken for continuing education credit more than once from the same entity and/or instructor during a renewal period.
   (2) Educational courses taken for disciplinary reasons shall not count towards the normal continuing education requirements for licensees.
(l) **Required number of continuing education hours.** The required number of continuing education hours for a licensee shall be as follows:
   (1) As a condition of a license activation or active reinstatement, each license with an expiration date of June 30, 2014 and thereafter, with the exception of those exempt as set out in Title 59, 858-307.2, shall provide evidence of completion of twenty-one (21) clock hours of Commission approved subject matter, or its equivalent, as determined by the Commission. Such hours shall have been taken in the same license term for which the license is to be issued, with the exception of a licensee whose hours were not used in the preceding license

term. In that case, the hours taken in the preceding license term shall count towards an applicable license activation or active reinstatement.
(2) Each licensee shall have completed of said twenty-one (21) clock hours of continuing education six (6) clock hours of required subject matter as directed by the Commission.
(3) The required subject matter, or its equivalent, as determined by the Commission, shall consist of at least one (1) clock hour in all following subjects each license term: Professional Conduct, Broker Relationships Act, Fair Housing, Contracts and Forms, Code and Rule Updates and Current Issues. The remaining fifteen (15) clock hours may consist of elective subject matter as approved by the Commission.
(4) Any licensee may complete the Broker in Charge course as approved by the Commission consisting of fifteen (15) clock hours in lieu of the required subject matter.
(5) Any Broker who holds or has held a license type of Broker Manager (BM), Proprietor Broker (BP), or Branch Broker (BB) during any portion of their current license term shall be required to successfully complete the Broker in Charge course as approved by the Commission consisting of fifteen (15) clock hours, or its equivalent, as approved by the Commission. In addition, to complete the continuing education requirement of twenty-one (21) clock hours such broker shall complete at least two (2) of the six (6) required subject matter, equal to at least six (6) clock hours, as referenced in paragraph (3) of this subsection.
(6) Any broker that lapsed or renewed inactive in their previous license term or current license term who applies for reinstatement or activation and held in their previous or current license term the license type of Broker Manager (BM), Proprietor Broker (BP), or Branch Broker (BB) must complete the Broker in Charge course and two (2) of the six (6) required subject matter equal to at least six (6) hours prior to their license being reinstated active or reactivating.

605:10-3-7. Provisional sales associate post-license education requirement
(a) **Purpose.** The purpose of the provisional sales associate post-license education requirement is to provide an educational program through which real estate provisional sales associate licensees can become more competent, knowledgeable and perfect their ability to engage in real estate activities for which they are licensed. Such activities involve facts and concepts which licensees must be knowledgeable in order to safely and confidently conduct real estate negotiations and transactions in the public's best interest.
(b) **Goals.** The goals of the provisional sales associate post-license education requirements are:
(1) To provide newly licensed individuals with the opportunity to obtain current information and knowledge to enable them to conduct real estate negotiations and transactions in a legal and professional manner in order to better protect public interest.
(2) To assure that licensees are provided with relevant information pertaining to practices which directly relate to real estate business.
(3) To assure that the provisional sales associate is provided with information regarding new and/or changing laws and regulations which affect the real estate business.
(4) To assure that the consumers interest is protected from unknowledgeable licensees.
(c) **Objectives.** The objectives of post-license education are to:
(1) Assist newly licensed individuals by having available a practical educational program wherein the information attained can be put into practice.
(2) To help licensees expand and enhance their knowledge and expertise so as to continually be effective, competent, and ethical as they practice real estate.
(3) To encourage licensees to gain additional education for specialization in particular areas of real estate.
(d) **Subject content.** On and after July 1, 1993, a provisional sales associate shall be required to successfully complete prior to the first license expiration date, forty-five (45) clock hours of post-license education or its equivalent as determined by the Commission. Such course of study shall be referred to as the Provisional Post-License Course of Real Estate, Part II of II and shall encompass the following areas of study:
(1) Real Estate Marketplace
(2) Marketing Real Estate
(3) Personal Marketing
(4) The Qualifying Process
(5) Prospecting and Negotiating
(6) Financing Real Estate, Investments and Exchanges
(7) Financial Documents

(8) Duty to Account
(9) Title Search
(10) Risk Management
(11) At least three (3) clock hour of Broker Relationships with Parties to a Transaction
(12) Property Management
(13) At least (3) clock hours of Laws and Regulations Affecting Real Estate Practice, including Code and Rules
(14) Disciplinary Action
(15) At least (3) clock hours of Contracts and forms
(16) At least (3) clock hours of Professional Conduct and Ethics
(17) At least (3) clock hours of Fair Housing.

(e) **Equivalent course content.** The Commission may approve and/or accept any offering or combination of offerings which consists of forty-five (45) clock hours or more or its equivalent as determined by the Commission provided by an entity which meets the purposes, goals and objectives of the provisional sales associate post-license education requirement.

(f) **Offerings.**
   (1) The Commission may accept the following offerings as proof of meeting the post-license education requirement:
      (A) Any offering which is approved and presented by those entities enumerated in Title 59, O.S., subsection B, of 858-307.2 of the "Code."
      (B) Any offering in real estate, or directly related area, approved and/or accepted by the real estate regulatory agency in another state; provided such offering is not excluded elsewhere in this Chapter.
      (C) Any offering in real estate, or directly related area, not accepted in paragraphs (A) or (B) of this subsection, which can be determined by the Commission to be in compliance with the intent of the rules of this Chapter.
      (D) The Commission has the authority to disapprove any offering which fails to meet the purposes, goals and objectives of this Section.

(g) **Licensee responsible for notification to Commission.** Each provisional sales associate shall be responsible to furnish evidence to the Commission of having successfully completed a Commission approved forty-five (45) clock hour post-license education course or its equivalent as determined by the Commission. Upon successful completion of the post-license education requirement, evidence must be submitted on or before license expiration and on a form approved by the Commission.

(h) **Failure to complete post-license education requirement prior to license expiration.** A provisional sales associate who fails to complete the post-license education requirement prior to the first expiration date of the provisional sales associate license, shall not be entitled to renew such license.

(i) **Evidence of completion.** As evidence of having completed the education requirement, each provisional sales associate shall present one or more of the following as required by the Commission:
   (1) A certificate, and/or documents, statements and forms, as may reasonably be required by the Commission, or
   (2) A certified transcript; however, if such offering is taken as an accredited C.E.U. (Continuing Education Unit) a certificate may be accepted in lieu of the transcript.

(j) **Attendance and successful completion required for in-class credit.** To complete any in-class offering, a person must physically be present during all of the offering time and successfully complete all course requirements and an examination.

(k) **Successful completion of materials and examination required for distance education credit.** To complete a distance education offering, a person must successfully complete all course requirements to include all modules and an examination.

(l) **Course limitations.** The following course limitations shall apply:
   (1) A provisional sales associate shall only be given credit for courses specifically approved by the Commission.
   (2) Educational courses taken for disciplinary reasons do not count towards the normal post-license education requirement.

(m) **Extension of time for completion of post-license course for provisional sales associate that has received orders for active military service.** A provisional sales associate that has received orders for active military service may request an extension of time to complete the post-license education requirement if the request is received in writing prior to the expiration of the license. The request must be accompanied by a copy of the military orders for active military service. The extension of time shall be one (1) year from the date of return from active military service. In conformance with §858-309, a licensee on active military service shall request an inactive status prior to each term for which the license is to be issued. If an extension is approved, a provisional sales associate shall be allowed to renew their license by requesting an inactive status in writing prior to each term for which the license is to be issued.

605:10-5-1. Approval of pre-license course
(a) **Course approval.** Any person or entity seeking to conduct an approved course of study shall make application and submit documents, statements and forms as may reasonably be required by the Commission. The request shall include the following:
   (1) Completed course application.
   (2) Application fee of One Hundred Twenty-five Dollars ($125.00) for each course.
   (3) An approved course syllabus encompassing the contents enumerated in 605:10-3-1 and divided by instructional periods, the name, author and publisher of the primary textbook, or a statement stating the entity will use OREC syllabus and other items as may be required by the Commission.
(b) **Course offering requirements.**
   (1) An entity not conducting an applicable approved course within any thirty-six (36) month period shall automatically be removed from approved status. In such event, the person and/or entity must re-apply as an original applicant.
   (2) If a course of study is to be conducted in the name of a corporation, the application shall include the names and addresses of all directors and officers.
   (3) An approved entity shall immediately report any changes in information in regards to the application previously filed with the Commission.
(c) **Denied applications.** No portion of the fees enumerated in this section are refundable. If an instructor, entity or course application is not approved, the applicant may appeal the decision by filing a written request for a hearing before the Commission. The hearing procedure shall be that as outlined in 605:10-1-3 titled "Appeal of administrative decisions; procedures."
(d) **Advertising course offerings.** No person or entity sponsoring or conducting a course of study shall advertise the course as approved prior to the course receiving approval from the Commission. Further, no person or entity sponsoring or conducting a course of study shall advertise that it is endorsed, recommended or accredited by the Commission although such person or entity may indicate that a course of study has been approved by the Commission.
(e) **Instructor application and approval requirements.** An individual determined by the Commission to possess one or more of the following qualifications may, upon receipt of an application and evidence of education and/or experience, be considered for approval as an approved instructor. Each application for approval must be accompanied by a Twenty-Five Dollar ($25.00) application fee and documentation required for compliance necessary to verify citizenship, qualified alien status, and eligibility under the Personal Responsibility and Work Opportunity Reconciliation Act of 1996. In order to qualify, an individual must possess proof of one of the following:
   (1) A bachelor's degree with a major in real estate from an accredited college or university.
   (2) A bachelor's degree from an accredited college or university, and at least two (2) years of applicable active experience within the previous ten (10) years as a real estate broker or sales associate.
   (3) A real estate broker or sales associate licensed in Oklahoma with a minimum of five (5) years applicable active experience within the previous ten (10) years as a real estate broker or sales associate and proof of high school education or its GED equivalent.
   (4) An individual determined by the Commission to possess a combination of education and/or applicable active broker or sales associate experience in real estate or real estate related fields which constitutes an equivalent of one or more of the qualifications in paragraphs (1), (2), or (3) of this subsection.
(f) **Course content examination.** Final approval will be considered after the instructor applicant has paid the appropriate examination fee and successfully completed an applicable examination with a passing score of 80% or more. If an instructor applicant has successfully taken an applicable license examination with a passing score of 80% or more within thirty (30) days of filing an instructor application, the passing score may be utilized to meet the applicable examination requirement in this section.
(g) **Instructor renewal requirements.**
   (1) In order to maintain approved status an instructor must comply with the following:

(A) Attend a Commission directed Instructor Renewal Course every twenty-four (24) months or successfully complete nationally recognized teacher modules consisting of at least 3 clock hours of credit as approved by the Commission.
 (B) Complete one of the following:
  (i) Furnish evidence that the instructor has taught a Commission approved pre-license course, or any other real estate related course(s) the Commission determines to be equivalent, within a required thirty-six (36) month period;
  (ii) Successfully pass the applicable sales or broker examination with a score of 80% or more; or
  (iii) Furnish evidence to the Commission that the instructor has audited an in-class pre-license course, in its entirety, that must be validated by the school instructor or director.
 (C) Any instructor not meeting the requirements of this subsection will be required to re-apply as an original instructor applicant.
(h) **Guest instructors.** Guest instructors may be utilized for in-class instruction provided an approved instructor is also present during presentations. Total guest instruction and lectures shall not consume more than thirty percent (30%) of the total course time.
(i) **Instructor and entity requirements.**
 (1) **Instructor must be present.** An approved instructor must be present in the same room during all in-class course instruction for students to receive credit toward course completion.
 (2) **Retention of records.** An instructor/entity shall maintain enrollment records and roll sheets which include number of hours completed by each student for seven (7) years.
 (3) **Course completion certificate.** Each individual successfully completing a course of study approved by the Commission shall be furnished a certificate prescribed or approved by the Commission certifying completion. The Commission shall accept from a college or university a certified transcript or a course completion certificate as prescribed by the Commission.
 (4) **Commission authorized to audit and inspect records.** A duly authorized designee of the Commission may audit any offering and/or inspect the records of the entity at any time during its presentation or during reasonable office hours or the entity may be required to provide the records to the Commission.
 (5) **Clock hours and breaks.** Not more than one clock hour may be registered within any one sixty (60) minute period and no more than ten (10) minutes of each hour shall be utilized for breaks.
 (6) **Class size limited.** Instructor ratio to students shall not exceed sixty (60).
(j) **Facility requirements.** The offering entity shall ensure that all classroom facilities have adequate lighting, seating space and technology to meet the needs of the student. The classroom area shall be free of distractions and noise.
(k) **Disciplinary action.** An approved course of study, director, and/or instructor may be withdrawn or disciplined as outlined in Title 59, O.S., Section 858-208, paragraph 6 either on a complaint filed by an interested person or the Commission's own motion, for the following reasons, but only after a hearing before the Commission and/or a Hearing Examiner appointed by the Commission:
 (1) In the event the real estate license of a director is suspended or revoked, the course of study shall automatically be revoked.
 (2) In the event the real estate license of an instructor is suspended or revoked.
 (3) Failure to comply with any portion of the Code or the rules of this Chapter.
 (4) Failure of an approved entity to maintain a 50% or better pass/fail ratio on the Commission examinations.
 (5) Falsification of records and/or application(s) filed with the Commission.
 (6) False and/or misleading advertisement.
 (7) Any other improper conduct or activity of the director, instructor, or entity as may be determined by the Commission to be unacceptable.

605:10-5-1.1. Approval of a post-license course

(a) **Course approval.** In accordance with Section 858-302 of the License Code, the Commission shall determine and approve the education content of the forty-five (45) clock hour post-license course content or its equivalent. Any person or entity seeking to conduct an approved course of study shall make application and submit documents, statements and forms as may reasonably be required by the Commission. The request shall include the following:
 (1) Completed course application.
 (2) Application fee of One Hundred Twenty-five Dollars ($125.00) for each course.

(3) An approved course syllabus encompassing the contents enumerated in 605:10-3-7 and divided by instructional periods, with the name, author and publisher of the primary textbook.

(b) **Course offering requirements.**
 (1) An offering entity not conducting the approved course within any thirty-six (36) month period shall automatically be removed from approved status. In such event, the person and/or entity must re-apply as an original applicant.
 (2) If a course of study is to be conducted in the name of a corporation, the application shall include the names and addresses of all directors and officers.
 (3) An approved entity shall immediately report any changes in information in regards to the application previously filed with the Commission.

(c) **Denied applications.** No portion of the fees enumerated in this Section are refundable. If an instructor, entity or course application is not approved, the applicant may appeal the decision by filing a written request for a hearing before the Commission. The hearing procedure shall be that as outlined in 605:10-1-3 titled "Appeal of administrative decisions; procedures."

(d) **Advertising course offerings.** No person or entity sponsoring or conducting a course of study shall advertise the course as approved prior to the course receiving approval from the Commission. Further, no person or entity sponsoring or conducting a course of study shall advertise that it is endorsed, recommended or accredited by the Commission although such person or entity may indicate that a course of study has been approved by the Commission.

(e) **Instructor application and approval requirements.** An individual determined by the Commission to possess one or more of the following qualifications may be considered for approval as an instructor upon receipt of an application and evidence of education and/or experience. Each application must be accompanied by a One Hundred Dollar ($100.00) application fee, and documentation required for compliance necessary to verify citizenship, qualified alien status, and eligibility under the Personal Responsibility and Work Opportunity Reconciliation Act of 1996. In order to qualify, an individual must possess proof of one of the following:
 (1) Possession of a bachelor's degree in a related field.
 (2) Possession of a valid teaching credential or certificate from Oklahoma or another jurisdiction authorizing the holder to instruct in an applicable field of instruction at the entity.
 (3) Five (5) years full-time experience out of the previous ten (10) years in a profession, trade, or technical occupation in the applicable field of instruction.
 (4) An individual determined by the Commission to possess a combination of education and/or experience in a field related to that in which the person is to instruct, which constitutes an equivalent to one or more of the qualifications in (1), (2) or (3) of subsection (e) of this section.

(f) **Instructor renewal requirements**
 (1) In order to maintain approved status, an instructor must comply with the following:
  (A) Attend a Commission directed Instructor Renewal Course, or its equivalent, every twenty-four (24) months. An exception to this rule may be given by the Commission if such instructor is licensed or certified through another regulatory body.
  (B) Instructors approved solely for distance education courses must complete three (3) hours every twelve (12) months of instructor training as accepted by the Commission and sign a statement that changes to current law and rules have been reviewed and that the instructor has made applicable amendments to the course material.
 (2) Any instructor not meeting the requirements of this subsection will be required to re-apply as an original instructor applicant.

(g) **Guest instructors.** Guest instructors may be utilized provided an approved instructor is also present during presentations. Total guest instruction and lectures shall not consume more than thirty percent (30%) of the total course time.

(h) **Instructor and entity requirements.**
 (1) **Instructor must be present.** An approved instructor must be present in the same room during all course instruction for students to receive credit toward course completion.
 (2) **Retention of records.** An instructor/entity shall maintain enrollment records and roll sheets which include number of hours completed by each student for a period of seven (7) years.
 (3) **Course completion certificate.** Each individual successfully completing a course of study approved by the Commission shall be furnished a certificate prescribed or approved by the Commission certifying completion.

The Commission shall accept from a college or university a certified transcript or a course completion certificate as prescribed by the Commission.
- (4) **Course notification to Commission.** An entity conducting an approved post-license education offering shall, within seven (7) days of the completion thereof, successfully submit to the Commission the list of name(s), license number(s) and other personal identifiers of those licensees who have successfully completed said offering. The information shall be submitted to the Commission by way of electronic format as required by the Commission, along with other information which may reasonably be required.
- (5) **Commission authorized to audit and inspect records.** A duly authorized designee of the Commission may audit any offering and/or inspect the records of the entity at any time during its presentation or during reasonable office hours or the entity may be required to provide the records to the Commission.
- (6) **Clock hours and breaks.** Not more than one clock hour may be registered within any one sixty (60) minute period and no more than ten (10) minutes of each hour shall be utilized for breaks.
- (7) **Class size limited.** Instructor ratio to students shall not exceed sixty (60).
- (i) **Facility requirements.** The offering entity shall ensure that all classroom facilities have adequate lighting, seating space and technology to meet the needs of the student. The classroom area shall be free of distractions and noise.
- (j) **Disciplinary action.** An approved course of study, director, and/or instructor may be withdrawn or disciplined as outlined in Title 59, O.S., Section 858-208, paragraph 6 either on a complaint filed by an interested person or the Commission's own motion, for the following reasons, but only after a hearing before the Commission and/or a Hearing Examiner appointed by the Commission:
  - (1) In the event the real estate license of a director is suspended or revoked, the course of study shall automatically be revoked.
  - (2) In the event the real estate license of an instructor is suspended or revoked.
  - (3) Failure to comply with any portion of the Code or the rules of this Chapter.
  - (4) Falsification of records and/or application(s) filed with the Commission.
  - (5) False and/or misleading advertisement.
  - (6) Any other improper conduct or activity of the director, instructor, or entity the Commission determines to be unacceptable.

605:10-5-2. Approval of a continuing education course
- (a) **Approval and expiration of application.** An entity seeking to conduct an approved continuing education course shall make application for the approval or renewal of each course. Such approval or renewal shall expire at the end of the thirty-sixth (36) month including the month of issuance.
- (b) **Application form.** Entities seeking approval of a course or group of courses totaling thirty-six (36) hours or less shall submit an application on a form prescribed by the Commission along with a nonrefundable fee of seventy dollars ($70.00). Each application is limited to thirty-six (36) hours and shall be submitted on a separate application and accompanied by a non-refundable fee of seventy dollars ($70.00). Such application shall be made on a form prescribed by the Commission. Each application shall include, but is not limited to, the following information:
  - (1) The name(s), address(es), and telephone number(s) of the sponsoring entity, the owner(s), and the coordinator/director responsible for the quality of the course.
  - (2) The title(s) of the course or courses.
  - (3) The number of hours in each course.
  - (4) A copy of each course's curriculum, including comprehensive course objectives, a detailed outline of the course subject matter and instructor(s) for each course.
  - (5) The method the entity will use to evaluate the course offering.
  - (6) The procedure the entity will use to monitor attendance.
  - (7) A personal resume indicating name(s) and qualifications of the instructor(s).
  - (8) Any other relevant information useful in determining that the entity is presenting a course which will meet the definition, purposes, goals and objectives adopted by the Commission.
  - (9) A statement attesting to the fact that in accepting approval as a continuing education entity, the entity will protect and promote the purposes, goals and objectives of continuing education as stated in the License Code and Rules.
- (c) **Commission course approval notice.** The Commission shall within sixty (60) days after receipt of an application inform the entity as to whether the course has been approved, denied, or whether additional information is needed to determine the acceptability of the course.

(d) **Course renewal requirements.** Upon expiration of the time period, as stated in sub-paragraph (a) of this rule, an application for renewal of any course or group of courses by an entity shall also be accompanied by a non-refundable application fee of Seventy Dollars ($70.00) for a thirty-six (36) month period. Renewal applications shall be subject to the same requirements as original applications; however, the renewal application shall be submitted prior to expiration of the course(s).

(e) **Change of information notice requirement.** Whenever there is any change in a course, the entity shall notify the Commission prior to the effective date of the change. Such change shall not be considered approved until written notice is received from the Commission.

(f) **Advertising of course offering.** An entity advertising a course as being approved for continuing education credit shall state in such advertisement, "Approved by the Commission for (correct number) hours of continuing education credit." No entity sponsoring or conducting a course of study shall advertise the course as approved prior to the course receiving approval from the Commission. Further, no entity sponsoring or conducting a course of study shall advertise that it is endorsed, recommended or accredited by the Commission.

(g) **Course requirements and limitations.**
  (1) A course will not be approved by the Commission if its duration is less than one (1) clock hour or its equivalent as determined by the Commission.
  (2) To meet the statutory requirement, a clock hour shall equal sixty (60) minutes, with no more than ten minutes of each hour utilized for breaks.
  (3) An entity conducting an approved continuing education course shall, within seven (7) days of the completion thereof, successfully submit to the Commission the list of name(s), license number(s) and other personal identifiers of those licensees who have successfully completed the course. The information shall be submitted to the Commission by way of electronic format as required by the Commission, along with other information which may reasonably be required.
  (4) Each licensee successfully completing a course shall be furnished a completion certificate, prescribed or approved by the Commission.
  (5) Each course shall be presented in a facility necessary to safely and properly present the course.
  (6) An approved instructor must be present in the same room during all in-class course instruction for students to receive credit toward course completion. If an instructor is presenting a Commission approved in-class course offering which is delivered to the licensees by way of electronic means to receiving sites other than where the instructor is presenting, the Commission may require that each receiving entity site have an in-class person monitoring the class in lieu of a Commission approved instructor.

(h) **Recruitment disallowed.**
  (1) A coordinator/director or instructor shall not allow the classroom to be used by anyone to advertise and/or recruit new affiliates for any firm. The coordinator/director shall cause the following statement to be posted in the classroom in such a manner as will be readable by all participants: "No recruiting for employment opportunities for any real estate brokerage firm is allowed in this class. Any recruiting on behalf of, or permitted by, the Instructor should be promptly reported to the Oklahoma Real Estate Commission."
  (2) An instructor shall not wear any identification relating to a specific name or identity of a real estate firm, a group of companies or franchises while in the class or on the premises.

(i) **Instructor application and approval requirements:** An individual may, upon receipt of an application and evidence of education and/or experience, be considered for approval as an instructor for a three (3) year period including the month of approval. Each application for approval must be accompanied by a Ten Dollar ($10.00) application fee. In order to qualify, an individual must possess proof of one of the following:
  (1) Possession of a bachelor's degree in a related field.
  (2) Possession of a valid teaching credential or certificate from Oklahoma or another jurisdiction authorizing the holder to instruct in an applicable field of instruction.
  (3) Five (5) years full-time experience out of the previous ten (10) years in a profession, trade, or technical occupation in the applicable field of instruction.
  (4) An individual determined by the Commission to possess a combination of education and/or experience, in a field related to that in which the person is to instruct, which constitute an equivalent to one or more of the qualifications in (1), (2) or (3) of this subsection.

(j) **Denied application; appeal.** If the Commission is of the opinion that a proposed continuing education offering does not qualify under the Code and/or Rules of the Commission, the Commission shall refuse to approve the offering and shall give notice of that fact to the party applying for approval within fifteen (15) days after its decision. Upon written request from the denied party, filed within thirty (30) days after receipt of the notice of denial, the

Commission shall set the matter for hearing to be conducted within sixty (60) days after receipt of the request. The hearing procedure shall be that as outlined in 605:10-1-3, titled "Appeal of administrative decisions; procedures."

(k) **Disciplinary action.** The Commission may withdraw or discipline as outlined in Title 59, O.S., Section 858-208, paragraph 6 the approval of a coordinator/director, instructor, offering or entity either on a complaint filed by an interested person or on the Commission's own motion, for any of the following reasons, but only after a hearing before the Commission and/or a Hearing Examiner appointed by the Commission:
   (1) In the event the real estate license of an instructor and/or coordinator/director is revoked or suspended.
   (2) Failure to submit all documents, statements and forms as may be reasonably required by the Commission.
   (3) Falsification of records and/or applications filed with the Commission.
   (4) False and/or misleading advertising.
   (5) Failure to revise an offering so as to reflect and present current real estate practices, knowledge, and laws.
   (6) Failure to maintain proper classroom order and decorum.
   (7) Any conduct which gives the coordinator/director, instructor or entity presenting the offering an unfair advantage over other brokers and/or real estate companies.
   (8) Failure to comply with any portion of the Code or rules of this Chapter.
   (9) Any other improper conduct or activity of the director, instructor, or entity the Commission determines to be unacceptable.
(l) **Retention of records.** An instructor/entity shall maintain enrollment records and roll sheets which include number of hours completed by each student for seven (7) years.
(m) **Commission authorized to audit.** A duly authorized designee of the Commission may audit any offering and/or inspect the records of the entity at any time during its presentation or during reasonable office hours or the entity may be required to provide the records to the Commission.
(n) **Licensee/Instructor course credit.**
   (1) A licensee who is the instructor of an approved offering for continuing education shall be credited with one (1) hour for each hour of actual instruction performed.
   (2) An instructor may not receive continuing education credit for instructing an offering more than one time during a license term.
   (3) Records of such instruction shall be reported and maintained in the same manner as prescribed for participants elsewhere in the rules of this Chapter.
(o) **Guest instructors.** Guest instructors may be utilized for in-class instruction provided an approved instructor is also present during presentations. Total guest instruction and lectures shall not consume more than thirty percent (30%) of the total course time.

605:10-5-3. Standards for Commission approved real estate courses
(a) **Approved instructor.** Each in-class course offering shall be conducted by a Commission approved instructor. Each entity conducting a distance education course offering shall have available a Commission approved instructor. The instructor shall be available during normal business hours as posted by the instructor to answer questions about the course material and provide assistance as necessary.
(b) **Student must attend entire in-class instruction or complete all modules required for distance education instruction.** In order for an entity to certify a student as passing an approved course the student must either: (1) attend the required number of hours of in-class instruction; or (2) complete all instructional modules required for distance education instruction.
(c) **Student must successfully complete a prelicense, postlicense or distance education course offering examination.** In order for an entity to certify a student as passing an approved prelicense, postlicense or distance education course, the student must successfully complete an examination covering the contents of the course material.
(d) **Student transfers.** Except with the prior approval of the Commission, a student transferring from one course to another may not count any portion of the student's attendance or work in the former course toward passing the course. A student who enrolls in an entity which offers a Commission approved course may not transfer credit for a course or courses completed in that series to another entity unless the receiving entity offers the identical series of courses and the receiving entity agrees to accept and examine said student throughout successful completion.
(e) **Course examinations.** Each approved prelicense provisional sales associate course and postlicense course offering shall conclude with an end-of-course examination consisting of no less than two hundred (200) questions administered by the approved entity. Each approved prelicense broker course shall conclude with an end-of-course examination consisting of no less than two hundred and fifty (250) questions administered by the approved entity.

Each approved distance continuing education course offering shall conclude with an end-of-course examination consisting of no less than seven (7) questions for each clock hour. End-of-course examination questions may not be the same as any previously used questions covering the respective course content.

(f) **Successful completion.** In order for a student to successfully complete a prelicense, postlicense or distance education course, the entity must require that the student complete all class material and/or modules and achieve a passing score of at least eighty percent (80%) on the entity's final examination. An entity shall require the student to complete sufficient material or modules to ensure mastery of the course offering, and shall require the student to complete the end-of-course examination. An entity may allow any student who fails to achieve a passing score the opportunity to take another examination without repeating instruction.

(g) **Grading standards.** In order for an entity to certify a student as passing an approved course, the student must meet the minimum grading standards established by this Section and the entity. On graded examinations for which this Section sets specific requirements, the entity's policy shall at least equal those requirements as listed in this Section. Other grading standards shall be in accordance with generally accepted educational standards. An entity shall publish grading standards and give them to a student in a written form at the beginning of the course.

(h) **Commission may impose sanction.** The Commission may impose any sanction permitted by law or Rules of the Commission on the approval of any entity, director and/or instructor which fails to provide proper security for their course evaluation or examination and for failing to comply with standards as set out in this Chapter.

(i) **Each entity must post notice.** Each entity must post or provide a notice that is easily observed by any person desiring to enroll in a prelicense course. The notice must at least include the following language: Oklahoma Statutes, Title 59, Section 858.301.1 "Effective November 1, 2009, state law prohibits the issuance of a real estate license to any person who has been convicted, pled guilty or pled nolo contendere to a felony for a pre-determined number of years based on the classification of said felony. For clarification, please contact the Commission and/or review the cited section of law as referenced herein. Additionally, if the applicant has delinquent unpaid child support or students loans, the applicant must check with the Real Estate Commission before enrolling in this class. The Commission will allow the applicant to seek preapproval prior to enrolling in a pre-license course."

(j) **Additional distance education course requirements.**
  (1) Each course shall contain suitable learning objectives.
  (2) Overview statements must be included for each course providing a quick preview of what is contained in the offering.
  (3) A complete set of questions and an answer key for all examinations must be provided to the Commission with each course application. An answer key may not be included in any course materials provided to the student.
  (4) From the date of enrollment, the course shall have a validity period of six (6) months in which to allow successful completion to be attained.
  (5) Entities must include information with the course material that clearly informs the student of the completion time frame, passing and examination requirements, and any other relevant information necessary to complete the course.
  (6) Each course must include a statement that the information presented in the course should not be used as a substitute for competent legal advice.
  (7) Course offerings must be sufficient in scope and content to justify the hours requested for approval.

(k) Each entity shall promote the Basic Course of Real Estate as Part I of a two part series and the Provisional Postlicense Course of Real Estate as Part II of that series. Applicants are to be advised that Part II of the series is not to begin until after license issuance and shall be completed prior to their first license expiration.

(l) All materials that are distributed to students in any class must be current and up-to-date with the License Code and Rules and state or federal laws.

605:10-7-1. License issuance

No real estate licensee shall begin operations in the real estate business without first having been issued his or her numbered active license certificate. This includes all original licenses, activations, reinstatements and all license types being changed from an associate to a broker or branch office broker, as defined in the rules.

605:10-7-1.1. Documentation required for compliance necessary to verify citizenship, qualified alien status, and eligibility under the Personal Responsibility and Work Opportunity Reconciliation Act of 1996

License renewals and reinstatements. Individuals who submit an application on or after July 1, 2002, shall be required to provide documentation necessary to verify compliance of citizenship, qualified alien status, and eligibility under the Personal Responsibility and Work Opportunity Reconciliation Act of 1996. Failure to provide this documentation shall result in disapproval of the application. If an individual fails to provide proof of citizenship within sixty (60) days from the date of reissuance of their license or approval, the individual will be placed inactive until the Commission receives current proof of citizenship or qualified alien status.

605:10-7-2. License terms and fees; renewals; reinstatements
(a) **License term and fees.** Each original license issued under the Code shall be issued to expire at the end of the thirty-sixth (36) month including the month of issuance. Each original provisional sales associate license issued under the Code shall be issued to expire at the end of the twelfth (12th) month including the month of issuance. Fees are non-refundable and are as follows:
  (1) For an original broker license and each subsequent license renewal, to include corporations, associations or partnerships, the fee shall be Two Hundred and Ten Dollars ($210.00).
  (2) For an inactive original broker license and each subsequent inactive license renewal, with the exception of corporations, associations or partnerships, the fee shall be One Hundred and Twenty-five Dollars ($125.00). In order to activate a license that was renewed inactive in the same license term, the licensee shall pay One Hundred and Thirty Dollars ($130.00). Thereafter, any future request to activate in the same license term shall be in accordance with Rule 605:10-7-4.
  (3) For an active original sales associate license and each subsequent active license renewal the fee shall be One Hundred and Fifty Dollars ($150.00).
  (4) For an inactive original sales associate license and each subsequent inactive license renewal the fee shall be Ninety-five Dollars ($95.00). In order to activate a sales associate license that was renewed inactive in the same license term, the licensee shall pay One Hundred Dollars ($100.00). Thereafter, any future request to activate in the same license term shall be in accordance with Rule 605:10-7-4.
  (5) For an original provisional sales associate license that is non-renewable the fee shall be Seventy Dollars ($70.00).
  (6) For an original branch office license and each subsequent license renewal the fee shall be One Hundred and Twenty-five Dollars ($125.00).
  (7) For each duplicate license or pocket card, where the original is lost or destroyed, and a written request is made, a fee of Seven Dollars and fifty cents ($7.50) shall be charged.
  (8) The Fifteen Dollar ($15.00) Education and Recovery Fund fee, shall be added and payable with the license fee for an original license and for each subsequent license renewal. Exceptions to this rule are: 1) a provisional sales associate license fee shall be Five Dollars ($5.00) for their twelve (12) month license term; and, 2) a branch office shall not pay the fee.
(b) **Terms cannot be altered.** Terms shall not be altered except for purposes of general reassignment of terms which might be necessitated for the purpose of maintaining an equitable staggered license term system.
(c) **Expiration date.** The actual expiration date of a license shall be midnight of the last day of the month of the designated license term. A person who allows their license to expire shall be considered an applicant and subject to a national criminal history record check, as defined by Section 150.9 of Title 74 of the Oklahoma Statutes.
(d) **Late penalty.** All renewals shall be filed on or before midnight of the tenth day of the month in which said license is due to expire, except in the event that date falls on a Saturday, Sunday or holiday; in such case, the next Commission working day shall be considered the due date for all renewals except electronic online renewal wherein this exception would not apply. Any such renewal application filed after such date shall be subject to a late penalty fee of Ten Dollars ($10.00).
(e) **Actual filing of license renewal.** A license shall lapse and terminate if a renewal application and required fees have not been filed with the Commission by midnight of the date on which the license is due to expire, except in the event that date falls on a Saturday, Sunday or holiday; in such a case, the next Commission working day shall be considered the due date. A renewal application and required fees are considered filed with the Commission on the date of the United States postal service postmark or the date personal delivery is made to the Commission office.
(f) **Reinstatement of license.** Any licensee whose license term has expired shall be considered for reinstatement of such license upon payment of an amount equal to the current examination fee in addition to the license and late penalty fee(s) for each delinquent license period(s). The following documents and fees must be submitted:
  (1) **Lapsed less than one year.** In the case of a license lapsed less than one year:
    (A) License and late penalty fee.
    (B) Reinstatement fee.
    (C) National criminal history check.

(D) Documents as required by the Commission
(2) **Lapsed more than one year but less than three years.** In the case of a license lapsed more than one year but less than three years:
   (A) License and late penalty fee.
   (B) Reinstatement fee.
   (C) National criminal history check.
   (D) A completed reinstatement application.
   (E) Successful completion of the appropriate licensing examination.
   (F) A statement that the applicant has read a current License Code and Rules booklet.
   (G) Documents as required by the Commission.
(3) **Lapsed more than three years.** If an application is submitted more than three (3) years subsequent to the most recent year of licensure, the applicant shall be regarded as an original applicant.

(g) **Reinstatement of a provisional sales associate license wherein post-license education was completed prior to license expiration date.** An applicant who successfully completed the post-license education requirement before their first license expiration date and failed to renew their license on or before such date shall be eligible to reinstate the license as a sales associate according to 605:10-7-2 (f), (1) through (3).

(h) **Reinstatement of a provisional sales associate license wherein post-license education was not completed prior to license expiration date.** An applicant who has not successfully completed the post-license education requirement prior to the first license expiration date shall not be eligible to reinstate such license and shall apply and qualify as an original applicant.

(i) **Reinstatement of revoked license.** An applicant may not apply for re-license or reinstatement of license for a minimum of three (3) years from the effective date of license revocation, except for an applicant whose license was automatically revoked pursuant to Sections 858-402 or 858-604 of Title 59, Oklahoma Statutes. Upon the passage of the three (3) year period, the applicant shall be required to comply with the requirements of an original applicant.

(j) **Reinstatement of an automatically revoked license.** An applicant who has had their license automatically revoked, pursuant to Section 858-402 or 858-604 of Title 59 of the Oklahoma Statutes, shall be required to comply with the requirements of (f) of this section. In addition, reinstatement will not be granted until all outstanding amounts due the Commission have been paid in full.

(k) **Reinstatement of a surrendered or cancelled license.** A surrendered or cancelled license applicant may be reinstated provided the applicant has received approval for re-issuance from the Commission. The following forms and fees must be submitted:
   (1) **Reinstatement with term of license still current.** A surrendered or cancelled license applicant whose license term is still current:
      (A) Applicable reinstatement fee equal to the current examination fee.
      (B) Re-issuance fee equal to the transfer of license fee.
      (C) Documents as required by the Commission.
      (D) Criminal history background check.
   (2) **Reinstatement with term of license expired.** A surrendered or cancelled license applicant whose license term has expired shall be required to comply with the requirements of (f) of this section.
   (3) **Reinstatement of provisional sales associate with term of license expired.** A surrendered or cancelled provisional sales associate whose license term has expired shall be required to comply with the following:
      (A) If a provisional sales associate completed the post-license requirement on or before the first license expiration date, the applicant shall be eligible to reinstate the license according to 605:10-7-2 (f), (1) through (2).
      (B) If a provisional sales associate did not complete the post-license requirement on or before the first license expiration date, the applicant shall be required to apply and qualify as an original applicant.

(l) **Continuing education requirement.** Each licensee with the exception of those as listed in Title 59, O.S., Section 858-307.2 (D) seeking renewal of a license must submit evidence that they have completed the continuing education requirements enumerated in Section 858-307.2 of Title 59. An applicant seeking active reinstatement of a lapsed license must submit evidence that all continuing education requirements have been completed for each term in which an active license is requested.

(m) **Sales to broker license fee prorated.** If a real estate sales associate or provisional sales associate qualifies for a license as a real estate broker, the unused license fee shall be credited to the broker license fee. The unused license fee credit shall commence with the first full month following the month in which the broker license is to be issued.

(n) **License expires after effective date of national criminal history check.**

(1) Any licensee who allows their license to expire shall be required to submit to a national criminal history check; however, such individual shall be allowed to proceed with reinstatement of such license pending receipt by the Commission of a completed fingerprint card, application Part A, and fee as stated elsewhere in these rules for the background search. If, the Commission does not receive a completed Part A of the application and completed finger print card and fee within thirty (30) days from the date of request by the Commission, the license will be placed inactive and a hold placed on the license until receipt by the Commission of the aforementioned items. Thereafter, upon receipt by the Commission, the license may be reactivated so long as appropriate reactivation forms and fees, as stated elsewhere in these rules, have been received by the Commission. However, if the finger print card is rejected for the purposes of a national criminal history check, the Commission will provide written notice to the licensee and the licensee must submit a new and unique fingerprint card to the Commission within thirty (30) days of receipt of such notice or the license will be placed on inactive status.

(2) A provisional sales associate who completes the Provisional Post-License Course prior to their first license expiration date but fails to timely renew the license shall be eligible to apply under the requirement under the preceding paragraph. However, after a period of three (3) years from the date of the license expiration such applicant shall no longer be eligible to apply under this section.

(o) **Issuance of license from provisional sales associate to sales associate.** A provisional sales associate is required to furnish to the Commission evidence of successful completion of the Provisional Post-license Course of Real Estate, Part II of II education requirement as set forth in Section 858-302 of Title 59, of the Oklahoma Statutes. Upon successful completion of the Provisional Post-license Course of Real Estate, Part II of II education requirement, the provisional sales associate must submit the appropriate document(s) to the Commission prior to the provisional sales associate's license expiration date for issuance of a renewable sales associate license. The Commission shall not issue the provisional sales associate a renewable sales associate license until the end of the provisional sales associate's license term and until the provisional sales associate has submitted evidence of successful completion of the forty-five (45) clock hour post-license course requirement and submitted all required form(s) and fee(s) as required by the Commission.

(p) **Active sales associate to inactive broker license - no remaining credit to be given.** In the event an active sales associate within six (6) months of obtaining their original license, reinstatement or license renewal qualifies for an inactive broker license, the Commission shall not credit the difference in the license fees.

(q) **Licensee on active duty as a member of the Armed Forces of the United States.**
  (1) In accordance with Title 59, O.S., Section 4100.6 of the Post-Military Service Occupation, Education and Credentialing Act while a license holder is on active duty the license may be renewed without payment of the license and education and recovery fund fee and meeting the continuing education requirement. Such waiver shall be requested in writing to the Commission prior to license expiration along with evidence of the order for active duty. The license issued pursuant to this rule may be continued as long as the licensee is a member of the Armed Forces of the United States on active duty and for a period of at least one (1) year after discharge from active duty. Upon discharge from active duty and a request for license activation, the licensee shall submit to the Commission evidence of successful completion of the continuing education requirement for the current license renewal term.
  (2) If a licensee on active duty does not request such a waiver in writing and the license expires, the applicant may, by written request provide the Commission documentation as required in subparagraph (1) of this subsection; however, no later than one (1) year after discharge from active duty.
  (3) In the event a license expires during the events as noted herein, the Commission shall waive the criminal history background check and license examination.
  (4) **Member of the National Guard or reserve component of the armed forces.** In accordance with Title 72, Chapter 1, Section 48.2 Extension and Renewal of Professional Licenses, any licensee whose license expires while on active duty as a member of the National Guard or reserve component of the armed forces shall be extended until no later than one (1) year after the member is discharged from active duty status. Upon the Commission receiving a copy of the official orders calling the member or reservist to active duty and official orders discharging the member or reservist from active duty all licensee fee and continuing education shall be waived for this time period as well as the criminal history background check and license examination.

(r) **Reinstatement for corporation, association or partnership.**
  (1) A corporation, association or partnership that has lapsed for less than three (3) years that wishes to reinstate must submit:
    (A) License and late penalty fees.

(B) Reinstatement forms and documents as required by the Commission.
(C) If the corporation or association has been lapsed for more than sixty (60) days, a current "Certification of Good Standing."
(2) Any corporation, association or partnership that has lapsed for than three (3) years must submit an original application to be considered for licensure.

(s) **Reinstatement for branch offices.**
(1) A branch office that is lapsed for less than three (3) years that wishes to reinstate must submit:
(A) License fee and late penalty fees.
(B) Reinstatement forms and documents as required by the Commission.
(2) Any branch office that has lapsed for more than three (3) years must submit an original application as a new branch office.

605:10-7-3. Placement of license on inactive status

In conformance with Section 858-309 of the Code a licensee who at any time fails to comply with all Code and Rule requirements for active license status shall be placed on inactive status. If a licensee fails to comply with a request for documentation from the Commission, based on another appropriate statutory or rule requirement which affects the license, the Commission shall place the license inactive. At any time the licensee complies with all requested requirements, the license shall be issued on active status.

605:10-7-4. Request for activation or re-issuance of license
(a) **Requirements.** All requests for activation or re-issuance of a license must be accompanied by the appropriate documents and fee of Twenty-five Dollars ($25.00) as required by the Commission. Upon activation of an inactive license wherein the licensee paid the reduced inactive license fee rate, the licensee shall be required to pay the remaining active license fee as outlined in 605:10-7-2.
(b) **Multiple change requests on same license.** In the event a licensee's request involves more than one change to the license at the same time, and each individual change requires a separate fee elsewhere in the rules of this Chapter, the Commission shall only require that one fee be charged to reissue the license if the request is done in a timely manner.
(c) **Continuing education required for activation.** A licensee requesting activation of a license must have complied with the continuing education requirement as set forth in Section 858-307.2 of Title 59 of the Oklahoma Statutes and rule 605:10-3-6. Further, upon a licensee's request for activation being completed and processed, the licensee shall then be required to complete the continuing education requirement for the next license term for which the license is to be renewed active or activated.
(d) **Active status requested, however, Commission unable to activate for reasons as stated in statutes elsewhere.** In the event a licensee requests an active original license, subsequent license renewal, or activation to be issued on active status and for reasons beyond the Commission's control the licensee is unable to obtain an active license at that time, the fees as received by the Commission shall be retained and not refunded. Once the licensee corrects the problem with the appropriate regulatory agency and such agency authorizes the issuance of an active license, the Commission will then, upon receipt of an activation fee and required documentation, issue an active license.

605:10-7-5. Name changes
(a) **Name change request.** Any change of name of a licensee or licensed firm must be filed in the Commission office within ten (10) days of such change. Filed shall mean the date of the United States postal service postmark or the date personal delivery is made to the Commission office. The licensee or firm shall return the license certificate to the Commission office along with the request for such name change. Upon any request for a change of name there shall be paid a fee to the Commission of Twenty-five Dollars ($25.00) for each license to be changed. The Commission may require additional documents as may reasonably be required by the Secretary-Treasurer.
(b) **Group name changes.** Under certain circumstances as determined by the Commission, the Commission may place a cap of Seven Hundred Fifty Dollars ($750.00) on group transactions requesting licenses to be reissued. To qualify, such request must be received complete and require no further correspondence and/or documents except for the issuance of the licenses.

605:10-7-6. Certification of license history
   Each request for a certification of license history shall be in the form of a letter to the Commission accompanied by a fee of Fifteen Dollars ($15.00).

605:10-7-7. Branch offices
(a) **Each additional office must be licensed.** If a broker desires to do business from more than one office location, the broker must license each additional office location as a branch office by submitting forms and fees as required by the Commission. The license shall be maintained in the branch office and available upon request.
(b) **Associate's license issued to branch office.** An associate's license shall be issued to and maintained in the office to which the associate is assigned.
(c) **Broker to designate a branch office broker to act.** A broker shall designate a branch office broker, other than himself or herself, to act as broker for each location, to supervise the activities of the branch office. The branch office shall be licensed in conformance with Section 858-310 of the Code. The branch office broker may be designated to perform all duties and sign documents on behalf of the broker with respect to the branch office at the discretion of the broker. Such designation shall be in writing and filed with the Commission. The branch office broker assumes the responsibility in conjunction with the broker, for all associates assigned to the branch office.
(d) **Broker may act as branch office broker; restriction.** A broker may act as the branch office broker if the branch office is located at the same location as the main office upon the appropriate documents and fees being filed with the Commission.
(e) **Reappointment of branch office broker.** In the event of the death, disability, retirement or cessation of employment for any reason by the designated branch office broker, and the branch office is to continue business, the main office broker shall appoint a new branch office broker and file the appropriate documents with the Commission within ten (10) days of the occurrence of the event.
(f) **Branch office must utilize the same name or trade name of main office.** A branch office may utilize a trade name which is different than the main office so long as the broker registers the name(s) with the Commission.

605:10-7-8. Corporation licensing procedures and requirements of good standing
(a) **Broker license requirement.** Each corporation who performs activities which require a real estate license pursuant to Title 59, O.S., Section 858-102 of the License "Code" shall apply as a real estate broker. Upon approval by the Commission, the corporation shall be granted a real estate broker license. In order to obtain a license, the corporation shall furnish to the satisfaction of the Commission, but not limited to, the following items:
   (1) Completed application form(s) and required fee(s).
   (2) Verification that the corporation is authorized to transact business as a corporation in the State of Oklahoma and that the corporation is in good standing in the State of Oklahoma.
   (3) Corporation must be in compliance with Title 59, O.S., Section 858-312.1 of the License "Code".
   (4) Corporation must have a managing corporate broker who holds a separate license as a real estate broker.
   (5) The designation of a managing corporate broker shall be established by sworn statement signed by the President of the corporation stating the date and place such action was effected.
   (6) In the event of the death, disability, retirement or cessation of employment for any reason of the managing corporate broker, the corporation shall be required to appoint a new managing corporate broker and such notice of change must be filed in the Commission office no later than five (5) working days of the occurrence of the event. The notice of change in a managing corporate broker must be accompanied by the appropriate documents as required by the Commission and a Twenty-five Dollar ($25.00) change of status fee.
   (7) The corporation is to notify the Commission in writing within ten (10) days of the date of a change in corporate officers.
(b) **Corporation and managing corporate broker responsible for acts.** The managing corporate broker in conjunction with the corporation is responsible for all acts of the corporation, including the acts of all associates associated with the corporation.
(c) **Corporation closing requirements or partial ceasing of real estate activities.** When a corporation discontinues a portion of real estate activities or ceases all real estate activities, the corporation is required to comply with the following:
   (1) Immediately notify the Commission.
   (2) Comply with Section 605:10-13-1 (n).

(d) **Group change information.** Under certain circumstances as determined by the Commission, the Commission may place a cap of Seven Hundred Fifty Dollars ($750.00) on group transactions requesting licenses to be issued. To qualify, such request must be received complete and require no further correspondence and/or documents except for the issuance of the licenses.

605:10-7-8.1. Partnership licensing procedures and requirements of good standing
(a) **Broker license requirement.** Each partnership who performs activities which require a real estate license pursuant to Title 59, O.S., Section 858-102 of the License "Code" shall apply as a real estate broker. Upon approval by the Commission, the partnership shall be granted a real estate broker license. In order to obtain a license, the partnership shall furnish to the satisfaction of the Commission, but not limited to, the following items:
  (1) Completed application form(s) and required fee(s).
  (2) A written statement signed by all partners attesting to the formation of a partnership and that it is in good standing in the State of Oklahoma.
  (3) Partnership must be in compliance with Title 59, O.S., Section 858-312.1 of the License "Code".
  (4) Partnership must have a minimum of two managing partners who each hold a separate license as a real estate broker.
  (5) The designation of the managing partners shall be established by sworn statement signed by the managing partners of the partnership stating the date and place such action was effected.
  (6) In the event of the death, disability, retirement or cessation of employment for any reason of the managing partner(s), the partnership is dissolved unless the partnership agreement provides otherwise. If the partnership agreement provides for the continuation of the partnership after the loss of a partner, the partnership shall be required to appoint a new managing partner and such notice of change must be filed in the Commission office no later than five (5) working days of the occurrence of the event. The notice of change in managing partners must be accompanied by the appropriate documents as required by the Commission and a Twenty-five Dollars ($25.00) change of status fee.
(b) **Partnership and managing partners responsible for acts.** The managing partners in conjunction with the partnership are responsible for all acts of the partnership, including the acts of all associates associated with the partnership. If a corporation or association is a partner of the partnership a letter must be submitted by the firm acknowledging that the managing member of the association or managing broker of the corporation is responsible for all acts of the partnership, including the acts of all associates associated with the partnership.
(c) **Partnership closing requirements or partial ceasing of real estate activities.** When a partnership discontinues a portion of the real estate activities or ceases all real estate activities, the partnership is required to comply with the following:
  (1) Immediately notify the Commission.
  (2) Comply with Section 605:10-13-1 (n).
(d) **Group change information.** Under certain circumstances as determined by the Commission, the Commission may place a cap of Seven Hundred Fifty Dollars ($750.00) on group transactions requesting licenses to be issued. To qualify, such request must be received complete and require no further correspondence and/or documents except for the issuance of the licenses.

605:10-7-8.2. Association licensing procedures and requirements of good standing
(a) **Broker license requirement.** Each association who performs activities which require a real estate license pursuant to Title 59, O.S., Section 858-102 of the License "Code" shall apply as a real estate broker. Upon approval by the Commission, the association shall be granted a real estate broker license. In order to obtain a license, the association shall furnish to the satisfaction of the Commission, but not limited to, the following items:
  (1) Completed application form(s) and required fee(s).
  (2) Verification that the association is authorized to transact business as an association in the State of Oklahoma and that the association is in good standing in the State of Oklahoma.
  (3) Association must be in compliance with Title 59, O.S., Section 858-312.1 of the License "Code".
  (4) Association must have a managing member or manager who holds a separate license as a real estate broker.
  (5) The designation of a managing broker member or manager shall be established by sworn statement signed by an authorized member or manager of the association stating the date and place such action was effected.

(6) In the event of the death, disability, retirement or cessation of employment for any reason of the managing broker member or manager, the association shall be required to appoint a new managing broker member or manager and such notice of change must be filed in the Commission office no later than five (5) working days of the occurrence of the event. The notice of change in a managing broker member or manager must be accompanied by the appropriate documents as required by the Commission and a Twenty-five Dollar ($25.00) change of status fee.

(b) **Association and managing broker member or manager responsible for acts.** The managing broker member or manager in conjunction with the association is responsible for all acts of the association, including the acts of all associates associated with the association.

(c) **Association closing requirements or partial ceasing of real estate activities.** When an association discontinues a portion of the real estate activities or ceases all real estate activities, the association is required to comply with the following:
  (1) Immediately notify the Commission.
  (2) Comply with Section 605:10-13-1 (n).

(d) **Limited liability company.** A limited liability company shall be considered as an association.

(e) **Group change information.** Under certain circumstances as determined by the Commission, the Commission may place a cap of Seven Hundred Fifty Dollars ($750.00) on group transactions requesting licenses to be issued. To qualify, such request must be received complete and require no further correspondence and/or documents except for the issuance of the licenses.

605:10-7-8.3. Sole Proprietor licensing procedures

(a) **Sole Proprietor.** A sole proprietor is a broker that is the sole owner of a real estate business/firm. To qualify for a sole proprietorship, the firm shall not conduct business in the name of an entity, i.e., corporation, association (Limited Liability Company) or partnership and the business/firm shall not be owned by any other person or entity. To apply as sole proprietor one must meet all requirements for a broker license and submit to the Commission the following:
  (1) Completed sole proprietor broker application form(s) and fee(s) as required by the Commission.
  (2) An associate release form if previously associated with a sponsoring broker.

(b) **Death, disability or retirement.** In the event of the death, disability or retirement of the sole proprietor, the sole proprietor firm shall cease business activities.

(c) **Broker responsible.** A sole proprietor broker is responsible for all acts of associates licensed with the firm.

(d) **Ceasing business activities.** When the sole proprietor discontinues a portion of the real estate activities or ceases all real estate activities, the sole proprietor is required to comply with the following:
  (1) Immediately notify the Commission.
  (2) Comply with Section 605:10-13-1 (n).

(e) **Group change information.** Under certain circumstances as determined by the Commission, the Commission may place a cap of Seven Hundred Fifty Dollars ($750.00) on group transactions requesting licenses to be issued. To qualify, such request must be received complete and require no further correspondence and/or documents except for the issuance of the licenses.

605:10-7-8.4. Managing broker, broker proprietor or branch broker's corporation or association formed for the purpose of receiving compensation

Within the meaning of subsection 14 of Section 858-312 of the "Code" payment of a commission by a broker to a managing broker's, broker proprietor's or branch broker's corporation or association does not constitute a payment of a fee (commission) to an unlicensed person provided the corporation or association and the managing broker, broker proprietor or branch broker abide by the following requirements:
  (1) The corporation or association shall not perform any act requiring a real estate license and shall not hold itself out as engaged in such activity.
  (2) The managing broker, broker proprietor or branch broker must have an active individual real estate license.
  (3) The broker of the branch broker must provide to the Commission a written statement approving of the branch broker's corporation or association.
  (4) The managing broker, broker proprietor or branch broker must be the majority stockholder and president of the corporation or majority member of the association.

(5) Ownership of a managing broker's, broker proprietor's or branch broker's corporation or association is limited to spouses and blood relatives.
(6) The corporation or association shall not advertise nor receive referral fees or commissions except from the broker.
(7) The managing broker, broker proprietor or branch broker must file a written statement with the Commission including the following:
   (A) A statement that the managing broker, broker proprietor or branch broker is the majority stockholder and president of the corporation or majority member of the association.
   (B) Names and relation of all officers/members and/or stockholders.
   (C) Verification that the association or corporation is in good standing with the Oklahoma Secretary of State.

605:10-7-9. Nonresident licensing
(a) **Nonresident licensed in another jurisdiction.** A nonresident applicant may apply to the Commission for a license to operate as a nonresident by submitting all appropriate documents as required by the Commission and furnish evidence that the applicant possesses a current active license in the applicant's resident jurisdiction or another jurisdiction in which the applicant has qualified for a license. No license shall be issued to any nonresident applicant at a higher level than the highest license of any current active license in the applicant's resident jurisdiction or another jurisdiction in which the applicant has qualified for a license. All nonresidents shall be required to complete the appropriate examination as required by the Commission No inactive license experience may be credited to qualify under this section. The Commission may issue a nonresident license if such nonresident has qualified and maintains a license in another jurisdiction and meets the following qualifications:
(1) A nonresident applicant who has been actively licensed as a sales associate or broker respectively for a minimum of two (2) years out of the previous five (5) years.
   (A) A nonresident applicant that applies under this paragraph must complete and submit the following:
     (i) Appropriate application(s).
     (ii) License certification(s) from the jurisdiction in which the applicant has held and/or currently holds a license.
     (iii) Criminal history background application, fingerprint card and fee.
     (iv) Examination fee and successful completion of the state portion of the examination.
     (v) Consent for service of jurisdiction form.
     (vi) Proof of completion of at least one (1) continuing education clock hour in each of the following Oklahoma-specific subjects: Broker Relationships Act, Contracts and Forms, and Code and Rule Updates.
   (B) Upon the Commission granting approval to the nonresident applicant for licensure in this jurisdiction, the applicant must complete and submit the following:
     (i) appropriate license application form(s) along with license and education and recovery fund fees.
(2) A nonresident applicant who has been actively licensed less than two (2) years as a sales associate or broker respectively out of the previous five (5) years must successfully complete the appropriate examination.
   (A) A nonresident applicant applying under this paragraph must complete and submit the following:
     (i) Appropriate application(s).
     (ii) License certification(s) from jurisdiction(s) in which the applicant has held and/or currently holds a license.
     (iii) Criminal history background application, fingerprint card and fee.
     (iv) Examination fee and successful completion of the entire appropriate examination.
     (v) Consent for service of jurisdiction form.
     (vi) Proof of completion of at least one (1) continuing education clock hour in each of the following Oklahoma-specific subjects: Broker Relationships Act, Contracts and Forms, and Code and Rule Updates.
   (B) Upon the Commission granting approval to the nonresident applicant for licensure in this jurisdiction, the applicant must complete and submit the following:
     (i) Appropriate license application form(s) along with license and education and recovery fund fees.
(b) **Nonresident agreement.** The Commission may enter into a nonresident agreement with another jurisdiction and thereby qualify actively licensed nonresident applicants for licensing in this jurisdiction provided the Commission

determines that the educational and experience requirements of the other jurisdiction are equivalent or equal to this jurisdiction; however, the applicant shall be required to comply with paragraph (a)(1)(A) and (B) of this section.

(c) **Nonresident applicant that is inactive in another jurisdiction.** A nonresident applicant who holds an inactive license in another jurisdiction and is unable to meet the requirement under paragraph (a) of this section may apply to the Commission for a license to operate as a nonresident provisional sales associate or broker by submitting all appropriate documents and successfully completing all requirements as required by the Commission.

(1) The nonresident applicant must complete and submit the following:
   (A) Appropriate application(s).
   (B) Criminal history background application, fingerprint card and fee.
   (C) Qualify as an original applicant by submitting proof of appropriate required education.
   (D) Examination fee and successful completion of the entire appropriate examination.
   (E) License certification(s) from the jurisdiction(s) in which the applicant holds or has held a license.
   (F) Consent for service of jurisdiction form.
   (G) Proof of completion of at least one (1) continuing education clock hour in each of the following Oklahoma-specific subjects: Broker Relationships Act, Contracts and Forms, and Code and Rule Updates.

(2) Upon the Commission granting approval to the nonresident applicant for licensure in this jurisdiction, the applicant must complete and submit appropriate license application form(s) along with license and education and recovery fund fees.

(d) **Consent for service of jurisdiction.** Prior to the issuance of a license to a nonresident, such nonresident shall file with the Commission a designation in writing that appoints the Secretary-Treasurer of the Commission to act as the licensed agent, upon whom all judicial and other process or legal notices directed to such nonresident licensee may be served. Service upon the agent so designated shall be equivalent to personal service upon the licensee. Copies of such appointment, certified by the Secretary-Treasurer of the Commission, shall be deemed sufficient evidence thereof and shall be admitted into evidence with the same force and effect as the original thereof. In such written designation, the licensee shall agree and stipulate that any notice or instrument which is served upon such agent shall be of the same legal force and validity as if served upon the licensee, and that the authority shall continue in force so long as any liability remains outstanding in this state. Upon receipt of any such process or notice the Secretary-Treasurer shall forthwith mail a copy of the same, by certified mail, to the last known business address of the licensee.

(e) **License history and application requirements.** Prior to the approval of the application, the nonresident must file with the Commission a certification of licensure from the real estate licensing jurisdiction of the licensee's resident jurisdiction and/or other jurisdictions in which the applicant has held or currently holds a license. The applicant shall pay the Commission the same examination fee and license fee as provided in the "Rules" for the obtaining of a resident sales associate or broker license in this jurisdiction. The certification of licensure shall be valid for sixty (60) days from date of issuance.

(f) **Approved application valid for ninety (90) days.** An approved application shall be valid for ninety (90) days.

(g) **Stipulations.** Nonresident licenses granted under the provisions of this section shall remain in force, only as long as such nonresident remains licensed in good standing in this jurisdiction or any other jurisdiction in which the nonresident is or has been licensed.

(h) **Co-brokerage arrangements.** A broker of this jurisdiction may participate in a cooperative brokerage arrangement with a broker of another jurisdiction provided that each broker conducts real estate activities only in the jurisdiction in which they are licensed.

(i) **Request for license transfer.** In the event a nonresident Oklahoma licensee desires to transfer the license and obtain a resident Oklahoma license or desires to transfer the license to another jurisdiction, the nonresident licensee shall be required to meet all applicable requirements and pay the appropriate change of address fee and submit all appropriate documents as required by the Commission. In the event a resident Oklahoma licensee desires to transfer the license and obtain a nonresident Oklahoma license, the licensee shall be required to pay the appropriate change of address fee and complete and submit all appropriate documents as required by the Commission.

(j) **Continuing education.** If a nonresident licensee completes the continuing education requirement of another jurisdiction for license renewal, the Commission will require proof of completion of at least one (1) continuing education clock hour in each of the following Oklahoma-specific subjects for license renewal: Broker Relationships Act, Contracts and Forms, and Code and Rule Updates. If a nonresident licensee is exempt from meeting a continuing education requirement in another jurisdiction then the licensee must meet the Oklahoma continuing education requirement as follow:

(1) Each licensee shall have completed of said twenty-one (21) clock hours of continuing education six (6) clock hours of required subject matter as directed by the Commission

(2) The required subject matter, or its equivalent, as determined by the Commission, shall consist of all following subjects each license term: Professional Conduct, Broker Relationships Act, Fair Housing, Contracts and Forms, Code and Rules Updates and Current Issues. The remaining fifteen (15) clock hours may consist of elective subject matter as approved by the Commission

(3) Any licensee may complete the Broker in Charge course as approved by the Commission consisting of fifteen (15) clock hours in lieu of the required subject matter.

(4) Any Broker who holds or has held a license type of Broker Manager (BM), Proprietor Broker (BP), or Branch Broker (BB) during any portion of their current license term shall be required to successfully complete the Broker in Charge course as approved by the Commission consisting of fifteen (15) clock hours, or its equivalent, as approved by the Commission. In addition, to complete the continuing education requirement of twenty-one (21) clock hours such broker shall complete at least two (2) of the six (6) required subject matter, equal to at least six (6) clock hours, as referenced in paragraph (2) of this subsection.

(5) Any broker that lapsed or renewed inactive in their previous license term or current license term who applies for reinstatement or activation and held in their previous or current license term the license type of Broker Manager (BM), Proprietor Broker (BP), or Branch Broker (BB) must complete the Broker in Charge course and two (2) of the six (6) required subject matter totaling six (6) hours prior to their license being reinstated active or reactivating.

605:10-7-10. Resident applicants currently or previously licensed in other jurisdictions

(a) **Requirements.** In order to qualify under previously licensed procedures, an applicant must complete and submit all appropriate documents as required by the Commission and furnish evidence that the applicant possesses or has possessed a license in good standing in another jurisdiction. Applications approved for resident applicants currently or previously licensed in other jurisdictions shall be valid for ninety (90) days. The Commission may issue the applicant a license if such previously licensed applicant meets all of the requirements of either paragraphs (1), (2), (3) or (4) of this subsection:

(1) If a nonresident agreement exists between Oklahoma and the jurisdiction in which the applicant qualified for a license, the Commission shall qualify the licensed applicant through the nonresident agreement. In order to qualify under this paragraph an individual must furnish evidence that the license from the former jurisdiction has not been inactive more than six (6) months prior to application to this jurisdiction.
  (A) An applicant applying under this paragraph must complete and submit the following:
    (i) Appropriate application(s).
    (ii) License certification(s) from the jurisdiction(s) in which the applicant has held or currently holds a license.
    (iii) Criminal history background application, fingerprint card and fee.
    (iv) Examination fee and successful completion of the state portion of the examination.
    (v) Proof of completion of at least one (1) continuing education clock hour in each of the following Oklahoma-specific subjects: Broker Relationships Act, Contracts and Forms, and Code and Rule Updates.
  (B) Upon the Commission granting approval to the applicant for licensure in this jurisdiction, the applicant must complete and submit the appropriate license application form(s) along with license and education and recovery fund fees.
  (C) An applicant qualifying under this paragraph will be issued either a sales associate, broker associate or broker license.

(2) If a nonresident agreement does not exist, the applicant shall be required to furnish evidence of two (2) years of active experience respectively as a sales associate or broker out of the previous five (5) years. In order to qualify under this paragraph an individual must furnish evidence that the license from the former jurisdiction has not been inactive more than six (6) months prior to application to this jurisdiction.
  (A) An applicant applying under this paragraph must complete and submit the following:
    (i) Appropriate application(s).
    (ii) License certification(s) from the jurisdiction(s) in which the applicant has held or currently holds a license.
    (iii) Criminal history background application, fingerprint card and fee.

(iv) Examination fee and successful completion of the state portion of the examination.
(v) Proof of completion of at least one (1) continuing education clock hour in each of the following Oklahoma-specific subjects: Broker Relationships Act, Contracts and Forms, and Code and Rule Updates.
(B) Upon the Commission granting approval to the applicant for licensure in this jurisdiction, the applicant must complete and submit the appropriate license application form(s) along with license and education and recovery fund fees.
(C) An applicant qualifying under this paragraph will be issued either a sales associate, broker associate or broker license.

(3) An applicant who does not possess the required two (2) years active experience out of the previous five (5) years respectively as a sales associate or broker, or an applicant who does not meet all of the requirements of either paragraphs (1) or (2) of this subsection, shall be required to apply as an original applicant.
(A) An applicant applying under this paragraph must complete and submit the following:
(i) Qualify as an original applicant by submitting appropriate required education and application.
(ii) License certification(s) from the jurisdiction(s) in which the applicant has held or currently holds a license.
(iii) Criminal history background application, fingerprint card and fee.
(iv) Examination fee and successful completion of the entire appropriate examination.
(v) Proof of completion of at least one (1) continuing education clock hour in each of the following Oklahoma-specific subjects: Broker Relationships Act, Contracts and Forms, and Code and Rule Updates.
(B) Upon the Commission granting approval to the applicant for licensure in this jurisdiction, the applicant must complete and submit the appropriate license application form(s) along with license and education and recovery fund fees.
(C) An applicant qualifying under this paragraph will be issued either a provisional sales associate, broker associate or broker license.

(4) In accordance with Title 59, O.S., Section 4100.4 of the Post-Military Service Occupation, Education and Credentialing Act, the Commission shall, upon satisfactory evidence of equivalent education, training and experience by an applicant for licensure, accept the education, training and experience completed by the applicant as a member of the Armed Forces or Reserves of the United States, National Guard of any jurisdiction, the Military Reserves of any jurisdiction, or the Naval Militias of any jurisdiction, and apply it in the manner most favorable toward satisfying the applicant's qualifications for examination and license issuance.
(A) An applicant applying under this paragraph must complete and submit the following:
(i) Appropriate application(s).
(ii) Satisfactory evidence of education, training and experience obtained by the applicant as a member of the military Armed Forces or Reserves of the United States.
(iii) License certification(s) from the jurisdiction(s) in which the applicant has held or currently holds a license.
(iv) Criminal history background application, fingerprint card and fee.
(v) Examination fee and successful completion of the entire appropriate examination.
(B) Upon the Commission granting approval to the applicant for licensure in this jurisdiction, the applicant must complete and submit the appropriate license application form(s) along with license and education and recovery fund fees.
(C) An applicant qualifying under this paragraph will be issued either a provisional sales associate, broker associate or broker license.

(b) **May be required to meet additional requirements.** If, in the opinion of the Commission, there is question as to the competence of the previously licensed applicant, the individual may be required to meet additional educational courses and/or successfully complete the Oklahoma examination.

(c) Military spouse applicant - 120 day temporary permit. In accordance with Title 59, O.S., Section 4100.5 the Commission shall expedite the issuance of a 120 day permit to an applicant:
(1) Who is actively licensed in real estate in another jurisdiction;
(2) Whose spouse is an active-duty member of the Armed Forces or Reserves of the United States;
(3) Whose spouse is subject to military transfer to this state; and
(4) Who left employment in another state to accompany their spouse to this state.

Expedite licensure means to issue the applicant a temporary permit to perform licensed activities for a period of 120 days to allow the person to successfully complete all application requirements as required by the Commission and any specific requirements in this state that were not required in the jurisdiction in which the person was licensed, i.e., criminal history background check and successful passage of the Oklahoma portion of the examination. An extension of the 120 days may be granted up to an additional 60 days if written justification is submitted by the applicant to the commission and the delay of license issuance was not the fault of the applicant.

605:10-9-1. Place of business and broker requirements
(a) **Place of Business.** Each broker shall maintain a specific place of business, and supervise a brokerage practice which is available to the public during reasonable business hours. Each broker shall be available to manage and supervise such brokerage practice and comply with the following:
  (1) The broker's license, as well as those of all licensees associated with the broker, must be maintained in the place of business as registered with the Commission and available upon request.
  (2) The place of business shall consist of at least one enclosed room or building of stationary construction wherein negotiations and closing of real estate transactions of others may be conducted and carried on with privacy and wherein the broker's books, records and files pertaining to real estate transactions of others are maintained.
  (3) Each broker shall register for each place of business a physical address and office telephone number.
(b) **Branch offices.** If a broker maintains one or more places of business, the additional places of business shall be referred to as a branch office. Each associate's license shall be issued to and available upon request in the office to which the associate is assigned whether that be the main place of business or branch office.
(c) **Office located at residence.** The office may be in the residence of the broker.
(d) **Associates not permitted to have an office.** Associates are not permitted to have a place of business, but must be registered with a place of business maintained and registered in the name of the broker.
(e) **Licenses issued to place of business.** All licenses will be issued to the street address of the place of business, unless the United States postal service refuses to deliver mail when addressed in such manner.
(f) **Broker may be broker for more than one firm.** A broker may be the broker for more than one firm so long as the firms are at the same location.
(g) **Broker is responsible for acts of unlicensed assistants.** A broker is responsible for all real estate related activities of any unlicensed assistant working within the firm.

605:10-9-2. Office identification
(a) **Office identification sign.** Each licensed real estate broker holding an active license certificate, except those registered as being associated with a broker who is in compliance with this Section, shall erect and maintain a sign on or about the entrance of his or her office and all branch offices, which sign shall be easily observed and read by persons about to enter any of said offices.
(b) **Specifications of sign.** Each sign shall contain the name of the broker or trade name registered with the Commission, and if a partnership, association or corporation, shall contain the name or trade name of such firm. The sign must indicate that the party is a real estate broker and not a private party, to include, but not limited to, "company", "realty", or "real estate", as the case may be, all in letters not less than one (1) inch in height. Legal abbreviations following the trade name or name under which the broker is licensed shall be acceptable as long as they are easily identifiable by the public as such.

605:10-9-3. Trade names
Each licensed broker or entity must register in writing to the Commission all trade names used in connection with real estate activities prior to the trade name being advertised or displayed in any way. Further, each broker is to notify the Commission in writing of all deleted or unused trade names.

605:10-9-4. Advertising
(a) **Requirements and prohibitions.**
   (1) A broker, when advertising, must use their registered business trade name or the name under which the broker is licensed; however, yard signs must also include the broker's office telephone number. A firm shall not register or use a trade name of another licensed firm. In addition, the advertisement must indicate that the party is a real estate broker and not a private party, to include, but not limited to, "agency", "company", "realty", or "real estate", as the case may be. Legal abbreviations following the trade name or name under which the broker is licensed shall be acceptable as long as they are easily identifiable by the public as such.
   (2) No real estate advertisement shall show only a post office box number, telephone number or street address.
   (3) A broker, when operating under a franchise name, shall clearly reveal in all office identification and in all advertising other than institutional type advertising designed to promote a common name, the franchise name along with the name of the broker or business trade name as registered with the Commission. A franchise name shall not be the complete business trade name. All institutional type franchise advertising shall indicate that each office is independently owned and operated.
   (4) A licensee shall not advertise, either personally or through any media, to sell, buy, exchange, rent, or lease property when such advertisement is directed at or referred to persons of a particular race, color, creed, religion, national origin, familial status or handicap. The contents of any advertisement must be confined to information relative to the property itself, and any advertisement which is directed at or referred to persons of any particular race, color, creed, religion, national origin, familial status, age or handicap is prohibited.
   (5) Any advertising in any media which is misleading or inaccurate in any material fact or in any way misrepresents any property, terms, values, services, or policies is prohibited.
   (6) A licensee shall not advertise any property for sale, rent, lease, or exchange in any media unless the broker has first secured the permission of the owner or the owner's authorized representative and said permission has a definite date of expiration.
   (7) **Social networking.** A licensee who is engaged in licensed activities through social networking mediums must indicate their license status and include their broker's reference as required elsewhere in this rule.
   (8) A licensee shall not use a yard sign at the licensee's personal residence as a marketing tool, to make it appear the real property is for sale, lease or rent when such is not the case.
   (9) A broker may, or authorize an associate to, promote a seller incentive with the consent of the seller. The publicity must clearly indicate the incentive is being offered by the seller and not by the licensee and that the promotion only applies to a seller's particular property or properties.
(b) **Associates advertising.**
   (1) An associate is prohibited from advertising under only the associate's name.
   (2) All advertising by an associate must be under the direct supervision of the associate's broker.
   (3) In all advertising, the associate must include the name of the associate's broker or the name under which the broker operates, in such a way that the broker's reference is prominent, conspicuous and easily identifiable. If approved by a broker, an associate may include in the advertisement:
      (A) The associate's personal insignia of which such approval is to be maintained by the broker and which cannot be construed as that of a firm's name.
      (B) The associate's personal nickname or alias which must be registered at the Commission prior to its use and which cannot be construed as that of a firm's name.
      (C) An associate's contact information.
      (D) A team name approved by the broker, as long as the broker's reference is prominent, conspicuous, and easily identifiable, and which cannot be construed as that of a firm's name. The broker's reference must be in close proximity to the team name reference.
      (E) A slogan which cannot be construed as that of a firm's name.
      (F) A domain/website name that is registered with the broker. Within this domain/website, the broker's reference shall appear on every individual page and/or frame.
   (4) An associate's contact information may be added to a yard sign if the yard sign contains the registered name or trade name and office telephone number of the broker so long as it is approved by the broker.
   (5) Open house or directional signs used in conjunction with broker's signs do not have to contain the name or trade name of the associate's broker and broker's telephone number.
(c) **Licensee acting as owner, purchaser or direct employee of owner.**

(1) When a licensee, either active or inactive, is purchasing real estate or is the owner of property that is being sold, exchanged, rented or leased and such is being handled either by the licensee or marketed through a real estate firm, the licensee is required to disclose in writing on all documents that pertain to the transaction and in all advertisements that he or she is licensed. On all purchase or lease contracts the licensee is to include their license number.

(2) A licensee who is not acting in the capacity of a licensee but is engaged in buying, selling, leasing or renting real estate as a direct employee for the owner or as an officer for an entity is not required to indicate in the advertising that he or she is licensed.

605:10-9-5. Broker change of address or office telephone number

(a) **Change of business address or office telephone number.** Any change of business address or office telephone number of a broker must be filed in the Commission office within ten (10) days of such change. Filed shall mean the date of the United States Postal Service postmark or the date personal delivery is made to the Commission office. The broker shall return his or her certificate to the Commission along with those of all licensees in his or her association with a request for a change of address. Upon any request for a change of address there shall be paid a fee to the Commission of Twenty-five Dollars ($25.00) for each license to be changed. No fee shall be charged for adding or deleting an office telephone number.

(b) **Group change of address.** Under certain circumstances as determined by the Commission, the Commission may place a cap of Seven Hundred Fifty Dollars ($750.00) on group transactions requesting licenses to be issued. To qualify, such request must be received complete and require no further correspondence and/or documents except for the issuance of the licenses.

(c) **Change of home address.** A broker is required to notify the Commission of his or her current home address. Such change shall be filed in the Commission office within ten (10) days of such change. No fee is required to change the licensee's record; however, a fee of Twenty-five Dollars ($25.00) will be charged if the change requires a new license to be issued.

605:10-9-6. Death or disability of broker

Upon the death or inability of a broker to act as a broker the following procedures shall apply:

(1) In the case of a corporation, association or partnership, the provisions of 605:10-7-8 relating to corporations, 605:10-7-8.2 relating to associations, and 605:10-7-8.1 relating to partnerships shall apply.

(2) In the case of a sole proprietor all brokerage activity must cease and a family attorney or representative should perform the following:
  (A) Notify the Commission in writing of the date of death or disability.
  (B) Advise the Commission as to the location where records will be stored. Such records may be assigned to another broker.
  (C) Return the broker's license certificate and pocket identification card and all license certificates of those associated with the broker to the Commission and advise the Commission as to the circumstances involving any not returned.
  (D) Notify each listing and management client in writing that the broker is no longer in business and that the client may enter a new listing or management agreement with the firm of his or her choice.
  (E) Notify each party and co-broker to any existing contracts.
  (F) Retain trust account monies under the control of the administrator, executor or co-signer on the account until such time as all parties to each transaction agree in writing to disposition or until a court of competent jurisdiction issues an order relative to disposition.
  (G) Notify the Commission of the date the trust account will be closed.
  (H) All advertising in the name of the firm must be terminated and offering signs removed within thirty (30) days of death or disability of the broker.

(3) In the case of a corporation, association or partnership which ceases all brokerage activity, the provisions of paragraph (2) of this Section apply.

605:10-9-7. Requirements for cessation of real estate activities

(a) **Requirement.** Unless specifically approved otherwise by the Commission a real estate firm shall, when ceasing a portion of real estate activities or ceasing all real estate activities, comply with Section 605:10-13-1 (m).
(b) **Ceasing a portion of real estate activities.** To cease a portion of real estate activities refers to closing a department within a firm wherein, to include but not limited to, separate accounting, trust/escrow accounts and trade names were established and utilized.
(c) **Firm not active in performing real estate activities.** If a firm is not active in performing real estate activities, such firm shall comply with Section 605:10-13-1 (m), (1), (A) through (C.)

605:10-9-8. Branch office closing instructions

The Commission must receive in writing, the requirements listed in this Section at the time notice is given to the Commission that the branch office has closed; however, a written request may be submitted to the Commission for approval to extend the period for submitting such documents and information. Unless specifically approved otherwise by the Commission, a real estate branch office shall be closed by the main office broker in the following manner:

(1) Notify the Commission in writing of the date the branch office will close and advise as to the location where records will be stored and retained for a minimum of five (5) years in conformance with 605:10-13-1 (1).
(2) Return the branch office license certificate and pocket identification card along with all license certificates of those associated with the branch office to the Commission and advise the Commission as to the circumstances involving any not returned.
(3) Release forms must be filed for all licensees affiliated with the branch office.
(4) The branch office broker must either transfer his or her license to a firm of his or her choice or place his or her license on inactive status.
(5) If the main office is not going to service the branch office's existing listing and management clients, as well as parties and co-brokers to existing contracts, notice is to be sent in writing advising all parties of the date the branch office will close and advise each client that he or she may enter a new listing or management agreement with a firm of his or her choice.
(6) All advertising in the name of the branch office must be terminated and offering signs removed within thirty (30) days of office closing.
(7) Trust account funds and pending contracts must be maintained by the responsible broker until final proper disbursal or until new agreements are secured from all parties for transfer of the funds and/or contracts. The Commission is to be notified in writing of any accounts that are closed.

605:10-11-1. Acts of associates

(a) **Requirement.** All acts performed by an associate under the provisions of the "Real Estate License Code" shall be done only in the name of the associate's broker.
(b) **Limitation.** An associate shall not be allowed to work for more than one broker at the same time.
    (1) An exception to this subsection would be if the associate's broker agreed to loan the associate to another broker for a specific duty to be performed, such as:
        (A) Sitting at an open house.
        (B) Calling an auction or performing other auction related duties.
        (C) Any other specific duty as requested in writing and approved by the Commission.
    (2) The broker is responsible for all acts performed by the associate while the associate is performing a specific duty for another broker.
(c) **An associate is responsible for acts of unlicensed assistants.** An associate who employs an unlicensed assistant is responsible in conjunction with the broker for all real estate related activities of the unlicensed assistant.

605:10-11-2. Associate licenses

(a) **License issuance and change request.** Each associate license shall be issued to the associate's broker, who shall retain custody of such license. Upon an associate leaving the association of the broker, the associate's license shall be returned to the Commission, together with a release executed by the broker. Any change of association from one firm to another or relocation from one office to another within a firm by an associate must be filed in the Commission office within ten (10) days. The associate's new broker shall be required to file a consent agreement to sponsor said associate on a form provided by the Commission. An associate requesting an association or office change shall be required to pay a fee of Twenty-five Dollars ($25.00).

(b) **Broker refusal to release associate.** In the event a broker refuses for any reason to release an associate, the associate shall notify the broker by certified mail of the disassociation and furnish the Commission a sworn statement that the notification has been sent to the broker. Upon receipt by the Commission of the aforementioned statement, the Commission shall release the licensee.

(c) **Group change requests.** Under certain circumstances as determined by the Commission, the Commission may place a cap of Seven Hundred Fifty Dollars ($750.00) on group transactions requesting licenses to be reissued. To qualify, the request must be received complete and require no further correspondence and/or documents except for the issuance of the licenses.

(d) **Associates transfer.** When an affiliated associate leaves a broker for whom the associate is acting, the broker shall immediately cause the license of that associate to be forwarded to the Commission along with a release of association form. The broker shall make every attempt to notify the associate of the disassociation.

(e) **Active associate may continually act.** An active associate transferring from one broker to a new broker may continually act if the change is done in a timely manner and in compliance with the ten (10) day notification requirement and other applicable rules of this Chapter.

(f) **Compensation due a disassociated associate.** A previous broker may pay compensation due a disassociated associate directly to the associate and not be required to make such payment through the associate's new broker. However, any agreements between the associate and prior broker requiring further activities to be performed in connection with the compensation to be received, can only be performed with consent and acknowledgement of the new broker.

(g) **Change of home address.** An associate is required to notify the Commission office of his or her current home address. The change shall be filed in the Commission office within ten (10) days of the change. No fee is required to change the licensee's records; however a fee of Twenty-five Dollars ($25.00) will be charged if the change requires a new license to be issued.

605:10-11-3. Associate's corporation or association formed for the purpose of receiving compensation

Within the meaning of subsection 14 of Section 858-312 of the "Code" payment of a commission by a broker to an associate's corporation or association does not constitute a payment of a fee (commission) to an unlicensed person provided the corporation or association, the associate and the broker, abide by the following requirements:
  (1) The associate's corporation or association shall not perform any act requiring a real estate license and shall not hold itself out as engaged in such activity.
  (2) The associate must have an active individual real estate license.
  (3) The broker of the associate must provide the Commission a written statement approving of the associate's corporation or association.
  (4) The associate must be the majority stockholder and president of the corporation or majority member of the association.
  (5) Ownership of an associate's corporation or association is limited to spouses and blood relatives.
  (6) The associate's corporation or association shall not advertise nor receive referral fees or commissions except from the associate's broker.
  (7) The broker and associate must complete and sign a Commission approved form that includes the following:
    (A) A statement that the associate is the majority stockholder and president of the corporation or majority member of the association.
    (B) Names and relation of all officers/members and/or stockholders.
    (C) Verification that the association or corporation is in good standing with the Oklahoma Secretary of State.

605:10-13-1. Duty to account; broker
(a) **Deposit and account of trust/escrow funds.**
  (1) The obligation of a broker to remit monies, valuable documents and other property coming into his or her possession within the meaning of subparagraph six (6), Section 858-312 of the "Code" shall be construed to include, but shall not be limited to, the following:
    (A) Shall deposit all checks and monies of whatever kind and nature belonging to others in a separate account in a financial institution wherein the deposits are insured by an agency of the federal government.

(B) The broker is required to be a signor on the account.
(C) The account must be in the name of the broker as it appears on the license or trade name as registered with the Commission and styled as a trust or escrow account and shall be maintained by the broker as a depository for deposits belonging to others.
(D) All escrow funds shall be deposited before the end of the third banking day following acceptance of an offer by an offeree unless otherwise agreed to in writing by all interested parties.
(E) The broker shall maintain such funds in said account until the transaction involved is consummated or terminated and proper accounting made.
(F) The broker shall at all times, maintain an accurate and detailed record thereof.
(2) Funds referred to in this subsection shall include, but are not limited to earnest money deposits, money received upon final settlements, rents, security deposits, money advanced by buyer or seller for the payment of expenses in connection with closing of real estate transactions, and money advanced by his or her principal or others for expenditures on behalf of subject principal.

(b) **Commingling prohibited.** A broker may not keep any personal funds in the trust account except amounts sufficient to insure the integrity of the account and cover any charges made by the financial institution for servicing the trust or escrow account.

(c) **Interest bearing account.** A broker shall not be prohibited from placing escrow monies in an interest bearing account; however, he or she must disclose in writing to all parties that the account bears interest and identify the party receiving the interest. The Commission does not prohibit the broker from receiving the earned interest. In the event the interest is credited to the broker, the broker should, upon final consummation of the transaction, immediately disburse the interest from the account or insure that the amount does not exceed a reasonable amount to cover normal financial institution charges. The broker is required to maintain complete and accurate records of the interest earned. The interest bearing account must be a demand type account; this prohibits the use of certificate of deposit or other types of time deposits as trust/escrow accounts.

(d) **Trust account not mandatory unless funds or items are held.** A broker shall not be required to maintain a trust or escrow account unless monies or other depositable items belonging to others are accepted by the broker and require the broker to place the monies or items in the broker's trust account.

(e) **Trust accounts must be registered with commission.** A broker shall be required to notify the Commission in writing of all trust or escrow accounts, security deposit accounts, rental management operating accounts, and interest bearing accounts in which trust funds are held. Further, if a broker is a signor on a principal's account, the broker shall register that account as a trust account. A broker shall inform the Commission in writing of any accounts which are closed and no longer in use.

(f) **Settlement statement to be furnished.** A broker shall insure that a signed settlement statement is furnished in each real estate transaction wherein he or she acts as broker, at the time such transaction is consummated.

(g) **Payment of funds.** A broker shall pay over all sums of money held by him or her promptly after the closing of any transaction, provided, that upon any hearing to suspend or revoke his or her license under this Section, the failure to pay over any sums of money held by him or her within three (3) days after a closing shall be prima facie evidence of a violation by such person under the provisions of this Section.

(h) **Return of earnest money or items.** In the event a transaction does not consummate, a broker shall promptly disburse the earnest money or items to the proper party in accordance with the terms of the contract. In the event a dispute arises prior to the disbursement, the broker shall follow rule 605:10-13-3 or may file an interpleader action with the appropriate court.

(i) **Documents, items, or monies furnished to all parties.** A broker shall insure the timely delivery or return of all documents, items or monies to a party to a transaction wherein the broker or the broker's associate have provided services.

(j) **Inform all parties pertaining to escrow being held.** A broker shall insure that all parties of each transaction are informed of the details relating to the escrow including, but not limited to, a statement as to the nature of a non-depositable item, the value of the item, and in whose custody the item is being placed.

(k) **Bookkeeping system required.** A broker shall maintain a bookkeeping system i.e., canceled checks, check book, deposit receipts, general accounts ledger, etc. which will accurately and clearly disclose full compliance with the Law relating to the maintaining of trust accounts.

(l) **Record retention.** A broker shall maintain all records and files for a minimum of five (5) years after consummation or termination of a transaction. In the case of trust account records the five years shall commence with the date of disbursal of funds. Records as referenced in this paragraph shall be destroyed in a secure manner.

(m) **Requirements for storage of records on alternative media.** The Real Estate Commission establishes the following requirements for storage of trust account and transaction records stored on alternative media. Alternative media is defined as media that uses an electronic device to store or retrieve the information that pertains to the trust account and transaction documentation. This requirement applies to any computer technology utilized by the broker to create, store or retrieve the aforementioned documentation, whether the computerized device is internal or external to the broker's computer equipment. If a broker utilizes his own equipment or a third party vendor to create, store or retrieve this information, the broker shall ensure that the documentation is maintained and able to be retrieved for the five (5) year time period as required by the Commission.
   (1) Trust account records shall be maintained by the broker in their original format for a minimum of two (2) years. Trust account records may then be transferred to an alternative media for the remaining required record retention time.
   (2) Records, with the exception of trust account records, may be transferred at any time to an alternative media for the remaining required retention time.
   (3) After documents are converted to alternative media, a quality assurance check shall be done to ensure that every document was imaged and can be reproduced in a legible and readable condition on a display device.
   (4) After the quality assurance check is completed, the original documents may be destroyed.
   (5) A broker shall maintain the alternative media and a means of viewing and retrieving records, and shall provide a true, correct and legible paper copy to the Commission upon request.
   (6) A broker shall store copies of the alternative media and the equipment used to read the media in an environment and at a level of quality conducive to maintain the ability to reproduce the media throughout the retention period. Reproduce means a process in which a document can be converted from the alternative media to a paper copy that is legible and able to be read.
(n) **Cessation of real estate activities.** Upon a firm ceasing a portion of real estate activities or ceasing all real estate activities the broker shall:
   (1) Notify the Commission in writing of the effective date of such action and advise as to the location where records will be stored and comply with the following:
      (A) Return the broker's license certificate and pocket identification card and all license certificates of those associated with the broker to the Commission and advise the Commission as to the circumstances involving any not returned.
      (B) Release forms must be filed for all licensees affiliated with the firm.
      (C) The broker must either transfer to a new firm or place his or her license on inactive status.
   (2) Notify in writing all listing and management clients, as well as parties and co-brokers to existing contracts advising them of the date of cessation of real estate activities.
   (3) All advertising in the name of the firm must be terminated and offering signs removed within thirty (30) days of cessation of real estate activities.
   (4) Funds in trust accounts and pending contracts must be maintained by the responsible broker until consummation of transaction and final proper disbursal of funds. Upon final disbursements of funds the broker is required to close the account and notify the Commission in writing that the account is closed.
   (5) In the event the responsible broker is unable to continue to maintain the funds and/or pending contracts, funds and/or pending contracts may be transferred to another authorized broker, entity or legal representative until consummation and proper disbursal of funds. In this event, the broker must submit a request in writing to the Commission for approval to transfer the contracts and/or funds. Upon written approval by the Commission, the broker must secure approval and obtain new agreements from all parties for transfer of the contracts and/or funds.
   (6) If funds, items and/or contracts are transferred to another authorized broker, entity or legal representative and approved by the Commission, the broker transferring such shall be required to compile a record of the following, retain a copy for his or her file and give a copy to the receiving authorized broker, entity or legal representative:
      (A) A copy of the written approval from the Commission authorizing the transfer of the contracts and/or funds.
      (B) The name and address of the authorized broker, entity or legal representative.
      (C) A trust account reconciliation sheet indicating ledger balance and financial institution balance at time of transfer to include the name of each depositor, amount of deposit, date, and purpose of the deposit.
      (D) A statement indicating that written agreements were obtained from all parties to each transaction agreeing to the transfer of the funds and/or contracts to another responsible broker, authorized entity or legal

representative and that each depositor was notified of the effective date of transfer, and the name of the responsible person or entity.
- (7) Any firm merger shall have a thirty (30) day time period in which to provide the Commission the documentation as referenced in subparagraph (n) of this rule. Firm merger means that a licensed firm has been acquired by another licensed firm and the firm that was acquired is ceasing a portion or all of its licensed activities.

(o) **Security breach of personal information.**
- (1) Security breach of personal information as defined in Title 24, Oklahoma Statutes, Sections 161-166 means the unauthorized access and acquisition of unencrypted and unredacted computerized data that compromises the security or confidentiality of personal information maintained by a licensee as part of a database of personal information regarding multiple persons. Personal information means the first name or first initial and last name in combination with and linked to any one or more of the following data elements:
  - (A) social security number,
  - (B) driver license number or state identification card number issued in lieu of a driver license, or
  - (C) financial account number, or credit card or debit card number, in combination with any required security code, access code, or password that would permit access to the financial accounts.
- (2) The breach of information would not include information that is lawfully obtained from publicly available information, or from federal, state or local government records lawfully made available to the general public.
- (3) In the event personal information is breached, the licensee is required to send notice to the Commission and to all concerned persons whose information was breached by an unauthorized person or source as required in Title 24, O.S., Section 162 . The licensee is required to comply with all requirements within the Security Breach Notification Act or be subject to disciplinary action by the Commission.

605:10-13-2. Duty to account; associate

The obligation of an associate to remit monies, valuable documents and other property coming into his or her possession within the meaning of subsection six (6), Section 858-312 of the Code shall be construed to include but shall not be limited to the following:
- (1) Shall turn over all documents, files and monies deposited, payments made, or things of value received by the associate to his or her broker promptly; and
- (2) Shall deliver a copy of all instruments to any party or parties executing the same when such has been prepared by the associate or pertains to the consummation of a transaction in which he or she participated.
- (3) Shall not be authorized to open or maintain a trust or escrow account, or be a signer on a trust or escrow account wherein the associate is providing licensed activities as defined in the License Code and Rules.

605:10-13-3. Special escrow disbursement

- (a) In the event a dispute arises prior to the disbursement of any monies or other valuables held by a broker in escrow in connection with a real estate purchase contract, the broker shall continue to retain said money or valuables in escrow until he or she has a written release from all parties consenting to its disposition or until a civil action is filed to determine its disposition at which time he or she may pay or turn it into the court.
- (b) In the absence of a pending civil action and upon the passage of thirty (30) days from the date of final termination of the contract, it shall not be considered grounds for disciplinary action by the Commission against a broker for a broker to disburse escrow monies or valuables to either purchaser or seller when the disbursement has been based on a good faith decision by the broker that the opposite party has failed to perform as agreed, such disbursement to be made, however, only after fifteen (15) days written notice to all parties concerned setting forth the broker's proposed action.

605:10-15-1. Disclosure of beneficial interest or referrals

- (a) No licensee shall, without disclosing such fact in writing to all parties on both sides of the transaction, either:
  - (1) Accept or receive any fee, commission, salary, rebate, kickback or other compensation or consideration allowed by law in connection with the recommendation, referral or procurement of any product or service, including financial services.

(2) Own any beneficial interest in any entity which provides any product or service, including financial services to home owners, home buyers or tenants, in connection with the sale, lease, rental or listing of any real estate. Activities or interests of associates shall ordinarily be disclosed to his or her broker who shall have the primary responsibility to make written disclosures covered by this Section to the parties.

(b) If any associate owns any beneficial interest in any entity which provides any product or service, including financial services, to home owners, home buyers, or tenants, the associate shall disclose the nature and extent of such interest to his or her broker. The obligation to make such disclosure shall be a continuing one.

(c) Notwithstanding the provisions of this Section, disclosure of a beneficial interest shall not be required if either:
(1) The beneficial interest consists solely of a stock or other equity ownership in a publicly traded company where such ownership is less than one percent (1%) of the total equity value of such entity.
(2) Such beneficial interest consists solely of a stock or other equity interest in a privately held company in which the aggregate ownership of all licensees employed by the firm otherwise required to make the disclosure does not exceed ten percent (10%) of the equity value of the company and where the licensee is not an officer, director, managing partner or otherwise directly or indirectly is in control of the entity which provides any product or service covered by this Section.

(d) No particular form of disclosure shall be prescribed by the Commission. All disclosures required by this Section shall be made:
(1) Either prior to or at the time that any recommendation, referral or procurement of any product or service is made in instances in which the licensee may receive any compensation or consideration in connection therewith.
(2) At or before the time that it becomes apparent to the licensee that any entity in which the licensee owns any beneficial interest may provide any product or service in instances in which the disclosure of any such ownership is required under this Section. All disclosures required by this Section shall be judged by the standard of whether the disclosure was adequate to inform all parties on both sides of the transaction of the existence of a beneficial interest covered by this Section or, if a party claims not to have been adequately informed, whether the form and manner in which the disclosure was made was adequate under the circumstances to inform a person of ordinary intelligence and understanding, not possessing expertise in real estate or financial matters, of the existence of any fee, compensation, salary, rebate, kickback or other compensation or consideration or the ownership of a beneficial interest in an entity providing products or services covered by this Section.

(e) The failure by a licensee to observe any provision of this Section shall be deemed to be a violation of subsections 2, 3, 8 and 15 of Section 858-312 of the Code and in the case of an associate, a violation of subsection 4 of Section 858-312 of the Code as well.

605:10-15-2. Broker Relationships Act to become effective November 1, 2013

(a) **Broker Relationships Act effective November 1, 2013.** A new law, Title 59, O. S., Sections 858-351 through 858-363 of the License Code, becomes effective on November 1, 2013, which law shall be referred to as the Broker Relationships Act.

(b) **Brokerage service agreement defined.** The term "brokerage service agreement" shall mean an oral or written agreement to provide brokerage services entered into by a real estate broker and a person who is a party to a real estate transaction and shall include, but not be limited to, listing agreements, buyer broker agreements and property management agreements.

(c) **Validity of a brokerage service agreement existing before and on November 1, 2013.** A brokerage service agreement entered into prior to November 1, 2013, shall remain in full force and effect until the agreement expires or is otherwise terminated by an agreement of the parties.

(d) **Providing services to more than one party to the transaction.** When a firm provides brokerage services to more than one party to the transaction, the broker shall provide written notice to those parties that the broker is providing brokerage services to more than one party. When a firm provides brokerage services to both sides of the transaction, the firm shall ensure compliance with the duties and responsibilities in Title 59, O.S., Section 858-353 along with all other requirements of the License Code and Rules.

(e) **Services provided to a tenant.** When a broker provides brokerage services to a landlord under a property management agreement, the services provided to the tenant by the broker shall not be construed as creating a broker relationship between the broker and the tenant unless otherwise agreed to in writing; however, the broker owes to the tenant the duties of honesty and exercising reasonable skill and care.

605:10-15-3. Requirements for furnishing psychological factors

Psychologically impacted property is any property where the existence of certain circumstances, suspicions or facts may create emotional or psychological disturbance or concerns to a prospective purchaser/lessee, with the potential of influencing a buying/leasing decision. Therefore, the obligation of a real estate licensee to obtain information as stated in Title 59, O.S., Section 858-513A (1) and (2) shall be performed in the following manner:

(1) Purchaser/lessee must be in the process of making a bona fide offer.
(2) Licensee must receive request in writing from purchaser/lessee.
(3) Purchaser's/Lessee's written request must state that such factor is important to the decision of the purchaser/lessee.
(4) Licensee shall make inquiry of the owner by submitting the written request to the owner.
(5) Licensee shall report any findings to the purchaser/lessee with the consent of the owner.
(6) If the owner refuses to furnish information requested, the licensee shall so advise the purchaser/lessee.
(7) Further, if a purchaser/lessee is requesting information as to whether or not an occupant of the real estate is, or was at any time suspected to be infected, or has been infected with Acquired Immune Deficiency Syndrome, or any other disease which falls under the privacy laws, the information can only be obtained in accordance with the Public Health and Safety Statute, Title 63, O.S., 1988, Section 1-502.2A.

605:10-15-4. Residential Property Condition Disclosure Act forms

(a) **Development and amendment of forms.** In accordance with Oklahoma Statutes, Title 60, Section 833 the Commission shall develop and amend by rule the forms for the Residential Property Condition Disclosure Statement and Residential Property Condition Disclaimer Statement. Effective July 11, 2008 the disclosure statement is amended and all disclosure forms executed prior to July 11, 2008 will remain in force and valid until expiration of the 180 days from the date noted thereon.
(b) **Availability of forms.** The forms shall be available to the public upon request on and after July 1, 1995.
(c) **Copy of form format.** The Residential Property Condition Disclosure Statement as referenced in this section is set out in Appendix A at the end of this Chapter. The Residential Property Condition Disclaimer Statement as referenced in this section is set out in Appendix B at the end of this Chapter.

605:10-17-1. Commissions and disputes

(a) The Commission shall not establish the rate of commissions to be charged for real estate services and shall have no interest therein.
(b) At its discretion, the Commission may dismiss or postpone any investigation or hearing which essentially involves a dispute not affecting the public interest until or unless such dispute is resolved.
(c) The Commission shall entertain a complaint against a broker charging a violation of subsection 18 of Section 858-312 of this "Code" only if the complaining licensee submits with his or her complaint evidence that a court of competent jurisdiction has ruled in his or her favor relative to the subject and awarded judgment against the broker.

605:10-17-2. Complaint procedures

(a) **Complaint may be filed by public or Commission's own motion.** A complaint alleging misconduct on the part of a licensee or any person unlicensed pursuant to the Code who violates provisions of the Code may be filed by any person in writing on a form for such supplied by the Commission, or may be ordered by the Commission on its own motion. The Commission will accept a complaint alleging misconduct on a form not supplied by the Commission if such form is notarized by a notary public.
(b) **Complaint notification; licensee response.** When a complaint has been filed the licensee or unlicensed person pursuant to the Code shall be immediately notified and shall be required to file an adequate written response within fifteen (15) days of the notice.
(c) **Investigation and/or investigative session.** Subsequent to the fifteen (15) day answer period, a field investigation or preliminary investigative session may be conducted to ascertain whether or not charges should be lodged and a formal hearing ordered. Such investigation or investigative session shall be under the supervision of the Secretary-Treasurer of the Commission. He or she may designate an attorney who will act as prosecutor for the Commission to examine the results of the field investigation and/or conduct a preliminary investigative session.

The prosecutor so designated may in the name of the Commission subpoena witnesses, take testimony by deposition and compel the production of records and documents bearing upon the complaint.

(d) **Findings reported to Commission.** At the completion of the investigation or investigative session, a written report accompanied by findings, if any, shall be submitted to the Commission. Following receipt of the report, the Commission shall determine whether or not the apparent evidence warrants lodging formal charges and ordering a formal hearing, and if a formal hearing is ordered all parties shall then be furnished with copies of any written report accompanied by findings, if any.

605:10-17-3. Complaint hearings; notice and procedures

(a) **Summary suspension.** If the Commission finds that public health, safety, or welfare imperatively requires emergency action, and incorporates a finding to that effect in its order, summary suspension of a license may be ordered pending proceedings for revocation or other action within thirty (30) days. The summary suspension shall remain in effect until further order by the Commission.

(b) **Formal hearing ordered; notification.** Except as provided in (a) of this section, the Commission may issue a disciplinary order only after a hearing of which licensee or unlicensed person pursuant to the Code affected shall be given at least fifteen (15) days written notice, specifying the offenses of which the licensee or unlicensed person pursuant to the Code is charged. Such notice may be served as provided by law for service of notices, or by mailing a copy by certified mail to the last known address. If the licensee is an associate associated with a broker, the Commission in like manner shall notify the broker with whom associated.

(c) **Formal hearing location.** The hearing on such charges shall be set at such time and place as the Commission through its Secretary-Treasurer may prescribe and the notice in (b) of this section shall specify this time and place.

(d) **Formal hearing before Commission; hearing examiner or selected panel.** The Secretary-Treasurer shall schedule each formal disciplinary hearing before a Hearing Examiner, a selected panel of the Commission, or the Commission as a whole. In the case of a proceeding conducted by the Commission as a whole or a panel of the Commission, the Chairman or his/her designee shall preside. Designated counsel shall advise the Chair as to rulings upon the questions of admissibility of evidence, competence of witnesses and any other question of law where such ruling is required or requested.

(e) **Request for postponement.** Once a hearing has been scheduled, the Secretary-Treasurer may for sufficient cause postpone or reschedule a hearing upon proper motion or request having been filed with the Commission office seventy-two (72) hours prior to the hearing.
  (1) Each postponement request must be in writing and must state the specific reason(s) for the request.
  (2) The Commission may require official documentation supporting such request.
  (3) An emergency postponement request shall be considered at the time of the emergency.
  (4) The granting of a continuance whether general or emergency, shall not be interpreted to deny the Commission the power to impose summary suspension if the Commission finds that public health, safety, or welfare imperatively requires emergency action, and incorporates a finding to that effect in its Order, summary suspension of a license may be ordered pending proceedings for revocation or other action within thirty (30) days.

(f) **Hearings public; witnesses may be excluded.** All hearings shall be public except that upon motion of either party, witnesses may be excluded from the hearing room when such witness is not testifying.

(g) **Court reporter.** A court reporter shall be present to record the proceedings on behalf of the Commission. Any person desiring a copy of the transcript of the proceedings, may purchase such from the reporter.

(h) **Formal hearing procedures.** The designated attorney for the State shall present the State's case. The respondent may present his or her own evidence or may present such through his or her own counsel. If the charges against the respondent resulted from a complaint filed by a party present at the hearing, the complaining party may be a witness for the State. In order that the hearing will not be encumbered by evidence having no bearing on the issues, testimony by all witnesses will be limited to matters relevant to the issues involved. The order of procedure shall be as follows:
  (1) Recitation of the statement of charges by the person presiding.
  (2) Opening statement by the State.
  (3) Opening statement by the respondent.
  (4) Presentation of the State's case followed by cross-examination and questioning by the Hearing Examiner or Hearing panel.

(5) Respondent's presentation followed by cross-examination and questioning by the Hearing Examiner or Hearing panel.
(6) Closing arguments by the State.
(7) Closing arguments by the respondent.

(i) **Order; hearing before commission.** If the case be heard by the Commission as a whole, the Commission shall deliberate and render a decision with confirmation of such decision in writing in the form of an Order distributed to all parties by mail.

(j) **Proposed order consideration; hearing before hearing examiner or panel.** In the case of a hearing conducted by a panel of the Commission or by a Hearing Examiner, following the hearing, the Hearing Examiner or attorney sitting as counsel to the panel shall prepare a proposed Order to be considered by members of the Real Estate Commission at a future meeting.

(k) **Proposed order notification; written exceptions.** Affected parties will be furnished copies of the proposed Order and notified as to the date the proposal will be considered by the Commission for adoption. At the same time, notice will also be given to the parties that written exceptions or requests to present oral exceptions or arguments, if any, should be submitted on or before a designated date pursuant to Section 311, of Title 75, Oklahoma Statutes. Upon adoption of the Order by the Commission as a whole, the adopted Order shall be distributed to all parties.

(l) **Actual notification pertaining to this Section.** For purposes of this Section, notice shall be deemed to have been given at the time that notice is deposited in the United States mail with proper postage thereon and mailed to the last known address of the notified person, or date when such notice is served in person by a person duly authorized as a representative of the Commission.

(m) **Violation found.** If the Commission shall determine that any licensee or unlicensed person pursuant to the Code is guilty of violation of the "Code," such person may be disciplined in the manner as prescribed in such "Code."

605:10-17-4. Prohibited dealings

Within the meaning of subsection 8 of Section 858-312 of the "Code," untrustworthy, improper, fraudulent or dishonest dealing shall include, but not be limited to, the following:

(1) The making of a brokerage service contract without a date of termination.
(2) Purchasing of property by a licensee for himself or herself or another entity in which the licensee has an interest as defined in 605:10-15-1 (c), if such property is listed with the broker or the broker's firm, without first making full disclosure thereof and obtaining the approval of the owner, or the failure by the licensee to exert the licensee's best effort in order to later purchase or acquire the property for themselves or another entity in which they have an interest as defined in 605:10-15-1 (c).
(3) Repeated misrepresentations, even though not fraudulent, which occur as a result of the failure by the licensee to inform himself or herself of pertinent facts concerning property, as to which he or she is performing services.
(4) Procuring the signature to a purchase offer or contract or to any lease or lease proposal which has no definite purchase price or lease rental, or no method of payment, termination date, possession date or property description.
(5) The payment of any fees or amounts due the Commission with a check that is dishonored upon presentation to the bank on which the check is drawn.
(6) Lending a broker's license to an associate; permitting an associate to operate as a broker; or failure of a broker to properly supervise the activities of an associate. A broker permitting the use of the broker's license to enable an associate licensed with the broker to, in fact, establish and conduct a brokerage business wherein the broker's only interest is the receipt of a fee for the use of the broker's sponsorship.
(7) Failure to make known in writing to any purchaser any interest the licensee has in the property they are selling.
(8) Failure of the licensee to inform the buyer and seller in writing at the time the offer is presented that the buyer and seller will be expected to pay certain closing costs, such as discount points and approximate amount of said costs.
(9) Failing, upon demand in writing, to respond to a complaint in writing, or to disclose any information within licensee's knowledge, or to produce any document, book or record in licensee's possession or under licensee's control that is real estate related and under the jurisdiction of the Real Estate Commission, for inspection to a member of the Commission staff or any other lawful representative of the Commission.
(10) Failure to reduce a bona fide offer to writing, where a proposed purchaser requests such offer to be submitted.

(11) Failure to submit all written bona fide offers to an owner when such offers are received prior to the seller accepting an offer in writing.
(12) Any conduct in a real estate transaction which demonstrates bad faith or incompetency.
(13) Failing to act, in marketing a licensee's own property, with the same good faith as when acting in the capacity of a real estate licensee.
(14) An associate who does not possess the license of a broker or branch office broker but is intentionally acting in the capacity of a broker or branch office broker.
(15) Discouraging a party from obtaining an inspection on a property.
(16) Allowing access to, or control of, real property without the owner's authorization.
(17) Knowingly providing false or misleading information to the Commission during the course of an investigation.
(18) Interfering with an investigation by means of persuading, intimidating or threatening any party or witness, or tampering with or withholding evidence relating to the investigation.
(19) Knowingly cooperating with an unlicensed person or entity to perform licensed real estate activities as required by Title 59 O.S. Section 858-301.
(20) Failing to disclose any known immediate family relationship to a party to the transaction for which the broker is providing brokerage services.
(21) Failure by a broker to ensure all persons performing real estate licensed activities under the broker are properly licensed.
(22) An associate shall not perform licensed activities outside their broker's supervision.
(23) Failing to maintain documents relating to a trust account or real estate transaction for the time period as required by Rule 605:10-13-1.

605:10-17-5. Substantial misrepresentation

Substantial misrepresentation within the meaning of paragraph 2 of Section 858-312 of the "Code" includes, but is not limited to:
(1) The recommendation or use by a licensee of a fictitious or false instrument for the purpose of inducing any lender or Government Agency to loan or insure any sum of money.
(2) Failure to disclose to a buyer or other cooperative licensee or firm a known material defect regarding the condition of a parcel of real estate of which a broker or associate has knowledge.
(3) The use by a real estate broker of the name or trade name of a licensee whose license has been revoked or currently on suspension.
(4) Representing to any lender, guaranteeing agency or any other interested party, either verbally or through the preparation of false documents, an amount in excess of the true and actual sales price of the real property or terms differing from those actually agreed upon by the parties to the transaction.

605:10-17-6. Requirements for suspended/revoked licensee

(a) A suspended/revoked licensee must return their license certificate and pocket identification card to the Commission office on or before the date the suspension/revocation becomes effective.
(b) When the suspension/revocation period becomes effective, the licensee shall comply with the following requirements:
  (1) A suspended/revoked licensee shall not engage in any activity which requires a real estate license, as defined in Section 858-102.
  (2) When a broker's license is suspended/revoked, associates under the suspended/revoked broker's supervision will automatically be placed "inactive" for the duration of the suspension/revocation period unless the licensee requests to be transferred to another broker.
  (3) If the suspended/revoked broker has a branch office, the license for the branch office will be placed inactive unless otherwise ordered by the Commission; and all licensees associated with the branch office will automatically be placed "inactive" for the duration of the suspension/revocation period unless the licensee requests to be transferred to another broker.
  (4) If a managing corporate broker of a corporation is suspended/revoked for an act which was on behalf of the corporation, the broker license of the corporation will be placed inactive unless otherwise ordered by the Commission; and all licensees associated with the corporation will automatically be placed "inactive" for the duration of the suspension/revocation period unless the licensee requests to be transferred to another broker.

(5) If the managing partner(s) of a partnership is suspended/revoked for an act which was in behalf of the partnership, the broker license of the partnership will be placed inactive unless otherwise ordered by the Commission; and all licensees associated with the partnership will automatically be placed on "inactive" for the duration of the suspension/revocation period and the other broker will be placed "inactive" unless he or she requests his or her license to be transferred out of the partnership.

(6) If a managing broker member of an association is suspended/revoked for an act which was in behalf of the association, the broker license of the association will be placed inactive unless otherwise ordered by the Commission; and all licensees associated with the association will automatically be placed "inactive" for the duration of the suspension/revocation period unless the licensee requests to be transferred to another broker.

(7) A suspended/revoked licensee shall only receive compensation during the suspension/revocation period for acts which were performed during the period in which the licensee was actively licensed.

(8) Listings must be cancelled by a suspended/revoked broker between the time the Order of suspension/revocation is received and the effective date of suspension/revocation, as listings will be void on the date the suspension/revocation becomes effective.

(9) A suspended/revoked broker shall not assign listings to another broker without the written consent of the owner of the listed property.

(10) A suspended/revoked broker shall not advertise real estate in any manner, and must remove and discontinue all advertising.

(11) The telephone in a suspended/revoked broker's office shall not be answered in any manner to indicate the suspended/revoked broker is currently active in real estate.

(12) All pending contracts, items or monies placed with the suspended/revoked broker must be transferred to another responsible broker as approved by the Commission and in compliance with Section 605:10-13-1 (n).

(13) A suspended/revoked licensee shall be required to comply with Section 605:10-13-1 (n) and provide the required information to the Commission prior to the effective date of suspension/revocation.

(14) A representative of the Commission shall visit the office of any suspended/revoked broker prior to the effective date of the suspension/revocation to insure compliance with the requirements of (1) through (13) of this subsection.

605:10-17-7. Cessation of licensed activities upon loss of license

(a) A revoked, suspended, cancelled, surrendered or lapsed licensee is prohibited from performing licensed activities upon the effective date of loss of license.

(b) A revoked or suspended licensee shall comply with Section 605:10-17-6.

(c) A broker whose license was cancelled, surrendered or lapsed shall comply with Section 605:10-13-1 (m.)

*Seller only to complete

APPENDIX A. RESIDENTIAL PROPERTY CONDITION DISCLOSURE STATEMENT

Notice to Seller: Oklahoma Law (the "Residential Property Condition Disclosure Act," Title 60, O.S., §831 et.seq., effective July 1, 1995) requires Sellers of 1 and/or 2 residential dwelling units to complete this form. A Seller must complete, sign and date this disclosure form and deliver it or cause it to be delivered to a purchaser as soon as practicable, but in any event no later than before an offer is accepted by the Seller. If the Seller becomes aware of a defect after delivery of this statement, but before the Seller accepts an offer to purchase, the Seller must deliver or cause to be delivered an amended disclosure statement disclosing the newly discovered defect to the Purchaser. If the disclosure form or amendment is delivered to a Purchaser after an offer to purchase has been made by the Purchaser, the offer to purchase shall be accepted by the Seller only after a Purchaser has acknowledged receipt of this statement and confirmed the offer to purchase in writing.

Notice to Purchaser: The declarations and information contained in this disclosure statement are not warranties, express or implied of any kind, and are not a substitute for any inspections or warranties the Purchaser may wish to obtain. The information contained in this disclosure statement is not intended to be a part of any contract between the Purchaser and Seller. The information and statements contained in this disclosure statement are declarations and representations of the Seller and <u>are not the representations of the real estate licensee.</u>

LOCATION OF SUBJECT PROPERTY_____

SELLER IS ____ IS NOT ____ OCCUPYING THE SUBJECT PROPERTY.

Instructions to the Seller: (1) Answer ALL questions. (2) Report known conditions affecting the property. (3) Complete this form yourself. (4) If an item is not on the property, or will not be included in the sale, mark "None/Not Included." If you do not know the facts, mark "Do Not Know if Working." (5) The date of completion by you may not be more than 180 days prior to the date this form is received by a purchaser.

ARE THE ITEMS LISTED BELOW IN NORMAL WORKING ORDER?

Appliances/Systems/Services	Working	Not Working	Do Not Know if Working	None/Not Included
Sprinkler System				
Swimming Pool				
Hot Tub/Spa				
Water Heater ___ Electric ___ Gas ___ Solar				
Water Purifier				
Water Softener ___ Leased ___ Owned				
Sump Pump				
Plumbing				
Whirlpool Tub				
Sewer System ___ Public ___ Septic ___ Lagoon				
Air Conditioning System ___ Electric ___ Gas ___ Heat Pump				
Window Air Conditioner(s)				
Attic Fan				
Fireplaces				
Heating System ___ Electric ___ Gas ___ Heat Pump				
Humidifier				
Ceiling Fans				

Appliances/Systems/Services	Working	Not Working	Do Not Know if Working	None/Not Included
Gas Supply ___ Public ___ Propane ___ Butane				
Propane Tank				
Electric Air Purifier				
Garage Door Opener				
Intercom				
Central Vacuum				
Security System ___ Rent ___ Own ___ Monitored				
Smoke Detectors				
Dishwasher				
Electrical Wiring				
Garbage Disposal				
Gas Grill				
Vent Hood				
Microwave Oven				
Built-in Oven/Range				
Kitchen Stove				
Trash Compactor				
Source of Household Water ___ Public ___ Well ___ Private/Rural District				

Buyer's Initials _____ Buyer's Initials _____   Seller's Initials _____ Seller's Initials _____

(OREC—11/15)

LOCATION OF SUBJECT PROPERTY_____

IF YOU ANSWERED Not Working to any items on page one, please explain. Attach additional pages with your signature.
_____
_____

Zoning and Historical

1. Property is zoned: (Check One) ___ residential ___ commercial ___ historical ___ office ___ agricultural ___ industrial ___ urban conservation ___ other ___ unknown

2. Is the property designated as historical or located in a registered historical district?   Yes _____   No _____

Flood and Water

	Yes	No
3. What is the flood zone status of the property? _____		
4. What is the floodway status of the property? _____		
5. Are you aware of any flood insurance requirements concerning the property?		
6. Are you aware of any flood insurance on the property?		
7. Are you aware of the property being damaged or affected by flood, storm run-off, sewer backup, draining or grading problems?		
8. Are you aware of any surface or ground water drainage systems which assist in draining the property, e.g. "French Drains?"		
9. Are you aware of any occurrence of water in the heating and air conditioning duct system?		
10. Are you aware of water seepage, leakage or other draining problems in any of the improvements on the property?		

Additions/Alterations/Repairs

	Yes	No
11. Are you aware of any additions being made without required permits?		
12. Are you aware of any previous foundation repairs?		
13. Are you aware of any alterations or repairs having been made to correct defects or problems?		
14. Are you aware of any defect or condition affecting the interior or exterior walls, ceilings, roof structure, slab/foundation, basement/storm cellar, floors, windows, doors, fences or garage?		
15. Are you aware of the roof covering ever being repaired or replaced during your ownership of the property?		
16. Approximate age of roof covering, if known _____ number of layers, if known _____		
17. Do you know of any current problems with the roof covering?		
18. Are you aware of treatment for termite or wood-destroying organism infestation?		
19. Are you aware of a termite bait system installed on the property?		
20. If yes, is it being monitored by a licensed exterminating company? If yes, annual cost $_____		
21. Are you aware of any damage caused by termites or wood-destroying organisms?		
22. Are you aware of major fire, tornado, hail, earthquake or wind damage?		
23. Have you ever received payment on an insurance claim for damages to residential property and/or any improvements which were not repaired?		
24. Are you aware of problems pertaining to sewer, septic, lateral lines or aerobic system?		

Environmental

	Yes	No
25. Are you aware of the presence of asbestos?		
26. Are you aware of the presence of radon gas?		
27. Have you tested for radon gas?		
28. Are you aware of the presence of lead-based paint?		
29. Have you tested for lead-based paint?		
30. Are you aware of any underground storage tanks on the property?		
31. Are you aware of the presence of a landfill on the property?		
32. Are you aware of existence of hazardous or regulated materials and other conditions having an environmental impact?		
33. Are you aware of existence of prior manufacturing of methamphetamine?		
34. Have you had the property inspected for mold?		
35. Are you aware of any remedial treatment for mold on the property?		
36. Are you aware of any condition on the property that would impair the health or safety of the occupants?		

Buyer's Initials _____   Buyer's Initials _____   Seller's Initials _____   Seller's Initials _____

(OREC—11/15)

LOCATION OF SUBJECT PROPERTY _____

Property Shared in Common, Easements, Homeowner's Associations and Legal	Yes	No
37. Are you aware of features of the property shared in common with the adjoining landowners, such as fences, driveways, and roads whose use or responsibility has an effect on the property?		
38. Other than utility easements serving the property, are you aware of any easements or right-of-ways affecting the property?		
39. Are you aware of encroachments affecting the property?		
40. Are you aware of a mandatory homeowner's association? Amount of dues $_____ Special Assessment $_____ Payable: (check one) _____ monthly _____ quarterly _____ annually Are there unpaid dues or assessments for the property? _____ YES _____ NO If yes, what is the amount? $_____ Manager's Name _____ Phone Number _____		
41. Are you aware of any zoning, building code or setback requirement violations?		
42. Are you aware of any notices from any government or government-sponsored agencies or any other entities affecting the property?		
43. Are you aware of any surface leases, including but not limited to agricultural, commercial or oil and gas?		
44. Are you aware of any filed litigation or lawsuits directly or indirectly affecting property, including a foreclosure?		
45. Is the property located in a fire district which requires payment? If yes, amount of fee $_____ Paid to Whom _____ Payable: (check one) _____ monthly _____ quarterly _____ annually		
46. Is the property located in a private utility district? Check applicable _____ Water _____ Garbage _____ Sewer _____ Other If other, explain _____ Initial membership fee $_____ Annual membership fee $_____ (if more than one utility attach additional pages)		
Miscellaneous	Yes	No
47. Are you aware of other defect(s) affecting the property not disclosed above?		
48. Are you aware of any other fees or dues required on the property that you have not disclosed?		

If you answered YES to any of the items on pages two and three, list the item number(s) and explain. If needed, attach additional pages with your signature(s), date(s) and location of the subject property. _____

On the date this form is signed, the seller states that based on seller's **CURRENT ACTUAL KNOWLEDGE** of the property, the information contained above is true and accurate.

Are there any additional pages attached to this disclosure? (circle one): YES   NO   If yes, how many? _____

_____   _____
Seller's Signature   Date   Seller's Signature   Date

A real estate licensee has no duty to the Seller or the Purchaser to conduct an independent inspection of the property and has no duty to independently verify the accuracy or completeness of any statement made by the Seller in the disclosure statement.

The Purchaser understands that the disclosures given by the Seller on this statement are not a warranty of condition. The Purchaser is urged to carefully inspect the property, and, if desired, to have the property inspected by a licensed expert. For specific uses, restrictions and flood zone status, contact the local planning, zoning and/or engineering department. The Purchaser acknowledges that the Purchaser has read and received a signed copy of this statement. This completed acknowledgement should accompany an offer to purchase on the property identified. This is to advise that this disclosure statement is not valid after 180 days from the date completed by the Seller.

_____   _____
Purchaser's Signature   Date   Purchaser's Signature   Date

The disclosure and disclaimer statement forms and the Oklahoma Residential Property Condition Disclosure Act information pamphlet are made available at the Oklahoma Real Estate Commission (OREC), Denver N. Davison Building, 1915 N. Stiles, Suite 200, Oklahoma City, OK 73105, or visit OREC's Web site www.orec.ok.gov.

(OREC—11/15)

APPENDIX B. RESIDENTIAL PROPERTY CONDITION DISCLAIMER STATEMENT FORM

Seller instructions: Oklahoma Law (the "Residential Property Condition Disclosure Act," 60, O.S. Section 831 et. seq., effective July 1, 1995) **requires a seller** of 1 and 2 residential dwelling units **to deliver, or cause to be delivered, a disclaimer statement to a purchaser as soon as practicable, but in any event before acceptance of an offer to purchase if you, the seller: 1) have never occupied the property and make no disclosures** concerning the condition of the property; <u>and</u> **2) have no actual knowledge of any defect** concerning the property.

If, however, you occupied the property or **know of a defect in regard to the property,** you must complete and deliver, or cause to be delivered, a "Residential Property Condition Disclosure Statement" to the purchaser.

Also, if you become aware of a defect <u>after</u> delivery of this disclaimer statement to a purchaser, but before you accept an offer to purchase, you must complete and deliver, or cause to be delivered, a "Residential Property Condition Disclosure Statement" to a purchaser.

Completion of this form by you **may not be more than 180 days prior to the date this form is received by a purchaser.**

Note: If this disclaimer statement **is delivered to a purchaser after an offer to purchase has been made by the purchaser,** the offer to purchase **shall be accepted by you only after** a purchaser has acknowledged receipt of this statement and confirmed the offer to purchase.

> Defect means a condition, malfunction, or problem that would have a materially adverse effect on the monetary value of the property, or that would impair the health or safety of future occupants of the property.

(For more information on the requirements of the law, please refer to the Residential Property Condition Disclosure Information Pamphlet.)

Seller's Disclaimer Statement

The undersigned seller states that seller has <u>never</u> occupied the property located at _____
_____, **Oklahoma; makes <u>no</u> disclosures concerning the condition of the property; AND has <u>no</u> actual knowledge of any defect.**

Seller's Signature	Date	Seller's Signature	Date

Purchaser's Acknowledgment

The purchaser shall sign and date this acknowledgment. The purchaser is urged to carefully inspect the subject property and, if desired, to have the property inspected by an expert. The purchaser acknowledges that purchaser has read and received a signed copy of this statement. This completed acknowledgement should accompany an offer to purchase you make on the property identified above.

Purchaser's Signature	Date	Purchaser's Signature	Date

Note to seller and purchaser: A real estate licensee has no duty to the seller or purchaser to conduct an independent inspection of the property and has no duty to independently verify the accuracy or completeness of any statement made by the seller in this disclaimer statement.

The disclosure and disclaimer statement forms and the Residential Property Condition Disclosure Information Pamphlet are made available by the Oklahoma Real Estate Commission, 1915 N. Stiles Ave., Suite 200 (Denver N. Davison Building), Oklahoma City, Oklahoma 73105-4919. Visit the Commission's web site: www.orec.ok.gov

OREC (07-2014)

CL. 17

TEST YOUR UNDERSTANDING

Regulations Affecting Real Estate

1. The Oklahoma Real Estate Commission is under the Sunset Law which requires the State Legislature to review its performance and either terminate it or extend it for
    1. 3 years.
    2. 5 years.
    3. 7 years.
    4. 10 years.

2. All members of the OREC shall be citizens of the U. S. and shall have been residents of the State of Oklahoma for
    1. 3 years.
    2. 4 years.
    3. 5 years.
    4. 6 years.

3. OREC commissioners are appointed by the
    1. OAR.
    2. House of Representatives.
    3. Governor with the advise and consent of the Senate.
    4. State Supreme Court.

4. Once confirmed by the Senate, OREC commissioners serve a term of
    1. 2 years.
    2. 3 years.
    3. 4 years.
    4. 5 years.

5. Each member of the OREC is paid
    1. travel expenses only.
    2. fifty dollars per day and travel expenses.
    3. one hundred dollars per meeting.
    4. two thousand dollars per month.

6. The fine for practicing real estate without a license is
    1. $10,000 or the commission whichever is greater.
    2. $5,000 or the commission whichever is greater.
    3. $3,000 or the commission whichever is greater.
    4. $1,000 or the commission whichever is greater.

7. A real estate licensee may be fined by the Commission no more than
    1. $5,000 for all violations resulting from a single incident.
    2. $4,000 for all violations resulting from a single incident.
    3. $2,000 for all violations resulting from a single incident.
    4. $1,000 for all violations resulting from a single incident.

8. A violation of the Oklahoma Real Estate License Code and Rules is
    1. a felony.
    2. grand larceny.
    3. a misdemeanor.
    4. a federal felony.

9. The OREC maintains a standing committee to
    1. review and revise rules.
    2. draft and revise residential real estate purchase contracts.
    3. review and revise ethical standards.
    4. None of the above.

10. **In the exercise of its powers and duties, the OREC shall comply with**
    1. Regulation Z
    2. Regulation X.
    3. Administrative Procedures Act.
    4. Uniform Commercial Code.

11. **Which of the following is NOT required to have a real estate license to perform some very limited real estate activities?**
    1. Owner.
    2. Attorney-in-fact.
    3. Attorney-at-law.
    4. All of the above.

12. **The Oklahoma Real Estate License Code specifies that it is acceptable for any person who is a resident of a residential rental unit may be paid a "resident referral fee" of not more than**
    1. $500.
    2. $100.
    3. $50.
    4. None of the above.

13. **In order to apply for a provisional sales associate license, an applicant must**
    1. be 18 years old or older.
    2. successfully complete the required pre-license course.
    3. be of good moral character.
    4. All of the above.

14. **The provisional sales associate license is for a period of**
    1. 1 year.
    2. 2 years.
    3. 3 years.
    4. 4 years.

15. **The Oklahoma Real Estate Commission office**
    1. is in Oklahoma City only.
    2. has Oklahoma City and Tulsa branches.
    3. has Oklahoma City, Tulsa and Lawton branches.
    4. None of the above.

16. **A provisional sales associate must successfully complete a 45-hour post-license course during**
    1. first year of licensure.
    2. second year of licensure.
    3. third year of licensure.
    4. fourth year of licensure.

17. **A passing score on the provisional sales associate's examination is**
    1. 70%.
    2. 75%.
    3. 80%.
    4. 85%.

18. **In order to qualify for a broker license, OREC Code requires the applicant to**
    1. successfully complete a 90-hour course.
    2. have two years active licensure as a provisional and/or sales associate.
    3. pass the broker examination with 75% accuracy or more.
    4. All of the above.

19. A broker license is issued for
    1. 1 year.
    2. 2 years.
    3. 3 years.
    4. 4 years.

20. OREC issues licenses to
    1. associations.
    2. branch offices.
    3. corporations.
    4. all of the above.

21. A real estate licensee in another state
    1. may apply for an Oklahoma nonresident license.
    2. apply for a temporary Oklahoma Real Estate License.
    3. must have an office in Oklahoma.
    4. None of the above.

22. A broker who is licensed in another state
    1. must never do real estate business in Oklahoma.
    2. may enter into a cooperative brokerage agreement with an Oklahoma Broker.
    3. must seek approval of the Oklahoma Secretary of State.
    4. must seek approval of the Oklahoma Securities Department.

23. With the exception of the first, entry-level provisional sales associate license, Oklahoma real estate licenses are normally issued for
    1. 1 year.
    2. 2 years,
    3. 3 years.
    3. 4 years.

24. In order to renew an active real estate sales associate or broker's license, an active licensee must complete
    1. 12 hours of continuing education.
    2. 9 clock hours of continuing education.
    3. 30 clock hours of continuing education.
    4. 21 clock hours of continuing education.

25. In order to renew an active real estate license, each licensee is required to complete certain required courses. Which, if any, of the following are required courses?
    1. Fair Housing.
    2. Professional Standards.
    3. Broker Relationships Act.
    4. All of the above.

26. Which of the following are not required to complete the continuing education requirements?
    1. A licensee who wishes to remain on inactive status.
    2. A licensee who holds a PSA license.
    3. A nonresident licensee who maintains a current license in another state and has satisfied the continuing education requirements in that state.
    4. All of the above..

27. A person shall not be permitted to file an application for re-issuance of a license after revocation of the license within
    1. 3 years of the effective date.
    2. 4 years of the effective date.
    3. 5 years of the effective date.
    4. 6 years of the effective date.

28. When a licensee requests the OREC to place a license on inactive status, the licensee must
   1. continue to pay renewal fees.
   2. make the request in writing.
   3. complete forms furnished by OREC.
   4. All of the above.

29. OREC requires proprietary brokers to maintain a specific place of business which
   1. complies with all local laws.
   2. is available to the public during reasonable hours.
   3. Both 1 and 2.
   4. Neither 1 nor 2.

30. If the OREC fines a licensee for a violation, the licensee has
   1. 15 days to pay or the fine doubles.
   2. 30 days to pay or the fine doubles.
   3. 45 days to pay or the fine doubles.
   4. to ay the fine immediately.

31. Concerning the Sex Offenders Registration Act, the OREC Code
   1. imposes no duty on licensees to disclose information about sex offenders.
   2. imposes a duty on licensees to disclose information about sex offenders.
   3. does not address the Sex Offenders Registration Act.
   4. None of the above.

32. According to the OREC Rules, the primary purpose of the OREC is to
   1. safeguard the public interests.
   2. provide quality service by assisting and providing resources.
   3. investigating and sanctioning licensed activities.
   4. All of the above.

33. The OREC operates under the Open Records Act which allows
   1. OREC to open records for inspection.
   2. OREC open records to be copied.
   3. OREC to charge for copies.
   4. All of the above.

34. OREC makes a directory of Oklahoma real estate licensees available
   1. in printed form available at OREC offices.
   2. in printed form available upon request.
   3. on the OREC web cite under "Licensee look up". *website*
   4. none of the above.

35. The membership of the OREC Contract Forms Committee is made up of
   1. three members appointed by the OREC.
   2. three members appointed by the BAR Association.
   3. five members appointed by the OAR.
   4. All of the above.

36. If the OREC receives an "insufficient funds" check
   1. it may be considered a violation of the "Code."
   2. OREC will charge a $35.00 fee.
   3. OREC may deny other services.
   4. All of the above.

37. The OREC requires applicants for real estate licenses to be of "good moral character." Which of the following does the OREC consider when evaluating "good moral character?"
 1. Convictions.
 2. Bankruptcy.
 3. License denied in another state.
 4. All of the above.

38. If the OREC denies an application for a real estate license, the OREC will notify the applicant of the denial within
 1. 10 days.
 2. 15 days.
 3. 20 days.
 4. 30 days.

39. The OREC examination fee for a provisional sales associate's license is
 1. $60.
 2. $70.
 3. $80.
 4. $90.

40 The state examination fee for a broker license is
 1. $65.
 2. $75.
 3. $85.
 4. $95.

41. Persons taking the OREC examination may take it
 1. on a computer.
 2. as a written (paper and pencil) exam not on a computer.
 3. Either 1 or 2.
 4. Neither 1 nor 2.

42. If an applicant fails to pass the appropriate examination, the OREC
 1. requires a one month waiting period before taking the test again.
 2. requires a one week waiting period before taking the test again.
 3. has no waiting period before taking the test again.
 4. will not allow re-takes of the examination.

43. An applicant who has failed the exam may review the failed exam within
 1. 10 days.
 2. 20 days.
 3. 30 days.
 4. 40 days.

44. Ultimate responsibility for notifying the OREC of a continuing education offering is on
 1. the licensee.
 2. the school.
 3. the broker.
 4. None of the above.

45. To complete any in-class continuing education offering, a person must be present
 1. 80% of the time.
 2. all of the time.
 3. 75% of the time.
 4. None of the above.

46. If a provisional sales associate fails to take the required post license (part II) course during the first year of licensure,
    1. he/he may take it during the second year.
    2. he/she may substitute an accounting course.
    3. he/she cannot renew the license.
    4. None of the above.

47. OREC may extend time for completion of the provisional sales associate post license course
    1. for military service.
    2. for an acceptable written reason.
    3. if the associate's broker makes a written request for an extension.
    4. All of the above.

48. No real estate licensee shall begin operation in the real estate business without
    1. joining a multi-list system.
    2. having been issued a license.
    3. attending at least one Commission meeting.
    4. joining the REALTORS Association.

49. The Personal Responsibility and Work Opportunity and Reconciliation Act of 1996, requires that licensees document
    1. citizenship.
    2. qualified alien status.
    3. Either of the above.
    4. Neither of the above.

50. A licensee whose license has lapsed shall be considered for reinstatement if the licensee
    1. pays an amount equal to the current examination fee.
    2. pays licensee fee and late penalties.
    3. provides documents as required by the Commission
    4. All of the above.

51. If a broker moves to a new office, OREC requires all licenses be re-issued to the new address. OREC charges a fee of
    1. $10 for each license with a maximum fee of $100 for all licenses.
    2. $20 for each license with a maximum fee of $100 for all licenses.
    3. $25 for each license with a maximum fee of $750 for all licenses.
    4. $30 for each license with a maximum fees of $1,000 for all licenses.

52. a broker may have
    1. no more than three branch offices.
    2. no more than five branch offices.
    3. no more than ten branch offices.
    4. as many branch offices as desired.

53. Any change of a license of licensed firm must be filed in the OREC office within
    1. 5 days of such change.
    2. 10 days of such change.
    3. 15 days of such change.
    4. 20 days of such change.

54. If a licensee works out of a branch office, the licensee's license must be issued to
    1. the home office.
    2. the branch office.
    3. Either 1 or 2.
    4. Neither 1 nor 2.

55. **A branch office manager**
   1. may be a sales associate.
   2. does not have to have a license.
   3. must have a broker license.
   4. must be designated by OREC.

56. **A broker may have an office in his home if**
   1. OREC approves.
   2. the corporation approves.
   3. not contrary to local zoning laws.
   4. None of the above.

57. **A broker may be the broker for more than one firm if**
   1. the firms are in the same place.
   2. he has an identical twin.
   3. the Secretary of State's Office issues a certificate of good standing.
   4. Both 1 and 3.

58. **If an associate hires an unlicensed assistant**
   1. only the associate is responsible for the assistant's activities.
   2. the broker is responsible for the assistant's activities.
   3. unlicensed assistants are not legal.
   4. only licensed assistants are legal.

59. **Each real estate office shall erect a sign**
   1. on or about the office entrance.
   2. which contains the company name.
   3. in which all letters are at least one inch high.
   4. all of the above.

60. **When an associate advertises, the advertisement must**
   1. not be done only under his/her name.
   2. include the name of the broker or the company name.
   3. under the direct supervision of the broker.
   4. all of the above.

61. **If a proprietary broker dies or becomes disabled**
   1. the company must close.
   2. OREC has a list of instructions for this event.
   3. OREC has no specific requirements.
   4. none of the above.

62. **In the event a broker refuses or for any other reason will not release an assocate,**
   1. the associate has no recourse.
   2. the associate shall notify the broker by certified mail of the disassociation.
   3. must furnish the Commission a sworn statement that the notification of disassociation has been served to the broker.
   4. Both 2 and 3 above.

63. **An active associate transferring from one broker to a new broker**
   1. must wait until the license is issued to the new broker.
   2. must notify the NAR of the change.
   3. may continually act if the change is done in a timely manner.
   4. none of the above.

64. **When as associate changes his/her home address, the Commission must be notified within**
   1. 10 days.
   2. 20 days.
   3. 30 days.
   4. does not need to notify the Commission as long as the office address does not change.

65. When a complaint is filed with the OREC against a licensee, the licensee must respond within
   1. 10 days.
   2. 15 days.
   3. 20 days.
   4. 30 days.

66. Good faith money paid under a contract for the sale of real estate is
   1. called "earnest money" and is paid by the buyer.
   2. may be held by a third party until closing.
   3. Both 1 and 2.
   4. Neither 1 nor 2.

67. The amount of earnest money deposit is usually
   1. a standard figure.
   2. determined by the broker.
   3. a percentage of the sales price.
   4. negotiated between the seller and the buyer.

68. The usual procedure is to deposit an earnest money payment
   1. by the end of the next banking day following completion of a firm contract.
   2. by the end of the third banking day following completion of a firm contract.
   3. within a reasonable time.
   4. any time prior to closing.

69. If a broker accepts an earnest money deposit from a buyer, which of the following is true?
   1. The deposit money does not belong to the licensee.
   2. In every case, all money deposited must immediately be delivered to the seller.
   3. Money deposited by the buyer is always returnable to the buyer.
   4. In case of dispute between the buyer and the seller, the broker always decides to whom the deposit is to be given.

70. A broker's trust account is used
   1. for the deposit of earnest money only.
   2. in lieu of a general account.
   3. for the deposit of money belonging to others.
   4. to compensate the broker for expenditures.

71. When money is deposited in a trust account, part of which will be used to pay the broker's commission
   1. the broker can withdraw his/her rightful share of the money before the real estate transaction is consummated or terminated.
   2. accurate records must be kept on the account.
   3. Both A and B.
   4. Neither A nor B.

72. When customer funds are placed in a trust account, the broker is
   1. free of personal liability for the amount of the deposit because of the state statutes governing trust account liability.
   2. free of liability for any loss because of the recovery fund provisions.
   3. only liable for the amount of the commission as stated in the listing contract.
   4. liable under the law for the full amount thereof.

73. Copies of all written instruments on a real estate transaction that are prepared by a licensee must be
   1. distributed to all signers of the instrument.
   2. maintained by the real estate broker.
   3. duplicate originals.
   4. All of the above.

74. The obligation of associates to turn over all monies deposited, payments made, or things of value received by an associate to the sponsoring broker promptly is found under
   1. Acts of Sales Associates.
   2. Prohibited Dealings.
   3. Substantial Misrepresentation.
   4. Duty to Account.

75. Non-depositable escrow items may be accepted
   1. only if the associate or broker agrees to care for same.
   2. if evaluated.
   3. if evaluated and placed with an authorized escrow agent.
   4. if evaluated, placed with an authorized escrow agent and all parties are informed.

76. When placing earnest deposits in the operating account of a company, a broker
   1. must take all necessary measures to assure that the balance never falls below the amount of such deposits.
   2. must keep separate records.
   3. is guilty of commingling.
   4. must do so by the end of the third banking day after acceptance.

77. An associate brings an offer to purchase with an earnest money check to the broker. The offer by the buyer is accepted by the seller. The next day the broker is notified by the seller that, through no fault of the associate, the buyer and seller have decided to cancel the sale, and the broker is instructed to return the deposit to the buyer. The broker
   1. can keep one-half of the deposit and give the other half to the seller.
   2. has grounds for suing the seller, but must return the deposit to the buyer.
   3. can retain the deposit as compensation for services rendered.
   4. can keep one-half of the deposit and return half to the buyer.

78. Brokers can be censured for commingling funds if they deposit earnest money to anything other than
   1. their general real estate operating accounts.
   2. their personal accounts because a portion of the money was due them.
   3. separate checking accounts designed as trust accounts.
   4. separate savings accounts.

79. A real estate broker sold a property late Friday evening and obtained a $4,000 deposit in cash. Afraid of losing the money over the weekend, a night deposit was made into a personal checking account. This action would most closely relate to
   1. conversion.
   2. commingling.
   3. misrepresentation.
   4. reasonable caution.

80. Property taxes are
   1. prepaid.
   2. unjust.
   3. paid in arrears.
   4. overdue.

81. Hazard insurance is always
   1. prepaid.
   2. accrued.
   3. excessive.
   4. unreasonable.

82. Documentary tax stamps cost
   1. 75 cents per thousand dollars on the gross sales price.
   2. 75 cents per $500, or portion there of, on the gross sales price.
   3. $1.50 per $500, or portion there of, of new money in the transaction.
   4. $1.10 per $1,000 on new money.

83. Sam seller sold his duplex for the sum of $40,635 on an assumption type sale. When the transaction was closed, the mortgage assumed was $20,000. What was the cost of documentary tax stamps attached to the deed?
   1. $61.50.
   2. $41.50.
   3. $31.50.
   4. None of these.

84. The settlement statement may be defined as the
   1. notice which appears at the bottom of the abstract.
   2. final accounting of the transaction dealing with real estate taxes, insurance, etc.
   3. recording of the completion of the transaction with the proper authorities.
   4. statement which conveys title to real property

85. Ultimate responsibility for accurate settlement cost statements rest with the
   1. title company.
   2. listing broker.
   3. sales associate.
   4. parties to the transaction.

86. The settlement statement will disclose the amount of money
   1. the seller will receive at the closing.
   2. the buyer must bring to the closing
   3. Both 1 and 2.
   4. Neither 1 nor 2.

87. The seller normally pays the cost of the
   1. abstracting.
   2. real estate commission.
   3. documentary tax stamps.
   4. all of these.

88. In preparing the settlement statement, generally the
   1. seller pays the cost of bringing the abstract up to date.
   2. buyer pays an attorney to render an opinion of title.
   3. Both 1 and 2.
   4. Neither 1 nor 2.

89. Which of the following is not a power and duty of the Oklahoma Real Estate Commission?
   1. To hold examinations of persons who shall apply for the issuance of license to them, and to promulgate such rules and regulations as it may deem proper.
   2. To cause the prosecution of any person who violates any of the provisions of the "Code."
   3. To serve as a board of arbitration to settle disputes among brokers, associates, or
   4. To issue licenses to persons who have passed examinations and who otherwise meet license requirements.

90. The Oklahoma Real Estate Commission has the right and power
   1. to arbitrate disputes between licensees.
   2. to set a maximum commission rate allowed to be charged to the public.
   3. to request records and files of a licensee suspected of violation of the Code or Rules.
   4. All of the above.

91. If a broker and an associate have a dispute over a sales commission which cannot be settled by other means, they should
   1. try to get the Oklahoma Real estate Commission to settle it first.
   2. bring action in an appropriate court.
   3. drop the issue.
   4. slug it out.

92. The percentage charged by a broker as the fee for finding a buyer is established by the
    1. Oklahoma Real Estate Commission.
    2. Corporation Commission.
    3. Broker and seller through negotiations.
    4. The National Association of REALTORS.

93. The Oklahoma Real Estate Commission is made up of
    1. one representative from an approved real estate school.
    2. five licensed real estate brokers.
    3. one member representing the consumer public.
    4. all of the above.

94. Which of the following is true about the Oklahoma Real Estate Commission?
    1. No more than two members may be from the same congressional district.
    2. They are appointed by the Governor with the advice and consent of the Senate.
    3. They are appointed to four-year terms.
    4. All of these.

95. Which of the following does the Oklahoma Real Estate Commission not have the power to do?
    1. Place an offending licensee on probation or issue a reprimand.
    2. Suspend or revoke any license issued by it.
    3. Impose a jail sentence.
    4. Require a licensee to obtain further education.

96. Which is exempt from the requirement to have a real estate license?
    1. A property owner selling a home.
    2. A legal guardian selling on behalf of an incompetent person.
    3. A resident manager of an apartment complex.
    4. All of the above.

97. For a broker to act for more than one party in a real estate transaction without the knowledge and consent of all parties is
    1. ethical.
    2. grounds for disciplinary action.
    3. contrary to the Statute of Frauds.
    4. all right if no party suffers monetary damage.

98. Sales associates may represent other brokers in cooperative sales if their brokers
    1. have knowledge of the transaction.
    2. give consent.
    3. Both 1 and 2.
    4. Neither 1 nor 2.

99. Real estate sales associates may lawfully accept bonus commissions for the completion of difficult sales
    1. if the seller wishes to give one.
    2. if they pay the taxes on them.
    3. only through their employing broker.
    4. if they receive them from the buyer.

100. Brokers collect earnest money because it
    1. shows good faith in the buyer.
    2. shows good faith in the seller.
    3. is part of their commission.
    4. is the consideration.

101. If a broker's license is revoked after a hearing at the OREC, the broker has the right to appeal to the
   1. district court.
   2. Oklahoma Association of REALTORS.
   3. count clerk.
   4. local board of REALTORS.

102. In Oklahoma
   1. licensees may place their licenses on inactive status indefinitely.
   2. in order to renew a license, the licensee must be re-examined.
   3. real estate licenses are renewed annually.
   4. twenty-one hours of continuing education are required annually.

103. The Oklahoma Real Estate Education and Recovery Fund assessment is
   1. $10.00 per year.
   2. $15.00 per three year license term.
   3. $30.00 for three year license term.
   4. $40.00 every other year.

104. Payments from the recovery fund for claims are limited to
   1. $25,000 for any one claimant..
   2. $50,000 for any transaction.
   3. $50,000 for all claims against one licensee.
   4.. All of these

ANSWERS

NOTE: The answers to all of the questions in this chapter are from the Oklahoma Real Estate License Code and Rules

1. 2	57. 1
2. 1	58. 2
3. 3	59. 4
4. 3	60. 4
5. 1	61. 2
6. 2	62. 2
7. 1	63. 3
8. 3	64. 1
9. 2	65. 2
10. 3	66. 3
11. 4	67. 4
12. 2	68. 2
13. 4	69. 1
14. 1	70. 3
15. 1	71. 2
16. 1	72. 4
17. 2	73. 4
18. 4	74. 4
19. 3	75. 4
20. 4	76. 3
21. 1	77. 2
22. 2	78. 3
23. 3	79. 2
24. 4	80. 3
25. 4	81. 1
26. 4	82. 2
27. 1	83. 1
28. 4	84. 2
29. 3	85. 2
30. 2	86. 3
31. 1	87. 4
32. 4	88. 3
33. 4	89. 3
34. 3	90. 3
35. 4	91. 2
36. 4	92. 3
37. 4	93. 4
38. 2	94. 4
39. 1	95. 3
40. 2	96. 4
41. 3	97. 2
42. 3	98. 3
43. 3	99. 3
44. 1	100. 1
45. 2	101. 1
46. 3	102. 1
47. 1	103. 2
48. 2	104. 4
49. 3	
50. 4	
51. 3	
52. 4	
53. 2	
54. 2	
55. 3	
56. 3	

DISCLOSURES AND ENVIRONMENTAL ISSUES

GOVERNMENT ENVIRONMENTAL ISSUES (TC)

A. **Environmental Protection Agency.**

The Environmental Protection Agency (EPA) is a federal agency which attempts are to monitor and control all forms of pollution. Some of the primary laws the EPA is charged with administering include:

Resource Conversation and Recovery Act of 1976 **(RCRA)**

Comprehensive Environmental Response, Compensation and Liability Act of 1980 **(CERCLA)**

Superfund Amendments and Reauthorization Act of 1986 **(SARA)**

The Clean Air Act

The Clean Water Act

The Federal Endangered Species Act

Residential Lead-Based Paint Hazard Reduction Act of 1992

Hazardous Solid Waste Amendments of 1984 (HSWA)

In addition to the Federal Environmental Protection Agency, each state has a state agency charged with responsibilities to assist EPA in administering and enforcing federal and state environmental laws and regulations.

In Oklahoma, the name of this agency is the Department of Environmental Quality (DEQ). DEQ routinely samples and tests air, water, solid waste, and hazardous waste materials throughout the state as required by applicable laws and regulations. It also addresses other Oklahoma environmental issues as needed.

B. *Comprehensive Environmental Response, Compensation, and Liability Act* **(CERCLA).**

The 1980 Comprehensive Environmental Response, Compensation and Liability Act, sometimes called "*Superfund*" or "CERCLA," indicates that lack of negligence or fault is not a defense in environmental issues. Owners, lessors, and even those who transport hazardous materials have been held liable.

Under the provisions of CERCLA present owners and operators, past owners and operators, those who transport hazardous substances and those who generate hazardous substances are financially liable for waste cleanup.

C. **Environmental Hazards. (TC)**

There are a number of chemicals or biological or even radioactive materials that may contaminate soil, surface or ground water and pose great health and/or safety risks to people, plants and animals.

Though these are most frequently thought of in connection with commercial and industrial activities, there are many residential properties where commercial activities have been conducted. Some of these may have created hazardous waste.

In addition, properties within one-half mile of dumps, land fills, waste sites, petroleum storage or delivery facilities and other possible pollution sources may cause even residential properties to become a risk for buyers, sellers and brokers.

The Environmental Protection Agency maintains a list of locations that are known hazardous sites. Properties within one half mile of one of the sites is cause for concern.

1. **Lead-Based Paint. (TC)**

   Lead-based paint became one of the hottest issues concerning environmental hazards over a decade ago. A lead-based paint disclosure is required. In 1996 a new regulation about lead-based paint went into effect. It requires real estate licensees and owners of properties to disclose to potential buyers all known lead-based paint hazards.

   Many houses and apartments built before 1978 have paint that contains lead (called lead-based paint). Lead from paint, chips, and dust can pose serious health hazards if not taken care of properly.

   Since 1996, federal law has required that individuals receive certain information before renting, buying, or renovating pre-1978 housing. Landlords must disclose known information on lead-based paint hazards before leases take effect. Leases should include a federal form about lead-based paint. Sellers or landlords must disclose known information on lead-based paint hazards before selling or renting a house. Sales contracts should include a federal form about lead-based paint.

   Federal law requires sellers, landlords, and renovators to give potential buyers and tenants a copy of a pamphlet, *"Protect Your Family From Lead in Your Home."* The law provides that tenants and buyers have a ten-day period to have the property inspected for the presence of lead-based paint. The law particularly targets properties constructed before <u>1978</u>. Real estate licensees have a particular responsibility to make this information available to members of the public.

2. **Mold. (TC)**

   Mold is a fungus normally found in moist locations. Most people have no reaction to common molds. However, some people have an allergic sensitivity to it.

   The presence of mold may render the property uninhabitable for these people. In recent years several high-profile lawsuits have drawn attention to the hazards which may be present with certain varieties of mold. Since mold may be present in locations not normally visible, some people with mold sensitivity should seek a mold inspection.

3. **Meth Labs. (TC)**

   The manufacture of illegal drugs on a property may so pollute the property as to make it uninhabitable. The ***Drug Enforcement Act*** (Section 881) allows enforcement agencies to confiscate real or personal property used in illegal drug activities. The manufacture of methamphetamine is a drug contributing to the problem.

   Since the process of "meth" manufacture pollutes the property, it creates a health hazard to subsequent occupants.

   If a licensee is aware of the possibility of "meth" having been manufactured on a property, it should be thoroughly investigated and not sold or leased until any conditions which represent a health hazard have been disclosed.

4. **Polychlorinated Biphenyls (PCBs). (TC)**

   PCBs where commonly used as insulating material in electrical equipment such as transformers and the ballasts in florescent light fixtures until 1979.

   Leaking electrical equipment may allow PCBs to contaminate soil, water and food. PCBs are a known carcinogen. It is believed they do not constitute a great threat to humans unless ingested.

5. **Ground Water. (TC)**

   Ground water is that water which accumulates below the surface of the land. It sometimes accumulates in pools called aquifers. Water which has not yet "pooled" in an aquifer or channel may be called percolating water. The water table is that level below which there is no longer percolating water.

   In Oklahoma, landowners have what is known as overlying rights. Farmers, for example, wishing to pump subsurface water from an aquifer will secure a permit from the Oklahoma Water Resources Board.

   Some communities and rural residents use underground water (wells) for their primary source of potable water.

Wells on rural property may be potential sources of problems. Water from municipal water supplies is usually safe. However, water from a well, even one that is filtered, may not be.

6. **Underground Storage Tanks. (TC)**

Underground storage tanks are defined by EPA as tanks which have 10% or more of its volume underground. These tanks have been used for the storage of petroleum products and other hazardous substances. When these tanks begin leaking, they may contaminate groundwater. In this event the owners of the leaking underground storage tanks (LUSTS) are in violation of several environmental laws.

These laws include the ***Resource Conservation and Recovery Act***, the ***Hazardous and Solid Waste Amendment Act*** and the ***Superfund And Reauthorization Act of 1986*** (SARA). Leaking underground storage tanks represent a large liability for the owner. **SARA** defines who is liable to pay for the cleanup of environmentally impacted properties.

The Leaking Underground Storage Tanks Trust Fund oversees cleanup by owners and to pay when responsible parties are unknown or unfound.

7. **Carbon Monoxide. (TC)**

Carbon Monoxide is an odorless, colorless, tasteless gas which, in sufficient quantities, kills. It can be present in residential properties where the plenum in the central heat unit develops cracks.

Carbon Monoxide is a product of the combination of gas and other heating fuels. It may be discovered by a Carbon Monoxide detection unit which all homes should have.

8. **Formaldehyde. (TC)**

Formaldehyde is a colorless compound with an exceedingly strong odor. It is classified by the Environmental Protection Agency as a "Probable Carcinogen." Formaldehyde is found in many building materials.

In past years urea foam insulation was used to insulate uninsulated homes. It contained Formaldehyde. Residents of such "Retro-insulated" houses began to suffer headaches and other physical reactions as the Formaldehyde fumes permeated the houses. Obviously, this kind of insulting material was discontinued.

Contact with Formaldehyde may cause skin rash, headaches and other physical problems.

9. **Radon. (TC)**

Radon is a naturally occurring gas, the molecules of which may attach to dust particles. These particles may be inhaled, attach to the linings of the lungs and emit radioactive particles.

10. **Asbestos. (TC)**

Asbestos is any one of a number of fibrous materials which is extremely durable and fire resistant. Asbestos fibers, when inhaled, may cause cancer or asbestosis, a degenerative disease of the lungs. Asbestos was used in many kinds of buildings, including residences, until the early 1970's.

11. **Brownfields. (TC)**

A brownfield is a tract of real property which has pollutants or potential pollutants present which complicate its reuse, expansion or redevelopment.

The EPA began its Brownfields Program in 1995. Its purpose is to empower local governments and others in cleanup and redevelopment of these properties. It is estimated that there are more than 450,000 brownfields in the U.S.

The Brownfields Program is a grant program created by the ***Business Liability Relief and Brownfield Revitalization Act***. This act has assisted public and private organizations to promote brownfield cleanup and reuse.

12. ***Telephone Consumer Protection Act (TC)***

The ***Telephone Consumer Protection Act*** went into effect on December 20, 1992. It is for the purpose of protecting consumers from unsolicited sales calls. It prohibits sales calls to emergency numbers, hospital and health care facilities.

The soliciting company may not call a residence before 8:00 A.M. or after 9:00 P.M.

If a consumer has the residence or cell phone listed on the "Do Not Call" list, a significant fine may be possible on the calling party.

THE IMPORTANCE OF A HOME INSPECTION (TC)

Home inspections, are not regulated by the Oklahoma Real Estate Commission. However, the Commission strongly encourages licensees to insist that purchasers receive a home inspection. The main purpose of a home inspection is to identify current problems with a piece of property and to educate Buyers about potential future problems.

A "home inspection" according to the Oklahoma Health Department's Rules means a visual examination of any or all of the readily accessible physical real property and improvements to real property consisting of four or fewer dwelling units, including structural, lot drainage, roof, electrical, plumbing, heating and air conditioning and such other areas of concern as are specified in writing to determine if performance is as intended.

A "home inspection report" means a written opinion of the functional and physical condition of property written by the licensed home inspector pursuant to home inspection. Such a report must be performed by a licensed "Home Inspector" which means, an individual licensed pursuant to the ***Home Inspection Licensing Act*** who, for compensation, conducts home inspections.

Not only should a Buyer have a home inspection, but a purchaser should also have a wood-destroying organism inspection. Most lending companies require a wood-destroying organism inspection prior to closing.

If the purchaser does not want to have a home inspection, it is advisable to have the Buyer waive his/her right, in writing and document the transaction file.

Remember, even recommending a home inspector could result in increased risk exposure to the licensee. The Buyer should choose his/her own home inspector. The Buyer is paying the home inspector for professional advise with respect to the condition of the property he/she is considering purchasing. Licensees should not attempt to thwart that relationship either by downplaying the importance of deficiencies noted by property inspectors, or by making disparaging comments about the Buyer's choice of property inspectors.

Further, the Commission has added an additional ***Prohibited Act*** wherein a licensee who discourages a purchaser from having a home inspection could be subject to disciplinary action.

The Commission suggests that parties to the transaction be present during the home inspection. Often times, the Seller can assist the home inspector and the Buyer can learn important information about the property. All parties should receive a copy of the inspection. After reviewing the report, if the Buyer has any questions the Buyer should call the home inspector to clarify any misunderstanding.

One of the biggest reasons for fallouts of contracts is the lack of understanding on the part of the Buyer and the Seller as to the purpose of the home inspection. The licensee should first discuss with their party that the contract does not allow the Buyer to request items to be repaired if they are cosmetic, such as: painting walls, cleaning carpets, requesting upgrades, etc.

If the licensee will educate the Buyer and Seller about the objective of a home inspection and the importance of such before entering into the contract and assist them in understanding the language in the contract regarding inspections it will make the transaction go more smoothly. Remember, that a home inspector conducts a general inspection, not a technically exhaustive inspection.

It is a good idea to have a re-inspection after repairs have been completed.

A home inspection is protection for the consumer and the licensee.

Effective July 1, 2003, home inspectors are regulated through the Oklahoma State Department of Health. The Commission has added on their front web page easy access to check to see if the home inspector that is being utilizing is properly licensed www.orec.state.ok.us, click on "list of licensed home inspectors."

COVENANTS, CONDITIONS AND RESTRICTIONS (CC&Rs) (TC)

Covenants, Conditions and Restrictions are recorded, against the property and generally empower a homeowner's association to control certain aspects of property use within the development. By purchasing a home in such a development, the Buyer agrees to be bound by the CC&Rs, therefore, CC&Rs form an enforceable contract. An association, homeowners as a whole, and individual homeowners can enforce the contract. These restrictions are to be made available to the Buyer prior to closing. Buyers should consult legal counsel if uncertain of the application of particular provisions in the CC&Rs.

The Real Estate Commission does not make reference to CC&Rs in the *License Code and Rules*, however, these should assist the Buyer with questions regarding the do's and don'ts of the property, to including: putting up a fence, adding a storage building, and adding a room addition to the home. (This is not an all-inclusive list.) Such restrictions could prohibit certain businesses being performed from the property location, i.e., day care, automotive repair, etc.

HOMEOWNERS' ASSOCIATION (HOA) (TC)

A homeowner's association is governed by *Articles of Incorporation, Bylaws, Rules and Regulations*, and often have building control standards. The HOA is in place to enforce these rules to preserve the value of homes in a condominium or planned community.

What makes a development a condominium or planned community are the "common areas." The common area is a community ownership of real estate for use by community residents. The common property is actually deeded as undivided interest to the condominium owners. In a planned community, the ownership of the common property vests in the homeowner's association.

If purchasing a resale home in a condominium or planned community, the seller or the HOA must provide the Buyer with a disclosure containing a variety of information. The disclosure should contain information regarding the principal contact for the association, amount of assessment dues, the money held by the association as reserves and, if the statement is being furnished by the association, a statement as to whether the records of the association reflects any alterations or improvements to the unit that violate the declaration. Also, the disclosure should contain information regarding pathways, tree cutting, and maintenance.

HOME WARRANTY POLICY (TC)

A home warranty plan may or may not be part of the sale of a home. In the event a home warranty plan is offered with a home, Buyers should read the warranty document for coverage and limitation information. Be aware that pre-existing property conditions <u>generally are not</u> covered under such policies. This comes into play if a home inspection is performed on the property and a problem is found and not corrected. There is a great possibility that such home warranty plan will not cover pre-existing issues.

Remember, if the licensee is to receive a referral for the recommendation of the home warranty plan, the licensee has to disclose his or her beneficial interest or referral.

COUNTY ASSESSOR'S RECORDS

The County Assessor's records contain a variety of valuable information including the assessed value of the property for tax purposes and some of the physical aspects of the property, such as the reported square footage which should always be verified by the Buyers for accuracy. Not all County Assessor's Offices are computerized. The Oklahoma County Assessor's Office web site is at www.oklahomacounty.org/assessor/, which is an excellent source of information on properties. The licensee can discover tax information, tax rates and on some properties, the lot size information and a layout of the home on the property.

Warning—The County Assessor's Office has stated that their records may not reflect the actual information of the property.

COUNTY CLERK'S OFFICE

The purpose of the County Clerk's Office is to provide a facility for the recordation of important documents, such as, deeds, contracts for deeds, trusts, wills, etc. for the purpose of giving notice to the world of their existence—in other words **Constructive Notice**. This is also includes the filing of the *Uniform Commercial Codes* (UCC's). The UCC has an important impact on the economy and upon the rights of the public, in this state and throughout the United States. The volume of international, interstate and multi-state transactions pursuant to the UCC requires that the administration of the UCC be conducted in a manner that promotes both local and multi-jurisdictional commerce by striving for uniformity in policies and procedures among the various states. The web site for the Oklahoma County Clerk's Office is www.oklahomacounty.org. For other county information go to www.state.ok.us/osfdocs/county.html.

TERMITES AND OTHER WOOD DESTROYING ORGANISMS (TC)

Oklahoma is a termite-infested State; therefore, it is a necessity to have an inspection completed for termites. Not only are there termites, but also there are other wood destroying organisms. A Wood Beatle which, is a little tiny black bug, will drill holes right through wood and leave a pile of sawdust.
An inspection cannot only tell if there are current problems, but can tell if treatment has been completed in the past.

Most termites that feed on wood or other items that contain cellulose are called Subterranean Termites. Items such as paper, fiberboard, and even some fabrics, are a lunch for these termites. They nest in the soil to obtain moisture, and also will nest in wood that is often wet. Any wood that has direct contact with the ground is a feasting area for termites. This is why wood should never be stored next to your foundation—firewood is a good example.

If wood is above the ground, termites will build tunnels to reach the wood and these tunnels can extend for 50-60 feet. Sometimes termites will enter a structure through expansion joints in concrete slabs or where utilities enter a house. Not only will termites eat through the studding in a home they will eat the paper around the sheet rock and have been known to eat pictures hanging on the walls.

A Seller when completing the ***Residential Property Condition Disclosure Statement*** is required to answer specific questions regarding termites or other wood-destroying organism infestation. Further, if a licensee has actual knowledge regarding infestation, the licensee is required to disclose such to the Buyer or the cooperative licensee or company. A Buyer should always be encouraged to obtain a wood infestation report when purchasing real property in Oklahoma.

Prices for inspection, estimates and treatments can vary between companies. A proper inspection should include a written report that notes the location of any problem areas and a diagram of the structure. Should treatment be necessary, an estimate is needed showing a complete description of where and how the treatment will be completed and the cost of the treatment.

ADDITIONAL DISCLOSURES AND INSPECTIONS (TC)

A licensee should always encourage a Buyer to perform all inspections in connection with the home purchase. It is a prohibited act for a licensee to discourage a Buyer from performing such inspections. *The License Code* also requires a licensee, who has knowledge of a defect to disclose such defect to a Buyer, or the cooperating licensee or company.

It is extremely important that the Buyer(s) perform <u>all</u> available property inspections.

Repairs and New Construction: (TC)

The Seller is required to disclose this information on the property condition disclosure form under the section, "Additions/Alterations/Repairs." If the Seller fails to disclose information on the form and the licensee has knowledge, the licensee is required by law to disclose any information that is not disclosed by the Seller.

Even though a home may be a new home, some builders feel it is not necessary to have a home inspection completed by a licensed home inspector; however, this should be the choice of the purchaser. Even though a home is new, people make mistakes, including builders. After the first year, parts of a home warranty will no longer be there and it's better to be safe than sorry. Older homes should always have an inspection and licensees should encourage Buyers to have one. If a purchaser desires not to have an inspection, the wise licensee will have the Buyers sign a waiver that they do not wish to have an inspection and document the file with such.

The Roof: (TC)

The Seller is required to disclose the age of the shingles and whether or not there is a defect with the roof on the property condition disclosure form under the section, "Additions/Alterations/Repairs." An inspector or appraiser might recommend having the roof further inspected by a Roofing Contractor. If the roof is ten (10) years old or older, a roof inspection by a roofer is highly recommended. Insurance companies are also looking at roofs for insurability and they too may require new roof shingles be installed or have it inspected by a roofer. If the Seller fails to disclose information on the form and the licensee has knowledge, the licensee is required by law to disclose any information that it is not disclosed by the Seller.

Swimming Pools and Spas:

A Seller is required to disclose whether or not there is a defect with the pool or spa on the property condition disclosure form. It may be necessary, in this case, to have a pool or spa company inspect the pool or spa and/or evaluate any problem. The pool inspector might determine that the cleaning system is not working properly. The Home Inspector will exclude the pool or spa from their general inspection. It may be necessary, in this case, to have a pool or spa company inspect the pool or spa and/or evaluate any problem.

Each city and county has its own swimming pool barrier ordinance. Permits are probably required for installation. Utility easements can also present a problem.

One couple bought a home that had a pool recently installed. Neither the pool company nor the homeowner had checked for utility easements when installing the pool. The electric company informed the new Buyers, two weeks after closing, that the pool had to be removed immediately because it had been installed **under** the power lines in the utility easement. Not only can things not be built **under** the power lines they cannot be built **over** power lines. This is an example why the buyer should be encouraged to perform all available inspections.

Sewer & Septic Tanks (TC)

A Seller is required to answer whether the sewer system is public, septic or a lagoon. In the case where a house has been left vacant, the Buyer should be encouraged to perform all available inspections. It is not always easy to verify if a home is connected to a city sewer and a plumber or home inspector may be able to verify if it is connected and to what.

Water Wells:

The Seller must disclose whether the source of household water is public, private, or a well. The Department of Environmental Quality (DEQ) can perform a test on well water to determine if it is safe for drinking. The licensee or Buyer may take a water sample to the DEQ for testing. A test is always advised, especially if the property has sat vacant for any length of time. Usually on a new loan, the lender will require an inspection or letter from DEQ and a water quality test. Results of these reports should be given to the interested parties. Information regarding Superfund Sites, where the soil and groundwater have been contaminated by improper disposal of contaminants, may also be found at the DEQ web site. The DEQ web site is **www.deq.state.ok.us**.

Previous Fire/Flood:

The Seller must disclose this information on the property condition disclosure form. Remember, if the licensee has knowledge that such property had previous fire or flood damage and the Seller does not disclose such on the disclosure form, the licensee is required to disclose the information to the buyer or the cooperating licensee or company.

Property Boundaries:

If the property boundaries are of concern, a survey may be warranted. There is a difference in a survey and a lender's inspection certificate. Some people believe if they receive a lenders inspection certificate it is the same as a survey; however, it is not the same. A true survey is called a pin survey where the surveyors actually go out and measure the property and each corner of the property is pinned with a stake made of metal, wood or concrete. There may be concerns of encroachments or easement areas, which could be a problem, if a purchaser wanted to install an in-ground swimming
pool or put in a permanent storage building and they were not aware of the easement or encroachment areas on a neighbor's property. DEQ's Land Protection Division's web site is **www.deq.state.ok.us/lpdnew/**.

Mold (TC)

A Seller must disclose this information on the property condition disclosure form if they have the property inspected for mold and if they have had any remedial treatment for mold on the property. Mold has always been with us, and it is rare if a home does not have some mold. However, over the past few years a certain kind of mold has been identified as a contributor to illnesses. Allergic individuals may experience symptoms related to mold. Mold growth is found underneath materials where water has damaged surfaces, or behind walls.

This is another reason that licensees should encourage a Buyer to perform all available inspections to include a mold inspection if they are highly allergic. The DEQ is also a great resource for persons wanting information on mold, the elimination, or treatment for it. The DEQ web address is: www.deq.state.ok.us.

Additional Problems of Concern:

In addition to mold, there are other indoor air quality concerns such as, radon gas and carbon monoxide poisoning. The home inspector, if requested, may address both of these problems and an additional fee may be charged. This is not a part of their normal inspection of a home. The EPA has a host of resource materials and pamphlets available at www.epa.gov and The Oklahoma Department of Environmental Quality's Air Quality Division's web site is **www.deq.state.ok.us/AQDnew.**

Flood Plain Status: (TC)

If a community does not belong to the National Flood Insurance Program (NFIP) flood insurance is not available to members of that community. Individuals may purchase flood insurance through local property and casualty insurance companies if their Community belongs to the NFIP.

When a homeowner makes application for flood insurance, there is a five-day waiting period before the insurance goes into effect.

If the property is in a flood zone, an additional annual insurance premium of several hundred dollars may be required. If the property is in an area deemed to be at high risk, the lender may require the Buyer to obtain flood hazard insurance. More flood information may be found at www.okflood.org and www.hazardmaps.gov.

Square Footage:

Be clear about statements made in regard to square footage. Numerous complaints are filed at the Commission regarding this issue. Indicate on documentation where information was obtained on the square footage information, i.e., Seller, county records, etc. If the consumer indicates that he/she specifically wants a certain amount of square feet, the licensee should advise them to measure the property themselves to insure they get what they want. County records and Seller's quotes have been found to vary tremendously. Even the Multiple Listing Service (MLS) has a disclaimer statement that indicates that such square footage may not be accurate.

HOMEOWNER'S INSURANCE

The American dream of home ownership brings with its fulfillment, risk. The possibility of loss of the home due to its physical destruction or damage is a very real prospect. Therefore, along with the growth in American home ownership since the end of World War II, there has been a corresponding growth in homeowner insurance.

The purpose of insurance is to shift the risk of loss from the individual to a large number of people who are exposed to similar risks. By sharing these risks, the individual's cost for protection is reduced to an affordable level.

A Buyer of property will be required to choose an insurance company to insure his/her property. There are times wherein a Buyer will assume the Seller's property insurance policy--recent problems have evolved regarding this. Claims submitted by the new Buyers have been denied by the insurance company stating that the previous Seller had already submitted a claim on that issue and evidently had not repaired such. If a Buyer chooses to continue the policy that a Seller has in place, the Buyer should check the past claim history on the property.

Once an insurance company knows that a property is vacant the homeowner's policy more than likely contains a clause, which states the property may not be protected. This clause may become extremely significant in those listings where in the principal is out of town. Coverage may drop off to cover fire only and the company may require a vacancy permit. Eventually, cancellation will occur and, possible, a higher risk policy may be required.

Virtually all policies contain a section called "Limits of Liabilities" and a "Personal Property Exclusions List." There will also be a Loss of Use clause should the property become severely damaged enough to make it uninhabitable or only partial use of the property. There will also be a Liability Coverage clause for bodily damage or property damage.

A licensee who handles property management or property that is rented during the listing period, needs to be aware that the property owner's personal homeowner's policy will not cover the renters' contents. Renters need to purchase a policy for their own personal property and liability protection.

Also, Condominium Insurance is a variation of homeowner insurance. However, condominium insurance only covers he solely-owned space and coordinates the policy with that of the condominium association.

Mobile Home Insurance is a form of homeowner's insurance, but provides a slightly unusual condition. Some insurance companies will only insure a mobile home, if it is permanently affixed to the land. Other insurance companies will insure the mobile home if it is owned and the land on which it sits may be rented. Since the mobile home is, in fact, mobile, there are likely to be some unique clauses concerning risks when moving the home. Does the policy cover damages while in transit?

Unless the licensee is a licensed insurance agent, he/she should avoid giving advice or making recommendations concerning insurance.

If a licensee makes a referral with the intention or expectation of receiving compensation due to such referral, then the licensee must disclose in accordance with Rule 605:10-15-1.

MOBILE HOMES/MANUFACTURED HOMES

A licensee needs to be aware of Oklahoma Statutes Title 47, Motor Vehicles, Chapter 62A, Section 581--Definitions. This law requires anyone who sells a mobile/manufactured home to have a manufactured home dealer's license. A real estate broker is exempt from having to obtain a "manufactured home dealer's license" only if the real estate broker is selling both the mobile/manufactured home and the real estate it is attached to.

The definition of a "manufactured home dealer's license" is any person who, for a commission or with intent to make a profit or gain of money or other thing of value, sells, offers to sell, or attempts to negotiate a sale or exchange of interest in, new or used manufactured homes, or that is engaged wholly or in part in the business of selling any new and unused, or used, or both new and used manufactured homes.

Title 47 O.S. Section 581(5)(b) exempts certain individuals from this definition, including "any Oklahoma licensed real estate broker or associate when buying or selling used mobile homes as a part of a real estate business." Therefore, if the real property and the attached mobile/manufactured home are sold or bought together, this would qualify as an exemption.

Oklahoma Statutes Title 47, Statute 1110 E states; if a manufactured home is permanently affixed to real estate, the original document of title may be surrendered to the Tax Commission or a motor license agent for cancellation. When the document of title is surrendered, the owner shall provide the legal description or the appropriate tract or parcel number of the real estate and other information as may be required on a form provided by the Tax Commission. The Tax Commission may not cancel a document of title if a lien has been registered or recorded. There is a fee involved that must be attached to the application for cancellation of title.

The Tax Commission or motor license agent shall notify the owner and any lien holder that the title has been surrendered to the Tax Commission and that the Tax Commission may not cancel the title until the lien is released. Once released, The Tax Commission will then forward the information to the County Assessor's Office of the county where the real estate is located and indicate whether the original document of title has been cancelled. Therefore, if a licensee is going to sell a mobile home, it may be a good idea to inquire if the owners have filed for a release of title to ensure they are selling real estate and not personal property. Mobile homes that are not permanently attached to the land are considered personal property.

Oklahoma Law Title 47, State Statutes 1110, states that a Notice of Cancellation of title on mobile homes may be done provided there is no lien on the mobile home at the time of cancellation.

Ch. 18

TEST YOUR UNDERSTANDING

1. When a real estate licensee is filling out the Seller's Property Condition Disclosure form, he/she must be sure
    1. all the blanks are filled in.
    2. the seller is present when the form is being filled out.
    3. the OREC has a file copy.
    4. the licensee is the seller.

2. Once the seller has completed the Seller's Property Condition Disclosure form, it is good for
    1. 60 days.
    2. 90 days.
    3. 120 days.
    4. 180 days.

3. If a seller becomes aware of a defect after delivery of the Seller's Property Condition Disclosure form, he/she may
    1. not do anything, it is too late.
    2. promptly deliver an amended form to the buyer which discloses the defect.
    3. send an amended copy to the OREC.
    4. None of the above.

4. Home Inspectors are regulated by the
    1. Department of Homeland Security.
    2. Department of Housing & Urban Development.
    3. Oklahoma Real Estate Commission.
    4. Construction Board.

5. It is perfectly acceptable for a licensee to
    1. choose a home inspector for the buyer(s).
    2. discourage the buyer(s) from getting a home inspector.
    3. allow the buyer(s) to choose the home inspector.
    4. also be a home inspector and inspect houses the licensee has sold.

6. Covenants, Conditions and Restrictions may regulate
    1. the kind of fence a home owner installs.
    2. the kind of storage building placed on the lot.
    3. the type of roof covering that may be put on the house.
    4. All of the above.

7. A home warranty plan is an insurance policy. The important part of the policy to read is the
    1. exclusions.
    2. expanded coverage.
    3. loss expectation clause.
    4. mortgagee exception clause.

8. The County Assessor's records usually contain
    1. assessed value.
    2. reported square feet.
    3. physical aspects of the property.
    4. all of the above.

9. The County Clerk's Office is for the purpose of recording documents for constructive notice. Which of the following may be recorded in the County Clerk's Office?
    1. Deeds.
    2. Contracts for Deeds.
    3. Trusts and Wills.
    4. All of the above.

ANSWERS AND EXPLANATIONS

1. 4 The only time a licensee should fill out the Seller's Property Condition Disclosure or Disclaimer for is when he/she is the seller.

2. 4 After 180 days a new form should be prepared.

3. 2 An amended form is necessary when a previously unknown or previous non-expected defect is discovered.

4. 4 The Construction Board licenses Home Inspectors.

5. 3 Allowing the buyer(s) to choose the home inspector helps reduce some of the licensee's liabilities.

6. 4 CC&R's may cover all of these and many more.

7. 1 Reading he Exclusions Section of any insurance policy is helpful if one wishes to know what is not covered by the policy agreement.

8. 4 The County Assessor's Records will contain all of this information and additional information as well.

9. 4 The County clerk's Office will record all of these documents and various other ones.

PROPERTY MANAGEMENT AND LEASING

LEASEHOLD ESTATES (TC)

Leasehold estates are possessory interests created by the establishment of landlord-tenant relationships. They may last for a definite time period or for as long as the parties are willing to continue their relationship. For the duration of the lease, the lessee possesses or occupies the land with the understanding that the landlord retains full ownership of the real property. The lessor retains the reversionary rights plus the right to collect compensation. Because title does not accompany such estates, leases are considered to be personal property.

In addition to the fact that most leases contain a clause against the assignment or subletting without prior consent of the lessor, Oklahoma statutes prohibit assignment or subletting without permission from the landlord. In the absence of such restraint, tenants could indiscriminately transfer leases, introducing "strangers" to the landlord.

In an assignment, the entire interest in the property of the assignor is transferred to the assigns or assignees. The transferee comes into privity of estate with the lessor, meaning that each remains liable to the other on the covenants of the original lease. In subleasing, a lease is given by a lessee for a portion of the leasehold interest with the lessee retaining sole reversionary interest. The main difference between subletting and assigning, so far as the landlords are concerned, is that they cannot directly sue the sublessee where it is possible to bring suit against the assignee.

Estate for Years (TC)

An estate for years is a leasehold estate expressed in terms of specific starting time and a specific ending time. The duration can be any length of time. An estate for years does not automatically renew itself.

Periodic Tenancy (TC)

A tenancy from period to period is an estate which continues for a fixed period (year, month, week) and for successive similar periods unless terminated by either party by property notice. The most common example of a periodic estate is the month to moth apartment rental. It is also called tenancy from year to year.

Tenancy at Will (TC)

A tenancy at will may be terminated at the will of either the landlord or the tenant and has no other specified length of duration. Oklahoma statute has changed the common law in that estates at will are treated much the same as tenancy from period to period. If, for example, a tenant at will is applying monthly rent, then a thirty day notice requirement must precede termination of the lease, just as in a tenancy from month to month.

Tenancy at Sufferance (TC)

Tenancy at sufferance exists when a tenant, without the consent of the landlord, fails to surrender possession after termination of the lease. This is the lowest estate in real estate and no notice of termination may be required for the landlord to evict the tenant. Designed to protect the tenants from being classified as trespassers on one hand, it also prevents their acquisition of title by adverse possession on the other.

Gross Lease (TC)

A gross lease is one in which the landlord agrees to pay the expenses relating to the property such as taxes and utilities and the tenant agrees to pay a fixed amount of rent each rental period.

Net Lease (TC)

A net lease is one in which the tenant agrees to pay for repairs, taxes, utilities, insurance, etc., in addition to a fixed or base rental fee.

Ground Lease (TC)

A ground lease is one in which only the land is being rented. These are usually longer term leases for periods of up to 99 years. Generally, the ownership of the land and the ownership of any buildings on the land are separate. The rent on the land is frequently on a net arrangement and is adjusted for inflation periodically.

Option Clauses (TC)

An option clause in a lease gives the tenant the option to purchase the rented property at some future time should he so decide. The price is normally determined in advance. Some leases have option clauses allowing the tenant an escape if the venture does not succeed. The lease may terminate or, the tenant has the option of continuing the lease for another year or two depending upon the success of his business.

Assignment and subletting (TC)

Most contracts, including leases may be "assigned" to another party. The assignor, the original tenant, transfers his rights under the lease to the assignee. The assignment transfers whatever rights the assignor has. Unless released from the contract, the assignor may remain liable for the lease.

The subletting of a leasehold interest does not transfer all of the tenant's rights as in an assignment. The sublessee acquires, typically, the right of possession for which he pays rent directly to the sublessor, the original tenant. The original tenant (sublessor) then is responsible for paying rent to the landlord.

Some leases may have clauses forbidding assignment or subleasing.

Termination of tenancy (TC)

Most leases terminate with the expiration of the stated time period. The tenant vacates the property and the landlord again takes possession. However, a new lease period may be negotiated.

MANAGEMENT

On-site Management

The on-site duties of the property manager include those things which must be accomplished on the property. This will include things like showing the property, interviewing a prospective tenant, negotiating and signing leases, tenant relations, collecting rents, property cleaning upon vacation and eviction. These duties may include repair and maintenance. The resident manager is responsible for safety and security issues as well.

Off-site management

The off-site duties of the property manager include those things the manager must leave the property to accomplish. These may include accounting, payroll, bills, and other related responsibilities. These off-site duties may also include training programs, hazard and liability insurance acquisitions, bidding for contract services, and even suggestions about selling the property for the owners.

Training

The task of training property managers frequently becomes an on-the-job activity. Therefore, many property management operations have their own training programs. In some cases, there are organizations such as the Central Oklahoma Apartment Association which helps provide training for property managers.

RENT COLLECTION

Property management is the business of operating a piece of real estate in order to safeguard the owner's investment while providing for the physical safety and well being of the residents. Only through constant and professional rent collection procedures can this dual aim be realized.

Unfortunately, actual rental income is based not on the number of occupied units or square feet, but, rather, on the number of paying residents. Rental income is applied primarily to meet operating costs of a property. When it is delayed or absent and monthly income is decreased, management's effectiveness is greatly jeopardized. In fact, non-payment of rent can actually increase operating costs, as added expenses for legal process actions must be added.

The maintenance budget generally must be reduced when income is down, as essential fixed costs such as mortgage, insurance, and taxes take first priority. Rent delinquency, therefore, can hamper an effective maintenance program. Much too often, non-payment of rent severely interrupts smooth and efficient management programs. Property managers can be forced into positions where they must stall for time, paying one company at the expense of another, in an effort to prevent necessary services and supplies from being terminated.

Allowing poor rental payment habits to develop can also be a disservice to the resident who pays on time. Eventually their rents will have to be increased to compensate for those who do not pay punctually. Furthermore, allowing a resident to get behind in his/her rental payments can do him/her a disservice. Once in arrears, few can afford the increase or additional payments that would be necessary to bring rental accounts current.

Rent Collection Policy

Each resident must be notified at the time he/she signs the lease that rent payments shall be paid in full and monthly in advance on or before the first calendar day of each month and delivered to the management office.

Some property managers require that a full month's rent be paid in advance prior to move-in. Others may require that if less than a full month rent is to be paid upon move-in, several days rent is to be paid. Some allow the deposit to be paid in monthly installments along with the monthly rent. This is a matter of company policy and, as such, should be spelled out in the company policy manual.

A property manager should not be reluctant to ask a tenant for the rent. When the moved into the property and educated in a matter of fact way, tenants tend to understand that the rent is due and payable on the contract (lease) terms.

Rent is frequently considered delinquent if it is not received on the first day of any given month. However, some firms offer a "grace period" of two or three days.

Most often, the rent is collected at the property by the manager. However, some residents prefer to mail their rent checks. In this case, the proper address for mailing must be given to each resident and they must be notified of any changes.

As a part of company policy, some property management firms prefer all rent to be paid by personal check, certified check or money order and refuse to accept third party checks.

Delinquent Rent Policy

If the lease agreement (contract) calls for the rent to be due on the first of the month and the company allows a two day grace period, this means that, if the rent is not collected by the third day of the month, the property manager might strongly consider preparation of a delinquency notice.

Some Suggested Procedures to Follow:

1. Prepare a five day Notice to Quit.

2. Deliver original copy of Notice to Quit to delinquent resident in person.

3. If unable to deliver in person, change to a 10 day Notice to Quit and post in a sealed envelope on the door of the dwelling.

4. Send one copy of the 10 day Notice to Quit to the tenant by registered mail with return receipt requested.

5. If the rent has not been paid within 5 working days on the 5 day Notice to Quit or within 10 day of the 10 day notice, proceed with the eviction process.

EVICTION PROCESS

Before any eviction proceeding is initiated, management should make every attempt to avoid such action. If a tenant shows a willingness to correct he situation, an agreement may be negotiated. It is important that management be consistent in handling any eviction situations. If eviction proceedings have been started on one tenant for failure to heed a certain agreement in the lease, then the same procedure should be enacted for any subsequent tenant under similar violations.

Causes for Eviction

Eviction is the legal process whereby a resident or tenant is forced to terminate his/her tenancy. Many lease agreements include a clause which permits management to terminate any tenancy for sufficient cause. A manager must know what steps should be taken if an eviction situation a rises.

Necessary in a legal eviction proceeding is proving that the resident in question is guilty of a breach or threatened breach of the lease. Non-payment of rent is the most commonly cited ground for eviction. Termination of tenancy may be caused by failure to heed any of the many paragraphs of the lease or rules and regulations.

Documentation of all instances of violation must be maintained by the manager because it may become necessary to support a case in court. In the case of violations of occupancy restrictions or rules and regulations, managers should make several personal and written contracts with a violator prior to taking any steps to terminate tenancy. Copies of letters to a violator should be maintained in a file as supportive evidence. In the case of a resident who has not paid his/her rent, the importance or maintaining accurate rental ledgers and rent reports is obvious. These records may be needed to prove that management is correct in asserting that the resident is delinquent.

SERVICE NOTICE TO QUIT

The first step in an eviction proceeding is delivery of a formal, written notice to the violator to vacate within a stated number of days. This document usually is called a "Notice to Quit." In the case of a rental delinquency, this may be called a "Notice to Pay or Quit." In the case of rental delinquencies, the number of days stated on the notice is five days. If, for some reason, notice to a resident cannot be served in person, then the number of days becomes ten, and the notice must be mailed. For violations of community policies, the apartment resident must be given ten days written notice.

Legal service requirements have been met when one or more of the following have been done:

1. A five-day notice is delivered in person, in writing.

2. A 10-day notice is sent to the resident's address by Certified Mail with Return Receipt Requested and a copy is posted to the resident's door.

In all cases, a "Notice to Quit" must be completely filled out, stating the exact amount of money owed and/or the exact violation for which eviction proceedings have commenced.

TAKING LEGAL ACTION

Sometimes "Notices to Quit" are ineffective and further legal action must be taken. In the case of delinquencies, this is known as unlawful detainer action. Unlawful detainer is the term applied to the occupancy of a premise for which payments are being withheld.

When all reasonable techniques have been exhausted, legal eviction proceedings will be referred to legal counsel. The decision to take such action with tenants is made by the property manager. The matter, complete with all pertinent information, is then turned over to an attorney. The attorney becomes responsible for heeding local legal procedures. The attorney must have proper and accurate documentation.

In the case of delinquencies, this documentation includes a ledger card (showing rents), lease, rental application, copies of any notices of delinquencies and affidavits of service, and other relevant material. In the case of other lease violations, this documentation will include warning letters to the violators, written complaints from other residents, etc.

When the matter is turned over to legal counsel, a letter to this effect should be sent to the resident notifying him/her that eviction proceedings have been authorized. If the resident does not vacate or make up his/her delinquency at this time, a court hearing or trial will be necessary. It is at this point that the maintenance of accurate, written records will be tested. If management prevails, the court will issue an order to evict. Once this order has been issued, many such tenants will bring their payments up to date to avoid eviction or they may move out voluntarily.

Many managers are agreeable to any resident who offers to set up a schedule to pay over-due rent even if legal action has begun. Any such agreement must be in writing and signed by both parties. Generally, arrangements are permissible if the resident shows the willingness to pay. However, if promises are broken, the property manager must move quickly to evict.

Property managers should be careful in accepting rental payments after eviction proceedings have been started. Any acceptance of rent could cancel the "Notice to Pay or Quit" and proceedings would have to begin again.

THE EVICTION PROCESS: OKLAHOMA LAW

The first step in the eviction process is delivery of a formal, written notice, "Notice to Quit." This may be made in duplicate or triplicate for the property manager's records. "The Notice to Quit" is a demand for payment of delinquent dollars including any and all delinquent dollars from prior months.

The "Notice to Quit" is to be served on the 3rd day after rent is delinquent and may be either a five-day or ten-day notice. Some property managers add "et. Al." (meaning "and others") after the tenant name(s) to include all persons residing at that address.

Should the property manager deliver the notice personally to a family member over the age of 12, it becomes a five-day notice.

If the notice cannot be delivered personally, due to the tenant not being home, not answering the door, etc., it can be posted to the door of the residence. If the notice is posted, the copy must be sealed in an envelope with the tenant's name and address or apartment number on it. The property manager must then mail the original copy to the tenant by certified mail or obtain a certificate of mailing.

After the requisite five or ten days have passed and the tenant has not tendered the full amount as stated on the notice, upon the sixth or eleventh day, a summons and petition may be filed at the court house.

When the summons and petition is filed, a court date and judge is established. The property manager will be required to have the summons and petition served upon the tenant by a process server, certified mail or Deputy Sheriff. There is a filing fee to be paid at the time the summons and petition are filed and an additional charge for service fee.

When appearing before the judge, the property manager will be asking for the dollar amount expended for the filing fee and service fee (court costs). Judgment will include dollars of rent through the date of the court hearing, court costs and any proven damages claimed in the petition if the decision is rendered in favor of the property manager.

If the tenant is still in possession of the residence on the date of the court hearing, the property manager must request an Execution and Writ of Assistance. After the hearing, when the judge has signed and granted possession and damages, the Journal Entry (the judge's declaration of dollar amounts granted to the plaintiff) must be filed in order for the judgment to be recorded on record. Execution and Writ of Assistance are taken back to be filed with the court clerk. There is usually an additional fee for the filing of this form. The Journal Entry and Writ will be stamped by the court clerk.

The Execution and Writ of Assistance will then be taken to the Sheriff's office or may be personally delivered by the property manager. The Writ gives the tenant three days from the date the Sheriff has posted the Writ on the tenant's door to get out of the property.

If the tenants are not out of the property in three days, the Sheriff and the property manager or the property manager's maintenance person, will meet at the property. The Sheriff will observe while the door lock is changed. Property managers should never lock a tenant out before the arrival of the sheriff.

Late Charges

Late charges may be levied as an incentive for prompt payment and to cover consequent extra account costs. Company policy may include a two or three day grace period, but this policy must be included in the company policy manual and all tenants must be informed of this potential penalty prior to being given possession of the residence.

Collection After Move-Out

There tend to be two occasions when a property manager may attempt to collect rents after the tenant has moved out. This may be when the Sheriff has had to physically move a tenant or when the tenant "skips out" without the property manager's knowledge.

In these cases, the property manager may take the necessary steps to obtain a judgment against the tenant. While a judgment is not "cash" it will likely keep the tenant from making a major purchase requiring a credit report until the judgment has been cleared.

Oklahoma allows wage garnishment. If the property manager knows where the tenant is employed, this may be the best method of collection.

The property manager should report tenants who have moved out without paying to the credit bureau. The credit bureau will ask for documentation.

When such a tenant pays the monies owed, it is the responsibility of the property manager to report the debt was paid to the credit bureau.

Collection Agencies

In the event the property manager decides to turn the problem of collection over to a collection agency, the collection agency will also require documentation. The property manager should retain originals and give the collection agency copies.

The rates charged by collection agencies vary.

The property manager must keep a record of every person turned over for collection. This record should include the tenant's name, the name of the collection agency, the date the account was turned over to the agency, the amount to be collected and provision of dates and amounts that may be collected.

When the account has been fully paid, the file should be marked, "paid."
The amount paid to the collection agency will be taken from the amount collected. The property manager will receive, if the account is collected, the debt minus the charges made by the collection agency.

LANDLORD AND TENANT REGARDING <u>NON</u>-RESIDENTIAL RENTAL PROPERTY (TC)
41 O.S. 2001, §§51-52, 61
(Any of the following could be on the state portion of the test.)
§51. Abandonment or surrender of non-residential rental property—Definitions.

As used in this act:
    1. "Landlord" means the owner, lessor or sublessor of a non-residential rental property, but does not mean an "owner" as defined by Section 192 of Title 42 of the Oklahoma Statutes;

    2. "Non-residential rental property" means any land or building which is rented or leased to a tenant for other than residential purposes and the rental agreement of which is not regulated under the provisions of the ***Oklahoma Residential Landlord Tenant Act***, Section 101 et seq. of Title 41 of the Oklahoma Statutes or the ***Self-Service Storage Facility Lien Act***, Section 191 et seq. of Title 42 of the Oklahoma Statutes; and

    3. "Tenant" means any person entitled under a rental agreement to occupy the nonresidential rental property.

    §52. Abandonment or surrender of nonresidential rental property—Disposition of personal property of tenant—Notice—Storage costs—Liability of landlord—Application of proceeds of sale.

A. If a tenant abandons, surrenders possession of, or is evicted from nonresidential rental property and leaves good, furnishings, fixtures, or any other personal property on the premises of the non-residential rental property, the landlord may take possession of the personal property ten (10) days after the tenant receives personal service of notice or fifteen (15) days after notice is mailed, whichever is latest, and if the personal property has no ascertainable or apparent value, the landlord may dispose of the personal property in a reasonable commercial manner. In any such case, the landlord has the option of complying with the provisions of subsection B of this section.

B. If the tenant abandons, surrenders possession of, or is evicted from the nonresidential rental property and leaves goods, furnishings, fixtures, or any other personal property of an ascertainable or apparent value on the premises of the nonresidential rental property, the landlord may take possession of the personal property and give notice to the tenant, demanding that the personal property be removed within the dates set out in the notice but not less than fifteen (15) days after delivery or mailing of such notice, and that if the personal property is not removed within the time specified in the notice, the landlord may sell the personal property at a public sale. The landlord may dispose of perishable commodities in any manner the landlord considers fit. Payment by the tenant of all outstanding rent, damages, storage fees, court costs and attorney's fees shall be a prerequisite to the return of the personal property. For purposes of this section, notice sent by registered or certified mail to the tenant's last known address with forwarding requested shall be deemed sufficient notice.

C. After notice is given as provided in subsection B of this section, the landlord shall store all personal property of the tenant in a place of safe-keeping and shall exercise reasonable care of the personal property. The landlord shall not be responsible to the tenant for any loss not caused by the landlord's deliberate or negligent act. The landlord may elect to store the personal property on the premises of the nonresidential rental property that was abandoned or surrendered by the tenant or from which the tenant was evicted, in which event the storage cost may not exceed the fair rental value of the premises. If the tenant's personal property is removed to a commercial storage company, the storage cost shall include the actual charge for the storage and removal from the premises to the place of storage.

D. If the tenant makes timely response in writing of an intention to remove the personal property from the premises and does not do so within the later of the time specified in the notice provided for in subsection B of this section or within fifteen (15) days of the delivery or mailing of the tenant's written response, it shall be conclusively presumed that the tenant abandoned the personal property. If the tenant removes the personal property within the time limitations provided in this subsection, the landlord is entitled to the cost of storage for the period during which the personal property remained in the landlord's safekeeping plus all other costs that accrued under the rental agreement.

E. If the tenant fails to take possession of the personal property as prescribed in subsection D of this section and make payment of all amounts due and owing, the personal property shall be deemed abandoned and the landlord may thereupon sell the personal property in any reasonable manner without liability to the tenant.

F. Notice of sale shall be mailed to the owner and any other party claiming any interest in said personal property, if known, at their last-known post office address, by certified or registered mail at least ten (10) days before the time specified therein for such sale. For purposes of this section, parties who claim an interest in the personal property include holders of security interests or other liens or encumbrances as shown by the records in the office of the county clerk of the county where the lien would be foreclosed.

G. The landlord or any other person may in good faith become a purchaser of the personal property sold. The landlord may dispose of any personal property upon which no bid is made at the public sale.

H. The landlord may not be held to respond in damages in an action by a tenant claiming loss by reason of the landlord's election to destroy, sell or otherwise dispose of the personal property in compliance with the provisions of this section. If, however, the landlord deliberately or negligently violated the provisions of this section, the landlord shall be liable for actual damages.

I. Any proceeds from the sale or other disposition of the personal property, as provided in subsection B of this section, shall be applied by the landlord in the following order:

1. To the reasonable expenses of taking, holding, preparing for sale or disposition, giving notice and selling or disposing thereof;

2. To the satisfaction of any properly recorded security interest;

3. To the satisfaction of any amount due from the tenant to the landlord for rent or otherwise; and

4. The balance, if any, shall be paid into court within thirty (30) days of the sale and held for six (6) months and, if not claimed by the owner of the personal property within that period, shall escheat to the county.

§61. Computation of time

The time within which an act is to be done, as provided for in Title 41 of the Oklahoma Statutes, shall be computed by excluding the first day and including the last day. If the last day is a legal holiday as defined by Section 82.1 of Title 25 of the Oklahoma Statutes, it shall be excluded. The provisions of this section are hereby declared to be a clarification of the law as it existed prior to the effective date of this act and shall not be considered or construed to be a change of the law as it existed prior to the effective date of this act. Any action or proceeding arising under Title 41 of the Oklahoma Statutes prior to the effective date of this act for which a determination of the period of time prescribed by this section is in question or has been in question due to the enactment of Section 20, Chapter 293, O.S.L. 1999, shall be governed by the method for computation of time as prescribed by this section.

RESIDENTIAL LANDLORD AND TENANT ACT (TC)

41 O.S. 2001, §§101-136, as amended through April 22, 2003

§101. Short Title

This act shall be known and may be cited as the *"Oklahoma Residential Landlord and Tenant Act."*

§102. Definitions

1. "Building and housing codes" means any law, ordinance or governmental regulation concerning fitness for habitation or the construction, maintenance, operation, occupancy, use or appearance of any premises or dwelling unit;

2. "Deposit" means any money or other property required by a landlord from a tenant as a security and which is to be returned to the tenant upon termination of the rental agreement, less any deductions properly made and allowed by this act;

3. "Dwelling unit" means a structure, or that part of a structure, which is used as a home residence or sleeping place by one or more persons, and includes any site, space or lot leased to the owner or resident of a manufactured or mobile home;

4. "Good faith" means honesty in fact in the conduct of the transaction concerned;

5. "Landlord" means the owner, lessor, or sublessor of the dwelling unit or the building of which it is a part, manufactured or mobile home site, space or lot, and it also means a manager of the premises who fails to comply with the disclosure provisions of Section 116 of this title;

6. "Occupant" means any person who abides within a dwelling unit, or any person who owns or occupies a manufactured or mobile home, but who is not a tenant or an unemancipated minor child of a tenant, and who is not legally obligated by the terms of a rental agreement;

7. "Organization" means a corporation, government, governmental subdivision or agency, business trust, estate, trust, partnership or association, two or more persons having a joint or common interest and any other legal or commercial entity;

8. "Owner" means one or more persons, jointly or severally, in whom is vested:

    a. all or any part of the legal title to the property, or
    b. all or part of the beneficial ownership and a right to present use and enjoyment of the property, and such term includes a mortgagee in possession;

9. "Person" means an individual or organization;

10. "Premises" means a dwelling unit and the structure of which it is a part, the facilities, and appurtenances therein, the site, space or lot leased to the owner or resident of a mobile or manufactured home, and the grounds, areas and facilities held out for the use of the tenant generally or the use of which is promised to the tenant;

11. "Rent" means all payments, except deposits and damages, to be made to the landlord under the rental agreement.

12. "Rental agreement" means all agreements and valid rules and regulations adopted under Section 126 of this title, which establish, embody or modify the terms and conditions concerning the use and occupancy of a dwelling unit and premises;

13. "Roomer" or "boarder" means a tenant occupying a dwelling unit:

    a. which lacks at least one major bathroom or kitchen facility, such as a toilet, refrigerator or stove,
    b. in a building
       (1) where one or more of such major facilities are supplied to be used in common by the occupants of the roomer or boarder's dwelling unit and one or more other dwelling units, and
       (2) in which the landlord resides;

14. "Single-family residence" means a structure used and maintained as a single dwelling unit. A dwelling unit, including those with common walls, shall be deemed a single-family residence if it has direct access to a street or thoroughfare and shares neither heating facilities, hot water equipment, nor any other essential facility or service with any other dwelling unit; and

15. "Tenant" means any person entitled under a rental agreement to occupy a dwelling unit.

§103. Application of Act

A. Except as otherwise provided in this act, this act applies to, regulates and determines rights, obligations and remedies under a rental agreement, wherever made, for a dwelling unit located within this state.

B. Any agreement, whether written or oral, shall be unenforceable insofar as said agreement, or any provision thereof, conflicts with any provision of this act.

§104. Arrangements not covered by act

Unless created to avoid the application of this act, the following arrangements are not governed by this act:

1. Residence at an institution, public or private, if incidental to detention or the provision of medical, geriatric, educational, counseling, religious or similar service;

2. Occupancy under a contract of sale or contract for deed of a dwelling unit or the property of which it is a part, if the occupant is the purchaser or a person who succeeds to his interest;

3. Occupancy by a member of a fraternal or social organization in a structure operated for the benefit of the organization;

4. Transient occupancy in a hotel, motel or other similar lodging;

5. Occupancy by an owner of a condominium unit or a holder of a proprietary lease in a cooperative; and

6. Occupancy under a rental agreement covering premises used by the occupant primarily for agricultural purposes.

§105. Mitigation of damages—Rights, obligations and remedies—Enforcement

A. An aggrieved party under the provisions of this act has a duty to mitigate damages.

B. Any right, obligation or remedy declared by this act is enforceable in any court of appropriate jurisdiction including small claims court and may be prosecuted as part of an action for forcible entry or detainer unless the provision declaring it specifies a different and limited effect. In any action for breach of a rental agreement or to enforce any right or obligation provided for in this act, the prevailing party shall be entitled to reasonable attorneys' fees.

§106. Settlement of claim

A. claim or right arising under this act or a rental agreement, if disrupted in good faith, may be settled by agreement and requires no further consideration.

§107. Good faith performance or enforcement

Every duty under this act and every act which must be performed as a condition precedent to the exercise of a right or remedy under this act imposes an obligation of good faith in its performance or enforcement.

§108. Beneficial owner to maintain premises

Any agreement, assignment, conveyance, trust deed or security instrument which authorizes a person other than the beneficial owner to act as landlord of a dwelling unit shall not relieve the beneficial owner of the duty to conform with this act and any other law, code ordinance or regulation concerning the maintenance and operation of the premises.

§109. Rent
A. In the absence of agreement, the occupants of a dwelling unit shall pay to the landlord as rent the fair rental value for the use and occupancy of the dwelling unit.

B. Rent shall be payable at the time and place agreed to by the parties. Unless otherwise agreed, the entire rent shall be payable at the dwelling unit at the beginning of any term of one (1) month or less, while one (1) month's rent shall be payable at the beginning of each month of a longer term.

§110. Term of tenancy
Unless the rental agreement fixes a definite term in writing, the tenancy is week-to-week in the case of a roomer or boarder who pays weekly rent, and in all other cases month-to-month.

§111. Termination of tenancy
A. Except as otherwise provided in the *Oklahoma Residential Landlord and Tenant Act*, when the tenancy is month-to-month or tenancy at will, the landlord or tenant may terminate the tenancy provided the landlord or tenant gives a written notice to the other at least thirty (30) days before the date upon which the termination is to become effective. The thirty day period to terminate shall begin to run from the date notice to terminate is served as provided in subsection E of this section.

B. Except as otherwise provided in the *Oklahoma Residential Landlord and Tenant Act*, when the tenancy is less than month-to-month, the landlord or tenant may terminate the tenancy provided the landlord or tenant give to the other a written notice served as provided in subsection E of this section at least seven (7) days before the date upon which the termination is to become effective.

C. Unless earlier terminated under the provisions of the *Oklahoma Residential Landlord and Tenant Act* or unless otherwise agreed upon, a tenancy for a definite term expires on the ending date thereof without notice.

D. If the tenant remains in possession without the landlord's consent after the expiration of the term of the rental agreement or its termination under the *Oklahoma Residential Landlord and Tenant Act,* the landlord may immediately bring an action for possession and damages. If the tenant's holdover is willful and not in good faith the landlord may also recover an amount not more than twice the average monthly rental, computed and prorated on a daily basis, for each month or portion thereof that said tenant remains in possession. If the landlord consents to the tenant's continued occupancy, a month-to-month tenancy is thus created, unless the parities otherwise agree.

E. The written notice, required by the *Oklahoma Residential Landlord and Tenant Act*, to terminate any tenancy shall be served on the tenant or landlord personally unless otherwise specified by law. If the tenant cannot be located, service shall be made by delivering the notice to any family member of such tenant over the age of twelve (12) years residing with tenant. If service cannot be made on the tenant personally or on such family member, notice shall be posted at a conspicuous place on the dwelling unit of the tenant. If the notice is posted, a copy of such notice shall be mailed to the tenant by certified mail. If service cannot be made on the landlord personally, the notice shall be mailed to the landlord by certified mail. For the purpose of this subsection, the word "landlord" shall mean any person authorized to receive service of process and notice pursuant to Section 116 of this title.

§112. Duties of parties upon termination of tenancy
Except as otherwise provided in this act, whenever either party to a rental agreement rightfully elects to terminate, the duties of each party under the rental agreement shall cease and be determined upon the effective date of said termination, and the parties shall thereupon discharge any remaining obligations under this act as soon as practicable.

§113. Rental Agreements
A. A rental agreement may not provide that either party thereto:

1. Agrees to waive or forego rights or remedies under this act;

2. Authorizes any person to confess judgment on a claim arising out of the rental agreement;

3. Agrees to pay the other party's attorney's fees,

4. Agrees to the exculpation, limitation or indemnification of any liability arising under law for damages or injuries to persons or property caused by or resulting from the acts or omissions of either party, their agents, servants or employees in the operation or maintenance of the dwelling unit or the premises of which it is a part, or

5. Agrees to the establishment of a lien except as allowed by this act in and to the property of the other party.

B. A provision prohibited by subsection A of this section and included in a rental agreement is unenforceable.

§113a. Disclosure of flood or flooding problems in rental agreement

A. If the premises to be rented has been flooded within the past five (5) years and such fact is known to the landlord, the landlord shall include such information prominently and in writing as part of any written rental agreements. Failure to provide such information shall entitle any tenant who is a party to the rental agreement to sue the landlord of the premises in a court of appropriate jurisdiction and to recover the personal property damages sustained by the tenant from flooding of the premises.

B. For the purpose of this section, "flooded and flooding" shall mean general and temporary condition of partial or complete inundation of normally dry land areas and structures upon and areas from the overflow of lakes, ponds, streams, river, creeks and any other inland water.

§113.1. Denial or termination of tenancy because of guide, signal or service dog

A landlord shall not deny or terminate a tenancy to a blind, deaf, or physically handicapped person because of the guide, signal, or service dog of such person unless such dogs are specifically prohibited in the rental agreement entered into prior to November 1, 1985.

§114. Alienees—Rights, obligations and remedies

Alienees of landlords and tenants shall have the same legal rights, obligations and remedies as their principals.

§115. Damage or security deposits

A. Any damage or security deposit required by a landlord of a tenant must be kept in an escrow account for the tenant, which account shall be maintained to the State of Oklahoma with a federally insured financial institution. Misappropriation of the security deposit shall be unlawful and punishable by a term in a county jail not to exceed six (6) months and by a fine in an amount not to exceed twice the amount misappropriated from the escrow account.

B. Upon termination of the tenancy, any security deposit held by the landlord may be applied to the payment of accrued rent and the amount of damages which the landlord has suffered by reason of the tenant's noncompliance with this act and the rental agreement, all as itemized by the landlord in a written statement delivered by mail to be by return receipt requested and to be signed for by any person of statutory service age at such address or in person to the tenant if he can reasonably be found. If the landlord proposes to retain any portion of the security deposit for rent, damages or other legally allowable charges under the provisions of this act or the rental agreement, the landlord shall return the balance of the security deposit without interest to the tenant within thirty (30) days after the termination of tenancy, delivery of possession and written demand by the tenant. If the tenant does not make such written demand of such deposit within six (6) months after termination of the tenancy, the deposit reverts to the landlord in consideration of the costs and burden of maintaining the escrow account, and the interest of the tenant in that deposit terminates at that time.

C. Upon cessation of a landlord's interest in the dwelling unit Including, but not limited to, termination of interest by sale, assignment, death, bankruptcy, appointment of receiver or otherwise, the person in possession of the tenant's damage or security deposits at his option or pursuant to court order shall, within a reasonable time:

1. Transfer said deposits to the landlord's successor in interest and notify the tenants in writing of such transfer and of the transferee's name and address; or

2. Return the deposits to the tenants.

D. Upon receipt of the transferred deposits under paragraph 1 of subsection C of this section, the transferee, in relation to each deposits, shall have all the rights and obligations of a landlord holding such deposits under this act.

E. If a landlord or manager fails to comply with this section or fails to return any prepaid rent required to be paid to a tenant under this act, the tenant may recover the damage and security deposit and prepaid rent, if any.

F. Except as otherwise provided by the rental agreement, a tenant shall not apply or deduct any portion of the security deposit from the last month's rent or use or apply such tenant's security deposit at any time in lieu of payment of rent.

G. This section does not preclude the landlord or tenant from recovering other damages to which he may be entitled under this act.

§116. Person to accept service or notice—Identity of owner and manager—Failure to comply with section

A. As a part of any rental agreement the lessor shall prominently and in writing identify what person at what address is entitled to accept service or notice under this act. The landlord or any person authorized to enter into a rental agreement on his behalf shall disclose to the tenant in writing at or before the commencement of the tenancy the name and address of:

1. The person or persons authorized to manage the premises;

2. The owner or owners of the premises; or

3. The name and address of a person authorized to act for and on behalf of the owner for the purpose of receipt of service of process and receiving and receipting for notices.

The information required to be furnished by this section shall be kept current and this section extends to and is enforceable against any successor owner, landlord or manager.

B. A person who fails to comply with this section becomes a landlord for the purposes of this act and an agent of each person who is otherwise a landlord for:

1. Receipt of service of process and receiving and receipting for notices and demands; and

2. Performing the obligations of a landlord under this act and under the rental agreement and expending and making available for the purpose all rents collected from the premises.

§117. Commencement of tenancy—Delivery of possession—Wrongful possession

A. At the commencement of the term a landlord shall deliver full possession of the premises to the tenant in compliance with the rental agreement and Section 118 of this title. Except as otherwise provided in this act, the landlord may bring an action for possession against any other person wrongfully in possession and may recover his damages.

B. A rental agreement may provide reasonable limitations upon use of a dwelling unit or premises by a tenant or occupant. A landlord shall have the right to demand that an occupant vacate the dwelling unit or the premises or both if such occupant breaches any conditions of the rental agreement which would be enforceable against the tenant. If a landlord makes a written request to the tenant or to the occupant for the occupant to depart from the dwelling unit or the premises or both, the occupant shall comply. If the occupant wrongfully fails to comply within a reasonable time, the occupant shall, upon conviction, be deemed guilty of a trespass and may be punished by a fine of not to exceed Five Hundred Dollars ($500.00) or by confinement in the county jail for a period of not to exceed thirty (30) days or by both such fine and imprisonment.

C. An occupancy limitation of two (2) persons per bedroom residing in a dwelling unit shall be presumed reasonable for this state. The two-person limitation shall not apply to a child or children born to the tenants during the course of the lease.

§118. Duties of landlord and tenant

A. A landlord shall at all times during the tenancy:

1. Except in the case of a single-family residence, keep all common areas of his building, grounds, facilities and appurtenances in a clean, safe and sanitary condition;

2. Make all repairs and do whatever is necessary to put and keep the tenant's dwelling unit and premises in a fit and habitable condition;

3. Maintain in good and safe working order and condition all electrical, plumbing, sanitary, heating, ventilating, air-conditioning and other facilities and appliances, including elevators, supplied or required to be supplied by him.

4. Except in the case of one-or two-family residences or where provided by a governmental entity, provide and maintain appropriate receptacles and conveniences for the removal of ashes, garbage, rubbish and other waste incidental to the occupancy of the dwelling unit and arrange for the frequent removal of such wastes; and

5. Except in the case of a single-family residence or where the service is supplied by direct and independently-metered utility connections to the dwelling unit, supply running water and reasonable amounts of hot water at all times and reasonable heat.

B. The landlord and tenant of a dwelling unit may agree by a conspicuous writing independent of the rental agreement that the tenant is to perform specified repairs, maintenance tasks, alterations or remodeling.

§119. Conveyance of property—Attornment of tenant

A. A conveyance of real estate, or of any interest therein, by a landlord shall be valid without the attornment of the tenant, but the payment of rent by the tenant to the grantor at any time before written notice of the conveyance is given to the tenant shall be good against the grantee.

B. The attornment of a tenant to a stranger shall be void, and shall not affect the possession of the landlord unless it is made with the consent of the landlord, or pursuant to a judgment at law, or the order or decree of a court.

C. Unless otherwise agreed and except as otherwise provided in this act, upon termination of the owner's interest in the dwelling unit including, but not limited to, termination of interest by sale, assignment, death, bankruptcy, appointment of a receiver or otherwise, the owner is relieved of all liability under the rental agreement and of all obligations under this act as to events occurring subsequent to written notice to the resident of the termination of the owner's interest. The successor in interest to the owner shall be liable for all obligations under the rental agreement or under this act. Upon receipt by a resident of written notice of the termination of the owner's interest in the dwelling unit, a resident shall pay all future rental payments, when due, to the successor in interest to the owner.

D. Unless otherwise agreed and except as otherwise provided in this act, a manager of premises that includes a dwelling unit is relieved of liability under a rental agreement and this act as to events occurring after written notice to the tenant of the termination of his management.

§120. Failure of landlord to deliver possession of dwelling unit to tenant

A If the landlord fails to deliver possession of the dwelling unit to the tenant, rent abates until possession is delivered and the tenant may terminate the rental agreement by giving a written notice of such termination to the landlord, whereupon the landlord shall return all prepaid rent and deposit, or the tenant may, at his option, demand performance of the rental agreement by the landlord and maintain an action for possession of the dwelling unit against any person wrongfully in possession and recover the actual damages sustained by him.

B. If a person's failure to deliver possession is willful and not in good faith, an aggrieved person may recover from that person an amount not more than twice the monthly rental as specified in the rental agreement, computed and prorated on a daily basis, for each month, or portion thereof, that said person wrongfully remains in possession.

§121. Landlord's breach of rental agreement—Deductions from rent for repairs—Failure to supply heat, water or other essential services—Habitability of dwelling unit

A. Except as otherwise provided in this act, if there is a material noncompliance by the landlord with the terms of the rental agreement or a noncompliance with any of the provisions of Section 118 of this act which noncompliance materially affects health or safety, the tenant may deliver to the landlord a written notice specifying the acts and omissions constituting the breach and that the rental agreement will terminate upon a date not less than thirty (30) days after receipt of the notice if the breach is not remedied within fourteen (14) days, and thereafter the rental agreement shall so terminate as provided in the notice unless the landlord adequately remedies the breach within the time specified.

B. Except as otherwise provided in this act, if there is a material noncompliance by the landlord with any of the terms of the rental agreement or any of the provisions of Section 118 of this act which noncompliance materially affects health and the breach is remediable by repairs, the reasonable cost of which is less than One Hundred Dollars ($100.00), the tenant may notify the landlord in writing of his intention to correct the condition at the landlord's expense after the expiration of fourteen (14) days. If the landlord fails to comply within said fourteen (14) days, or as promptly as conditions require in the case of an emergency, the tenant may thereafter cause the work to be done in a workmanlike manner and, after submitting to the landlord an itemized statement, deduct from his rent the actual and reasonable cost or the fair and reasonable value of the work, not exceeding the amount specified in this subsection, in which event the rental agreement shall not terminate by reason of that breach.

C. Except as otherwise provided in this act, if, contrary to the rental agreement or Section 118 of this act, the landlord willfully or negligently fails to supply heat, running water, hot water, electric, gas or other essential service, the tenant may give written notice to the landlord specifying the breach and thereafter may:

1. Upon written notice, immediately terminate the rental agreement; or

2. Procure reasonable amounts of heat, hot water, running water, electric, gas or other essential service during the period of the landlord's noncompliance and deduct their actual and reasonable cost from the rent; or

3. Recover damages based upon the diminution of the fair rental value of the dwelling unit, or

4. Upon written notice, procure reasonable substitute housing during the period of the landlord's noncompliance, in which case the tenant is excused from paying rent for the period of the landlord's noncompliance.

D. Except as otherwise provided in the act, if there is a noncompliance by the landlord with the terms of the rental agreement or Section 118 of this act, which noncompliance renders the dwelling unit uninhabitable or poses an imminent threat to the health and safety of any occupant of the dwelling unit and which noncompliance is not remedied as promptly as conditions require, the tenant may immediately terminate the rental agreement upon written notice to the landlord which notice specifies the noncompliance.

E. All rights of the tenant under this section do not arise until he has given written notice to the landlord or if the condition complained of was caused by the deliberate or negligent act or omission of the tenant, a member of his family, his animal or pet or other person or animal on the premises with his consent.

§122. Damage to or destruction of dwelling unit—Rights and duties of tenant

A. If the dwelling unit or premises are damaged or destroyed by fire or other casualty to an extent that enjoyment of the dwelling unit is substantially impaired, unless the impairment is caused by the deliberate or negligent act or omission of the tenant, a member of his family, his animal or pet or other person or animal on the premises with his consent, the tenant may:

1. Immediately vacate the premises and notify the landlord in writing within one (1) week thereafter of his intention to terminate the rental agreement, in which case the rental agreement terminates as of the date of vacating; or

2. If continued occupancy is possible, vacate any part of the dwelling unit rendered unusable by the fire or casualty, in which case the tenant's liability for rent is reduced in proportion to the diminution in the fair rental value of the dwelling unit.

B. If the rental agreement is terminated under this section the landlord shall return all deposits recoverable under Section 115 of this act and all prepaid and unearned rent. Accounting for rent in the event of termination or apportionment shall be made as of the date of the fire or other casualty.

§123. Wrongful removal or exclusion from dwelling unit

If a landlord wrongfully removes or excludes a tenant from possession of a dwelling unit, the tenant may recover possession by a proceeding brought in a court of competent jurisdiction, or terminate the rental agreement after giving notice of such intention to the landlord, and in either case recover an amount not more than twice the average monthly rental, or twice his actual damages, whichever is greater. If the rental agreement is terminated, the landlord shall return all deposits recoverable under Section 115 of this act and all prepaid and unearned rent.

§124. Unlawful entry or lawful entry in unreasonable manner-Harassment of tenant-Damages

A. If the landlord makes an unlawful entry or a lawful entry in an unreasonable manner or harasses the tenant by making repeated unreasonable demand for entry, the tenant may obtain injunctive relief to prevent the recurrence of the conduct or, upon written notice, terminate the rental agreement. In either case the tenant may recover actual damages.

B. Neither injunctive relief nor damages shall be available to a tenant if the basis for the landlord's action is the landlord's execution of a writ in the manner prescribed by sections 1148.10A of Title 12 of the Oklahoma Statutes.

§125 Defective condition of premises-Report to landlord

Any defective condition of the premises which comes to the tenant's attention, and which the tenant has reason to believed is unknown to the landlord, shall be reported by the tenant to the landlord as soon as practicable.

§126. Tenant's use and occupancy of premises-Rules and regulations.

A. A landlord, from time to time, may adopt a rule or regulation, however described, concerning the tenant's use and occupancy of the premises. Such a rule or regulation is enforceable against the tenant only if:

1. Its purpose is to promote the convenience, peace, safety or welfare of the tenants in the premises, preserve the landlord's property from abusive use, or make a fair distribution of services and facilities held out for the tenants generally; and

2. It is reasonably related to the purpose for which it is adopted; and

3. It applies to all tenants in the premises in a fair manner; and

4. It is sufficiently explicit in its prohibition, direction or limitation of the tenant's conduct to fairly inform the tenant what such tenant must or must not do to comply; and

5. It is not for the purpose of evading the obligations of the landlord; and

6. The tenant has notice of it at the time such tenant enters into the rental agreement, or when it is adopted.

B If a rule or regulation is adopted after the tenant enters into the rental agreement and that rule or regulation works a substantial modification of such tenant's bargain, the rule or regulation so adopted is not valid and enforceable against the tenant unless he consents to it in writing.

§127. Duties of tenant

The tenant shall at all times during the tenancy:

1. Keep that part of the premises which such tenant occupies and uses as safe, clean and sanitary as the condition of the premises permits;

2. Dispose from such tenant's dwelling unit all ashes, garbage, rubbish and other waste in a safe, clean and sanitary manner;

3. Keep all plumbing fixtures in the dwelling unit or used by the tenant as clean and sanitary as their condition permits;

4. Use in a safe and nondestructive manner all electrical, plumbing, sanitary, heating, ventilating, air-conditioning and other facilities and appliances including elevators in the premises;

5. Not deliberately or negligently destroy, deface, damage, impair or remove any part of the premises or permit any person, animal or pet to do so;

6. Not engage in conduct or allow any person or animal or pet, on the premises with the express or implied permission or consent of the tenant, to engage in conduct that will disturb the quiet and peaceful enjoyment of the premises by other tenants;

7. Comply with all covenants, rules, regulations and the like which are in accordance with Section 126 of this title; and

8. Not engage in criminal activity that threatens the health, safety or right of peaceful enjoyment of the premises by other tenants or is a danger to the premises, and not engage in any drug-related criminal activity on or near the premises either personally or by any member of the tenant's household or any guest or other person under the tenant's control.

§128. Consent of tenant for landlord to enter dwelling unit-Emergency entry-Abuse of right of entry-Notice-Abandoned premises-Refusal of consent

A. A tenant shall not unreasonably withhold consent to the landlord, his agents and employees, to enter into the dwelling unit in order to inspect the premises, make necessary or agreed repairs, decorations, alterations or improvements, supply necessary or agreed services or exhibit the dwelling unit to prospective or actual purchasers, mortgagee, tenants, workmen or contractors.

B. A landlord, his agents and employees may enter the dwelling unit without consent of the tenant in case of emergency.

C. A landlord shall not abuse the right of access or use it to harass the tenant. Except in case of emergency or unless it is impracticable to do so, the landlord shall give the tenant at least one (1) day's notice of his intent to enter and may enter only at reasonable times.

D. Unless the tenant has abandoned or surrendered the premises, a landlord has no other right of access during a tenancy except as is provided in this act or pursuant to a court order.

E. If the tenant refuses to allow lawful access, the landlord may obtain injunctive relief to compel access or he may terminate the rental agreement.

§129. Tenant's breach of rental agreement-Wrongful abandonment.

A. Unless otherwise agreed, use by the tenant of the dwelling unit for any purpose other than as his place of abode shall constitute a breach of the rental agreement and shall be grounds of terminating the rental agreement.

B. If the tenant wrongfully quits and abandons the dwelling unit during the term of the tenancy, the landlord shall make reasonable efforts to make the dwelling unit available for rental. If the landlord rents the dwelling unit for a term beginning before the expiration of the rental agreement, said rental agreement terminates as of the commencement date of the new tenancy. If the landlord fails to use reasonable efforts to make the dwelling unit available for rental or if the landlord accepts the abandonment as a surrender, the rental agreement is deemed to be terminated by the landlord as of the date the landlord has notice of the abandonment. If, after making reasonable efforts to make the dwelling unit available for rental after the abandonment, the landlord fails to rerent the premises for a fair rental during the term, the tenant shall be liable for the entire rent or the difference in rental, whichever may be appropriate, for the remainder of the term. If the tenancy is from month-to-month or week-to-week, the term of the rental agreement for this purpose is deemed to be a month or a week, as the case may be.

§130. Abandoning, surrendering or eviction from possession of dwelling unit-Disposition of personal property

A. If the tenant abandons or surrenders possession of the dwelling unit or has been lawfully removed from the premises through eviction and leaves household goods, furnishings, fixtures, or any other personal property in the dwelling unit, the landlord may take possession of the property, and if, in the judgment of the landlord the property has an ascertainable or apparent value, the landlord may dispose of the property without any duty of accounting or any liability to any party. The landlord may dispose of perishable property in any manner the landlord considers fit.

B. If the tenant abandons or surrenders possession of the dwelling unit or has been lawfully removed from the premises through eviction proceedings and leaves household goods, furnishings, fixtures, or any other personal property in the dwelling unit, the landlord may take possession of the property, and if, in the judgment of the landlord the property has an ascertainable or apparent value, the landlord shall provide written notice to the tenant by certified mail to the last-known address that if the property is not removed within the time specified in the notice, the property will be deemed abandoned. Any property left with the landlord for a period of thirty (30) days or longer shall be conclusively determined to be abandoned and as such the landlord may dispose of said property in any manner which he deems reasonable and proper without liability to the tenant or any other interested party.

C. The landlord shall store all personal property of the tenant in a place of safekeeping and shall exercise reasonable care of the property. The landlord shall not be responsible to the tenant for any loss not caused by the landlord's deliberate or negligent act. The landlord may elect to store the property in the dwelling unit that was abandoned or surrendered by the tenant, in which event the storage cost may not exceed the fair rental value of the premises. If the tenant's property is removed to a commercial storage company, the storage cost shall include the actual charge for the storage and removal from the premises to the place of storage.

D. If the tenant removes the personal property within the time limitation provided in this section, the landlord is entitled to the cost of storage for the period during which the property remained in the landlord's safekeeping plus all other costs that accrued under the rental agreement.

E. The landlord may not be held to respond in damages in an action by a tenant claiming loss by reason of the landlord's election to destroy, sell or otherwise dispose of the property in compliance with the provisions of this section. If, however, the landlord deliberately or negligently violated the provisions of this section, the landlord shall be liable for actual damages.

§131. Delinquent rent

A. If rent is unpaid when due, the landlord may bring an action for recovery of the rent at any time thereafter or the landlord may wait until the expiration of the period allowed for curing a default by the tenant, as prescribed in subsection B of this section, before bringing such action.

B. A landlord may terminate a rental agreement for failure to pay rent when due, if the tenant fails to pay rent within five (5) days after written notice of landlord's demand for payment. The notice may be given before or after the landlord files any action authorized by subsection A of this section.

Demand for past due rent is deemed a demand for possession of the premises and no further notice to quit possession need be given by the landlord to the tenant for any purpose.

§132. Tenant's failure to comply with rental agreement or perform duties-Rights and duties of landlord

A. Except as otherwise provided in the *Oklahoma Residential Landlord and Tenant Act*, if there is a noncompliance by the tenant with the rental agreement or with Section 127 of this title which noncompliance can be remedied by repair, replacement of a damaged item, or cleaning and the tenant fails to comply as promptly as conditions require in the case of an emergency or within ten (10) days after written notice served as provided in subsection E of Section 111 of this title by the landlord specifying the breach and requiring that the tenant remedy it within that period of time, the landlord may enter the dwelling unit and cause the work to be done in a workmanlike manner and thereafter submit the itemized bill for the actual and reasonable cost or the fair and reasonable value thereof as rent on the next date rent is due, or if the rental agreement has terminated, for immediate payment. If the landlord remedies the breach as provided in this subsection, the landlord may not terminate the rental agreement by reason of the tenant's failure to remedy the breach.

B. Except as otherwise provided in the *Oklahoma Residential Landlord Tenant Act*, if there is a material noncompliance by the tenant with the rental agreement or with any provision of Section 127 of this title, the landlord may deliver to the tenant a written notice served as provide din subsection E of Section 111 of this title specifying the acts and omissions constituting the noncompliance and that the rental agreement will terminate upon a date not less than fifteen (15) days after receipt of the notice unless remedied within ten (10) days. If the breach is not remedied within ten (10) days from receipt of the notice, the rental agreement shall terminate as provided in the notice. If within the ten (10) days the tenant adequately remedies the breach complained of, or if the landlord remedies the breach according to the provisions of subsection A of this section, the rental agreement shall not terminate by reason of the breach. Any subsequent breach of the lease or noncompliance under this section shall be grounds, upon written notice to the tenant, for immediate termination of the lease.

C. Notwithstanding other provisions of this section, if there is a noncompliance by the tenant with the rental agreement or with any of the provisions of Section 127 of this title, which noncompliance causes or threatens to cause imminent and irremediable harm to the premises or to any person and which noncompliance is not remedied by the tenant as promptly as conditions require after the tenant has notice of it, the landlord may terminate the rental agreement by immediately filing a forcible entry and detainer action.

D. Any criminal activity that threatens the health, safety or right of peaceful enjoyment of the premises by other tenants committed by a tenant or by any member of the tenant's household or any guest or other person under the tenant's control or is a danger to the premises and any drug-related criminal activity on or near the premises by the tenant or by any member of the tenant's household or any guest or other person under the tenant's control shall be grounds for immediate termination of the lease.

§133. Lien on tenant's property

A landlord shall have a lien upon that part of the property belonging to the tenant which has a reasonable relationship as nearly as practicable to the amount of the debt owed, which may be in a rental unit used by him at the time notice is given, for the proper charges owed b the tenant, and for the cost of enforcing the lien, with the right to possession of the property until the debt obligation is paid to the landlord. Provided, however, that such lien shall be secondary to the claim of any prior bona fide holder of a chattel mortgage or to the rights of a conditional seller of such property, other than the tenant.

For the purposes of this section, property shall mean any baggage or other property belonging to the tenant which may be in the rental unit used by the tenant but which shall not include all tools, musical instruments or books used by the tenant in any trade or profession, all family portraits and pictures, all wearing apparel, any type of prosthetic or orthopedic appliance, hearing aid, glasses, false teeth, glass eyes, bedding, contraceptive devices, soap, tissues, washing machines, vaporizers, refrigerators, food, cooking and eating utensils, all other appliances personally used by the tenant for the protection of his health, or any baby bed or any other items used for the personal care of babies.

§134. Enforcement of lien

A landlord lien may be enforced as by any other general lien as provided in Section 91 of Title 42 of the Oklahoma Statutes.

§135. Construction of act
This act shall be liberally construed and applied to promote and effectuate its underlying purposes and policies.

§136. Removal of rented furniture-Procedure
A. Upon termination of a furniture rental agreement, the lessor or agent of the lessor shall not remove the furniture from possess or dwelling place of the lessee unless the lessee or an agent of the lessee is present. Such furniture shall be marked with either an identifying number or in some other distinguishable manner prior to removal. Before the furniture is removed, the lessor or his agent shall inspect the furniture and advise the lessee or the agent of the lessee of each specific item of damage. If furniture is removed when such person is not present or if the furniture is not inspected before removal, the entire amount of any security deposit held by the lessor shall be returned to the lessee.

B. If the lessor complies with the provisions of subsection A of this Section and recovers damages which the lessor has suffered due to the fault of the lessee if the lessor provides to the lessee a written itemized statement of damage delivered by mail, to be by return receipt requested and to be signed for by any person of statutory service age at such address. The lessor shall allow the lessee an opportunity to re-inspect the furniture in question before any security deposit may be retained or any additional damage charged made.

C. In the case of undamaged furniture, the lessor shall return any security deposit without interest to the lessee within thirty (30) days of the termination of the rental agreement, If the returned furniture is damaged, the lessor shall return the balance of any security deposit above the cost of damage, without interest, to the lessee within thirty (30) days of the inspection of the furniture by the lessee. If the lessee chooses to not inspect the furniture, the balance of the security deposit shall be returned to the lessee within thirty (30) days of the mailing of the written itemized statement of damage.

PROFFESIONAL ASSOCIATIONS

There are several professional associations available for people who wish additional training in property management. Some of them as follows:

Building Owners and Management Institute:

This is a professional association which specializes in office and related types of buildings. They offer many courses tailored for this specialty.

Accredited Residential Manager:

This is a certification program offered by the Institute of Real Estate Management. It is for property managers who manage apartment complexes, rental condominiums, single room occupancy, apartments or home owners' associations.

Institute for Real Estate Management:

This is an affiliation of the National Association of Realtors. They offer courses for managers of income producing properties, office buildings, retail properties, and multi-family developments.

Certified Property Manager (CPM):

This is an earned designation offering organization specializing in property management of all kinds.

Candidate Commercial Investment Management (CCIM):

This association offers a wide variety of commercial real estate courses.

TEST YOUR UNDERSTANDING

1. Leasehold estates are
    1. estates of trust.
    2. **possessory estates.**
    3. reversionary estates.
    4. titled estates.

2. Leasehold estates last for
    1. a definite period of time.
    2. for as long as the parties are willing to continue the relationship.
    3. **Either 1 or 2.**
    4. Neither 1 nor 2.

3. In the leasehold estate arrangement
    1. the lessor retains the reversionary rights.
    2. the lessor retains the right to collect rents.
    3. **Both 1 and 2.**
    4. Neither 1 nor 2.

4. A lessee generally may
    1. sublet as desired.
    2. **sublet only if the lease permits it.**
    3. sublet only for short periods of time.
    4. None of the above.

5. An estate for years
    1. has a specific starting time.
    2. has a specific ending time.
    3. can be for any agreed upon period of time.
    4. **All of the above.**

6. A periodic tenancy may be
    1. month-to-month.
    2. week-to-week.
    3. year-to-year.
    4. **Any of the above.**

7. A tenancy at will may be terminated at the will of
    1. the tenant.
    2. the landlord.
    3. **Either 1 or 2.**
    4. Neither 1 nor 2.

8. A tenancy at sufferance exits when
    1. the tenant is in possession of the property without the consent of the landlord.
    2. the tenant fails to surrender possession after the lease terminates.
    3. **Both 1 and 2.**
    4. Neither 1 nor 2.

9. tenancy at sufferance
    1. protects tenants from being classified as trespassers.
    2. prevents the tenant from acquiring the property through adverse possession.
    3. **Both 1 and 2.**
    4. Neither 1 nor 2.

10. **In a gross lease the landlord agrees to pay**
    1. taxes.
    2. utilities.
    3. Both 1 and 2.
    4. Neither 1 nor 2.

11. **A net lease is one in which the tenant agrees to pay**
    1. repairs.
    2. taxes and utilities.
    3. insurance.
    4. All of the above.

12. **A ground lease is one in which**
    1. only rural land and buildings may be included.
    2. only the land is leased.
    3. there is no such thing as a ground lease.
    4. a ground lease is only for 99 years.

13. **On-site property management duties include**
    1. showing the property.
    2. interviewing prospects.
    3. negotiating and signing leases.
    4. All of the above.

14. **Off-site property management duties include**
    1. accounting, payrolls, payment of bills.
    2. training programs for the property manager.
    3. acquiring hazard and liability insurance.
    4. All of the above.

15. **Rental income is based on**
    1. number of units.
    2. available square feet. — only paying
    3. number of paying tenants.
    4. rental of off-site facilities.

16. **Non-payment of rent can**
    1. increasing operating costs.
    2. have little effect on the budget.
    3. decrease management's workload.
    4. None of the above.

17. **Allowing poor rental payment habits to develop can**
    1. be a disservice to the residents who pay on time.
    2. cause rental rates to increase.
    3. Both 1 and 2.
    4. Neither 1 nor 2.

18. **Rent is generally required by the property manager to be paid**
    1. in advance.
    2. in arrears.
    3. paid as convenient for the tenant.
    4. paid on the property manager's birthday.

19. Which of the following would be the least acceptable form of rent payment?
   1. Personal check.
   2. Money order.
   3. Third-party check.
   4. certified check.

20. The first step in the eviction process is
   1. call the tenant on the phone.
   2. deliver a formal, written notice to the violator to vacate within a number of days.
   3. send a post card stating the alleged lease violation and demanding payment.
   4. None of the above.

21. Legal service requirement to vacate or quit the property will have been met when
   1. a five-day notice is delivered in person, in writing to the tenant.
   2. a ten-day notice is sent to the resident's address by certified mail with return receipt requested and a copy is posted on the resident's door.
   3. Either 1 or 2.
   4. Neither 1 nor 2.

22. Sometimes Notices to Quit are ineffective and further legal action must be taken. In the case of delinquencies this is known as
   1. specific performance.
   2. unlawful detainer action.
   3. special eviction action.
   4. tenant eradication.

23. To operate legally, property managers must have a real estate license unless
   1. they own the properties they are managing.
   2. are a resident manager.
   3. are the direct employee of the owner.
   4. Any of the above.

24. The Broker Relationships Act applies to property managers if
   1. they own the property they are managing.
   2. they are resident managers.
   3. they are managing the property for another person.
   4. All of the above.

25. A property manager's responsibilities include
   1. maintaining profitability.
   2. protect the owners fro liability.
   3. maintaining the property.
   4. All of the above.

26. A property management agreement
   1. is an agreement between the licensee and the property owner.
   2. is another term for a lease.
   3. is enforceable in court only when multiple properties are included.
   4. has nothing to do with the Broker Relationships Act.

27. When all other efforts to collect unpaid rent fail, property managers may utilize
   1. the local sheriff.
   2. a collection agency.
   3. an actuarial expert.
   4. a hit man.

28. When a landlord begins the eviction process, the usual first step in the process is called a notice
   1. to evacuate.
   2. to quit.
   3. to respond.
   4. to pay or leave.

29. The landlord is the same person as the
   1. lessor.
   2. lessee.
   3. mortgagee.
   4. mortgagor.

30. The tenant is the same person as the
   1. lessor.
   2. lessee.
   3. mortgagee.
   4. mortgagor.

31. An occupant
   1. owns the property.
   2. manufactures glasses for landlords.
   3. abides within the dwelling unit.
   4. there is no such person as an "occupant."

32. Payments to be made to the landlord other than deposits and damages are
   1. security deposits.
   2. escrow items.
   3. trust funds.
   4. rent.

33. The Oklahoma Residential Landlord and Tenant Act does not govern
   1. institutional residency.
   2. occupancy under a contract for deed.
   3. occupancy in a hotel.
   4. All of the above.

34. The Oklahoma Residential Landlord and Tenant Act provides that if the rental agreement does not specify the terms of the tenancy, the tenancy for all other than a roomer, the tenancy will be
   1. month-to-month.
   2. week-to-week.
   3. year-to-year.
   4. day-to-day.

35. The Oklahoma Residential Landlord and Tenant Act provides the landlord or the tenant may terminate a month-to-month tenancy with written notice to the other at least
   1. 30 days notice.
   2. 60 days notice.
   3. 90 days notice.
   4. 120 days notice.

36. If the tenancy is less than month-to-month, the landlord or tenant may terminate the tenancy with written notice of
   1. 5 days.
   2. 7 days.
   3. 9 days.
   4. 14 days.

37. The landlord is required to disclose if the premises to be rented has been flooded within the last
   1. 1 year.
   2. 5 years.
   3. 10 years.
   15 years.

38. When the landlord serves notice to terminate personally, the notice may be given to a family member who is over
   1. 10 years old.
   2. 12 years old.
   3. 18 years old.
   4. 21 years old.

39. The landlord shall not deny or terminate a tenancy because the tenant
   1. has set up a "meth" lab.
   2. has violated local zoning ordinances.
   3. has a guide dog.
   4. fails to pay rent.

40. Any damage or security deposit required by a landlord
   1. shall be maintained in the State of Oklahoma.
   2. must be in a federally insured financial institution.
   3. shall be kept in an escrow/trust account.
   4. All of the above.

41. The Oklahoma Residential Landlord and Tenant Act requires landlords to
   1. keep all common areas clean, safe and sanitary condition.
   2. make all repairs to keep property in a fit and habitable condition.
   3. keep all electrical, plumbing, ventilating, air conditioning, etc., in good working condition.
   4. All of the above.

ANSWERS AND EXPLANATIONS

1. 2 Leases are possessory estates. Ownership remains with the owner.

2. 3 Leasehold estates are negotiated between the lesser and lessor and may be for a fixed period and re-negotiated at termination.

3. 3 The owner retains ownership rights and has the right to collect rent as compensation.

4. 2 Some leases allow the original tenant to sublease his possessory rights to another.

5. 4 A good definition of an estate for years.

6. 4 A good definition of a periodic tenancy.

7. 3 A tenancy at will may be terminated with appropriate notice by either party.

8. 3 A good description of a tenancy at sufferance.

9. 3 Both are characteristic of a tenancy at sufferance.

10. 3 Usual terms in a gross lease.

11. 4 Usual terms of a net lease.

12. 2 The usual purpose of a ground lease.

13. 4 All on-site duties.

14. 4 All off-site duties.

15. 3 Income received.

16. 1 When rent payments are not made, operating costs are likely to increase.

17. 3 Poor rental rates may result in both.

18. 1 Not a good idea to collect rents in arrears.

19. 3 The level of risk increases with these kinds of checks.

20. 2 A written notice is the first step in the eviction process.

21. 3 Both these are available.

22. 2 A next step in the eviction process.

23. 4 Legal requirements.

24. 3 The Broker Relationships Act covers relationships between licensees and members of the public.

25. 4 All of these are property managers' duties.

26. 1 A pre-agreement is a contract.

27. 2 A service available to property managers.

28. 2 The usual first step.

29. 1 Landlord = Lessor.

30. 2 Tenant = Lessee

31. 3 A good definition in the law.

32. 4 A good definition in the law.

33. 4 All excluded by the law.

34. 1 A legal presumption.

35. 1 A legal provision.

36. 2 A legal provision.

37. 2 A legal provision.

38. 2 A legal provision.

39. 3 A legal provision.

40. 4 Required by the Oklahoma Landlord and Tenant Act.

41. 4 Required by the Oklahoma Landlord Tenant Act.

RISK MANAGEMENT

LENDER REQUIREMENTS

Since lenders have money at risk in homes on which they have loaned money, they will usually require the borrower to purchase hazard insurance which protects their interest in the property. In most cases, in the event of a loss to the property, the insurance company will put the name of the borrower and the lender on any settlement check.

Typically, the lender is not interested in medical and liability coverage. The lender is normally not concerned about this kind of risk.

If the borrower is unable to obtain insurance coverage on the property, the lender will probably not issue the loan.

REPLACEMENT COST (TC)

The replacement clause in many insurance policies is frequently a lender requirement. In this clause, the insurance company guarantees to make money available to replace or rebuild the structure at current market prices. A buyer/homeowner will typically prefer a policy with a replacement cost provision. This will offset appreciation of the real estate and inflation in building costs.

ASSUMPTION OF A POLICY

Sometimes the buyer will purchase the seller's existing homeowner's insurance policy. This will probably save the buyer from purchasing one year's insurance coverage in advance. Of course, the insurance company must accept the buyer before the closing. To do this the insurance company will issue an endorsement to the policy naming the buyer as the insured person. The insurable interest in the property is the financial interest in the property.

POLICY CANCELLATION OR SUSPENSION

The homeowner (insured) may terminate the policy at any time. This may cause a refund because insurance is usually paid in advance.

The insurance company also has the right to cancel the policy. Normally, the insurance company is required to give the homeowner a five-day notice. A refund of unused premium is also refunded.

LANDLORD/TENANT POLICY

Any landlord will be interested in maintaining adequate insurance on tenant-occupied property. If there is a loan on the property, the lender will require property damage coverage against the property to cover the lender's interest.

In addition to hazard coverage, most landlords will purchase liability coverage in the event of someone being injured on the property. This can usually be done with an endorsement to the hazard policy.

With the litigious atmosphere in the world, a landlord or any other property owner would be foolish not to have adequate, appropriate insurance coverage.

REAL ESTATE INSURANCE

HAZARD INSURANCE

The American dream of home ownership brings, with its fulfillment, risk. The possibility of loss of the home due to its physical destruction or damage is a very real prospect. Therefore, along with the growth in American home ownership since the end of World War II, there has been a corresponding growth in homeowner insurance.

The purpose of insurance is to "shift the risk of loss" from the individual to a large number of people who are exposed to similar risks. By "sharing" these risks, the individual's cost for protection is reduced to an affordable level.

KINDS OF POLICIES: COVERAGE

Probably no other kind of insurance is as standardized in America as is homeowners' insurance. There are four basic kinds of policies homeowners may buy. These are the **"HO 1," "HO 2," "HO 3," "HO 4," "HO 6," and "HO 8."**

Generally, the **HO 1** provides only basic coverage. A typical **HO 1** policy will cover losses from fire, lightening, wind, hail, explosion, riot or civil disturbance, aircraft, vehicles, smoke, vandalism, theft and breakage of glass windows.

The **HO 2** provides a broader spectrum of coverage. A typical **HO 2** policy will cover losses from fire, lightening, wind, hail, explosion, riot or civil disturbance, accumulation of snow, ice or sleet, water damage, water heating systems, freezing of plumbing, accidental electrical injuries, volcanic eruption.

The **HO 3** provides coverage for special circumstances. A typical **HO 3** policy will cover losses from fire, lightening, wind, hail, explosion, riot or civil disturbance, accumulation of snow, ice or sleet, water damage, water heating systems, freezing of plumbing, accidental electrical injuries, volcanic eruption and selected other risks (perils).

The **HO 4** is the tenants or renters' insurance broad form coverage.

The **HO 6** is for condominiums.

The **HO 8** is for older homes.

While homeowners' insurance is fairly standardized, there are enough differences to require the reading of individual policies to determine the exact quality and extent of coverage.

Exclusions

A list of typical exclusions includes flood, earthquake, war, and nuclear accident among others.

If the dwelling is left vacant, there is likely to be a clause in the policy which states the property may not be protected. This clause may become extremely significant in those listings wherein the principal is out of town. Coverage may drop off to cover fire only and the company may require a vacancy permit. Eventually, cancellation will occur and, possibly, a higher risk policy may be required.

In addition to not covering a vacant dwelling from losses due to freezing, most policies will not cover vacant dwellings from losses due to vandalism if it can be shown the property has been vacant.
If the dwelling collapses due to faulty construction, the insurance will probably not pay. The same is true if a natural phenomenon such as a sinkhole causes the collapse of the house.

Neglect of property will not be covered by most insurance policies.

Damage to property caused by a power failure will not be paid for.

Water damage will probably be covered in the exclusions of most policies. Constant seepage from pipes or appliances, seepage from a swimming pool, surface water, waves, overflows of backed-up sewers, underground streams may not be covered.

Most homeowners' policies do not cover against losses caused by acts of governmental bodies.

Coverage of Personal Property

The personal property of the insured, specifically, items owned and used by the insured, are normally covered. This coverage extends to personal property even if the loss occurs outside the dwelling. Most policies place severe limitations on the coverage of personal property. In most cases, personal property is covered only to its actual value, not its replacement value. Additional coverage may be purchased, however. For example, a homeowner who possesses a large amount of jewelry may purchase a "rider" for increased coverage specifically for the jewelry.

Many people in America have a city home and a "place at the lake," a secondary residence. Some insurance policies will cover personal property at the secondary residence only 10% to 50% of the coverage on the principal residence.

Limits of Liability

Virtually all policies contain a section called "Limits of Liabilities." This section places limits on the insurance company's liabilities.

Examples of limits of liabilities:

$200 on cash, valuable metals, bank notes kept in the residence.

$1,000 on boats, including the trailer.

$1,000 on trailers (not boat trailers).

$1,000 on jewelry.

$2,500 on property used by the homeowner in his/her business which is on the premises.
$2,000 on firearms.

$1,000 on deeds, letters of credit, notes, manuscripts, passports, tickets, stamps, etc.

This is not an all-inclusive list. Each policy must be read to determine the exact amounts and items included in the limited liabilities.

Personal Property Exclusions:

Some items of personal property typically excluded from coverage in most homeowners' policies include:

Pets;
Motorized vehicles, except those for handicapped persons and those not subject to registration;
Credit cards;
Bookkeeping records;
Computer software,
Aircraft parts.

Again, this is not an all-inclusive list. Each policy must be read to determine the exclusions on personal property.

Loss of Use

In the event the dwelling is damaged severely enough to make it uninhabitable, or the owner loses its use or partial use, most policies provide two ways for which this loss may be compensated. The insurance company may pay for additional living expenses to obtain habitation during repairs (living expenses) or the homeowner may receive "fair rental value" of the portion unusable until repairs are made.

Additional Coverage

Some **HO 3** policies have coverage of which the owner probably is totally unaware. For example, if the house catches on fire and the fire department charges a service fee, the **HO 3** policy may cover it. If a storm leaves the property covered with debris, the policy may cover its removal.

Liability Coverage

Many homeowners' policies cover the insured against claims or suits for damages caused by bodily damage or property damage. If the policy has this liability coverage, the company will likely pay up to the limit of liability if the insured is legally liable and provide legal defense.

EXCLUSIONS TO LIABILITY COVERAGE

Typical exclusions to the liability coverage of many homeowners' policies include war, communicable disease, workers compensation covered injuries, certain damage caused by boats or the operation of aircraft, business activities, bodily injury to the homeowner and his/her intentional acts.

Again, this is not an exhaustive list and each policy must be read to discover the actual exclusions and coverage.

Renters' Insurance

Renters' insurance provides coverage for personal property and liability protection.

Condominium Insurance

Condominium insurance is a variation of homeowners' insurance. Since condominium owners have sole ownership of a particular "living space" and a small interest in the common area of the condominium complex, condo insurance is a little different to regular homeowners' insurance.

The condo owner will purchase insurance for the solely-owned space and coordinate the policy with that of the condominium association.

The individual policy protects the property to which the condo owner has title. In addition, it covers portions of the common area, the insured's personal property and has some liability coverage.

Mobile Home Insurance

Mobile homes provide a slightly unusual condition. The mobile home may be permanently affixed to the land or may be owned by the insured, but the land on which it sets may be rented. Insurance companies may have a special mobile home policy or provide a modified homeowner policy. Many insurance companies will not "write" homeowner insurance coverage on a mobile home unless it is permanently affixed to the land.

Mobile home policies usually provide the same or similar coverage and exclusions as do those for site-built homes. However, since the mobile home is, in fact, mobile, there are likely to be some unique clauses in mobile homes policies. For example, there may be a clause concerning risks when moving the home. If, while in transit, does the policy cover damages? In addition, some policies provide for removal of a mobile home from a hazardous locale to a safer one.

Again, careful reading of the policy will reveal coverage.

Caveat To Real Estate Licensees: Unless the licensee is a licensed insurance agent, he/she should avoid giving advise or making recommendations concerning insurance.

Caution For Real Estate Licensees

For many years it has been a practice for some brokers to operate a real estate firm at the same location as their insurance firm. While, as a general practice, OREC finds this an acceptable method of operation, the disclosure of beneficial interests becomes significant.

Flood Insurance

The National Flood Insurance Program (NFIP) was created by Federal legislation in 1968. Prior to that time, the only protection people whose property was damaged by flood was possibly some type of government disaster relief.

Obviously, the danger of flooding is different for each community. Each community may join the National Flood Insurance Program (NFIP) or not, depending on that community's fear of floods.

If the community joins the NFIP, individuals in the community may purchase flood insurance. If the community does not join the NFIP, flood insurance is not available to members of the community. In NFIP member communities, individuals may purchase flood insurance through local property and casualty insurance agents.

Insurance companies who sell flood insurance are guaranteed against any losses they may incur above the premiums they receive by the Federal government.

Flood Insurance Rates and Coverage

Each insurance company has a copy of a FLOOD INSURANCE RATE MAP. This map illustrates the likelihood of flood in an area. Naturally, the greater the likelihood of flooding in an area, the higher the premium will be for the flood insurance.

When a homeowner makes application for flood insurance, there is a five-day waiting period before the insurance goes into effect.

Most structures that have a roof and walls may be covered unless they are built over water. Flood insurance covers the structure and its contents.

Coverage for flood insurance requires the joining community to begin measures to control flooding. Initially, flood insurance coverage is begun under the "emergency program." Coverage under this program is usually limited to $35,000. Once the community's flood control projects are developed, the coverage is shifted to the "regular program." Under the "regular program" coverage, most residences are covered up to $185,000 for the structure and $60,000 for the contents.

Coverage for small businesses under the "regular program" is limited to $250,000 for the structure and $300,000 for the contents.

Flood Defined

For the purposes of flood insurance a flood is defined as a "temporary condition of partial or complete inundation of normally dry land areas." This can be caused by the rapid accumulation of runoff or the overflow of inland waters. Mud slides and the collapse of land on a shoreline may be covered. In these cases the collapse must be caused by waves or currents and the mud slide must be caused by flooding of normally dry area.

Deductibles

As is the case with many other insurance programs, several packages with different levels of deductibles are available. Detailed information can be obtained by contacting an insurance agent or contacting the Federal Emergency Management Agency, Federal Insurance Administration, 500 C Street S. W., Washington, D.C. 20472, 1-800-638-6620. For information concerning the National Flood Insurance Program, interested persons may call **1-800-358-9616**.

TITLE INSURANCE (TC)

The American system of law recognizes more rights and interests in real estate ownership than it does in personal property. As a result of real estate's uniqueness, those who have an interest in real estate are properly concerned that their rights and interests in the property are clear at the time of purchase, that the transfer is effected expeditiously and correctly, and their interests in the property are safeguarded as much as is possible. The services provided by title insurance companies are designed to further these goals.

The traditional method of title transfer, until fairly recent years, was handled by conveyancers who were responsible for all aspects of the transaction. They conducted a title search for the purpose of determining the ownership rights of the seller and any liens or encumbrances that might exist. The conveyancer would then provide a signed abstract of the status of the title. Conveyancers are generally recognized as experts on real estate law even though they are not usually attorneys.

The function of attorneys in the traditional conveyancing of title is to render an "opinion of title." A title opinion is an opinion rendered by a qualified title examiner estimating the current title status of a particular parcel of real property.

The need for title insurance arose from the concern that traditional methods of conveying real property did not provide adequate protection for the parties involved.

Coverage

The function of most other forms of insurance is to provide financial indemnity through a pooling of risks for losses coming from unforeseen events, the purpose of title insurance is to eliminate losses caused by defects in title which come from events which have happened in the past.

If problems concerning the title do arise, and they are covered events, the title insurance company will pay the costs of defending the title against the claim.

A title insurance company will perform an extensive search of relevant public records to determine if any person other than the seller has any right, lien, claim of encumbrance on the title. Once a "title search" is done and all recorded claims and rights are determined, a policy of title insurance will be issued for a one-time premium. There are, frequently, no continuing premium payments.

An owner's title insurance policy is not the same as a lender's title insurance policy. An owner's title insurance policy will cover the insured as long as he/she and his/her heirs or devisees have an interest in the property.

A lender's title insurance policy provides protection for the lender as long as the lender (mortgagee) has an interest in the property.

Occasionally, an individual will make the assumption that since the lender has a title insurance policy, there is no need for the buyer to have one. A lender's title policy provides protection for the lender, not the property owner. An owner's title policy provides protection for the property owner, not the lender. Some states require buyers to sign a waiver if they elect to not purchase owner's title insurance stating they understand they have no title insurance coverage.

Typical coverage is likely to include:

Someone else owns an interest in the title

A document is not properly signed, sealed, acknowledged or delivered

Forgery, fraud, duress, incompetency, incapacity or impersonation

Defective recording of any document

Failure to have legal right of access

Restrictive covenants limiting owners use of the land

Lien on title because of mortgage, judgment, tax, special assessment, charge by homeowner's association

Liens for labor and material furnished before the policy date

Rights of others from leases, contracts, options

Other(s) having an easement on the property

Unmarketable title which allows others to refuse to perform a contract, lease or make a mortgage loan

Being forced to move the existing structure if it extends on adjoining land or easement, violates a restriction, violates a *zoning law*

Exclusions

A typical title insurance policy may include some of the following exclusions:

Governmental police power including building and zoning ordinances

Condemnation

Title risks the insured agrees to, knows about, that result in no loss, that affect title after policy date

Failure to pay mortgage

Unrecorded liens

This does not include all of the coverage and exclusions that may be found in a title insurance policy. For a complete list, each policy must be examined.

OKLAHOMA STATUTE

Title 46 Oklahoma Statutes, Section 19, 20 and 21. Title Protection.

Section 19. Definitions:

As used in this act:

1. "Buyer" means a person who purchases property through financing, in whole or in part, by a loan secured by the property;
2. "Mortgagee" means a person who provides financing, in whole or in part, to a buyer for the purchase of property and the financing is secured by the property;
3. "Person" means an individual, partnership, corporation, trust or other legal entity;
4. "Property" means real property which is either improved property or unimproved property which is purchased through financing by a loan for construction; and
5. "Title protection document" means a lawyer's title opinion, a title certificate, a title insurance policy or other written assurance as to the state of the title to property.

Section 20. Issuance of title protection document—Notice—Waiver

A. If a title protection document will be issued to the mortgagee, the mortgagee shall give to the buyer at the time of loan application written notice containing the following:

1. Whether the title protection document will provide protection to the buyer; and

2. That the buyer should seek independent, competent advice as to whether the buyer should obtain any additional title protection document. In the event said additional title protection is desired, it shall be obtained by the buyer in a timely manner in order to avoid undue delay of the closing under the terms of the contract of sale.

B. The requirements of this section shall not be subject to waiver by the buyer.

Section 21. Violation—Penalty

Any mortgagee who fails to comply with the provisions of this act shall be subject to a penalty in the amount of One Hundred Dollars ($100.00). the penalty imposed herein shall be recoverable by the buyer, plus all costs of any action, including a reasonable attorney fee, to recover the penalty.

ERRORS AND OMISSIONS INSURANCE

Errors and Omissions Insurance for real estate agents is very similar to Medical Malpractice Insurance for doctors. Both policies cover professional liability for failures to act by licensed specialists with specific skills and training. The policies are designed to protect the licensee from the financial consequences of claims brought by consumers of their services. If the consumer is displeased with the service performed, no matter how accurately and skillfully, the consumer may still file suit.

Real estate Errors and Omissions Insurance offers some protection against such suits. Once an Errors and Omissions Insurance company is notified of a claim, the insurance company has the responsibility of defending the claim as well as paying the settlement or judgment against the insured.

Coverage

A typical Errors and Omissions Policy will cover the insured against:

Claims arising from an error, omission or negligent act relating to rendering or failure to render professional services connected with those of a real estate licensee.

Claims for which a written claim is first made during the policy period.

Claims which are not specifically excluded from coverage such as those related to pollution or intentional wrong doings of a licensee (torts).

Limit of Liability

Virtually every insurance policy places a limit on the liability the insurance company is willing to assume. Errors and Omissions Insurance is no different. Some companies limit their liability to $100,000 for each claim. Some extend this limitation to greater amounts with increased premium levels.

Deductibles

Typical Errors and Omissions Insurance has two deductibles. Frequently, the deductible for defense costs may be a thousand dollars ($1,000) and the deductible for damages may be two or three thousand dollars.

The total cost to the insured for any claim that does not exceed the limit of liability will not exceed the total amount of the deductible.

Exclusions

Some typical exclusions included in Errors and Omissions Insurance may be claims caused by or arising from:

- the insolvency of the insured

- fraudulent, dishonest, or criminal acts intentionally committed by the insured

- bodily injury, illness, disease or death of any person

- damage or destruction of property

- libel, slander, defamation of character, false arrest

- wrongful entry or eviction

- property owned by the insured

- property that is polluted

This is not a complete list of exclusions. Each policy must be read to understand the exclusions contained in individual policies.

In the event of a claim, the insurance company must investigate and defend any claim, even if groundless, false or fraudulent, at its own expense.

Most Errors and Omissions Insurance covers the broker only if the claim is made during the period of the policy.

Ch. 20

TEST YOUR UNDERSTANDING

1. The purpose of homeowner's insurance is
    1. to shift the risk of loss from the individual to a large number of people who are approved for similar risks.
    2. avoid unnecessary profits.
    3. avoid liability.
    4. None of the above.

2. Homeowner's insurance policies may be designated
    1. liability plus.
    2. exclusives included.
    3. liability limited.
    4. HO-1, HO-2, HO-3, HO-4

3. Generally, the HO-1 policy provides
    1. basic coverage.
    2. broad spectrum coverage.
    3. coverage for special circumstances.
    4. renter's insurance.

4. In most cases, if a dwelling is vacant
    1. the coverage will remain in effect.
    2. the coverage will no longer be in effect.
    3. the coverage may be reduced.
    4. None of the above.

5. If the dwelling collapses due to faulty construction
    1. it will be covered in most insurance policies.
    2. it will not be covered.
    3. the coverage will be reduced.
    4. None of the above.

6. Most homeowner's policies do not cover
    1. flood.
    2. earthquake.
    3. nuclear accident.
    4. all of the above.

7. Most homeowner's policies make provisions in the event the dwelling is damaged enough to make it uninhabitable
    1. by not making any provisions for additional living expenses.
    2. by paying additional living expenses.
    3. by renting a concierge suite for the insured.
    4. None of the above.

8. If a fire department charges a service fee,
    1. a HO-1 will probably pay it.
    2. a HO-2 will probably pay it.
    3. a HO-3 will probably pay it.
    4. no insurance will pay it.

9. Many homeowners' insurance policies do not include coverage for
    1. communicable disease.
    2. damage caused by aircraft.
    3. bodily injury to the insured.
    4. All of the above.

329

10. Renters insurance provides coverage for
    1. liability protection.
    2. personal property.
    3. communicable disease.
    4. war and riot.

11. Some insurance on mobile homes may require
    1. removal to a safer location.
    2. annual inspections by the fire marshal.
    3. Both 1 and 2.
    4. Neither 1 nor 2.

12. In order to be able to purchase flood insurance, a homeowner's community
    1. joins the National Flood Insurance Program.
    2. makes flood insurance available through its central purchasing department.
    3. eliminates issuing building permits in flood zones.
    4. gets approval for all building permits from the Corps of Engineers.

13. Flood insurance may be purchased from
    1. Federal Flood Insurance Program.
    2. local branches of the Corps of Engineers.
    3. insurance companies.
    4. only the federal government.

14. Flood insurance premiums are determined by
    1. Congress.
    2. different levels of deductibles available through insurance companies.
    3. municipal government.
    4. None of the above.

15. The purpose of title insurance is
    1. to cover losses caused by title defects which came from events in the past.
    2. to cover losses caused by title defects which come from events in the future.
    3. Both 1 and 2.
    4. Neither 1 nor 2.

16. If problems concerning title arise, the title insurance company will
    1. make a cash payment to the mortgage company.
    2. make a cash payment to the mortgagor.
    3. pay the cost of defending the title against the claim.
    4. all of the above.

17. There are two kinds of title insurance policies. They are
    1. seller and buyer policies.
    2. high deductibles and low deductibles.
    3. mortgagor's policy and mortgagee's policies.
    4. There is only one kind of title insurance policy.

18. Which of the following is likely to be excluded from coverage by a mortgagor's title insurance policy?
    1. Restrictive covenants.
    2. Failure to have legal right of access.
    3. Defective recording of a document.
    4. Condemnation.

19. Real estate Errors and Omissions insurance is
    1. a required expense.
    2. an optional expense.
    3. only necessary when there is a complaint at the OREC.
    4. errors and omissions insurance is mandated by the OREC.

ANSWERS AND EXPLANATIONS

1. 1 Homeowners' insurance spreads the cost of losses over a large pool of insured in order that no one insured bears all of the loss.

2. 4 Homeowner's insurance policies generally are designated by the letters "HO."

3. 1 A HO 1 policy only provides basic property coverage.

4. 2 Usually, if a property is left vacant, the insurance policy will provide that there is no coverage.

5. 2 If a building collapses due to faulty construction, most insurance companies will not cover it.

6. 4 Most homeowners' policies will not cover any of these.

7. 2 Insurance policies provide for additional living expenses.

8. 3 Since a HO 3 policy is a broad-spectrum coverage, it will probably pay such a fee.

9. 4 Many policies will not cover any of these.

10. 2 Renters' insurance generally only covers the renters' personal property.

11. 3 Insurance companies may require removal of mobile homes to safer areas or refuse to write the policy.

12. 1 Flood insurance is available only in communities which have joined the National Flood Insurance Program.

13. 3 Flood insurance is sold by insurance companies in communities which have joined the National Flood Insurance Program.

14. 2 Flood insurance premiums are determined by insurance companies based upon their risks.

15. 1 Title insurance covers against title problems which existed prior to the date of the policy.

16. 3 Title insurance typically pays for the cost of defending title.

17. 3 title insurance may be purchased by mortgagees and/or mortgagors.

18. 4 Condemnation is a legal process related to the government's right of Eminent Domain.

19. 2 OREC does not require real estate companies to purchase Errors and Omissions Insurance.

… Ch. 21

BASIC REAL ESTATE MATH

1. If you list a 2,300 square foot house with 2 baths, a three car garage and a den for $184,000 with a 6% commission. The seller accepts a full price offer from another company. There is a 50/50 commission split between your company and the selling company. You get 70% of your company's share. How much is your share of the commission?

   1. $5,500
   2. $3,864
   3. $1,565
   4. $1,104

2. You sell a house for $120,000. The commission is $7,200. What is the commission rate?

   1. 4%
   2. 5%
   3. 6%
   4. 7%

3. You list a lot which is 170 feet by 300 feet. How many acres are in the lot?

   1. 1 acre
   2. 1.1 acres
   3. 1.17 acres
   4. 1.2 acres

4. You sell a lot which is 75 feet by 145 feet. What part of an acre is it?

   1. 1 acre
   2. ¼ acre
   3. ½ acre
   4. 1/3 acre

5. You sell a 2,300 square foot house for $192,000. What is the price per square foot?

   1. $83.48
   2. $84.04
   3. $85.00
   4. $85.91

6. You are building a strip shopping center. You make application to the local municipality's planning commission for a building permit. Part of the local commercial building requirements state that for every square foot of building space, you must provide one and one half square feet of parking area. If your building is to be one story 800 feet long and 75 feet wide, how many square feet of parking area is required?

   1. 100,000
   2. 90,000
   3. 80,000
   4. 70,000

333

7. You sell a commercial property for $275,000. The estimated annual income for this property is $30,000. What is the capitalization rate?

   1. 10.9%
   2. 9.2%
   3. 9.10%
   4. 9.02%

8. Sam sold his house for $134,000. What was the amount of the documentary (conveyance) tax?

   1. $198.00
   2. $199.00
   3. $200.00
   4. $201.00

9. Information from the county assessor's office shows the assessed valuation of Fred's property is $4,200. Homestead exemption is approved for the year on the property. The county tax levy for the area is 90 mills. How much is the ad valorem tax on Fred's property for the year?

   1. $378.00
   2. $288.00
   3. $169.00
   4. $278.00

10. Jack's house sold for $55,000 and the total commission was 6% of that amount. The broker received ¾ of the commission and he sales associate received ¼. How much was the sales associate's share?

    1. $3,300
    2. $2,475
    3. $825
    4. $1,650

11. A tract of land described as the SE ¼ of the SE ¼ of the NE ¼ of the NW ¼ contains how many acres?

    1. 25 acres
    2. 10 acres
    3. 5 acres
    4. 2.5 acres

12. Mary purchased a home for $145,000. She made a 20% down payment. What is her loan-to-value ratio?

    1. 80%
    2. 85%
    3. 90%
    4. 95%

13. The purchase price of Albert's new house was $200,000. With a 5% down payment, what is the loan-to-value ratio?

    1. 80%
    2. 85%
    3. 90%
    4. 95%

334

SOLUTIONS

1. 2. $184,000 times 6% equals $11,040, total commission. $11,040 divided by 2 equals $5,520, your company's share. $5,520 times 70% equals $3,864, your share.

2. 3. $7,200 divided by $120.00 equals 6%.

3. 3. 300 feet times 170 feet equals 51,000 square feet. 51,000 divided by 43,560 (number of square feet in one acre) equals 1.17 acres.

4. 2 75 feet times 145 feet equals 10,875 square feet. 10,875 square feet divided by 43,560 square feet equals ¼ acre.

5. 1. $192,000 divided by 2,300 square feet equals $83.48.

6. 2. 800 feet times 75 feet equals 60,000 square feet of building space. 60,000 square feet times 50% equals 30,000 square feet. 60,000 square feet plus 30,000 equals 90,000 square feet of parking area.

7. 1. The $30,000 annual income divided by $275,000 purchase price equals a 10.9% capitalization rate.

8. 4. $134,000 divided by 500 equals 268. 268 times 75 cents equals $201.00 documentary tax. Documentary tax is sometimes called "conveyance tax".

9. 2. $4,200 minus $1,000 for homestead exemption equals $3,200. $3,200 times .090 (millage rate) equals $288.00. 90 mills is equal to 9%.

10. 3. $55,000 times 6% equals $3,300. $3,300 minus 75% equals $825.00.

11. 4. Begin with 640 acres. ¼ of 640 acres is 160 acres. ¼ of 160 acres is 40 acres. ¼ of 40 acres is 10 acres. ¼ of 10 acres is 2.5 acres.

12. 1. $145,000 minus 20% down payment equals $116,000 loan amount. $116,000 divided by $145,000 equals 80%, the loan-to-value ratio.

13. 4. $200,000 minus 5% down payment equals $190,000 loan amount. $190,000 loan amount divided by $200,000 equals 95% loan-to-value.

Made in the USA
Lexington, KY
01 September 2017